THE TIME HAS COME

Debates over the Autocephaly of the OCA
Reflected in *St Vladimir's Quarterly*

The Time Has Come

Debates over the Autocephaly of the OCA Reflected in *St Vladimir's Quarterly*

Edited by
IONUT-ALEXANDRU TUDORIE

ST VLADIMIR'S SEMINARY PRESS
YONKERS, NEW YORK
2020

Library of Congress Control Number: 2019956059

COPYRIGHT © 2020

ST VLADIMIR'S SEMINARY PRESS
575 Scarsdale Road, Yonkers, NY 10707
1-800-204-2665
www.svspress.com

ISBN 978–088141–655–8 (hardback)
ISBN 978–088141–656–5 (electronic)

All Rights Reserved

Table of Contents

Introduction: The Time Has Come for All Orthodox of America
by Ionut-Alexandru Tudorie   ix

PART I
The Long Path from the Alaska Mission to Autocephaly (1794–1970)

1. Metropolitan Leonty, "Problems of the Eastern Orthodox Church in America" (1952)   3

2. John Meyendorff, "One Bishop in One City (Canon 8, First Ecumenical Council)" (1961)   11

3. Serge S. Verhovskoy, "The Unity of the Orthodox Church in America" (1961)   21

4. Alexander A. Bogolepov, "Conditions of Autocephaly" (1961)   35

5. William S. Schneirla, "The Future of American Orthodoxy" (1961)   69

6. Alexander Schmemann, "Problems of Orthodoxy in America: The Canonical Problem" (1964)   95

7. Dmitry Grigorieff, "The Orthodox Church in America from the Alaska Mission to Autocephaly" (1970)   119

PART II
And Beyond... (1970–2016)

1. Alexander Schmemann, "A Meaningful Storm: Some Reflections on Autocephaly, Tradition, and Ecclesiology" (1971)   149

2. John H. Erickson, "Autocephaly in Orthodox Canonical Literature to the Thirteenth Century" (1971)   179

3. John E. Rexine, "The Quest for Orthodox Church Unity in America" (1975)   197

4. John H. Erickson, "Concrete Structural Organization of the Local Church: The 1971 Statute of the Orthodox Church in America" (1976)   207

5. John Meyendorff, "Orthodox Unity in America: New Beginnings?" (1991)   219

6. Archbishop Peter L'Huillier, "Accession to Autocephaly" (1993)   235

7. Archimandrite Elpidophoros Lambriniadis, "Greek Orthodoxy, the Ecumenical Patriarchate, and the Church in the USA" (2010)   273

8. Paul Meyendorff, "A Response to Archimandrite Elpidophoros Lambriniadis" (2010)   291

9. Elizabeth H. Prodromou, "Historical Method and Competing Logics: A Response to Archimandrite Elpidophoros Lambriniadis" (2010)   299

10. Paul Meyendorff, "Fr John Meyendorff and the Autocephaly of the Orthodox Church in America" (2012)   311

11. Paul Meyendorff, "Ethnophyletism, Autocephaly, and National Churches—A Theological Approach and Ecclesiological Implications" (2013)   329

12. John H. Erickson, "Autocephaly and Autonomy" (2016)   343

13. Andrey Shishkov, "Church Autocephaly as Sovereignty: A Schmittian Approach" (2016)   363

Appendix 1: "Some Quotations" (1961)   389

Appendix 2: "Documents: The Autocephaly of the Orthodox Church in America" (1971)   395

INTRODUCTION
The Time Has Come for All Orthodox of America

Ionut-Alexandru Tudorie

IN AN OCTOBER 1960 article published in Russian in the monthly *The Russian American Orthodox Messenger* by Bishop John (Shahovskoy) of San Francisco (bishop: 1950–1961; archbishop: 1961–1973; 1975–1979), the reader can find one of the strongest statements regarding the needed unity of all the Orthodox in the U.S.:

> The time has come for all Orthodox of America, whatever their extraction may be, to understand that the United States of America cannot be considered a colony any more either in political or in ecclesiastical sense. The past is gone. This country has ceased to be an ecclesiastical colony of the English, the Dutch, the Swedes; it cannot remain a spiritual colony of the Greeks, the Serbs, the Romanians, the Russians, whether those of the U.S.S.R. or those *in exile*. Americans have indeed won the right (no less than the Cypriots, the Albanians or the Czechoslovaks) to have their own Orthodox Local Church, in conformity with the ecclesiastical canons.[1]

This passionate appeal for ecclesial unity instead of ethnic divisions comes as no surprise since it was voiced by one of the hierarchs representing the *Metropolia*, a self-governing Orthodox Church in the U.S. as early as

---

[1] "Ведемъ ли мы переговоры съ Московской Патріархіей? О нашей позиціи. – По поводу выступления Митрополита Бориса" [Are we negotiating with the Moscow Patriarchate? About our position. – Regarding the speech of Metropolitan Boris], *Русско-Американскій Православный Вѣстникъ / The Russian American Orthodox Messenger* 56.10 (October, 1960): 166–168, at 166.

1924, but it is worth noting that similar positions had also been articulated by the Ecumenical Patriarch Meletios IV Mataxakis (1921–1923; former Greek Archbishop in the U.S.: 1921–1922) and the Antiochian Archbishop of New York and Metropolitan of All North America, Anthony Bashir (1936–1966), to name but two personalities. Beyond the article's merits in articulating with force and precision a position that reflected the consensus of the leading representatives of the major Orthodox jurisdictions in North America, another reason to quote it stems from the fact that Archimandrite and later Bishop John served as Dean of St Vladimir's Seminary between 1939 and 1950. In this capacity he was the driving force behind the successive agreements with The General Theological Seminary and The Union Theological Seminary, places where St Vladimir's had its quarters for more than two decades.[2] It was not under his term, but a mere two years later, during Fr Georges Florovsky's service as Dean, that the academic reputation of this institution was boosted by the publication of the first issue of *St Vladimir's Seminary Quarterly* in the Fall of 1952. The journal proved instrumental for the mission of the Orthodox Church in North America and beyond, in addition to providing the faculty of St Vladimir's Seminary with the ideal platform to discuss the problems of Orthodoxy in America. One after another, Fr John Meyendorff, Serge S. Verhovskoy, Alexander A. Bogolepov, and Fr Alexander Schmemann openly wrote about the concept of autocephaly, the interpretation of canonical tradition, and the history of the Orthodox mission in North America. Starting as early as the first issue of *St Vladimir's Seminary Quarterly* (later *St Vladimir's Theological Quarterly*), the multifaceted topic of one Orthodox Church in America can be easily traced throughout successive issues, not only before April 1970, when the *tomos* of autocephaly was granted by the Moscow Patriarchate, but also after that. And so what better way to celebrate the fiftieth anniversary of this long-awaited moment in the life of the Orthodox Church

---

[2]"Chronicle of St Vladimir's Seminary: Historical Background," *St Vladimir's Seminary Quarterly* 1.1 (1952): 21–23; "Seminaries," *Orthodox America: 1794–1976: Development of the Orthodox Church in America*, general editor: Constance J. Tarasar (Syosett, NY, 1975), 205–210, at 208–210.

in America than a volume featuring a selection of the best articles on this very topic published in *St Vladimir's Quarterly*?

The articles are arranged chronologically and divided into two parts: the first one, "The Long Path from the Alaska Mission to Autocephaly (1794–1970)," comprising seven articles published between 1952 and 1970, offers the reader a much needed theological context for this very sensitive topic; the second part, "And beyond . . . (1970–2016)," consisting of thirteen articles published between 1971 and 2016, delves into the issues entailed by the reception process of autocephaly, starting right after April 1970 and reaching very recent analyses on autocephaly and autonomy in the Church.

It is appropriate and highly relevant that the volume should open with an inspiring article by Metropolitan Leonty, initially published in 1915 (when he was the Rector of the Seminary in Tenafly, New Jersey) and republished in the very first issue of *St Vladimir's Seminary Quarterly* in 1952, because in it the author successfully demonstrates that the major problem of Orthodox Christians in North America concerns their ethnic divisions. In the second article selected for the volume, Fr John Meyendorff seeks to solve the issue of parallel national Orthodox jurisdictions in the U.S. through a discussion of the canonical expression "one bishop in one city" (Council of Nicaea, canon 8, AD 325). In his article, Serge S. Verhovskoy identified once more that in 1961 "excessive nationalism" was still preventing a natural rapprochement of the different Orthodox jurisdictions in North America. A detailed analysis of the conditions of autocephaly, granted either by the Ecumenical Patriarchate or by the Mother Church, was provided by Alexander A. Bogolepov. Fr William Schneirla attempted to turn his face from the distant past to the future, discussing the major problems facing American Orthodoxy and acknowledging that "those who would preserve their separate national entities are fighting a battle already lost." One of the major actors of the autocephaly debate, Fr Alexander Schmemann, argued in his article that a strong emphasis on the Synod of bishops, the diocese, and the parish would be the answer to the "national pluralism." The article by Fr Dmitry Grigorieff is an overview of the Orthodox presence in North America, starting with the Alaska mission and going up to the time of receiving the *tomos* of autocephaly from the Moscow Patriarchate (April 1970).

The second part of the volume opens with another seminal article by Fr Alexander Schmemann, tackling the ecclesiastical storm provoked by the decisive gesture by the Mother Church of granting autocephaly to the Orthodox Church in America. The concept of autocephaly as expressed in the canonical literature up to the thirteenth century was the main focus of John Erickson's article, which brings a broader historical perspective to the April 1970 event. This is followed by a comparative review by John E. Rexine of two volumes published in 1973, one by the Greek scholar Panagiotes Trembelas and the other by Archimandrite Serafim Surrency. Although dealing with the 1971 Statute of the Orthodox Church in America, the analytical article by John Erickson includes valuable insights related to autocephaly and the reception process. The fall of communism in Eastern Europe in 1991 offered an excellent opportunity for Fr John Meyendorff to raise the question of the possible (and necessary) new beginnings in inter-Orthodox relations. Archbishop Peter L'Huillier, mirroring an article by Alexander Bogolepov, carefully interpreted for the reader examples of the different ways of granting autocephaly, so as to offer a compelling model for such a process. Archimandrite Elpidophoros Lambriniadis (now Greek Archbishop of America), in a paper presented at a conference organized at St Vladimir's Seminary in June 2010, clearly reiterated the position of the Ecumenical Patriarchate regarding the "uncanonical actions and developments . . . dictated by historical necessity." In response to Archimandrite Elpidophoros' article, both Paul Meyendorff and Elizabeth Prodromou challenged the primacy of the Ecumenical Patriarchate based on canon 28 of the Fourth Ecumenical Council (Chacedon, AD 451). Fr John Meyendorff's tireless efforts during the long negotiation with the different Orthodox jurisdictions in North America on the one hand, and on the other hand, the Moscow Patriarchate, were vividly recounted in an article by Paul Meyendorff. More recently (2013), the same author discussed the concepts of ethnophyletism in relation to autocephaly. Fr John Erickson provided for the reader a reevaluation of the inter-Orthodox dialogue on autocephaly and autonomy, two of the topics that were originally on the agenda of the Holy and Great Synod. Finally, Andrey Shishkov proposed a new approach based on Carl Schmitt's theory on sovereignty in order to determine who has the authority to grant autocephaly in the Church.

A rather limited number of citations from Orthodox authorities collected back in 1970, and a full dossier of correspondence and official documents related to the process of negotiations for granting autocephaly were added at the end of the volume as an Appendix.

The editorial work was restricted to minor tacit interventions here and there in order to correct chronology and typographical errors, and to ensure consistency in the footnote references. Any other intervention in the text (especially in the footnotes) was clearly marked with square brackets and the usual indication at the end [*Ed.*].

Although this book is a mere reprint of articles originally published in *St Vladimir's Quarterly*—some of them still informing current scholarly debate, but others completely and unjustly forgotten—it is our strong belief that this volume will highlight once more the active role of the faculty of St Vladimir's Seminary in the granting of the *tomos* of autocephaly and during the continuous reception process. It bears emphasis that the *Quarterly* was a platform for genuine intellectual dialogue, open to the positions formulated by the other side in the autocephaly debate. In the present tense context, when the concept of autocephaly is causing serious disruption within the Orthodox world, a new reading of the arguments produced by Fr John Meyendorff, Fr Alexander Schmemann, Archbishop Peter L'Huillier, or Fr John Erickson can help reach a reasonable solution.

PART I

The Long Path from the Alaska Mission to Autocephaly (1794–1970)

Problems of the Eastern Orthodox Church in America

Metropolitan Leonty

St Vladimir's Seminary Quarterly 1.1 (1952): 6–12

This article was written in 1915 when His Eminence was Archpriest Leonid Turkevich and was published in The Constructive Quarterly [3 (1915): 311–27—Ed.]. Despite the passage of the years and drastic historical changes, it retains much of its relevance to the situation of American Orthodoxy. It is presented here in a slightly revised and abridged form.

THE ORTHODOX CHURCH IN AMERICA has a long history, its beginnings reaching back to the late 18th century. At first no more than a mission of the Russian Church to the natives of Alaska, with the growth of emigration from the Orthodox lands of the Old World it has become the church of a considerable portion of the American people. Until the most recent years there has been an impressive increase in membership and Orthodox communities are spread over the whole continent. The ancient faith of the undivided Church is now an integral part of the religious life of the Americas, especially in the United States.

In the New World, Orthodoxy was forced to face a new situation, different in all respects from the familiar pattern in existence in the countries of Europe and the Near East from which the Orthodox emigrants came. Under the pressure of new and unfamiliar conditions it was required to manifest its creative and constructive power in adjustment to the new environment, without, however, compromising its principles or betraying its peculiar ethos.

First of all, we must stress the feeling of unity between the Orthodox of various national backgrounds, they brought with them an established tradition, ideals formulated in the early centuries of a Christian history and determined by the ecumenical councils that continue to lie unshaken at the basis of Orthodox life in America. Seeds preserved since the days of Byzantium begin to germinate in the soil of the New World. This unity of faith has surmounted national differences and survived the loss of political support common in European Orthodoxy.

Their entire content with the spiritual treasure which came down to them from their remote ancestors and was so well preserved shows the many-sidedness, catholicity, and humaneness of the Orthodox faith.

And so outside of any political support, Orthodoxy in America shows itself to be a confession of Christian faith as it was in the times of the undivided Church. In speaking thus, we say nothing new but merely bring out that which would not be noticeable on a non-American soil where there exist influences, national, political, and historically acquired, which would certainly dim its outlines and cause it to escape the attention of the observer; whereas in America the general applicability of Orthodoxy is the foremost feature that we notice. And indeed, besides the above-mentioned nations, there are other Orthodox in America, the aborigines of Alaska, the Creoles, Aleutians, Alaskan Indians, Eskimos, as well as immigrants from countries as remote from each other as Macedonia, Persia, and Japan.

To distinguish themselves from all religious denominations using the adjective Catholic, the Orthodox of America have to add to their original title of Catholic Orthodox Christians the name of their own nation as well as of the nation through which they receive their Catholic Orthodoxy. This is the origin of the sometimes exceedingly lengthy names of Orthodox provinces in America. By adding to the name of Catholic Orthodox the word Greek, the members of this Church intend to prevent the possibility of being suspected of bearing the historical stamp of another branch of Christendom, which in ancient days was centered in Rome and still continues to gravitate towards the local church of this city and province of Italy. Another Church with the same character of catholicity and at the same time obviously with historical, ethnographical, and even geographical features, is the church which is called Protestant Episcopal, though (merely from the point of view we have adopted in this article) it would be more correct to call it Anglican Catholic Protestant Episcopal. But, the most characteristic point of both the Roman Catholic and the Protestant Episcopal Church, practically, is not in their catholic foundation, and not even in their historical and national traits, but in the whole order of their life: with Roman Catholicism it is in the definitely worked out and rigorously applied demands of discipline of thought and action; and with the Episcopalians it is in the breadth and yet entire strictness of self-governing organizations.

The word *catholicity* doubtless has its origin in the centuries when the Greco-Roman rulers thought of themselves as the possessors of the "circle of the earth." Christianity, which filled the emptiness of this "circle of the earth" with the miraculous power which regenerated it for a new life, naturally inherited from the Greco-Roman world this same designation of its exterior character and thus the designation of *catholic* came to he possessed by the Church partly by way of historical development and still more by way of reference to the commandment of its Founder: "Go ye into all the world, and preach the Gospel to every creature" (Mk 16.15).

Consequently, the Christian Church comes out in history as a universal or catholic force whose activity is directed towards the spiritual possession of the universe. But though we retain the sense of the word catholicity, which means universality or being spread everywhere, we must not ignore its other significance, which was adopted by the Christian Church because of the very formation of the word, "gathered from all." This meaning already found its realization in the life of the Church through the calling of the representatives of all the Christian world to come to special councils with the object of solving problems of faith, morality, and church rule which concerned equally all the faithful of the Church. It is remarkable that the Christians of the Greek Catholic confession retain to this day rather the second significance of the word *catholic*, so that in their speech it is synonymous with "ecumenical," or having representatives from every part of the whole which is governed in its totality.

We also must note the general way in which unity is manifested in catholicity, and also what is the instrument and exterior gauge of realized unity. We may say that no such question existed in the world of the undivided Church, because the whole mass of people making part of it spoke the Greek language by preference, which is confirmed by the fact that the books of the New Testament were written in this tongue, it being the more popular, the more democratic. In the meanwhile, in the Western part of the Church the Latin language struck deeper and deeper root, as the general conversational and ecclesiastical tongue.

To this day this language remains the autocratic sacred language of the people who received the Catholic faith through the Roman Church, and who remain in union or rather submission to it. As far as the faithful of this church are concerned, it is exactly this language which is the most general sign of their belonging to Catholic Christianity. Under the banner of this language other names are lost and even become superfluous as far as nationality is concerned. Next after the oneness of belief and rule it may be said that the catholicity of the Roman Church is defined by the use of the sacred tongue of this church, the Latin tongue. As the binding cement of this church, this tongue becomes especially noticeable through the fact that those who do not consider it necessary to the expression of their religious needs are cut off by this very circumstance from the unity of this Church, becoming separate confessions according to nationalities.

At the same time, in the Episcopal we may take for a sign of union the mother tongue of Americans, so that there are quite a number of people who do not hesitate to give it the name of the American Church without the risk of being misunderstood. The unity of belief and government is realized in this denomination without much effort.

In comparison with religious denominations so characteristically different in the outward signs of their inner unity, the special catholic character of the Orthodox Church becomes strikingly clear.

First of all, we cannot fail to notice the stamp of the catholicity of the Orthodox Church in the fact that this church allows every national group of its members to use their own tongue in church without any confusion, mistrust, or sensitiveness. Greeks, Syrian Arabs, Persians, Slavs of various nationalities, Albanians, Eskimos, and in the later days the Japanese and the Chinese, hear the word of God, prayers, and divine services in a language they all understand. The contents and the ritual offered to all these nations being one and the same, Orthodoxy loses nothing from the use of so many different tongues, each tribe praising the Creator and Master of the Universe, the Triune God, in its own way. The Orthodox Church works on the principle of catholicity so trustingly that every nation in it is allowed to be governed by an independent Church of its own. Church unity suffers no detriment and is not shaken by such a superficial division, the Orthodox believes. Superior powers connect the local groups such as the unity of faith and signs of piety, the unity of the hierarchy and the sacraments, the unity of the presence of him who is "greater than all that is in the world" (1 Jn 4.4); who "is the head of the body, the church; who is the beginning the firstborn among the dead; that in all things he might have the preeminence" (Col 1.18); who is "with you always, even unto the end of the world" (Mt 28.20).

Consequently, the chief problem of the Orthodox Church in North America concerns the national churches which make a part of it. Are they to be governed independently of each other? But in this case the canonical demand of there being only one bishop for every town, in order that there should be no division of this town within itself, risk being broken (Council of Chalcedon, Canon 12). Or are they to be united by their submission to one representative according to the canonical rule, so that every Church should know its own intercessor (Apostolic Canon 34)? But in this case what will be the dominant exterior organ of intercommunion?

It would seem that the Orthodox Church must choose between the two chief directions taken by the religious life of America, the Roman Catholic and the Episcopal. Shall discipline be allowed to become the binding link between the different parts, even with the acceptance of a single sacred tongue (the Greek, for instance, or the Slavonic), following the example of the Roman Catholic Church? But in such a case the national character of the churches will suffer detriment.

Or else, shall the preponderance of the principle of self-government be allowed to develop, as in the Episcopal Church? But in this case could an exterior organ of union, that is, the language of the country, develop to its full power even in the narrow limits of pure ritual? In other words, in this case will not the Orthodox Church of America become simply the American Orthodox Church, without any distinction between national groups according to the origin of early immigrants from the old world? The existence of national difference, however, will prevent the language of the country from becoming the language of church practices for a long time to come, as at present it prevents all the languages in use among the various communities from becoming the sacred language. Yet the Americanization of the Orthodox in this country is developed enough to force the members of this Church to have recourse to the neutral language—which to a good many of them has become the natural language of all American citizens for all everyday affairs.

The one thing that still remains to be done is to condense into a single whole, and to harmonize the demands of Orthodox discipline with the lawful manifestation of the principle of ecumenicity, in order to enable the Orthodox Church to manifest on American soil its natural character of universal applicability and its creative faculty of uniting organically all the elements within it.

So far, the principle of nationality has stood firm, the language of communication between the various groups being the local English. The form, which this harmonization of the unity of discipline and the diversity of nationalities has to take, is the problem of the Orthodox Church in America in the very near future.

Thus, a sphere of immediate activity is already indicated for the Orthodox Church in America. It will not be a repetition of what has been done by Roman Catholicism, because the principle of catholicity will find a much wider expression, "for into the bosom of the one Church any language and any tribe will be admitted, without being deprived of its national peculiarities" (Rev 14.6). The Orthodox Church will strive in America, as it has striven everywhere else, to realize the commandment of the ancient psalm singer: "That thy way may be known upon earth, thy saving health among all nations" (Ps 67.2). To some extent the activity of the Orthodox Church will awaken in other religious groups a desire to reform or at least reexamine many phases which until now have remained somewhat vague. For instance, the question of the legality of nationality in pure Roman Catholicism is sure to come out in greater relief; also, the degree of original independence which it would be legal for every national group to attain in their religious affairs; also, more light will be shed on the question of democracy in religion.

In a word, because of its general accessibility and primitive purity and intactness, Orthodoxy may to a considerable degree become the very neutral spiritual medium which for so many Christian denominations in America has become obscured.

Generally speaking, things are attracted towards each other from motives of their nearness in space and their inner affinity, especially if there is no obstacle raised by some unusual condition of their existence. Everything in America helps the rapprochement, the trust, the cooperation between various confessional groups in all their religious affairs. It only remains to define the nearness and the affinity existing between these groups in order to allow their mutual gravitation to show itself to the full. Once you have taken this point of view, you can immediately become aware of the natural nearness between the representatives of Orthodoxy in North America and their next of kin who had been forced by historical conditions to place themselves outside the Orthodox Church, without, however, losing altogether the signs of their belonging to that Church. Such are, first of all, the Russians and the Slavs who entered into the Unia with the Roman Catholic Church as long ago as the sixteenth century, preserving their Greek ritual almost intact and their mother language in all church services. And this is exactly the point on which the endeavors of North American Orthodoxy have been concentrated, trying to facilitate the return within its pale of all the religious national bodies which heretofore were part of the papal church in a merely mechanical way. As gradually they leave to join the Orthodox Greek Eastern Catholic Church, the Latin Western Catholic Church becomes relieved of all the elements which are alien to it and enters into the natural boundaries belonging to the region of Latin nationalities. In this case, Orthodoxy works at equalizing values in regions of church interests. The degree in which the legality of preserving nationality in religious affairs is the true essence of Orthodoxy will define the degree in which its presence and activity in North America is bound to awaken the sense of national foundations in other religious bodies, inducing them to become clearer and more definite.

However, this is the second, or perhaps even the third, stage of the solution of the problems of Orthodoxy in America.

We perceive much more clearly the first stage of the development of Orthodoxy's problems in relation to the Episcopal Church. The rapprochement between the latter and the Orthodox Church has been brought about by spiritual kinship and affinity, demonstrated by the national coloring of both, admitted in theory and practice, as well as the theoretical confessional kinship proclaimed quite distinctly at least by a few individuals who express the consciousness of the two churches.

We have not as yet become identical and are as yet far from inter-communion in the sacraments, yet no one can deny the fact of mutual affection and friendliness between us, of which unfortunately there is so little where problems of religion are concerned. Insofar as the Episcopalians are in possession of the correct idea of what the participation of national elements should be in the life of the Church, the Orthodox see quite clearly that between them there can be no strife and no animosity. Insofar as they neglect to preserve doctrine in the shape which the individual ecumenical Church has established, the Episcopalians are not Orthodox, but insofar as they decidedly protest against further digression from this doctrine and preserve the episcopate as the true gauge of their integrity and undividedness, they retain their nearness to Orthodoxy. The Orthodox have sensed the impulse which moves the Episcopalians towards rapprochement and further union: and when the time comes to establish the union in principle, in theory, and in metaphysics, there will be no difficulty.

Until now it would seem that the way of differentiation has been dominant in the history of humanity in general and of Christianity in particular. But it has reached the last stage of its development. The fragmentary condition of Christians in North America proves it altogether too clearly. The hour is near at hand for the integration of disintegrated parts. The bones that are dry and dusty, in the vision of the prophet Ezekiel, are affected by the invisible breath of God's spirit. The conclusion of the prophet's vision, that is, the resurrection of all the divided creatures, who seemed to be lifeless, is the hope and expectation of human individuals; and, what is immeasurably greater, it is the divine wish spoken in the prayer, "That they all may be one" (Jn 17.21).

One Bishop in One City
(Canon 8, First Ecumenical Council)[1]

John Meyendorff

St Vladimir's Seminary Quarterly 5.1–2 (1961): 54–62

No CANONICAL REGULATION has ever been affirmed by the Tradition of the Church with more firmness than the rule which forbids the existence of separate ecclesiastical structures in a single place. The strictly territorial character of church organization seemed practically self-evident to the fathers of all the councils and it is implied by all the canons dealing with ecclesiastical order. We will try to give here a brief analysis of this canonical legislation of the Church and a definition of its theological and spiritual meaning.

1. The Canons

The Orthodox Church has not, as yet, provided her faithful with a complete system of canonical legislation. It is even doubtful whether she will ever do so. The fullness of divine truth and life indeed abides in the Church, and no juridical system will ever be completely adequate to this living and organic reality, which true Christians know only by experience. What is then the real meaning of our canons? As soon as we are acquainted with their text, we discover that they usually have been issued in relation to specific situations and distortions of ecclesiastical life, which occurred in the past. In order to understand them fully it is necessary to be acquainted

---

[1] The French translation of this article was published in Jean Meyendorff, *Orthodoxie et catholicité* (Paris: Éditions du Seuil, 1965), 99–108 (title: "Sommes-nous vraiment l'Église une?"). Later on, the English version was reprinted twice in: John Meyendorff, *Orthodoxy and Catholicity* (New York: Sheed & Ward, 1966), 107–18; John Meyendorff, *Catholicity and the Church* (Crestwood, NY: St Vladimir's Seminary Press, 1983), 111–20.—*Ed.*

with the particular historical circumstances in which they were published. Then, the eternal and normative value of the canons becomes manifest. They appear as a kind of medicine applied by councils and Church Fathers to cure specific diseases of the ecclesiastical organism. This cure was a product of the eternal and permanent nature of the Church. It was, and still is, a witness of the unchangeable identity of the Church, its inner organization and structure being established upon the apostolic witness and provided with the constant presence of the Holy Spirit. The canons indicate to us how to apply to the changeable realities of human history this unchangeable and vivifying reality of the redemptive grace of God abiding in the Church. To consciously disregard the canons of the Church leads finally to corruption of church life, i.e., to ecclesiological heresy.

In order to understand correctly each canon of the Church, we must therefore first localize it in its proper historical setting, and then define the particular aspect of the eternal nature of the Church to which it corresponds. Regarding the question which now occupies us—the territorial structure of the Church in the Orthodox tradition—no serious question of interpretation arises and both the formulas and their meaning are absolutely clear.

Several Ecumenical Councils have issued decisions on the matter and the historical situation in which these decisions were made was not really different from ours. These decisions of the highest authority of the Church are obviously expressions of holy Tradition and we can safely affirm that by their very consistency they express the true and permanent nature of the Church.

The First Ecumenical Council, called in 325 in Nicaea by Emperor Constantine, mainly dealt with the doctrinal question of the Arian heresy, but it also had to pay attention to the remnants of various struggles which had divided Christians in the time of the persecutions. Among these dissensions was the schism of the "Novatians," a sect of puritans, refusing forgiveness to Christians who betrayed the faith during the persecutions and formally condemning second marriages. After peace was given to the Church by Constantine, many Novatians wished to return to the communion of the Church. Canon 8 of Nicaea defines the mode through which

Novatian communities were to be reunited. Since no question arose as to the validity of Novatian ordinations, the episcopal dignity was to be granted to their bishops, but only in places where no parallel orthodox hierarchy already existed. "But wherever there is a bishop of the catholic Church," proclaims the council, "it is obvious that, as the bishops of the Church will keep the dignity of bishop, the one called a bishop among the so-called puritans shall have the honor of a presbyter. . . . There may not be two bishops in the city."[2] It would obviously have been easier to solve the Novatian problem by giving the schismatic bishops some honorary title, or else by transferring them to some empty episcopal see, or by keeping them as heads of their churches, thus establishing two parallel, mutually recognized "jurisdictions" in the same place, but the council decided otherwise and solemnly proclaimed the principle of territorial unity of the Church.

In a somewhat different historical context, the Second Ecumenical Council (Constantinople, 381) formulated the same principle on the level of provincial ecclesiastical administration. The Church of Alexandria having, at that time, shown the tendency to intervene and perform ordinations in provinces which did not belong to its jurisdiction, especially in Constantinople, the council ordered in Canon 2 that, "The bishops are not to go beyond their own dioceses to churches lying outside of their bounds, nor bring confusion on the churches. . . . And let not bishops go beyond their dioceses for ordinations or any other ecclesiastical ministrations, unless they be invited. And the aforesaid canon concerning dioceses being observed, it is evident that the synod of every province will administer the affairs of that particular province as was decreed in Nicaea." The Third Ecumenical Council also declared, in relation to the Church of Cyprus: "None of the God-beloved bishops shall assume control of any province

---

[2]The major canonical texts of the Orthodox Church are easily available in English. The canons of the Ecumenical Councils are published by H. R. Percival, ed., *The Seven Ecumenical Councils of the Undivided Church: Their Canons and Dogmatic Decrees*, A Select Library of Nicene and Post-Nicene Fathers, second series, vol. 14 (Grand Rapids, MI: Eerdmans, 1956). Cf. also a translation of the standard canonical collection of the Greek-speaking churches, the *Pedalion* or *Rudder* compiled in the late 18th century by St Nicodemos of the Holy Mountain, which has been published recently in the United States: *The Rudder*, trans. Denver Cummings (Chicago: Orthodox Christian Educational Society, 1957).

which has not heretofore, from the very beginning, been under his own hand or that of his predecessors" (Canon 8). Finally, we find the same principle in Canon 20 of the Quinisext (Fifth-Sixth Ecumenical) Council [in Trullo]: "It shall not be lawful for a bishop to teach publicly in any city which does not belong to him. If any shall have been observed doing this, let him cease from his episcopate."

A single bishop in every local community, a single synod or council in every province, such is the absolute rule established by the fathers. In the course of centuries, the Church had to protect this rule against many attempts to alter it by the establishment of different principles of ecclesiastical administration. The importance and the authority of some churches led them to exercise a power over an area larger than their own ecclesiastical district, and to "bring confusion on the churches." We already saw the Second Ecumenical Council dealing with Alexandrian pretensions of this kind. The bishops of northern Africa, gathered in Carthage in 419, who were traditionally opposed to the interventions of Rome in their provincial affairs, wrote to Pope Celestine that "all matters should be terminated in the places where they arise" and that the fathers "did not think that the grace of the Holy Spirit would be wanting to any province." No bishop, patriarch, or pope can put himself above the council of bishops of a given province "unless it be imagined that God can inspire a single individual with justice, and refuse it to an innumerable multitude of bishops assembled in council."[3] The ecclesiastical affairs of a province cannot be solved from far off, "from behind the see," as the African bishops put it, since the only true aim of Christians is to promote and establish the Kingdom of God in every place, and not to serve the interests or ambitions of any particular church or individual.

The same territorial principle was applied in 692 by the Council "in Trullo" (Fifth-Sixth Ecumenical) to a case very similar to our contemporary situations: the Cypriot immigration in Asia Minor. Wars between the Arabs and Byzantines provoked shifts of population in the border regions and one of these shifts concerned, in 691, the larger part of the population

---

[3]NPNF² 14:510.

of Cyprus, which was transferred by Emperor Justinian II to the district of the Hellespont, near the sea of Marmara.

Ecclesiastically, the district possessed in Cyzicus its own metropolitan whose elections were confirmed by the Patriarch of Constantinople. Strictly speaking, the Cypriot bishops, who followed their flock in exile, should have submitted to this local jurisdiction. However, the archbishop of Cyprus, since the time of the Council of Ephesus (431), was the head of an autocephalous church. The general council of 692 decided to preserve his former right in his new jurisdictional area. The only way of doing it, without encroaching on the territorial unity of the Church, was to submit the metropolitan of Cyzicus to the former Cypriot archbishop and also to delegate to him the primatial rights of Constantinople over the area of Hellespont. Both actions were taken by the council (canon 39): "We decree . . . that new Justinianopolis[4] shall have the rights of Constantinople and whoever is constituted the pious and most religious bishop thereof shall take precedence of all the bishops of the province of the Hellespont and be elected by his own bishops according to ancient custom . . . the existing bishop of the city of Cyzicus being subject to the metropolitan of the aforesaid Justinianopolis. . . ."[5]

It is therefore quite obvious that the autocephalous status of the Church of Cyprus did not give her any right to establish her own ecclesiastical administration in places which already possessed a local ecclesiastical structure. The council did not admit the creation of a parallel Cypriot jurisdiction in Hellespont and preserved territorial unity. It solved quite radically a question of precedence, at the expense of the existing authorities—Constantinople and Cyzicus—but did not divide the Church. The pattern of ecclesiastical structure remained the same: one church, one bishop, one community in every single place. The canons of the Church

---

[4]Justinianopolis was then the name of Constantia, capital of Cyprus. The Cypriot settlement in Hellespont was called "new Justinianopolis."

[5]NPNF² 14:383; see also the commentary on this canon by Bishop Nikodim Milash, *Pravila Prvoslavnoi Tserkvi s tolkovanniami* [Rules of the Orthodox Church with interpretations], vol. 1 (St Petersburg, 1911), 524–25, and by Nicodemos of the Holy Mountain, in *The Rudder*, 335. The Cypriots later returned to their home island, but their Archbishop still keeps among his honorific titles that of "bishop of new Justinianopolis."

have always protected this simple principle against all attempts to create several separated ecclesiastical administrations in the same place or country, and also against the tendency of some big and important churches (Rome, Alexandria, Antioch) to deprive the local bishops of their authority and to affirm their own power over the rights of the local synods.

2. The Nature of the Church

The aim of the incarnation of the Son of God and the very purpose of his teaching, death, and resurrection was to establish between God and men a new relation, a new unity: "The glory which thou gavest me I have given them; that they may be one, even as we are one. I in them and thou in me, that they may be made perfect in one; and that the world may know that thou hast sent me" (Jn 17.22–33). Unity with God supposes also unity between men, a unity which is described here by Christ himself as visible to the world and as a witness concerning his own mission. It is by seeing the unity that Christians have among themselves that the world "knows" and "believes." This unity is not therefore only a spiritual and invisible reality, but it appears in the concrete visible life of the world. Without Christ's unity, Christians cannot truly fulfill their call, because the world cannot see in them the new life given in him.

This is the reason why at the very origin of the Church, "all that believed were together and had all things in common" (Acts 2.44). Christians gathered together regularly for the celebration of the Lord's Supper and nothing, not even the Roman persecutions, could prevent them from holding their assemblies because the very nature of their faith implied that God abided not in each of them individually, but in the entire Church, the Body of Christ. Only by being a member of this Body could the individual also be a member of Christ. Early Christians considered each church assembly, held in the name of Christ, i.e., in unity and love, as witness of Christ's victory over human egoism, selfishness, and sin. A father of the first century, St Ignatius, bishop of Antioch, wrote in a letter to the church of Ephesus: "Be zealous to assemble more frequently to render thanks [in Greek, *eucharistein*, i.e., 'celebrate the Eucharist'] and praise to God. For, when you meet together frequently, the powers of Satan are destroyed and danger from him is dissolved in the harmony of your faith."[6]

No other passage of early Christian literature gives a clearer indication of the very mystery of the Christian Church: by the power of the Holy Spirit, scattered and separated human beings are able to become, when they gather, a powerful and victorious transfigured reality: "Where two or three are gathered in my name, there am I in the midst of them" (Mt 18.20). This real presence of God in the assembly of the Church makes it possible that the various Christian ministries are really Christ's mysteries and this concerns first of all the episcopal function. Every Christian community is manifesting the Body of Christ in its fullness since this Body cannot be divided: "Wherever Jesus Christ is, there is the Catholic Church."[7] The function of the bishop is to fulfill in the assembly the ministry of the head, to sit where Christ sat among his disciples, to teach what he taught, to be the shepherd and the High Priest. "Let all follow the bishop," St Ignatius writes, "as Jesus Christ did the Father, and the priests, as you would the apostles.... Let that Eucharist be held valid which is offered by the bishop or by one to whom the bishop has committed this charge. Wherever the bishop appears, there let the people be."[8] There is no Church without the bishop, but the reverse being also true, there is no bishop outside the Church, since the head needs a body to fulfill its function. In the views of St Ignatius, which are confirmed by the entire tradition of the Church, it is in the Eucharist that the divinely instituted episcopal ministry finds its real meaning. However, the Eucharist is the sacrament of our unity with God

---

[6]*Ephesians* 6.13; *The apostolic Fathers*, trans. G. G. Walsh, The Fathers of the Church, vol. 1 (New York, 1947), 92.

[7]St Ignatius of Antioch, *Smyrneans* 8; ibid., 121. This is the earliest example of the adjective "catholic" applied to the Church in Christian literature. [Both letters of St Ignatius of Antioch cited here are now available in a new English translation: Ignatius of Antioch, *The Letters*, trans. Alistair Stewart, Popular Patristics Series 49 (Yonkers, NY: St Vladimir's Seminary Press, 2013). —*Ed.*]

[8]*Smyrneans*, ibid. In the time of St Ignatius, every Christian community (or "parish") was headed by a bishop who normally was the only celebrant of the Eucharist. Later, with the expansion of Christianity, the bishops started to delegate their privileges to priests on a permanent basis. The parish priest is nowadays the normal center of Church life on the parish level, but he cannot fulfill these functions unless he is appointed by the bishop.

and of our unity in Christ among ourselves. The bishop stands at the very center of this mystery. His sacramental functions in the Eucharistic liturgy are complemented by his pastoral responsibilities, which oblige him to assure in the practical life of the Church the unity given sacramentally by God in the Eucharist. His ministry is therefore one of reconciliation and unity.

All these aspects of orthodox ecclesiology constitute the foundation of our canonical legislation concerning church structure.

It is inadmissible to have two communities and two bishops in a single place, simply because Christ is one, and only one person can fill his place. This point is of a particular importance today, in our dialogues with Roman Catholics, who have begun to realize that the existence of one "vicar of Christ" for all the churches duplicates (if it does not suppress) the episcopal sacramental ministry of each particular local community.[9] In the Roman Church, there can be neither theological nor practical objection to maintaining in a single place several ecclesiastical jurisdictions, separated by rite, language, or nationality, because the criterion of their unity and the center of their ecclesiastical life is always to be found in Rome, outside their own limits. On the contrary, Orthodox ecclesiology, in affirming the catholic fullness of every local church, is bound to manifest catholic unity everywhere on the local level. The presence of Christ in the Church is guaranteed by the very gathering in his name, in the unity of the true faith and in conformity with true tradition, and not by an allegiance to some universal center.

What happens then when Orthodox Christians living side by side in the same city consider it normal to constitute several "churches"—the Russian, Greek, Serbian, or Syrian—which, of course, maintain their formal unity in faith and spirit, but not in practice? There is no doubt that such a situation is the greatest blow to our witness in the contemporary world and goes against the very nature of the Church of Christ. Any reference

---

[9]This point was dealt with by several authors in one of the last issues of the *Quarterly* devoted to "Primacy and Primacies in the Orthodox Church" (*St Vladimir's Seminary Quarterly* 4.2–3 [1960]). [Veselin Kesich, John Meyendorff, Alexander Schmemann, and Serge Verhovskoy authored four extensive articles on the above-mentioned topic.—*Ed.*]

to "spiritual unity" or "sacramental intercommunion" is of no relevance in this connection because Christ has established on earth a Church visibly one and because the meaning of spiritual communion consists precisely in giving us the strength and responsibility to accomplish visible unity.

Conclusion

The tradition of the Church being clear on this point both on the canonical and on the doctrinal level, the only question which may arise is whether strict territorial unity—one Orthodox bishop, one Orthodox Church in every place for all nationalities and groups—is practical and practicable in 1961 in America. I would answer this question in a twofold manner.

First, by historical evidence: until the early twenties of the present century, when the united Orthodox Church of America (in the Russian jurisdiction) began to disintegrate into an entire constellation of parallel national jurisdictions, it is impossible to find in the entire history of the Church any example of the territorial principle being overlooked. Do we have the right then to consider our present situation as normal?

Second, Orthodox canon law admits what is called the principle of "economy." The most competent canonists of our time are unanimous in defining this principle as a conscious relaxation by the ecclesiastical authorities of the letter of the canons in cases when a strict legalistic observance would do more harm than good to the entire body of the Church.[10] Let us therefore act slowly and carefully "for the good of the Church." For a relatively long period of time, we must give the greatest attention to the existence in America of various national groups preserving their national identity. This can easily be secured inside a united church. National organizations and societies will have to be maintained for the next few generations, and it is equally unavoidable that parishes, deaneries, and even dioceses will preserve for some time their national character, but a single church structure must unite and coordinate church life in America. Various concrete needs can be covered by the principle of "ecclesiastical economy,"

---

[10] N. S. Alivisatos, *Economy from the Orthodox Point of View* (in Greek) (Athens, 1949), 31–39; Hieronymos Kotsonis, *Problems of "Ecclesiastical Economy"* (in Greek) (Athens, 1957), 30–50, etc.

but division cannot remain a permanent norm, and, at the same time, it is to be remembered that the "good of the Church," which may justify temporal separation, requires also unity. The final and ultimate challenge to all of us begins when this "good of the Church" conflicts with the interests of our respective national groups. There is no doubt that, in this case, any Orthodox Christian, whether bishop, priest, or layman, is bound to put the will of God and the holy Tradition of the Church above the "human traditions" which were condemned by the Lord as soon as they conflicted with the law of grace. With wisdom and care, let us move towards the restoration of Orthodox canonical norms in America.

The Unity of the Orthodox Church in America

Serge S. Verhovskoy

St Vladimir's Seminary Quarterly 5.1–2 (1961): 101–103

LAST JUNE [1960—ED.] the primates of the Orthodox churches in America decided to create an all-American standing episcopal conference or synod "for the consideration and resolution of common problems, the coordination of efforts in matters of common concern, and the strengthening of the unity which is the essence of Orthodoxy" as it was said in the minutes. Eleven different commissions will be established by this synod. They will work in the fields of Christian education, theological schools, Orthodox chaplaincy in colleges, boy scout organizations, English translation of the services, chaplaincy in the armed forces, missionary activity, and fund raising. One of these commissions will deal with relations of the Orthodox Church in America with other denominations. Another will follow civil legislation of the United States on church affairs. The synod will direct the activity of the Council of Eastern Orthodox Youth Leaders of America.

One can but rejoice at the organization of the Pan-Orthodox Synod. And we must wish it great success. Nevertheless, this synod is only the first step toward final unification of Orthodoxy in America, and there are certainly many obstacles in obtaining this goal.

Many Orthodox Christians understand the necessity of unity, and it is known to all how destructive the effect of this division of Orthodoxy is regarding the fruitfullness of church activity, church discipline, education, relation with other denominations, etc. However, indifference to the unity of Orthodoxy is widely spread. Behind this indifference, there is one of the most dangerous defects in the life of the Orthodox clergy and people in America: indifference to everything beyond the limits of parish life.

Many Orthodox laymen and priests not only disregard whatever does not directly concern their parishes, but are even inclined to consider everything above parish life as dangerous for their parishes and not deserving confidence. Unity, cooperation, and obedience to the central authorities is often considered as harmful to the rights and interests of the parishes and particularly dangerous to their property rights. Among the bishops we also see a reticent attitude towards the problems of unification; the reasons for this reticence are probably various. But in any case, it is the duty of the episcopate to lead the Church toward unity, a good example of which we see in the organization of the synod.

We must also point out that the Orthodox of Western Europe and America are unfortunately accustomed to divisions. In Western Europe the Orthodox Church was never canonically organized because very few Orthodox lived there before the 1920s. In America there existed a strictly canonical organization before the Russian Revolution that created such a terrible turmoil in the Russian Church. Since the 1920s for forty years already a complete disunity reigns among the Orthodox in America. During this period almost one and a half generations have grown up. It is no wonder that the existence of numerous "jurisdictions" seems normal. It is dreadful that the people are so used to this evil. But even within some of these jurisdictions there is no unity. Parish separatism ruins church life. The canonical consciousness of many Orthodox approaches that of the Protestant congregationalists, who recognize the full independence of each parish, the union of which has the form of a federation. These parishes recognize only these obligations which they willingly accept. Some Orthodox in America openly proclaim that the parishes not only have the right to oppose their rectors and bishops, but that the decisions of the general councils of the Church are not binding to them. Anarchical ideas poison the life of our Church. The episcopate often feels helpless in the face of this evil.

Not only does parish separatism lead to the denial of the necessity for unity, but nationalism does so even more strongly. Too many Orthodox either consider nation higher than Church or Orthodoxy as a national religion and sometimes even as a nationalistic form of Christianity. The intelligentsia and hierarchy share this idea no less than do the people; therefore, it is difficult to overcome this deformation of the understanding of the relations between religion and nationality. From the point of view of church nationalism, the division of the church into national groups is the best form of its organization. This division is consciously asserted and supported although it contradicts Orthodox canons and was condemned by the Constantinopolitan patriarch as the heresy of phyletism.

The last obstacle in reaching the unity of Orthodox churches in America is the existence of clergymen irregularly ordained. Experience shows that the majority of Orthodox churches refuse to be in communion with this clergy, but thousands of Orthodox recognize it. The reason for this acceptance is again nationalism: the people are ready to accept any hierarchy, even irregularly ordained, if it is nationalistically minded. The Orthodox hierarchy would probably be willing to grant a regular ordination to this clergy for the sake of "economia."[1] We hope that this possibility will be used as it was by a bishop this year. A church with a falsely ordained hierarchy is in a position worse than in a schism: such a church has no apostolic succession of ministry and can be excommunicated from the Orthodox Church. This will necessarily also happen in America if the "self-ordained" hierarchy does not canonically regularize its position.

We have said that the newly-created synod is only a first step towards the perfect organization of the Orthodox Church in America. Cooperation between Orthodox jurisdictions is indeed highly desirable. But the very existence of many jurisdictions in one country contradicts the canons.

The Orthodox Church must be organized on the territorial principle, which requires that there should be only one church organization, or as we now say jurisdiction (diocese, metropolitan district, patriarchate), in every country. Before the 1920s there existed no case in the whole history of the Orthodox Church of the same territory being governed by several bishops, in other words, that there existed more than one diocese on the same territory.

---

[1] Economia is a principle by which the Church eases the strictness of its laws by condescension.

Until the present no one objected to this principle. Orthodox belonged everywhere to the same Church organization and were under the jurisdiction of the same bishop regardless of their origin, nationality, class, profession, and convictions concerning the affairs of this world. It happened at all times that Orthodox living in the same city were of various nationalities and generally differed in many respects, but before the present it occurred to no one to organize several independent jurisdictions in the same place on account of this fact. Parishes might use different languages. We know that in the second century already there were parishes of different nationalities in the same cities but they always belonged to the same diocese. When the Bulgarians wished to establish their own diocese in Constantinople, the patriarch condemned them. He was right although the Greek hierarchy itself sometimes sinned against Orthodox tradition by compelling other nations to have services in Greek and by imposing Greek priests and bishops on them. From the most ancient times variety of languages in the Church was considered completely normal and in apostolic times already clergymen could be of any nationality. In general, the Church does not condemn differences of secular character which might exist among us, but it does not establish its own organization on the basis of them.

Some believe that nationality is far deeper and more spiritual than is territory: nationality is connected with moral consciousness, love of our country and culture; territory is but a section of land, which has no spiritual meaning. Is it not better to establish the Church on more spiritual principles? This question is answered by our Lord in his teaching about love of neighbors. Our Lord teaches us to love all men, whoever they are. He affirms that the highest and deepest link between men is their unity in God and their faithfullness to him, which is the essence of the Church. The value of national relation and kinship is not denied by Jesus Christ, but He puts them in second place. The commandment about the love of men orders us to love our neighbors, that is, those with whom we are in direct relation and to whom we can do good. Let us remember the parable of the good Samaritan, which was told by Christ exactly for the purpose of explaining who is our neighbor. The thieves who wounded the Jew were probably of the same nationality as he was, as also were those who passed by indifferently. His neighbor became the Samaritan, a man of different nation, hostile to the Jews. He became a neighbor because providence brought him to the side of the wounded man and he did not remain indifferent to his suffering. Therefore, to love our neighbor means to love him with whom we are in direct relations even if he is our enemy. Inability, or to say better, lack of desire to love our neighbor is the inability or refusal to be Christian. In search for closeness with people of the same nationality one does not need to be a Christian. If Orthodox living in the same city do not want to belong to the same church organization, they ruin the very essence of the Church, which is to unite all neighbors in mutual love and faith in God. Thus, the territorial principle is not at all superficial. On the contrary it expresses the fundamental task of the Church, to unite all men, if only communion between them is possible in fact. If people of different nationalities are incapable of uniting even within the Church, they prove that they do not live as Christians but as men of this world.

When St Paul proclaimed that in the Church there are no Greeks or Jews, no bound or "free, no male or female, but Christ is all and in all" (Gal 3.28), he not only proclaimed the moral commandment of unconditional love among all Christians, but also pointed out the very essence of the Church, that is to be in Christ. In Christ we find communion with God, spiritual perfection, knowledge of truth and justice, the power of grace, love from God, reconciliation with him and with men, spiritual purity, and liberation from evil. The Orthodox faith, the life in grace (in particular the sacraments and services), moral law, and holiness; all this elevates us above this world and must be the content our Christian life regardless of the nation to which we belong and the form of our life and activity on the earth. The task of Church organization is to organize our common Christian spiritual life because the life of the Church must be Christian and spiritual and not simply one of the forms of worldly social activity. Therefore, the organization of the Church, by the very nature of its purpose, must be independent from everything worldly.

If the Church and its organization must be the same for everyone it does not mean that variety is excluded from this unity. There can be different forms of spiritual life (contemplative, active, mystical, moral, ascetic), although all these elements have to be present in some measure in the life of every Christian. There can be different tendencies in theology, especially developing one of its aspects. There can be variety in services and rites. Christians can use different languages. All the more we can have different political convictions and in general a different understanding of the problems of this world. But if such a variety is admissible in the Church it must not be a cause of division. Nevertheless, this is exactly what the Orthodox of Western Europe and America have been doing for the last forty years. We divide the Church according to nationality, language, or attitude towards the Communist governments. If some group founds a parish it is inclined to consider it as its own property, independent from any general organization of the Church. If we would really possess the spirit of the Church, we would create national, political and cultural organizations within Orthodox society, without trying to organize a special jurisdiction for each of them. No people would believe that if they found a parish it belongs to them independent from the Church, like some organization arising from the private initiative of a group of persons.

Let us discuss the general problems of the place of nationality in Orthodoxy. Since apostolic times the Church blessed patriotism, faithfullness to the state, the use of our own language. If it is good to love our people, the first duty of Christian patriotism is to convert our nation to Christianity, to make it really Christian, to create a national Christian culture and statehood. Christ and the apostles tried to convert their own, that is the Jewish people, first. However, the majority of the apostles finally consecrated their life to preaching among other nations. This fact shows that the love of other nations is not less natural and necessary for Christians than patriotism. It is generally easier to serve our own people but sometimes, as it was in the case of Jesus Christ and the apostles, our own nation is closed to Christianity while others are far more open.

The creation of a national Christian culture is a great and honorable task. The Russian culture of the nineteenth century was on the whole Christian and in this lies its great importance. However, the main task of the Church is in establishing a purely Christian culture directly connected with theology, church art, services, and spiritual life. The national element in such a culture is secondary. Such for example was the Byzantine church culture.

Many Orthodox sincerely believe that Orthodoxy itself is nothing more than a religious form of their national life. They admit the necessity for each nation to have a religion even if the latter is not considered important. To some nations this religion is Orthodoxy, therefore it is natural for all those belonging to these nations (for example Russians, or Greeks) to be Orthodox, and to be unfaithful to Orthodoxy for them is to be unpatriotic. Thus, religion is lowered to the significance of a simple addition to national life.

There is a more refined but equally incorrect understanding of the national character of religion. It consists in the recognition of an absolutely inseparable link between religion and nation. However important religion may be it is always necessarily national, being the highest creation of the national spirit. If one nation takes on the religion of another it falls under its spiritual influence. From this point of view Christianity is a form of Judaism and all Christian nations are in their religious aspect under the influence of ancient Israel. Orthodoxy becomes a Christian form of Hellenism. Religion outside a nation is an abstraction: in real religion everything is national and is connected to the development of the national spirit and history.

The only truth in this theory is that the relation between religion and nationality can indeed be very deep and that one nation may be converted by the missionaries of another. However, it is wrong that religion is the product of a national spirit. Even the so-called natural religions (except primitive paganism) were founded by great religious leaders and thinkers. Their influence on their people was far more considerable than the influence of environment was upon them where true religion is concerned its very truthfullness results from the fact that it is based on divine revelation! We believe in the revelation of the Holy Spirit and not of Jewish spirit; Orthodoxy is for us a doctrine preserved in its purity and explained by the God-bearing fathers, and not the creation of Hellenistic genius. True religion is the gift of God to men, although, once accepted by them it becomes a part of their life. Nations are born and die, are converted to the faith and lose it, but the Church remains and shall always remain the same. All the faithful, regardless of nationality belong to the one "holy nation" of God (1 Pet 2.9), participating in the Church which was founded not by men and nations but by God. In general, it is wrong to consider the Church as a worldly or purely human institution. Men and nations can grow spiritually in the Church. Because of their efforts and cooperation with God, the body of the Church can develop. However, its essence, that is, grace, truth, and the spirit of true life, is always of God and not of us or of this world.

The danger of nationalism in the Church is not only in its dividing character but also in the fact that it replaces little by little the spirit of Christianity by national traditions, interests, and even passions. The Church sometimes becomes an instrument of gaining national and political goals. The hierarchy more or less consciously blesses that which is desired by the people and state. Finally, the church is led by the nation and not the nation by the Church. Many inadmissible compromises are justified by the affirmation that they serve national interests.

The nationalism of Orthodox people in America inevitably has a double character: one is related to the former fatherland and one to the United States. The second is at present not as strong as the first, although Orthodox are politically absolutely loyal and become rapidly Americanized as far as education and way of life are concerned. The nationalism of the Orthodox people is shown mainly in the Church, in the closeness of those of the same origin, and in the particular interest which each group has for their former country. The last two forms of national feeling are completely natural, but the first can be both good and bad. It is good to be faithful to the Christian tradition of our nation but it is bad to divide the Church because of an excessive nationalism and to be indifferent to the Orthodox from other nations. On the other hand, it is only deplorable that many Orthodox know so little of their national culture (partly on account of lack of education) and that the second generation of American Orthodox forgets their own national language despite the fact that the knowledge of, for example, Russian and Greek, is appreciated everywhere. If there are some dangers in nationalism from the religious point of view, it does not mean that we must fight national Christian traditions. In the eyes of the people themselves the latter consist primarily in particular ways of celebrating the services (in language, music, rites, etc.). The problem of language must be freely solved by each parish, which can either use only one language or English and the national language simultaneously. The attitude of the Church toward national organizations must be positive, but an excessive or exclusive nationalism only must be condemned. The cooperation of all Orthodox national organizations is certainly very desirable.

It seems to me that taking the strength of nationalism among the Orthodox into consideration, it would be admissible for the sake of economia to have special vicariates or deaneries, uniting the parishes according to their nationality or language, within the limits of each diocese. The Orthodox Church in North America could be divided into no more than ten dioceses for this purpose, so that in each of them there would be a sufficient number of parishes to form national vicariates or deaneries.

Nevertheless, all the parishes existing in a certain territory must be united in only one diocese. This is the requirement of the dogma of the unity of the Church, of the canons regulating Church administration, and of Christian ethics, calling for the unity of all Christians regardless of their nationality. We must finally understand that the divisions in the Orthodox Church in Western Europe and America may be called at best a "spiritual illness" but more strictly speaking they are a betrayal of Orthodoxy.

The diocesan bishop must have the full authority granted to him by the canons. However, it would be natural and desirable to have periodical meetings of the suffragan bishops and deans of the diocese besides regular diocesan conventions of all the clergymen and lay representatives. The vicariates and deaneries could organize their own meetings.

The nationality of candidate for diocesan bishop could be considered as indifferent if this candidate would be accepted by the greater majority of the diocesan convention (for instance by more than 4/5 of voices). In the opposite case, a regulation could be established according to which each new bishop should be of a different nationality than the previous one.

The same principle could be applied to the election of the primate of the whole American Church. Thus, the danger that the government of the Church would be taken by one nationality would be eliminated. The head of the American Church should govern in cooperation with the council of all bishops which could be convened twice or thrice yearly.

Only a united Orthodox Church in America would be perfectly Orthodox and strong. Only a united Church could overcome the divisions, disorders, and the spirit of separatism which we so often meet. Only a united Church could be able to elevate rapidly the level of Church education by an organized and energetic effort. At present even the bishops very often feel helpless to encourage education. The clergy and laity are often indifferent to this problem. There is neither a sufficient number of well-trained personnel nor sufficient funds for this purpose. Ignorance of one's own faith is pernicious for the Church. For this reason thousands of Orthodox leave the Church or become so-called nominal believers. In general, our Church does only part of the work which is necessary to be done: there are very few Orthodox schools, very few books about Orthodoxy, no missions, monasticism is weak, Orthodox students in colleges do not receive sufficient religious guidance, the number of chaplains in the armed forces is insufficient, we have no Orthodox hospitals and Orthodox patients are sometimes neglected (e.g., in New York), welfare organizations are weak. Our Church is represented in interdenominational organizations not as it should be. All this is chiefly the consequence of bad organization and lack of experienced personnel. A united Church would certainly overcome all these defects.

At this time the significance of Orthodoxy in America is not great. In the eyes of Americans we are one of the secondary denominations which is divided into many organizations and is not very active. This would change if Orthodoxy were united. The United States is now one of the greatest powers on earth. A strong Orthodox Church in this country could have a great influence all over the world, and could help the Orthodox churches abroad far more than we now do. It is a real misunderstanding to believe that separate national jurisdictions in America can do more for their mother churches than could a united Orthodox Church.

When the Orthodox Church in the United States will become strong, great missionary possibilities will be open to it in this country itself, in Asia and possibly even in Africa, where there are already a few native parishes.

If Orthodoxy still has influence in the world it is on account of the interest which other confessions take in it. If the Orthodox would make the same effort to spread Orthodoxy as do other confessions for their own faith, our Church would have many thousands of converts and its general spiritual and theological influence would be considerably increased. We ourselves badly use the treasures of Orthodoxy and do not open them to others, like the wicked servant who buried his talent (Mt 25.14–30).

Would not unification of the Orthodox Church in America lead to its rapid Americanization? Is not Americanization dangerous for the Church?

We face the strange fact that many Orthodox are inclined to recognize the legitimacy of all nationalisms in the Church except American. For Americans who know English only and are not of Orthodox origin there is very often no room in our Church. In the whole United States there are only a few parishes which entirely use English and which do not declare themselves as belonging to any of the nationalities of the Old World, although even these are parts of some national jurisdiction. This situation is abnormal. I hope that there is no necessity to prove that Americans who have lost the link with their former nationality or are recently converted to Orthodoxy, have a full right not only to be Orthodox, but to have American parishes, which would be open to everybody preferring to use English. A denial of such a right and necessity would be contrary to Orthodox tradition since apostolic times. The number of such parishes even with a favorable attitude from the hierarchy would increase slowly. The majority of Orthodox parishes will not become purely American before two or three generations. This Americanization must be absolutely free and dependent on the free choice of parishioners and their priests.

The Americanization of the Orthodox Church would make the union of Orthodoxy psychologically easier and would widen the possibilities for educational and missionary work—the latter on condition of the creation of Orthodox literature in English and of the full translation of all services into English. We must not forget that without educational work in English we are unable not only to spread our Church but even to preserve it from the loss of part of our youth. Our American young people sometimes leave the Church because the spiritual richness of Orthodoxy is not sufficiently shown to them.

Without the full English text of Orthodox services the liturgical life of those who know only English is inevitably poor. Already at the present time the greatest part of the parishioners attends only the Liturgy. The exceptional spiritual value of the Orthodox services is thus lost to Americans; they are unable to use one of the most important sources of the spiritual, moral, and theological education. Even some of our clergymen seem to forget the power of spirituality and depth of theology which is contained in our services.

The dangers of Americanization are real, but they are already active. If our church would possess a better and stronger organization it would be much easier to fight them. These dangers are as follows: first, the loss of the language and culture of our old countries. Very few among our youth study the culture of their ancestors and even fewer work in this field. Professors of Russian, Greek, Serbian, etc. are mostly Americans having no original connections with these nations. Secondly, American education has many negative sides connected with contemporary ideas, psychology, pedagogy, literature, television etc. Our youth is defenseless against such negative influences because in the absence of Orthodox schools and publications it is brought up entirely in the American culture. The clergy often cannot help our youth in this respect because they sometimes possess neither a higher theological education nor an American college degree. Thirdly the insufficient attention to purely spiritual life which is spread through America undoubtedly affects the Orthodox also. Ambition, vainglory, and the habit to praise oneself and others under any pretext is also very common in our church. Finally, as we have already mentioned, there is a certain influence of American Protestantism on the ambitious anticlericalism of our laity and on the separatism of our parishes.

It is obvious that America not only has defects but also great positive qualities, for example, an exceptional vital power, an openness to all that is good, a love of activity and education, a pioneer spirit, a desire and ability to work together, to help each other, to be generous and responsive, to learn one's own defects. All these qualities are also very necessary for us

Orthodox. In energy, pioneering, education, organization, solidarity, generosity, and in mutual help we are often behind other Americans.

On the one hand, as we see, the dangerous sides of Americanism are already actual and will be the more active the weaker the organization of our church is. On the other hand, we cannot but desire to assimilate all that is good in America. In any case Americans have no less right to be Orthodox than does any other nation.

However, the unity of the Orthodox Church is necessary not for the purpose of Americanization and not because a rapid denationalization of Greeks, Russians, Syrians, and other Orthodox nationalities would be desirable, but for the benefit of the Church and in the name of our faithfullness to Orthodoxy. The present organization of our Church is contrary to Orthodoxy. Therefore, all Orthodox must wish that the first step made by our hierarchy toward unity would not be the last one. A kind of federation of the Orthodox churches in America is welcome as a transitory state only, but not as a final form of organization, which must be according to our dogmas and canons a complete unity of all Orthodox in one Orthodox American Church.

Conditions of Autocephaly (I)[1]

Alexander A. Bogolepov

St Vladimir's Seminary Quarterly 5.3 (1961): 11–37

1. The Establishment of a New Local Church as a Problem of Orthodox Canon Law

THE WAY IN WHICH NEW Orthodox local churches are established is of special significance for Orthodox canon law. As a legal problem, the establishment of a new church is significant, for opposite reasons, neither to Catholicism nor Protestantism.

According to Roman Catholic teaching, the Church is one, not only because all her members profess the same faith and join in a common worship, but also because they are united by the guidance of the infallible successor of St Peter, the Roman pontiff. The unity of the Roman Catholic Church eliminates the possibility of any lawful separation from her. No new church can be organized from the parts of the Roman Church and legitimately become independent. From the Roman point of view, the true Christian Church can exist only under the authority of the Pope of Rome, the visible head of the Church and Christ's vicar on Earth; those Christians who are outside of the Roman Church are heretics or schismatics. Ecclesiastical bodies existing separately from the Roman Catholic Church can

---

[1] This is the first of two articles dealing with the problem of ecclesiastical independence and its implications in America. [The promised second part of this text was never published in the *Quarterly*, but it was indeed included in Alexander A. Bogolepov's volume published two years later: *Toward an American Orthodox Church: The Establishment of an Autocephalous Orthodox Church* (New York: Morehouse-Barlow Co., 1963). The first part of the above-mentioned volume (first seven chapters; pp. 11–47) is a reprint of this very article, while the second (last three chapters; pp. 48–100) explores the implications of the canonical concept of autocephaly in the United States' context. A new edition of A. A. Bogolepov's volume, with a foreword by John H. Erickson, was published by St Vladimir's Seminary Press in 2001.—*Ed.*].

be united with her only on the condition of their complete subordination to the pope.

Unlike Catholics, Protestants recognize the possibility of organizing new religious communities. Since preaching the Word of God is considered the basic task of the Church, each group of believers may, in their struggle for the right understanding of the Gospel, organize their own community with their own clergy. In Protestant practice, the establishment of a new body of clergy presents no specific difficulties. It can even be established by the community itself. Since Protestantism recognizes the absolute supremacy of the Word, the Church is considered as founded on the teaching of Christ, that is "on Christ" but not "by Christ" and his apostles. In their fight against the Roman Catholic Church, the Protestants rejected the idea of the uninterrupted succession of the spiritual authority from the apostles. Only churches of the Anglican communion recognize the apostolic succession in principle. Since the appointment of pastors and ministers in the Protestant Church is not connected with the reception of hierarchal authority from the successors of the apostles, it does not, therefore, depend on an existing hierarchy but rather depends solely on the community of believers. From the point of view of the Protestant ecclesiology, nothing stands in the way of the separation of one or several communities from established Protestant churches and for the organization of new Protestant churches. Complications may arise from civil authorities concerning the activities of ecclesiastical associations of citizens, but not from the Protestant concept of the Church. In spite of the desire for unity, Protestantism is, in reality, not one Church but an aggregation of many Protestant churches and communities which differ from one another both in their teachings and their structures.

The Orthodox Church retained the concept of church unity which existed during the time of the seven Ecumenical Councils. She is a unity in plurality of sister churches, some of whom can have only the privileges of honor. Her unity does not consist in the subordination to one single head. She recognizes no one to have been empowered by Christ to be his vicar on earth and to have an indisputable authority above the whole of his Church. The deep spiritual unity of the sister churches consists in the unity of faith, church tradition, basic features of canonical structure and divine services, as well as in the recognition only of that hierarchy which inherited its authority from the apostles—from all the apostles, and not just from Peter. The Orthodox Church greatly values the connection of her hierarchy with the apostles and through them with Christ himself, and she firmly retains the principle of apostolic succession of hierarchal authority. With regard to the administration of internal affairs, the sister churches enjoy the right of self-government and have independent ruling bodies. Administrative independence is provided for by differences in local usages but it is connected with a strong adherence to the basic principles of faith and church order. The highest expressions of this unity were the Ecumenical Councils.

Since the time of the Ecumenical Councils, the unity of the Church has been expressed in meetings of the heads of the various churches as well as in their correspondence with one another and in letters notifying others as to their accession to their sees, in reciprocal visits, and in the exchanges of delegations. Besides all this, the previous intercommunion in sacraments and worship has always been retained in full. Bishops and priests of one local church worship together with the bishops and priests of another sister church; members of one Church partake in the sacraments and worship of other churches. In this way the community of spiritual life and the unity of the whole body of the Orthodox Church are secured, and an unrestricted subdivision of church structure as is found in the Protestant Church is thereby eliminated.

The first four Ecumenical Councils not only recognized the principle that the Church consists of several administratively independent local churches but they also established new local churches. In this way the possibility was given for establishing new local churches, whose number has never been limited.

The possibility that the number of local churches may expand creates the problem of establishing the canonical requirements for setting up such a new local church. This problem is more complicated in Orthodox canon law than it is for Protestants because under Orthodox canon law, the establishment of new independent self-governing local Orthodox churches is bound up with the observance of certain requirements, such as securing the apostolic succession of hierarchal authority and maintaining unity among the sister churches.

2. Canonical Requirements for Establishing a New Local Church

The requirements for establishing new local churches are closely connected with peculiar features of their canonical position. The Orthodox sister churches are autocephalous churches. We would search in vain for the word "autocephalous" in the canons adopted by the Ecumenical Councils. It was introduced by practice, and its meaning changed with the course of history. Later, the term "autocephalous" (in Greek—"himself the head") was used to denote a self-governing independent church, a concept that had already been elaborated by the Ecumenical Councils.

Having recognized each of the five civil dioceses of the prefecture of the East as independent churches, the Second Ecumenical Council determined that "The bishops of Alexandria, Antioch, Asia (Minor), Pontus, and Thrace," may "alone administer the affairs of their dioceses," without any interference from other ecclesiastical authorities (Canon 2). Defending the independence of the Church of Carthage, the African Council of 424 also insisted in its letter to Pope Celestine, "That all matters should be determined in the places where they arise." In addition, at the time that it recognized the independence of the churches of Cyprus from the Church of Antioch, the Third Ecumenical Council declared that, "The rulers of the holy churches of Cyprus shall enjoy, without dispute or diminution, . . . the right of performing for themselves the ordination of their excellent bishops" (Canon 8). Among the three bishops of Cyprus, who presented their petition to the Third Ecumenical Council, the newly elected head of the Church of Cyprus, Bishop Reginus, was also present at Ephesus. His election by the bishops of Cyprus was recognized as canonically valid: an autocephalous church can appoint her head herself. Therefore, there are two distinguishing marks of an autocephalous church:

(1) The right to resolve all internal problems on her own authority, independently of all other churches, and

(2) The right to appoint her own bishops, among them the head of the church.

Accordingly, a part of the Orthodox Church claiming to be autocephalous must be sufficiently mature to organize its own ecclesiastical life; it must have a sufficient number of parishes and parishioners, the possibility of training new clergymen, and a hierarchy canonically capable of making subsequent appointments of new bishops. As to the latter, canonically very important, requirement, the canons distinguish between (a) the appointment of a bishop, i.e., the designation of a person to hold the office of bishop, and (b) the ordination or consecration of the bishop. According to the 4th Canon of the First Ecumenical Council, the appointment of a bishop can be made by "at least" three bishops of the provincial council of bishops, and "then the ordination should take place." As to the ordination, it can be performed by as few as two bishops (Apostolic Canon 1), but it can take place only after the candidate had been appointed by the assembly of at least three ruling bishops, since the provincial council of bishops consists only of bishops who administer dioceses belonging to the metropolitan district. If the number of ruling bishops of one Orthodox region is less than three, then this region cannot be proclaimed "autocephalous," since it is canonically unable to provide new bishops for itself.

Authority to appoint and ordain a new bishop exists only when the three ruling bishops of an ecclesiastical region are themselves duly appointed and ordained, which means that they also had to be appointed and ordained by ruling bishops of one of the autocephalous Orthodox churches having the "right of performing for themselves the ordination of their excellent bishops" (Ephesus, Canon 8). Since no autocephalous church has the right to appoint bishops for any but her own dioceses, a bishop of a new church originally had to be appointed by ruling bishops of one of the established autocephalous churches to a diocese of that particular church. As a result, the whole church region claiming autocephalous status must be a part of an autocephalous Church, her diocese, or her mission.

This rule had been deeply rooted in the practice of the Orthodox Church. Before proclaiming her independence in 1448, the Russian Church had been a metropolitan district of the Church of Constantinople. In the 19th and 20th centuries, the newly established churches of Greece, Serbia, Romania, Bulgaria, and Albania, were also dioceses of the Patriarchate of Constantinople. The Polish Orthodox Church was formed from dioceses of the Russian Church. The Church of Czechoslovakia included diocesan districts which were under the jurisdiction of the churches of Russia and Serbia, as well as some former Uniate dioceses which came under the jurisdiction of Moscow. The autonomous churches of Finland and China originated from parts of the Russian Church.

New churches always originate from existing autocephalous churches, and the whole Orthodox Church is like a tree which sends its branches in different directions; nevertheless, all the branches are fed by one sap and live one life. In this way the uninterrupted succession from the apostles has really been preserved. Any ecclesiastical region which was not a part of an autocephalous local church and whose administration was not organized by that church, may not claim to be autocephalous.

The presence of three canonically approved bishops as well as the canonical origin from one of the autocephalous churches, however, gives the right to claim an independent ecclesiastical administration only if that region is located in a state independent of that of its mother church. This requirement developed in the course of long church practice, beginning with the 19th century. It derived from a system of establishing new churches during the time of the Ecumenical Councils. For practical considerations, ecclesiastical districts were established from the very beginning of the Christian era in conformity with the political division of the Roman Empire. Later on, this practice was confirmed by the 17th Canon of the Council of Chalcedon, which stated: "Let the order of the ecclesiastical parishes follow the political and municipal pattern." The same regulation was renewed by the 38th Canon of the Council in Trullo, which reads: "Let the order of things ecclesiastical follow the civil and public models." Since the political division of the Roman Empire was based on the territorial principle, the same territorial principle was also applied to the determination of the borders of ecclesiastical districts.

In the course of its historical development, the Roman Empire included in its boundaries some formerly independent states with a population consisting of different nationalities. Consequently, its political and administrative division reflected, to a certain extent, the national character of the countries absorbed. National peculiarities of the different regions were much more preserved in the lower administrative districts than in the higher ones, but the territorial principle was paramount whereas the national principle was always subordinate. Following the civil and public models, the administrative division of the Church also reflected, to some extent, the national composition of the Roman Empire.

The 34th Apostolic Canon mentions the national principle in the lower church districts; according to this canon, "The bishop of every nation (*ethnos*), must acknowledge him who is first among them." The language of this canon has been cited to support the contention that the nation should be the basis of Church organization; however, the Council of Antioch of 341 gave the most authoritative interpretation to the word "nation" (*ethnos*). Its Canon 9 explains "nation" (*ethnos*), not as meaning a people bound together by ties of blood, language, and customs, but as meaning a "province," as the administrative subdivision of the civil diocese of the Roman Empire. The 9th Canon of Antioch, which in effect reproduces the 34th Apostolic Canon, reads: "It behooves the bishops in every province (in Greek—*eparchia*) to acknowledge the bishop who presides in the metropolis." Thus, in the middle of the fourth century the territorial principle was recognized as paramount for the establishment and government of ecclesiastical districts, regardless of whether or not it conformed to the national principle. The national principle was significant only so far as it coincided with the territorial principle, but it could never override it.

Later in the history of Orthodox canon law, this correlation of the territorial and the national principles was interpreted to mean that a new autocephalous church could only be established for a nation lying within the borders of a state independent of the mother church. From the ninth century, this point of view was accepted by the new Balkan nations: Bulgaria, Serbia, and Romania. These had all received Christianity from Constantinople; the Church in these states had the same quality as that of

Byzantium, i.e., was a state-church. After these nations had acquired their independence, efforts were made to withdraw their churches from subordination to Constantinople and to establish them as independent church administrations. After all the others, the Russian Church went the same way.

In the *Kormchaya Kniga* (*The Rudder*) published by Patriarch Nikon in 1653, the establishment of these new churches, as well as the secession of the Russian Church from the Patriarchate of Constantinople, was justified. In the introductory chapters of the *Kormchaya Kniga* it was explained that the reception of Christianity from Constantinople does not mean that the Church must be subordinated to the Patriarch of Constantinople forever. If a nation has established an independent state, not subordinate to the Greek Empire, and if the local church gradually becomes stronger, it may in time become self-governing and independent. The initiative can be taken, as was the case with the Bulgarian Church, by the tsar, who very "justly" decided to nominate a Patriarch by the Bulgarian bishops' sobor in Trnovo. It is also possible to obtain the necessary consent of the Greek emperor and the patriarch, as occurred in Serbia, where the patriarch was appointed by the local bishops. As for Russia, the *Kormchaya Kniga* stressed the extreme significance of the Russian principality since ancient times and the subsequent high authority of the Russian tsar, describing the sublimity of the state of Moscow and the growth of its piety. As a strange inconsistency, it was pointed out that the Russian metropolitans were still ordained by the Patriarch of Constantinople and, despite the long distance, they had to go to Constantinople for their ordinations. The submission of all the Eastern churches to the Muslim Turkish rule was mentioned as a further obstacle to the Russian metropolitans' going to Constantinople (pp. 5–10); by all this the idea was emphasized that an independent Orthodox Church can be established in an independent state.[2]

Although it was not so pleasant for the patriarchal see of Constantinople, the above principle was generally recognized even by the latter at the Synod of 1593, in Constantinople. The question was raised at that

---

[2] A. Bogolepov, "On the 300th Anniversary of the *Kormchaya Kniga*," *The Russian American Orthodox Messenger* 4 (1953): 58, 59 (in Russian).

Conditions of Autocephaly (I)

synod whether canonical rules allow the establishment of a patriarchal see in Moscow, and whether the Russian Church could be recognized as autocephalous. An affirmative answer to this question was obtained through the interpretation of Canon 28 of Chalcedon, according to which the patriarchal see of Constantinople received its privileges because Constantinople was a royal city, honored with the sovereignty and the senate. The same argument was applied to the see of Moscow, which could also be recognized as worthy of the patriarchal dignity, since Moscow was a royal city of the Russian kingdom.[3]

The principle, "An autocephalous Church in an independent state," was later approved and developed in detail by the patriarch of Constantinople, Joachim III, in his letter concerning the recognition of the Serbian Church in 1879. The Letter of Patriarch Joachim III is an answer to the letters of the Serbian Prince Milan Obrenovich and Michael, the Metropolitan of Belgrade, requesting that the Serbian Church be granted independence. After having given careful consideration to this problem, Patriarch Joachim III, together with his Holy Synod, recognized that self-governing local churches may be established, "not only in conformity with the historical importance of the cities and countries in Christianity, but also according to political conditions of the life of their people and nations." Referring then to the 23rd Canon of Chalcedon and to other canons, as well as to the opinion of Patriarch Photius, Patriarch Joachim III reaffirmed: "The ecclesiastical rights, especially those of parishes, usually follow the political subdivision of the country and the government concerned."

(a) Whereas—the Letter goes on—the pious and God-protected principality of Serbia has, through God's providence, gained strength, has increased, and has attained complete political independence, and,

(b) Whereas, the most pious Prince Milan M. Obrenovich IV and His Eminence, Michael, Archbishop of Belgrade and Metropolitan of Serbia, on behalf of the honorable clergy and pious people,

---

[3] A. Kartashev, *The History of the Russian Church*, vol. 2 (Paris, 1959), 44 (in Russian).

requested us by letter to grant autocephalous and independent ecclesiastical status, conforming with the political independence of the state, the patriarch and the holy synod found that the request was well grounded and conformed to the spirit of the sacred canons and to church practice," and therefore decided—"To proclaim the holy Serbian Church autocephalous, independent and self-governing."[4]

The above decision is of extreme importance because the granting of autocephalous status is conditioned directly upon the location of the church in a politically independent state, so that the foundation of a new church under such circumstances is recognized as being "in conformity to the spirit of the sacred canons and to Church practice." The same idea was used by the ecumenical patriarch Gregory VII as a basis of his Patriarchal and Synodal Canonical Tomos of November 13, 1924. When referring to Canon 17 of the Fourth Ecumenical Council and Canon 36 of the Council in Trullo, Patriarch Gregory VII states that the structure of ecclesiastical affairs has to follow the political and public forms. These were the reasons to grant the autocephalous status to the Orthodox Church in the reestablished Polish state. Therefore, a church district of canonical origin having no fewer than three duly appointed ruling bishops may receive autocephalous status, if it be situated in a politically independent state.

It is true that the Letter of Patriarch Joachim III concerned the Serbian Church as a national one, but even in this case the national principle was again subordinated to the territorial; the Serbian Church was recognized as independent, as long as her members were within the borders of the state of Serbia, however, the Orthodox Serbs living outside the Serbian state, for example in Austria, were not regarded as belonging to the Serbian Autocephalous Church, and they were not granted her privileges. On the other hand, the political-territorial principle cannot prevent members of one nationality group, within the borders of an independent Church, from

---

[4]The content of the Letter of Patriarch Joachim III is given by Prof. I. Palmov in his report to the Pre-Sobor Committee of 1906. *Journals and Protocols of the Sessions of the Pre-Sobor Committee*, vol. 3 (St Petersburg, 1907), 236–37 (in Russian). See also N. Duchich, *History of the Serbian Church* (Belgrade, 1894), 232–36 (in Serbian).

living side by side with members of another ethnic group as citizens of the same state. In multi-national states, the political-territorial principle comes to the concept of a "nation-state," and may include all citizens of that state.

Later, the independence of a state as a prerequisite for obtaining autocephalous status was also stressed by Patriarch Alexis at the Moscow Conference of 1948. Actually, Patriarch Alexis only repeated the reasons mentioned in the *Kormchaya Kniga* by Patriarch Nikon, but at the same time he defined them more exactly and gave some additional reasons. His most important points were:

(1) The number of bishops in the Russian Church far exceeded the minimum canonically required for the establishment of an independent church;

(2) The Russian Church found herself within another state, which possessed an enormous territory and was quite independent of the state in which her mother church of Constantinople was located;

(3) Her faithful belonged to another nation, which had a different language, different habits, and different customs;

(4) It became more and more obvious that not only was there a need for having a Russian metropolitan as head of the Russian Church but also, for having the right of appointing him independently of the patriarch of Constantinople, by a council of Russian bishops.

Further on, just as in the *Kormchaya Kniga*, Patriarch Alexis mentioned the great distance between Constantinople and Moscow, the instability of the Greek Church in Orthodoxy, the fall of Constantinople into the hands of the Turks, which threatened the Church with the loss of the purity of her faith, and the fact that the Bulgarian and Serbian churches had long since received autocephalous status, although they were smaller than the Russian Church and were situated nearer to Constantinople.

The complete list of the prerequisites for establishing a new local church given by Patriarch Alexis is important because the patriarch indicated some additional conditions which might justify separation from a mother church.

Among several reasons for secession from the Greek Church, Patriarch Alexis mentioned the instability of the Greek Church in Orthodoxy. He asserted that the Russian Church could preserve the Orthodox faith pure and intact only by becoming completely independent of the Church of Constantinople.[5] This statement by Patriarch Alexis evidently rested upon Canons 13–15 of the First-Second Council of 861 in Constantinople. The canons permit and even approve withdrawing from communion with higher ecclesiastical authorities when they publicly preach a heresy already condemned by the holy councils or by the holy fathers.

Now, that the hierarchy of the Russian Church has been compelled to support the Communist government in both internal and external difficulties in return for its permission to reestablish the shattered hierarchal structure of the Church and for some freedom of performing divine services, the Russian hierarchy usually asserts that secession from the Russian Church can be lawful only if hierarchs would openly preach heresy (Letter of Locum Tenens, Metropolitan Sergius, December 31, 1927).[6]

The attempt to limit the reasons for separation to dogmatic problems or to treat canonical reasons as dogmatic is absolutely unjustified. The provisions concerning reasons for secession are not limited to Canons 13–15 of the First-Second Council in 861. They are also found in the Apostolic Canon 31, which gave the reasons for secession. It forbade the secession of a presbyter from his bishop, if he did it without first condemning his bishop (before the bishops' council) for doing something wrong not only with regard to "piety" but also with regard to "righteousness." The public preaching of heresy can be understood as an infringement of piety,

---

[5] *Acts of the Conference of the Heads and Representatives of the Autocephalous Orthodox Church in Moscow, 1948*, vol. 1 (Moscow, 1949), 11–13 (in Russian). [A French version of the Proceedings is also available: *Actes de la Conférence des chefs et des représentants des Églises Orthodoxes Autocéphales, réunis à Moscou a l'occasion de la célébration solennelle des fêtes du 500ème anniversaire de l'autocéphalie de l'Église Orthodoxe Russe (8–18 juillet 1948)* vol. 1–2 (Moscow: Éditions du Patriarcat, 1950–52).—*Ed.*]

[6] See also Archbishop Makarios, "To the Communion of the North American Metropolia and Moscow Patriarchate," *Yedinaya Tserkov* (1947): 9–40 (in Russian).

while the violation of righteousness includes violations of ecclesiastical order and the rules of organization and administration of the Church. The validity of the Apostolic Canons, recognized by Trullo and the Seventh Ecumenical Councils, is higher than that of the canons of the local First-Second Council of 861, which do not belong to the general canonical code of the Orthodox Church established by the Ecumenical Councils. Therefore, Canons 13–15 of the Council of 861 are no restriction on the broader meaning of the 31st Apostolic Canon and, hence, the reasons for secession can be dogmatic as well as canonical.

Patriarch Alexis also regarded the subordination of Constantinople to the Muslim yoke as a danger to the purity of the Orthodox faith. This subordination could not have been the immediate reason for the separation of the Russian Church from the Patriarchate of Constantinople. The Greek Metropolitan Isidore was deposed in Moscow in 1441, and in 1448 a new Russian Metropolitan Jonah was elected in his place by the Russian Sobor, whereas the city of Constantinople was captured by the Turks in 1453; the Russian Church became independent of the Church of Constantinople before that city's seizure by the Turks. But the Muslim yoke could still have been the reason for Moscow's maintaining its independence, which had been proclaimed earlier. The Russian apprehensiveness about injury to Orthodoxy in Constantinople under the Turks was, of course, exaggerated. However, the Russian Church faced the real danger that her head might become dependent on the Muslim sultan if Russian metropolitans were appointed in Constantinople. Like all appointments of bishops made by the ecumenical patriarch, the appointment of the metropolitan for Moscow would have had to be approved by the sultan. The Russian candidates would have been obliged to make a long trip to Constantinople, visit the sultan, and make to him the necessary payments in order to receive confirmation of their right to the Moscow see.[7] The dependence of the ecumenical patriarch upon the sultan could have impaired the free development of ecclesiastical life in the Moscow state. Patriarch Alexis rightly emphasized the dependence of the mother church on a non-Christian power as

---

[7] A. Kartashev, *The History of the Russian Church*, vol. 1 (Paris, 1959), 376 (in Russian).

one of the reasons for the establishment of an independent ecclesiastical administration.

If an ecclesiastical region not only fulfills the three principal requirements necessary for receiving autocephalous status (canonical origin, presence of at least three duly appointed bishops, and location in a state other than that of the mother church), but also has other reasons forcing it to separate from its mother church, then these additional reasons take on special importance; they reinforce its right of self-government. Such reasons may be: the mother church's support of heresy, violation of the basic principles of the canonical structure of the Church, as well as the subordination of the mother church to a civil government which deprives her of freedom. But all these circumstances are only additional reasons forcing a certain ecclesiastical region to use its canonical rights to complete independence and speeding up the process of separation from the mother church.

It must also be noted that Patriarch Alexis took a strong legal stand on the question. He gave a full account of the reasons for ecclesiastical independence in order to prove that the "Russian Church even in the first years of her existence had a right to more than she had received in the field of her Church administration," which means that she should have had a more independent administration than that which she had. In his conclusion Patriarch Alexis emphasized that the Russian Church "possessed all the canonical prerequisites not only for autonomous, but also for autocephalous status."[8] But if a church meets all the canonical requirements for autocephalous status, then justice requires that its claim be recognized and that it be included in the number of autocephalous churches. "Rights" always correspond with "duties" of others to act according to these rights.

---

[8] *Acts of the Conference of the Heads and Representatives of the Autocephalous Orthodox Churches in Moscow, 1948*, vol. 1 (Moscow, 1949), 11 (in Russian).

3. The Recognition of a New Local Church at the Time of the Ecumenical Councils

The recognition of autocephalous status is the final act in the establishment of a new and independent Church. From that moment on, she becomes a full and equal member of the community of autocephalous churches of the Orthodox Church. The introduction of a new member into this community is of common concern to all its members, as well as to the entire Orthodox Church. Therefore, such an innovation can only occur with the consent of all the other autocephalous churches.

During the time of the ecumenical councils all new independent church were recognized, or established, by ecumenical councils themselves. The independence of the Churches of Rome, Alexandria, and Antioch was recognized by the First Ecumenical Council. The churches of Thrace, Asia Minor, and Pontus were proclaimed independent by the Second Ecumenical Council. The independence of the Church of Cyprus was established by the Third Ecumenical Council. The Fourth Ecumenical Council subordinated the churches of Thrace, Asia Minor, and Pontus to the authority of the archbishop of Constantinople and, at the same time, founded the Church of Constantinople. The same council also proclaimed the Church of Jerusalem to be independent.

When the Ecumenical Councils ceased to convene, church practice from the 9th to the 20th centuries established two methods by which the existence of new churches was officially recognized: (1) By the mother church, and (2) By the ecumenical patriarch. Under either method, the other autocephalous churches joined in the recognition.

4. Recognition of a New Church by the Mother Church

The prerogative of the mother church to recognize a new church was strongly defended in a letter by Alexis, Patriarch of Moscow, to the ecumenical patriarch, Athenagoras (March 7, 1953). "Until rules have been established by which one part of a local church may be proclaimed autocephalous," this letter states, "legal force shall be attributed to the practice of establishing an autocephalous church by the decision of the council of bishops of her mother church, which alone has the right to decide on matters such as the granting of autocephalous, as well as autonomous, status to one of her parts. Of this fact numerous examples can be provided."⁹

As appears from this letter, "rules" for proclaiming one part of a local church autocephalous or autonomous have not yet been established and hence, the rights of the mother church are based upon the existing order, relying on "numerous examples," taken from church practice or church customs. But Church practices can have special legal force only if based on canons. In order to prove the privilege of the mother church to establish new local churches reference is usually made to the Apostolic Canon 31, as well as Canons 13, 14, and 15 of the First-Second Council of 861 in Constantinople (see The Letter of the Patriarchal Locum Tenens, Metropolitan Sergius of January 5, 1935 to Archbishop Benjamin, Patriarchal Exarch in America).

Apostolic Canon 31 prescribes that a presbyter be deposed who despises his own bishop, collects a separate congregation, and erects another altar without having any grounds for condemning his bishop with regard to piety or righteousness. Canon 13 of the First-Second Council also provides that any presbyter or deacon shall be subject to deposition if he, on the ground that his own bishop has been condemned for certain crimes, but before the Council of Bishops has examined the charges, should dare to secede from his communion. The same sanction was laid down in Canon 14 for a bishop who withdraws from communion with his metropolitan, and in Canon 15, for any presbyter, bishop, or metropolitan who breaks away from his patriarch. All these canons of the Council of 861 forbid the arbitrary withdrawal of clergymen from communion with their higher ecclesiastical authorities, except in the case when the bishop publicly preaches a heresy which has already been condemned by the holy councils. But none of these canons is concerned with establishing a new local church.

(1) They only mention personal acts of individual clergymen—the withdrawal by a deacon or presbyter from canonical communion with his bishop, by the bishop from communion with his metropolitan,

---

⁹*Zhurnal Moskovskoy Patriarchii* 5 [Journal of the Moscow Patriarchate] (1953): 4–8.

as well as by a metropolitan, bishops, or presbyters with their patriarch, regardless of whether the flock joins them. Even if a part of the flock follows them, the withdrawn part is canonically unable to continue an independent church life. By contrast, whenever a new church is established, it is not one presbyter, or one bishop, or metropolitan who withdraws from church communion, but rather an entire region, with its population and clergy, with no fewer than three bishops who withdraw not from communion but only from administrative dependence.

(2) The Council of 861 considered the withdrawal of a bishop or metropolitan from communion with his patriarch on a level with that of a presbyter from his bishop or patriarch. It is very clear that the Council of 861 was only concerned with internal strife (the secession of the adherents of Ignatius from Patriarch Photius) and did not provide regulations for the separation of a part of the Church situated in a country completely independent from Byzantium, whereas the founding of a new autocephalous church depends upon the location of a church in a region within the boundaries of a state other than that of its mother church.

(3) Apostolic Canon 31 and Canons 13–15 of the First-Second Council only deal with splits which occur as a result of charges brought forward against certain hierarchs. Where the withdrawal occurs before these charges are heard by the council of bishops, it is looked upon as a schism, an illicit, arbitrary split, and those found guilty are subject to ecclesiastical sanctions: deposition or excommunication. But the establishing of a new church from parts of the old Church may occur without any charges against the hierarchy of the mother church, simply on the grounds that this region has reached maturity for self-government and has fulfilled all canonical requirements necessary for the foundation of a new church.

All of the foregoing only proves that Apostolic Canon 31 and Canons 13–15 of the First-Second Council have no importance in the problem of establishing a new church, especially since that problem first arose only later. Hence, the privilege of the mother church to grant autocephalous status to one of her parts cannot be based on these canons. The canons and practices of the Orthodox Church clearly distinguish between the withdrawal of a presbyter, bishop, or metropolitan from the jurisdiction of higher church authorities and the establishment of a new local church. The first is an action of individual presbyters or bishops under the pretext that their superiors were guilty of misconduct, but before the case had been heard and determined by the Council of Bishops. The second—that is the establishing of a new local church—is the separation of one part of the Church (clergy and laity together) when it has no fewer than three duly appointed bishops and is located in an independent state other than that of its mother church. Although single presbyters and deacons cannot withdraw without the consent of their higher ecclesiastical authorities, that is no ground for concluding that the establishing of a new local church is likewise possible only with the consent of the head of the mother church and her council of bishops. There is a special procedure for the recognition of a new church.

The distinction between the separation of clergymen from communion with their superiors and the establishing of a new church is of great importance for the understanding of the canonical meaning of different types of separation in the Orthodox Church. While the withdrawal of clergymen from communion with their hierarchal superiors is generally an illicit and arbitrary action, the establishing of a new local church is not necessarily a schism but may be canonically lawful. Consequently, persons taking part in the canonical organization of a new church are not liable to punishment, as required by the First-Second Council of 861.

The opinion that the mother church alone is entitled to grant autocephalous status not only has no basis in the canons reviewed, but is also inconsistent with the principles of Orthodox canon law. If the council of bishops of the mother church "alone" has the right to grant autocephalous status to a part of herself, then necessarily, no other autocephalous church has any voice in this matter. If the council of bishops of the mother church does not recognize the autocephalous status of the new church, the other churches have no authority to do so; however, after autocephalous status has been granted by the mother church, all the sister churches, according to the letter of Patriarch Alexis of Moscow, must enter into canonical communion with that church, thus acknowledging the legality of the founding of the new church by the will of the mother church.

In the same letter, the Patriarch of Moscow expressed his bewilderment as to why, "[c]ontrary to the canons and tradition of the Church," the ecumenical patriarch did not enter into canonical communion with the Polish and Czechoslovakian churches, "despite the fact that their autocephalous status has been recognized by the Moscow Patriarchate as their mother church." Evidently, according to the letter of Patriarch Alexis, the sister churches must recognize the autocephalous status granted by the mother church. Thus, a change which ought to be decided by the whole community of autocephalous local churches becomes an internal problem of one of the autocephalous churches, and the latter confers upon herself a right which belongs to the entire community of local churches. Such an interpretation of the right of the mother church does not conform to the canonical principles of the ecumenical councils. The recognition of the autocephalous status of one of her parts by the mother church cannot deprive the sister churches of their independent right to pass on the legality of such a move. One member of the community of Orthodox churches cannot, on its own motion, introduce a new church into the community without the consent of all the other members, all of whom are equal. The Patriarchal see in Constantinople, just as every other autocephalous church, has the right to withhold recognition of the autocephalous status of a new church, as granted by her mother church. Therefore, the refusal of the ecumenical patriarch to enter into canonical communion with the Heads of the Polish and Czechoslovakian churches cannot be considered as an act "contrary to the canons and traditions of the Church," as claimed in the letter of the patriarch of Moscow of March 7, 1953. By declining to recognize the autocephalous status of these churches, the ecumenical patriarch was exercising the basic rights of every autocephalous church, and especially of the first among them.

The separation of a new church from an existing autocephalous church is usually a rather painful procedure; even for a church covering a large region, it is hard to lose one of her parts. In this connection, it is especially useful for the mother church to seek the opinion of her sister churches; they may have an opinion different from hers.

The Third Ecumenical Council in 431 recognized the Church of Cyprus as independent of the Church of Antioch, despite the claim of the Bishop of Antioch to ordain bishops for Cyprus as officers of the Antiochian Church. The life of the entire Orthodox Church is based on the intercommunion of all local churches, and each one of them has the right to decide independently on the eligibility of one of the parts of an autocephalous church to be self-governing.

5. The Recognition of a New Church by the Ecumenical Patriarch

The system of recognition of a new church by the ecumenical patriarch did not precede the system of recognition by the mother church. From the 19th to the 20th century both procedures were used together. The Patriarchate of Constantinople was also a mother church from which new churches separated. Their recognition by the head of their mother church at the same time was a recognition by the ecumenical patriarch. Autocephalous status was granted by the act of the one Church only, that is, by the decision of the patriarch of Constantinople and his Synod of Bishops. Contrary to the practice at the time of the ecumenical councils, the ancient Patriarchates of Alexandria, Antioch, and Jerusalem thereafter did not enjoy the same rights as the Church of Constantinople. Especially during the Turkish domination from the 15th to the 19th centuries, the representatives of those patriarchates were unable to resist the authority of the Patriarch of Constantinople.

A striking example of this inequality was the procedure by which the Patriarchate of Moscow was recognized. The ecumenical patriarch Jeremias II made that decision alone. When visiting Moscow in 1589 he recognized the patriarchal dignity of the see of Moscow and attended the enthronement of the newly appointed Russian Patriarch. Only later, in 1590 and then in 1593, were synods convoked in Constantinople to discuss the Russian question, partly upon the insistence of the Russian Government. The sessions of the Synod in 1590 were attended by Joachim, the Patriarch of Antioch, and by Sophronios, the Patriarch of Jerusalem. Meletios, the Patriarch of Alexandria, was present only at the sessions in 1593. The Synod of 1590 confirmed the personal decision of Patriarch Jeremias II. At the same time the patriarchs of Antioch and Jerusalem publicly acknowledged their subordination to the patriarch of Constantinople. By a Synodal decision the duty was imposed upon the new patriarch of Moscow "to respect the apostolic see of Constantinople as head and authority ... just as the other patriarchs respect him." Patriarch Meletios was displeased by this decision and sent Patriarch Jeremias a letter in which he wrote: "I know for certain that you were wrong to elevate the Moscow Metropolitanate to a Patriarchate because ... the right to decide on this matter belongs not to the Patriarch alone, but to the synod and even to the ecumenical synod (council). Therefore, Your Holiness," Patriarch Meletios continued, "should obtain the consent of the other brethren. ... Since our words do not lead you to anything good, but only bring you confusion, anger, and their consequences, I relieve Your Holiness from my reproaches and myself from trouble." In spite of his opinion, the patriarch of Alexandria did not openly reject the patriarch's decision. Finally, at the synod sessions in 1593, Patriarch Meletios publicly supported the previous decision of 1590 on the establishment of the Patriarchate of Moscow.[10]

Later on, in the 19th century, autocephalous status was granted to the churches of Greece (1850), Serbia (1879), and Romania (1885), by means of synodal tomos (decree) of the ecumenical patriarch.

What was the ecumenical patriarch's basis for exercising such extensive powers? No such basis could be expected in the canons of the Seven Ecumenical Councils; even the title "ecumenical" is not to be found in them. This title, first used in letters of Byzantine emperors, was canonically conferred upon the patriarch of Constantinople in 586 by the synod of the see of Constantinople, i.e., by the local law of the Church of Constantinople

---

[10] A Kartashev, *The History of the Russian Church*, vol. 2 (Paris, 1959), 41–45 (in Russian).

herself. Nevertheless, the title "ecumenical" was eventually accepted by all other Orthodox churches. Its significance had to be established by church practices and customs.

Although the history of the Patriarchate of Constantinople was full of tragic events, the powers of the patriarch himself were broadened by both the Byzantine emperors and the Turkish sultans. His authority with regard to other churches increased. The Byzantine emperors made the patriarch of Constantinople an intermediary between themselves and other patriarchs and bishops. The patriarchs of Alexandria, Antioch, and Jerusalem might be granted an audience with the emperor only upon the recommendation of the patriarch of Constantinople, and as a result, they became dependent upon him. The Turkish sultan proclaimed the patriarch of Constantinople the head and ruler of all Christians in the Ottoman Empire. The ancient patriarchs of Alexandria, Antioch, and Jerusalem were usually appointed by the sultan upon the recommendation of the patriarch of Constantinople and became dependent upon him even more than they were at the time of the Byzantine Empire.

The Eastern patriarchates: Alexandria, Antioch, and Jerusalem, fell under the control of Constantinople far more easily, since they had become extremely weak following the loss of some of their dioceses as a result of dogmatic controversies; they were destroyed by the invasion of the Arabs and by the crusaders. The patriarch of Constantinople helped them to restore the life of their churches. Sometimes the ancient patriarchal sees could not be filled and a titular patriarch, appointed by the ecumenical patriarch, resided in Constantinople. Together with the ancient patriarchates, the formerly independent churches of Bulgaria and Serbia also came under the jurisdiction of the ecumenical patriarch, in consequence of the subordination of their countries to the Turks. Thus, within the boundaries of the Turkish Empire a large multi-national Orthodox Church was formed, headed by the ecumenical patriarch, who not only used the honorific prerogatives established by the Ecumenical Councils (Second Ecumenical Council, Canon 3; Fourth Ecumenical Council, Canon 28) but also jurisdictional powers whose basis lay outside the canons.

When in the 19th century the national churches of Greece, Serbia, Bulgaria, and Romania began to secede from the Church of Constantinople one after another, the ecumenical patriarch alone had to decide on their canonical status. The establishing of a new church meant withdrawal from the jurisdiction of the ecumenical patriarch. Under such conditions it became accepted that a new church could be established with the consent of the ecumenical patriarch and his synod only, and that her independence might be recognized by him alone. Only the Russian Church was completely independent from Constantinople, but she too had seceded from her and regarded all new secessions as internal affairs of the Church of Constantinople.

Evidently it was the above practice of the Church of Constantinople to which Patriarch Alexis of Moscow referred in his letter of March 7, 1953. The canonical validity of that reference can be evaluated only after a judgment is reached on the problem of whether this church practice, which arose under peculiar political conditions, can serve as a general rule for all future periods.

A church practice cannot take on binding force simply because it has been followed for a long time. To become a church custom, a practice must be (a) in conformity to the basic principles of faith and church order, and (b) repeated freely. The binding force of a custom derives from church consciousness, which accepts a certain line of action as correct. Church consciousness can, of course, be evidenced in any action performed freely, without the use of force. The practice of establishing new churches solely with the consent of the patriarch of Constantinople was created on the basis of his powers obtained from the Byzantine emperors and the Turkish sultans. But all acts of state power are measures of compulsion, and a church practice based upon acts of state fails to attain the standing of a church custom for lack of one of the most important conditions—the freedom of formation. Sometimes the Church has no choice but to follow some laws and orders of the state, but civil laws can never be considered sources of canon law, which is created by the Church herself.

Likewise, the recognition of the prerogatives of the ecumenical patriarch by other local churches of the Ottoman Empire cannot support the canonical validity of such prerogatives, since those prerogatives were derived from the decrees of the Ottoman Empire, and the other churches were compelled to comply with those decrees. No recognition in any sense imposed by the state can be canonically valid, any more than acquiescence by the Church of Constantinople in arbitrary appointments and depositions of patriarchs and bishops by Byzantine emperors and Turkish sultans could bring about any alteration by prescription of the canonical procedure for their appointments and deposition.

Afterwards, when they had an opportunity to use the same sultan's authority to loosen their dependence upon the patriarch of Constantinople, the other ancient patriarchates succeeded in re-establishing the right of their bishops to elect their own patriarch: Jerusalem in 1844, Antioch in 1898, and Alexandria in 1899. The other churches separated themselves from the Church of Constantinople at the time of disintegration of the Ottoman Empire, and gradually became independent of the ecumenical patriarch.

The concept that recognition of a new church is the exclusive privilege of the ecumenical patriarch, or that his approval must precede any subsequent recognition by other local churches, is as inconsistent with the principles of the Orthodox canon law as the equally misunderstood right of the mother church discussed above. In both cases, the error would allow one local church to decide an inter-orthodox question, and the rights of that church are put above the rights of all the sister churches.

It must be admitted that the recognition of new local churches by the ecumenical patriarch was, canonically, the only possible way, after he became head and ruler of all Christians in the Turkish Empire, and when the establishment of a new church necessarily meant withdrawal from his jurisdiction. But under new conditions, when the number of autocephalous churches had increased considerably, that system cannot stand, since it is inconsistent with the canonical principles and practices of the times of the Ecumenical Councils. The Moscow Patriarch's attempt to base the right of the mother church to establish an autocephalous church upon the practice of the Church of Constantinople, which arose under particular historic conditions, seems to lack sufficient foundation.

6. The Recognition of New Churches Since the Beginning of the Twentieth Century

The theory of the exclusive right of a mother church to grant autocephalous status, so insistently defended by Patriarch Alexis, can be regarded as nothing but the transfer of the prerogatives of the Church of Constantinople to the new Russian mother church. It is easy to understand that these two principles had to collide, as they actually did after the First World War. At this time the insufficiencies of both principles were revealed and at the same time, fresh approaches to the problem of recognizing new autocephalous churches came to light.

From the middle of the 15th century to the beginning of the 19th century the life of the Orthodox Church proceeded in such a manner that not only did the ecumenical council cease to convene but even contact, based upon mutual equality, was lost among the autocephalous churches. During this period the concept disappeared of the Orthodox Church as a unity in plurality, as a community of equal autocephalous churches with only prerogatives of honor among them. This community could not exist so long as there were only two truly independent local churches: the Church of Constantinople and the Russian Church, the latter being degraded by her synodal structure compared with the old patriarchal dignity of the Church of Constantinople.

The re-establishment of the community of Orthodox local churches became possible only after the re-establishment of the independence of the ancient Eastern patriarchates and other churches which, during the period of Turkish rule, had become dependent upon Constantinople. As a result of several wars of liberation of the 19th century in which Russia took an active part, Greece, Serbia, Romania, and Bulgaria were freed from Turkish rule and started to organize their own independent churches. In spite of the protests of the patriarch of Constantinople, the Russian imperial government supported before the Sublime Porte the requests of the ancient patriarchates to elect their own candidates for the patriarchal sees in Jerusalem (1844), Damascus (1898), and Alexandria (1899). The re-establishment of the independence of these churches was possible owing to the influence of the Russian Church whose voice as a state church could more readily be heard since it coincided with the political interests of the Russian government. As a result of the disintegration of the Turkish Empire the community of free Orthodox churches was organized anew. At the beginning of the 20th century there were already ten local churches: Constantinople, Alexandria, Antioch, Jerusalem, Cyprus, Russia, Greece, Serbia, Romania, and Bulgaria. These local churches also undertook to display their own will, and the importance of the ecumenical patriarch in the matter of the recognition of new churches gradually ebbed.

The first time a dispute with the Patriarch of Constantinople was apparent was when the latter refused to recognize the Bulgarian Exarchate established by the Imperial Decree (Firman) of the Turkish Government in 1870. In 1872 the patriarch of Constantinople invited representatives of the churches of Russia and Serbia together with the patriarchs of the ancient Eastern churches to a council in Constantinople to censure the Bulgarian Church for this action. However, the Russian Holy Synod refused to participate in this council, claiming that the dispute was purely an internal affair of the Church of Constantinople. The Serbian Church also refused to participate. Later, the Russian Church did not associate itself with the decision of this Council of Constantinople of 1872. She avoided common celebration of the Divine Liturgy with Bulgarian clergymen for a long time, but members of the Bulgarian Church were always admitted to Communion and other sacraments in Russian churches and vice versa. In this case the rights of the mother church of Constantinople to grant autocephalous status were not questioned but censure of the Bulgarian Church was withheld.

A very clear case of non-recognition of the acts of the ecumenical patriarchal see in Constantinople occurred soon after the First World War, when the ecumenical patriarch recognized the establishment of new churches in the Republics of Estonia, Latvia, Finland, and Poland, which had separated from the Russian Church. In this case a separation of the functions of the Patriarch of Constantinople as the head of the mother church and as the ecumenical patriarch occurred. Now, he acted only as the ecumenical patriarch. "Since the most holy apostolic patriarchal see in Constantinople" considered it to be its duty "to care for the welfare of all the Orthodox churches which have been deprived of pastoral care,"[11] the ecumenical patriarch recognized the churches of Finland, Estonia, and Latvia as "autonomous" (in 1923) and the Church of Poland as "autocephalous" (in 1924).

The Russian Church considered all these acts as violations of her rights as a mother church which—according to the views of the Moscow Patriarchate—alone could grant autonomy or autocephalous status to a Church separating from her. With the changed political situation, the patriarch of Moscow succeeded in depriving these acts of the ecumenical patriarch of their effectiveness. After the Second World War, the Democratic Republics of Estonia and Latvia became Union Republics of the USSR, their churches were reunited with the Russian Church as her dioceses and they lost their autonomy. The effectiveness of Constantinople's grant of autocephalous status to the Church of Poland was nullified in another way. The Polish democratic government, which favored autocephalous status, was replaced (after the Second World War) by a government friendly to the Communist government of the USSR. The Moscow patriarch thereupon proclaimed Metropolitan Dionysius, the acting head of the Polish Autocephalous Church, to be suspended from his office and deprived of liturgical and canonical communion with the Russian Church to which he had formerly belonged. The administration of the Orthodox Church in Poland was assumed by a "Governing Board" of a few bishops. According to a petition of this board, the Moscow patriarch, in agreement with the council of russian Bishops, granted, "by the authority of the mother church," complete autocephalous status, instead of the "non-canonical and invalid autocephalous status" proclaimed by the tomos of the Patriarch of Constantinople. Athenagoras, the Patriarch of Constantinople, sought to regard the grant of autocephalous status by the Moscow Patriarch as a recognition of the 1924 act of the Church of Constantinople, and therefore proposed to re-establish Metropolitan Dionysius in his rights. But the Patriarch of Moscow did not accept this proposal. Referring to the right

---

[11] Tomos of the ecumenical patriarch Meletios concerning the autonomy of the Church of Estonia, July 1923.

of the mother church, the patriarch of Moscow denied the authority of the ecumenical patriarch to grant autocephalous status to a church which previously was not under the jurisdiction of the Church of Constantinople. The rejection went so far that the autocephalous status granted to the Polish Church "by a foreign patriarch" was declared completely invalid.

Continuing to develop the same idea of the prerogatives of the mother church, the Moscow Patriarchate recognized the autocephalous status of the Church of Czechoslovakia in 1951. Her autocephalous status had also been proclaimed by the Moscow Patriarchate without any previous consultation with the ecumenical patriarch. Nevertheless, the Czechoslovakian Church was later recognized not only by the churches behind the Iron Curtain, but also by the patriarchal sees of Alexandria and Antioch.

More serious disagreements arose between the Patriarchate of Constantinople and other autocephalous churches about the re-establishment of the Bulgarian Patriarchate. In this case, many local churches opposed the will of the Patriarch of Constantinople. The Bulgarian Church, after having been granted autocephalous status by the patriarch of Constantinople in 1945, decided to proclaim the restoration of the patriarchate on her own initiative. To receive recognition of her new status by all the other Orthodox local churches, by special letters the Holy Synod of the Bulgarian Church invited their representatives to take part in the enthronement of the new patriarch of the Bulgarian Church. The ecumenical patriarch received such an invitation as well. At the appointed time representatives of the local churches arrived in Sofia, but there was no representative from Constantinople. Soon a letter arrived from Athenagoras, the ecumenical patriarch, in which "the attributing to herself of patriarchal dignity and honor by the Bulgarian Church on her own accord" was considered "a deviation from the existing canonical and ecclesiastical order." According to this letter, the Bulgarian Church had to "seek her elevation to the patriarchal dignity through us"—i.e., the ecumenical patriarchal see—from the body of the presiding heads of the holy Orthodox churches. Besides, the letter made it clear that in passing on this application, the ecumenical patriarch would consider whether the Bulgarian Church had reached maturity and had manifested her constancy and loyalty to canonical principles.¹² In spite of the refusal of the ecumenical patriarch to recognize the Patriarchate of Bulgaria, it was recognized by the patriarchs of the ancient churches of Alexandria, Antioch, and Jerusalem, as well as by the churches of communist countries: Russia, Romania, Georgia, Poland, and Czechoslovakia, i.e., by the majority of the existing local churches.¹³

But the prerogatives of the mother church to grant autocephalous status did not receive universal recognition. The autocephalous status of the Polish and Czechoslovakian churches granted to them by their Russian mother church was not recognized by the Churches of Constantinople, Greece, or Cyprus. Despite its insistence upon the prerogatives of the mother church, the Moscow Patriarchate itself sometimes acted against the interests of other mother churches and thereby weakened this principle. In 1937 the Albanian Church received autocephalous status from her mother church, Constantinople. However, the Moscow Patriarchate maintained relations not with the Holy Synod established according to the Statute of 1937, but with the bishops friendly to the communist government of Albania. Later, with the consent of the government, a new synod, consisting of these bishops, replaced the Holy Synod which had originated on the basis of the statute approved by the Church of Constantinople. The Moscow Patriarchate recognized the new head of the Albanian Church, but the patriarch of Constantinople refused to recognize him and did not enter into canonical communion with him. The interests of the Serbian Patriarchate were also impaired by the Moscow Patriarchate on the establishment of the Church of Czechoslovakia. Some of the former parts of the Serbian Church within the boundaries of Czechoslovakia were included in the new church. And consequently, the Serbian Patriarch did not recognize the autocephalous status of the Church of Czechoslovakia.

---

¹²The Letter of His Holiness Athenagoras, archbishop of Constantinople and ecumenical patriarch, to Cyril, the Metropolitan of Plovdiv, president of the Holy Synod of the Bulgarian Church, of April 25, 1953, and the answer of the Holy Synod of the Bulgarian Patriarchate of December 31, 1953 in *Tserkoven Vesnik* (Church Bulletin), Sofia, January 22, 1954. The English translation was distributed at the Second Assembly of the World Council of Churches at Evanston, Illinois, USA.

¹³*Yedinaya Tserkov* [One Church] 10–12 (1953): 17.

Although the collision of two systems of recognition weakened both of them, the growing number of local churches and the strengthening of their mutual relations stressed the specific need to have a "first" among other members to whom they could apply for advice in their difficulties, and who could assist local churches to find a solution for their problems in the general interests of whole Orthodox churches. The appeals of the churches of Finland, Estonia, Latvia, Poland, and of the Russian metropolitan districts of Western Europe to the ecumenical patriarch after World War I indicate in any case the high prestige of the ecumenical patriarch in the Orthodox Church. As to the Church of Finland, the Moscow Patriarchate could not but recognize her autonomy in 1958, granted by the ecumenical patriarch, although this was made in complete disagreement with the claims of the Moscow Patriarchate concerning the prerogatives of the mother church.

As practice has evolved, the recognition of a new church and her introduction into the community of Orthodox local churches is now decided not by one mother church or by the ecumenical patriarch in Constantinople alone, but by all the autocephalous local churches together. The latter reserve the right to accept or disapprove the decision of the mother church or the ecumenical patriarch. The patriarchal dignity, as well as autonomous or autocephalous status, sometimes were recognized by local churches without previous approval of either the ecumenical patriarch (Bulgaria, Czechoslovakia, Albania) or the mother church (Poland, Finland, Estonia, Latvia). From the jurisdiction of a single local church this problem is coming to be decided by all the local churches, and thus the ancient principle of deciding this matter by the whole community of autocephalous churches is being revived. The recognition by the mother church can, of course, facilitate the later recognition by other local churches, but under present circumstances, the problem of which Church has the right to decide in the first instance, loses its sharpness. Sometimes the local churches recognized a new church after her mother church granted her autocephalous status, sometimes the ecumenical patriarch was first to act. The Bulgarian Church was elevated to the patriarchal dignity by many churches without previous recognition by the ecumenical patriarch or by the mother church, both being represented by the same Church of Constantinople. The appeal of the Bulgarian Church was forwarded not to the mother church or to the ecumenical patriarch but to all autocephalous churches simultaneously. In this manner a new way of initiating a request for recognition was shown.

The system of recognizing new churches by each particular local church is much slower than the system of recognition by an ecumenical council. As a result, individual local churches may for some time be not recognized by all the autocephalous churches but only by some of them. However, in time the Orthodox sister churches may drop their objections, as was done in connection with the Church of Finland in 1958. In 1961 the ecumenical patriarch also recognized the autocephalous churches of Poland and Czechoslovakia as well as the Patriarchate of Bulgaria.

7. The Proclamation of Her Own Independence by a New Church

Obstacles to the recognition of a new church and unsuccessful attempts to obtain it from the mother church have usually resulted in a Church herself proclaiming her own independence. If the proclamation is given practical effect, she becomes a *de facto* independent self-governing Church, practically enjoying the rights of an autocephalous church.

There are but few examples where, in a short time a mother church granted autonomous or autocephalous status to a subsisting part of herself. This occurred, e.g., when the ecumenical patriarch granted autonomy and later autocephaly to the Serbian Church in 1832 and in 1879, respectively. But in the past, the founding of a new church occurred mostly without the consent of the mother church. After that, canonical relations were usually broken off and sometimes the new church was even excommunicated. But later, there was no alternative for the mother church but to recognize the independence of the separated Church. The Patriarch of Constantinople, for example, had to recognize the self-proclaimed independence of the following churches in the 19th and 20th centuries: the Church of Greece—17 years after she had proclaimed herself autocephalous (1833–1850), the Romanian Church—21 years after (1864–1885), the Albanian Church—15 years after (1922–1937), and the Bulgarian Church—72 years after (1872–1945). In the 12th century the Patriarch of Constantinople recognized the Bulgarian Church 50 years after she had proclaimed herself independent (1185–1235); in the 14th century the Serbian Church was recognized 30 years after (1346–1375) and in the 16th century the Russian Church—almost 140 years after (1448–1589). In the 20th century the Patriarch of Moscow recognized the Finnish Church 35 years after she had been granted autonomy by the ecumenical patriarch (1923–1958).

The mother church usually regarded separation from her as arbitrary and uncanonical. It must, nevertheless, be noted that even the largest local churches when separating from the Church of Constantinople had to use the same arbitrary methods. This fact deprives them in turn of any right to condemn similar "arbitrary" separations of their own parts. We might expect that these churches might have later regretted their previous action and might even condemn them now. But they did not. On the contrary, the declaration of independence by a new church herself was authorized by the Conference of the Heads and Representatives of the Autocephalous Orthodox churches in Moscow in 1948. This Conference was convened on the invitation of Alexis, the Patriarch of Moscow, "on the occasion of the celebration of the 500th anniversary of the autocephaly of the Russian Orthodox Church." In 1448 the Council of Bishops of the Russian Church, which until that time had been one of the metropolitan districts of the Church of Constantinople, elected the Russian Bishop Jonah as the metropolitan of Moscow, without seeking the approval of the patriarch of Constantinople, and thereby laid the basis for the self-government of the Russian Church and her independence. Although the Russian Church was canonically recognized by the Church of Constantinople only in 1589, Alexis, the Patriarch of Moscow, dates the beginning of the autocephaly not from the time of this canonical recognition, but from the year when the Russian Church proclaimed her independence on her own motion, and against the will of the Church of Constantinople.

It is also important to emphasize that Metropolitan Germanos, the exarch of the ecumenical patriarch in Western Europe, taking part in this conference, stressed in his speech that the ecumenical patriarch and his holy synod "received with utmost joy the decision of the great Russian Church to celebrate the 500th anniversary of her autocephaly." From the viewpoint of the representative of the ecumenical patriarch, the autocephaly of the Russian Church also dates from the time she proclaimed herself independent, in 1448. The patriarchs of the Serbian and Romanian churches, and the exarch of the Bulgarian Church participated in the celebration. They all congratulated the Russian Church on the 500th anniversary of her autocephaly and independence. Greetings were also conveyed from the patriarch of Antioch, the catholicos-patriarch of the Church of Georgia, as well as from representatives of the churches of Poland and Albania.[14] In this manner, a proclamation of her own canonical independence by a new church herself, without the consent of her mother church, was accepted as lawful by the Russian Church as well as by representatives of the ecumenical patriarch and all the other autocephalous churches attending the Moscow Conference of 1948. The real meaning of this authorization can be properly understood if we remember the words of Patriarch Alexis during the general session of the Conference, where he declared that before the election of Metropolitan Jonah in 1448, the Russian Church "possessed all the canonical prerequisites . . . for autocephalous status." Therefore, the proclamation of independence may be made by a newly organized Church only if she meets all the usual requirements necessary for obtaining autocephalous status by other means.

The lack of formal recognition of a new church did not prevent some sister churches from maintaining liturgical and canonical relations with her. After the Russian Church had proclaimed her independence from the Church of Constantinople, her relations with the Eastern patriarchates were broken, but not for long. Soon they were reestablished. The connection of Moscow with the eastern Patriarchs was evidenced in her correspondence with them, in their letters and information about the personnel changes in the patriarchates, in their repeated visits to Moscow, and in financial assistance by Moscow to the needy churches of the East. The establishment of the Russian Patriarchate and the enthronement of the Russian patriarch in 1589 took place during one such visit of the Eastern

---

[14]*Acts of the Conference of the Heads and Representatives of the Autocephalous Orthodox Churches, 1948*, vol. 1 (Moscow, 1949), 18, 20, 23, 24, 29, 35 (in Russian).

patriarchs to Moscow. Although not recognized *de jure*, a new church may enjoy *de facto* recognition by other autocephalous local churches.

The Future of American Orthodoxy

William S. Schneirla[1]

St Vladimir's Seminary Quarterly 5.4 (1961): 24–42

IF THE WRITING OF HISTORY presents such pitfalls that the finished product may be said to be no more than a fable generally agreed upon, how much more rash is the enterprise of predicting the course of events that lie in the future. Prognostication for investors and statesmen has been a profitable endeavor throughout the centuries, but both political and financial empires have collapsed while seers or statisticians were cheerfully announcing a triumphant future. If some forthcoming mechanical computer is to transcend the inherent fallibilities of its human creators, man may one day peer confidently into tomorrow. Until that time the prophet deserves no respect beyond what may be accorded his past performances, and the notes that follow are not prophecies. They represent an attempt to suggest future possibilities, based on the interested observations of twenty years of American Orthodox life, both within and without the iconostasis. There is said to be safety in generalizations, so the broad generalizations which make up part of this survey may be its only refuge from the judgement of time.

Serious long-range planning is the work of specialists and these essays at prediction lay no claim to professional competence. But there are superficial currents apparent to everyone at work in the Church, and with respect to these anyone may point out the obvious. Some matters of current debate are simply touched upon, e.g., the struggle to preserve

---

[1] These notes are part of a longer article planned for the special issue of the *Quarterly* devoted to the Church in the United States. They lack organization, connective tissue, and the benefits of revision, but are offered in their present form before discussion of the special issue will have closed. It is a cause of particular regret that a section on the American youth societies was insufficiently complete to permit its inclusion.—W. S. S. [The dedicated issue of the *Quarterly* was not published, nor was Schneirla's longer article.—*Ed.*]

non-English languages, which might be illuminated by reference to the experience of heterodox bodies longer in the United States, and wide areas of the future are not discussed at all. Rather it is hoped that logical probability has been indicated in a few sectors.

The Jurisdictions Become a Church

By chance the American Orthodox Church finds itself splintered into many semi-autonomous administrative divisions generally coterminous with ethnic or linguistic communities of recent immigrants. There have been obvious advantages in this arrangement in the past. Cultural and language differences have not intruded in parish or diocesan life; nationalism has been available as a useful tool for combatting proselytism, engendering loyalty, and fostering solidarity; the treasures of many cultural traditions have been allowed to flourish and grow, presumably mediating much of value to the future one church. But the Church now stands on the threshold of unification, new generations need a Church that is native to this land and united for the difficult years of transition that lie immediately ahead. The first subject on the agenda of any discussion of the American future is always and inevitably the shape and timetable of the coming union.

Any approach to administrative unity of the national jurisdictions in the United States must begin with the understanding that the American Church was one until the effects of the Russian Communist coup radiated to this country in the 1920s. The Greeks had been reluctant participants from the first, and took the earliest opportunity to go their own way, while the other national bodies had flourished under a benevolent Russian leadership that combined a sympathetic appreciation of national differences with real contributions of money, service, and personnel. The Russian-Syrian attempt of the twenties and thirties to restore the shattered unity and create an autonomous American Church unrealistically assumed that the ideals of the canons would prove stronger than the budding nationalisms released by the First World War. Until the insistent demands of the Second World War dramatized the need for cooperation, the parochialism of the jurisdictions prevented any serious consideration of reunion, and when all of the sources are available for the historians who write the full story of the Federation of the early 1940s, it will be discovered that this venture was artificially imposed on communities unready for it. It collapsed once the imagined threat was over.

The national jurisdictions by and large are quite content to preserve their familiar isolations, and few of the faithful look far beyond the parish boundaries. The recently formed Standing Conference of Canonical Orthodox Bishops of the Americas was inspired by a few leaders and has not yet caught the imagination of the congregations, although it represents the normal first step in unification. But while both the people and hierarchs, with notable exceptions, are fearful of unification or indifferent to it, or hesitant, union is advanced by the current historical situation of the American Church.

Those who would preserve their separate national entities are fighting a battle already lost. Leaders might be blind, insensitive, or actually opposed, to the real requirements of the American Orthodox community, but these needs demand solution, and no amount of procrastination, temporizing, or diplomatic maneuvering can forever defer the day when common problems are confronted and satisfied by the united effort of the whole community. In such fields as religious education, chaplaincies, service organizations, relations with interdenominational bodies, and many other matters, the jurisdictions must cooperate. And it is here, where the formal resolution of canonical irregularities may be temporarily postponed, that working groups provide the growing points for eventual unification. In local centers, parishes of diverse backgrounds learn that opportunities for welfare benefits and necessary recognition are increased when the Church realizes itself and when nationalistic boundaries are ignored for practical advantage. Unification is already on the verge of accomplishment in some areas and it may be predicted with assurance that it will finally come about in general as the result of the living and working together that is a concomitant of limited efforts for one specific goal or one section of the nation.

Official motions must be made, and by their very nature they must move haltingly, with much patient retracing of the inevitable routes, but union is creeping in rapidly where necessity demands it as the price of efficiency, economy, and survival. Interjurisdictional cooperation is the open high road to unity. The time table? One American Church in about a dozen years, embracing all but a few pockets of nationalistic conservatism and a few eccentric leaders.

Autocephalous, Autonomous, or Outlawed?

A united American Church will be confronted at once with the need to relate itself to world Orthodoxy. If some effective link is not forged in the very course of the process of unification, and the ancient primatial sees are already observing the course of events with interest, the new church could find itself embarrassed by a defective fellowship with the Ecumenical Church. After the mutual drawing apart of the national branches of the Church in the western hemisphere a kind of provisional and unprecedented canonical adaptation developed. Some national organizations have maintained their position in the world Church by depending directly on sees of primary jurisdiction abroad, others have lacked such ties but have been admitted to indirect fellowship by the bodies that retained them. The canons know only geographical eparchies, not racial dioceses, and the overlapping jurisdictions of North and South America constitute a canonical monstrosity. Expediency has dictated the temporary preservation of the status quo, and on the whole the results are better than might have been expected. Two patriarchal sees claim exclusive primary jurisdiction in America: Constantinople on the grounds of the famous 28th Canon of Chalcedon, and Moscow on the basis of the 2nd Canon of Carthage, which provides that missionary settlement confers jurisdiction. In the nature of things as they are, it is not likely that a dispassionate interpretation of these or other ancient canons will provide the groundwork for the constitution of the American Church.

The most striking symptom of the history of the rise of autocephalous churches is the reluctance with which mother sees have granted even semi-independence. Almost without exception new administrative units have gained freedom at the cost of good relations with the mother sees, with mutual ill-will sometimes extending over decades. Primatial sees have willingly conceded the autonomy of units formerly dependent on other thrones, but have not often displayed the same tolerance toward their own dependencies. If the American Church were to take the traditional path to free fellowship in the world Church this would imply a longer or shorter period of practical ostracism.

There are elements present in the American picture militating against a repetition of the traditional pattern of agitation, petition, refusal, break, and ultimate reconciliation. A principal difference is the lack of American unity over against one foreign see. Moreover, it is improbable that the American clergy or laity would feel they could afford the ugly spectacles that seemed not to deter their ancestors in their search for independence in local matters. Revolution or an overt break would be a final desperate action.

Since World War II, it has been reported that the Moscow Patriarchate is willing to lend its active support to American plans for unification on a very liberal basis, but world political tensions place an initial rein on the potential response. The component elements in the total situation present the Ecumenical Patriarchate with an unparalleled opportunity to recover a position not inferior to that of its most brilliant era, with certain additional advantages. There would be some reservations in America, of course, with Slavic and other national prejudices foremost among the causes, but the deciding factor would be the ability of the ecumenical throne to demonstrate convincingly a responsible concern for non-Hellenic Orthodoxy. If the Patriarchate of Constantinople should prove itself ready to grant American autonomy—certainly autocephaly is too ambitious a first goal—with guarantees for the preservation of local rights, and a willingness to relegate the interests of Hellenism to a specialized Greek department, then it is apparent that it would eventually win the American Church. A self-image involving a truly international concern for the Church as the Church, in which the faith takes precedence over all other considerations, may or may not be among the capabilities of those who guide the Great Church, but the vision, or fantasy, is breathtaking in its prospects for Orthodoxy.

With two great Patriarchates to choose from, it does not appear that a unified American Church would have to wait long for recognition. It would be naive to expect one of the great world sees to take the leadership in American unification and autonomy or autocephaly if some representatives of Moscow had not already given evidence of real stature as Christian leaders in this respect.

The Church and Other Christians

Until recently the majority of the Orthodox lived in lands where the Church was a closed community, either with a monopoly on religious activity or well insulated from equally self-centered bodies. The real church was the national church, and theological essays published abroad or communion occasionally proffered to a heterodox tourist at home did not touch it. It was an island incorporated in world Orthodoxy but actually little affected by anything beyond its borders. Hierarchs and theologians formed in such an atmosphere cannot always adjust to life in a society in which the Church is a minority group surrounded by a multitude of sects historically remote from Orthodoxy. The easy temptation is to take comfortable refuge in the foreign-born minority community and to regard other religious bodies as if they were safely across a national frontier. They may then be dealt with by recourse to a sort of double standard in which the eventual reunion of Christendom is anticipated in statement and action, friends are made, mortgages are paid, and invitations are received to dinner at the club, sometimes followed by union vespers at the local community church.

Only in this perspective is it possible to understand the concessions which Orthodox representatives have made of principle at the expense of loyalty to the tradition and good common sense. It is unfair, and can become unwholesome, to suspect international plots and conspiracies behind all of the irresponsible acts that dot the history of Orthodox-heterodox relations in the west. Political advantage has sometimes been a motive on both sides, but it has not been the dominant agent in the process. Orthodox weakness, not Protestant guile or duplicity, has been at fault. A limited view of the ecclesiastical world and confusion in the face of the unfamiliar are the real villains.

More or less impulsive individual attempts to create good relations by exceptions to the canons have distressed or scandalized the faithful, but they could not commit the Church, and by their very inconsistency always fail of permanent results. A more promising avenue of approach to the non-Orthodox is the participation of the Church in the World Council of Churches and the National Council of churches. Contact with the first body must be cleared at the centers of primary jurisdiction abroad, and does not fall within the scope of a survey of the American scene, but the National Council of churches offers the Church the possibility of defining its position alongside the major segments of American Protestantism, with added opportunities for growing understanding and fellowship. Until the present time Orthodox involvement in the National Council of churches remains extremely ambiguous, and any reasonable prediction of the future must begin with an honest account of the succession of events leading to the curious impasse in which the Orthodox member jurisdictions now find themselves.

Orthodox membership begins with the application of the Syrian Archdiocese to the parent body, the Federal Council of churches, almost immediately after the consecration and installation of Metropolitan Antony Bashir in 1937. The step was taken on the personal initiative of Metropolitan Antony and was made in harmony with the keen desire for promoting inter-Christian cooperation which has been a feature of his entire ministry. He understood that membership was neither more nor less than a sincere symbol of good will on both sides and required no practical action from either party. At one time continued association was briefly thrown into jeopardy by concerted pressure from an ultra-conservative party of priests, who demanded clarification of the canonical and theological significance of membership, but the protesting party shortly thereafter lost its influential position in the archdiocese for other reasons. Prevalent policy is conditioned by the assumption that a sincere and friendly but cautious and passive affiliation will preserve valuable opportunities which can be fully realized when the American Church as a whole determines the form of its relationship. The laity of the archdiocese has been indifferent from the outset, while several clergy have accepted routine appointments.

The second jurisdiction to enter the Federal Council of churches was the Ukrainian diocese under the throne of Constantinople. The motives were practical on the part of the clergy who felt that the diocese would benefit from additional formal ties with the non-immigrant Christian bodies in the United States. In the preliminary interview with the Ukrainian delegates, an officer of the Council explained that council circles welcomed steps that would help identify it as more than a pan-Protestant body. Orthodox memberships were so valuable in this respect as to outweigh such considerations as budgetary or other contributions.

It is impossible to attribute motives to others, more especially corporate bodies, without hearing their testimony, and any convincing rebuttal of reasons alleged for conduct must offer some supporting evidence. For the remaining Orthodox jurisdictions, the apparent reasons for entering the National Council were all quite practical, and this is not a serious criticism, or a criticism at all, since the Council has a practical purpose.

This is the picture of the past. It is evident that Orthodox entry into the National Council and its predecessor, the Federal Council of churches, was generally accidental and unreflective, the work of individuals, hierarchs or others, who in these acts by no means represented some official tendency in the Church or even lay opinion, which is uninformed and indifferent in this field. The motives on both sides presumably differed markedly from those operative in the application of a Protestant denomination. No one would claim that subsequent Orthodox cooperation with the council or its member agencies has been more than nominal. This is illustrated by the many larger and smaller conferences between council officials and jurisdictional representatives called to interpret and develop Orthodox membership. No striking results have been achieved in terms of increased sharing in council programs. The effects of membership are not limited to direct association, however; many Orthodox rigorists challenge the whole premise of Orthodox presence in an association Protestant both in majority membership and concept. It was felt that the Syrian jurisdiction membership was one important factor in overcoming Anglo-Catholic objections to a degree that permitted the Protestant Episcopal Church to join the Federal Council. It may be equally true that Orthodox membership counts against the National Council of churches in very many sensitive Protestant circles: a provincial Lutheran synod once declined to join the World Council of Churches because it would find itself "kneeling beside the icon-worshippers" of the Orthodox Church.

There is no assurance that the future will not simply perpetuate the past, and that irresponsibility, accident, and the blindly shifting winds of circumstance will set the course of Orthodox-National Council relations, so that prediction is impossible. If the leadership of the American Church has attained sufficient maturity to control its destinies within the limits of possibility, then the course ahead may be discerned in its major outlines. Even now the Standing Conference of Bishops has determined on a program to regularize the nature of its future involvement in the National Council of churches by traditional Orthodox norms, and it will have an opportunity to provide the hierarchy with an instrument intended to insure that the continuing relations of the Church with the National Council will be fair to the Church's tradition as well as its future and will eliminate the ambiguities that now embarrass all participants.

If the future is to be purposeful some changes are necessary and their nature inevitable. The whole character of Orthodox membership, which is now on the basis of six separate jurisdictions, reflects the national administrative divisions of the American Church, but not its unity. Church membership may be transformed so that one office, with as many national subdivisions as are required, can speak to the Council for the Church. The office would logically profit from a written statement of policy from the bishops, and from the directions of a commission appointed by the bishops. It is unlikely that many in the Church will continue to regard with equanimity common statements which link several varieties of Protestants and the Orthodox jurisdictions, considered as separate denominations. It is probable that the Orthodox role will be one of cooperation in social welfare and similar projects and the cultivation of friendly relations with the Protestant member churches of the National Council. The authorization of joint statements frequently infringing on doctrine may well discontinue as American Orthodoxy becomes more theologically self-conscious. Effective Orthodox representation with Protestants on study groups or commissions charged with the preparation of statements with doctrinal connotations would necessarily confine many of them to the vaguest generalities of basic Christianity.

Some feel that inclusion in the National Council fosters the dependence already typical of some of the jurisdictions, rooted in centuries of existence under unfriendly majorities or created by decades of emigré existence. A vigorous and healthy Orthodoxy must meet government on its own, and must begin to plan and provide for an independent role in national and local affairs. It is dangerously convenient to rely on powerful friends in treating with statesmen or politicians, but there is no surer way of retarding the growth of self-reliance. In some respects, the unselfish and sincerely helpful support of non-Orthodox religious leaders and communities has removed stimuli that should have promoted maturity. Considerable sums granted for relief, education, salaries, and building have permitted Orthodox administrators to shirk their duty, and the membership to avoid the sacrificial giving that is the privilege as well as the penalty of commitment to the Church. Our unavoidable claims of ecclesiastical uniqueness must be supported by action when the bills are to be paid. Any influence, however well-intentioned, that robs the church of the stamina to face reality with her own strength is unwholesome in its effects. Jurisdictional divisions, limited planning, and parochialism have restricted giving, with the result that the Orthodox community has never yet employed a fraction of its potential resources for self-support and expansion.

Relations with the Roman communion in America have never presented a problem. Rome is uncompromisingly exclusive and aggressively missionary, and in America both characteristics have been intensified by her long struggle for social and civil equality. With the rise of a Roman middle class, and the weakening of the Protestant majority, Roman representatives now feel sufficiently secure to allow themselves an occasional objective look at other Christians. Some hierarchs and theologians are irenically disposed toward the Church, but the masses still lump the Orthodox with the Protestants and contact on the popular level is minimal and unimportant.

The existence of relatively large Uniate bodies (from whom most of the Slavic Orthodox in the United States were reconvened during the last century) has kept both Rome and the Church aware of each other as threats. As late as 1937, a new Orthodox jurisdiction was formed out of a half a hundred Uniate parishes, but the introduction of Uniate parochial schools and the diminution of the foreign-born generation has slowed the leakage from Rome to the Church. Orthodox who defect almost always prefer a Protestant body, so deep-seated is the fear of Roman autocracy.

Paradoxically, the Church and Rome, almost at one in dogma and discipline, are psychologically unable to meet on any level, while the Protestants and the American jurisdictions cooperate with the greatest of freedom. Unfortunately, it does not appear that Rome can afford any relaxation if she is to survive, and so the natural affinity that should foster alliance for common interests will not develop.

External Relations

Association with non-Orthodox will not and cannot be confined to official societies designed for that purpose. The faithful on the campus, in the armed forces or public institutions, and in community life are thrown into daily contact with members of other religious groups as well as with the indifferent and unbelievers. Ideally these contacts should provide the occasion of witnessing for the Church, and of making an Orthodox contribution. In fact, few of the laity are equipped to present the faith, either by training or psychologically. Typically, the well-informed will be those most familiar with a foreign expression of Orthodoxy, and the others will loyally avoid embarrassing rivalries or, if they have social pretensions, desert to the "real" American majority. Here the Church has a battle to win or lose, and it does not yet appear how it will be fought, or by whom the strategy will be drawn. Two conclusions are self-evident: first, a special program and ministry is required at the earliest possible moment, and second, the Church cannot expect alien shepherds to preserve her flock. In the years ahead, thousands of Orthodox isolated from the too few parishes located largely in the great cities will drift out of the Church.

Another question follows at once: will, or should, Americans of non-Orthodox antecedents drift into the Church? So far as our unchurched neighbors are concerned, it seems there can be no objection from the most reactionary. But it is sometimes said that Orthodoxy does not proselytize, i.e., convert Christians to the Church from the sects. Aside from the fundamentalists, who are numerous, Protestants generally proclaim that all churches are equal, but act as though some churches were more equal than others, with an understandable preference for their own denomination. Roman Catholics forthrightly proclaim their own uniqueness and invite all and sundry to join forthwith. In practice all non-Orthodox communions, without exception, are quick to save our people from their decadent, moribund, and superstitious Christianity when they can conveniently do so. One need not cite the existence of the "rice Christians" Protestant bodies of the Near East; every suburban church in the United States welcomes our people.

In the Ottoman Empire the Orthodox were tolerated to a surprising extent, and permitted considerable freedom in internal affairs. The one act that brought summary discipline was the conversion of Muslims. Thinkers and hierarchs conditioned in that world eventually learned to repress any disposition to missionary activity, so that in time this necessity became a theological virtue, and missionary vision in the Church until recently was the exclusive possession of the Russians. In America the Church offers the security of the most ancient tradition, combined with a reasonable freedom of thought and life that all but the most liberal Protestants can envy. As the Church loses her foreign aura, and our own ways of worship are fitted to the needs of the American born, Orthodoxy could appeal to many of our Christian fellow citizens. At long last the Church will be confronted by the necessity of acting on the divine imperative and inviting those with partial Christian traditions to supply what they lack from the wholeness of the apostolic faith. It is not too soon for the Church to set up a missionary strategy and launch experimental invitations. If it is urged that such a program must await the consolidation of our position and the service of our isolated believers and communities, it should be remembered that no other missionary minded religious body has postponed action because of perennial internal shortcomings.

Clergy and Laity

Early in the 19th century the Roman Church in the United States was torn by the "Trusteeism Controversy." Groups of immigrant believers had purchased property, built churches, and hired available itinerant priests before episcopal authority had arrived or was consolidated. By 1830, the Roman Church was virtually congregational in polity, and then the bishops reasserted the hierarchical principle; property and funds were transferred to the episcopate from lay "trustees," and the ancient power structure of traditional Christianity was restored. The Orthodox experience has been rather different, but it has brought us to the place at which Rome found itself just before the Trusteeism Controversy. The original Russian jurisdiction began on a sound canonical basis; in the Syrian diocese, for example, organized by the Russian Holy Synod, two trustees and the pastor managed the financial affairs and real estate of the parish, and the bishop had final and unquestioned control. With the Russian revolution and the consequent breakdown of hierarchical authority in American Orthodoxy, congregations developed independent corporations and bodies of lay trustees became the real masters of church polity. Bishops curried their favor, and the trustees hired and fired priests at will. This is popularly described as democracy, but in fact it results more frequently in an oligarchy on the parish level. One cannot oversimplify the process, in which the struggle for possession of Uniate property was influential, or simply condemn the result which was an ad hoc response by the faithful to practical neglect from a hierarchy absorbed in other interests and struggles. That the present system is uncanonical is not the least of its evils, but a more pernicious result has been the unwholesome effect on the recruiting and formation of candidates for the priesthood.

A priest sometimes appears to the younger generation as a man who labors for comparatively modest compensation at the mercy of fickle congregational approval or the whim of some lay demagogue whose social and cultural limitations confine the orbit of his exaggerated ego to parish polities. If this were true it would preclude any possibility of a prophetic ministry, confine planning to the most modest parochial goals, and stimulate the least desirable motives in laymen. Whether or not it is an accurate analysis of the contemporary structure of American Orthodoxy, the years ahead must see the normalization of our polity, and this requires a revision of the average parish constitution. American Orthodox will recall that Rome, with a generally greater sense of discipline, did not accomplish the necessary changes one hundred years ago without bitterness, confusion, and outright schisms, and will note that a movement toward enforcing the canonical standards in the Russian Metropolia is a current source of strain. Thus it may be that clergy and people will hesitate to precipitate a crisis and so the day of final reckoning will be postponed, but both our doctrine and the health of the American Church demand that this particular adjustment be made. As the real character of church membership is clarified and social pressures are relieved by the fading of the immigrant mind, an atmosphere may develop in which the change will evolve with a minimum of conscious effort either way.

Population

The weight of the Orthodox population has remained in the big cities so that the current decline in rural population is of little significance in calculating the future. The doubling of suburban growth on the other hand portends an evolving evil already begun. Too many city parishes, even some recently constructed, exist on the assumption that a large, centrally located plant can economically serve thousands of scattered faithful. Both parish trustees and contributing members realize that each new church represents a new budget load which must proportionately be reflected in individual and family pledges. Offerings to the priest for sacraments and sacramentals are naturally more numerous in a larger parish. But a geographically scattered parish is fatal to the habit of regular church attendance, detrimental to the church school, and has an adverse effect on a creative pastoral ministry. Mass production sacramentalism on the major feast days is an inadequate substitute for sustained parish life. In addition, shifting populations—and one person in five changes his address every year in this nation—can leave an expensive plant impossibly remote from the people it was built to serve. Two cathedrals and a number of parish churches in New York City are already miles away from the bulk of their membership.

The pattern of the future is probably indicated by the Cleveland project of the Greek Archdiocese, where four centers were deliberately planned to serve the drifting population once attached to one complex of buildings. In Detroit, Boston, Montreal, and Los Angeles a few Syrian churches and priests are serving people located all over large metropolitan areas.

The Future in Theology

Shortly after the Second World War a venerable prelate of some reputation as a dogmatist bluntly assured the members of an Orthodox symposium in New York, "We do not expect from America a theology." He never made his expectations explicit, but as he died still showing a marked reluctance to return to the land from where he presumably did expect a theology, it would seem to follow that liberty may have been an American offering he did not scorn. The rest of us must expect a theology from America, but it is questionable whether we have employed our liberty in its service with full seriousness.

It is normal to look to seminary faculties for theologians, but few would challenge the judgment that creative theology in the American Church began only with the migration of European scholars to North America after World War II. Excellent men taught and wrote before then, of course, and one cannot disregard the record of what might be called the "Buffalo School," in which Americans of non-Orthodox antecedents produced both scientific studies and popularizations for the laity. That the content of much of this was in the worst westernized tradition, conservative, and its guiding spirit extremely narrow and somewhat unrealistic, cannot diminish the fact that for many years the only productive American scholarship depended on the Buffalo circle.

At present we are well prepared theologically if Arius or Nestorius should be resurrected, but little is written to warn us about Tillich, or Richardson, or Pike. Our scholars tend to concentrate on issues that have not been especially dangerous to anyone since before the fall of Constantinople. There are notable exceptions, the recent number of the *Quarterly* devoted to the primacy is one,[2] but we are generally irenic to the point of blindness. Inter-Christian polemics are certainly not the primary task of the theologian, but there is no excuse for our failure to evaluate critically the major issues of current heterodox theology. Participation in the ecumenical movement, supposed dependence on the good will of some western agencies, a clear understanding of the terrible reality of the anti-Christian threat in the modern world, and an inherited reluctance to aggravate inter-Christian relations all contribute to the current preoccupation with safe subjects.

The better-known theologians of the American Church, including many of the younger men, were born and trained abroad. It may be assumed that life in the American Church and in the United States will stimulate adaptations or a synthesis which will acquire a new "American" Orthodox flavor. Through their students, administrative posts in the national jurisdictions, published works, and lectures these men are influencing the theological future, even where they have aroused opposition. A church largely east-European-peasant in background acquired gifted theological leaders whose training is at least equal to that of the non-Orthodox American theologians. The next generation will be conditioned by these men.

But there are other seedlings of the future. Probably the most creative theologians of today, at least those who are best known, are Russian in background. But there is no significant number of younger Russian-American students preparing for a future in any branch of theology. Quite the contrary is true of the Greek-Americans, many of whom are engaged in graduate study, or in teaching in secular colleges, in fields directly related to theology. In a half dozen years, the Greek-American community will have a large supply of men trained in good American schools in fields

---

[2][Here, the author refers to "Primacy and Primacies in the Orthodox Church," a special double issue of *St Vladimir's Seminary Quarterly* 4.2–3 (1960).—*Ed.*]

represented on any seminary curriculum. What percentage of this group began in the Greek Theological School, or some other Orthodox faculty, is uncertain, but these are men working for degrees at recognized institutions of learning.

One temptation of American Orthodox theology will be offered by the very friendliness of non-Orthodox theological circles. Cooperation in common enterprises with first-rate specialists of other traditions in a scientific spirit could either intensify the appreciation of Orthodox tradition or focus attention and interest on purely academic projects removed from the needs of a church seeking self-identification in the American religious world. This latter course might have greater appeal to scholars never exposed to a vital presentation of Orthodox theology, and removed from the ongoing life of the Church by professional preoccupations. One conclusion is certain, the fertilization of our theology from abroad, and the serious preparation of the younger men have saved us from the sectarian degeneration that otherwise could have been our destiny. A committed Orthodox believes that the inescapable weaknesses of heterodox theology confer an advantage on even a poor presentation of our tradition. As acquaintance with the content and spirit of our theology increases, our influence should keep pace with it.

Addendum to Theology

On the level that might be termed popular theology, writing aimed at what religious publishers call "the educated layman," the American Church is probably on the threshold of better things. Deterioration here is impossible simply because the Church is at the very bottom of the abyss. A quick glance at the parish pamphlet rack or a bookseller's catalogue is a disheartening experience, while full-length books are very scarce. The reader will find available two general categories of publications: highly technical theological and historical studies, often antiquarian in interest, or popular apologetical or devotional material evidently designed for retarded but deeply sentimental adolescents. Between the academic treatise and the hackneyed rehash of the catechism very little is offered.

It is not true that our publications reflect consumer needs, for every alert priest is preaching and teaching from heterodox works that provide some nourishment for his inquiring "educated laymen." Look at his bookcase the next time you are in his study.

Nothing is published, aimed at a popular audience, that provides an Orthodox evaluation of the questions modern men are asking. The old debate between science and religion, still vital for the layman; the modern search for meaning in religious and philosophical discourse; solutions to some moral problems that have arisen since the patristic period, or, if this is too much for a beginning, at least a courageous discussion of them. The sects, the "isms," the religious thinkers covered in the popular weekly news magazines, reach the Orthodox layman. Where will he find a balanced analysis from his own tradition? Bulgakov's "Orthodox Church" appeared in English thirty years ago and has not yet been replaced, not to speak of equaled, or superseded by necessary expansion. There can be but one outcome; the next few years will find American Orthodox theologians and apologists moving into this vacuum.

The hierarchy cannot commission nor can the laity demand creative writing. Great literature is not requisitioned or ordered by the page, although, parenthetically, the Orthodox record is striking. If the recognized literary classics of the past century and a half are surveyed, the Russian contribution is impressive, even excluding dissenters like Tolstoy and writers of dubious religious orientation such as Pasternak. Dostoevsky is of an almost unique stature among the novelists informed by one of the Christian traditions. First-rate creative writing clearly within a definite Protestant heritage is rare and the outstanding Roman Catholic authors of our time, especially the English, are almost all converts. American Orthodoxy would not seem to be a potential source of inspired authors for at least another generation, nor does the most urgent need demand literary artists. The Church needs craftsmen able to present the tradition palatably in respectable dress. The required skills and abilities can be taught and transmitted and a far-sighted hierarchy will address itself to this undertaking. Artistry must await the necessary appearance and union of appropriate conditions, but craftsmanship of sorts can be fostered.

Liturgy

The tone and system of life in modern secular industrialized America is utterly different from that in late Byzantium, or even in an agrarian Balkan society of a decade ago. It may well be that the culture in which the Church finds itself is an incarnation of that organism which the Gospel refers to as "this world." If it is, the prophetic judgements on this state of affairs are now no more than murmurs from within the Church. The heralds of judgement are evidently busy with other matters. Our church, which has been well represented in the coal fields of Pennsylvania through a long period of great labor agitation, evidently has conditioned no single student of social justice.

Our trumpet has given no certain sound either for or against the major symptoms, features, and characteristics of American life, but there is one field in which we are quite positive. Nothing obvious must be done to alter the several traditional ways of worship. Forms of worship which evidently spoke to and for far different populations in vastly different worlds are urged as an ancient tradition which can be modified only at the peril of our immediate dissolution.

This does not mean that Orthodox worship has not changed since the fourth century, or even the fourteenth, but it does seem to imply that changes must come obliquely, by custom and local variation, ignored and unrecognized until time has surreptitiously sanctified them. Greek worship and Russian worship are from two different worlds, especially when the one is sung to Turkish cadences and the other to Italian polyphony, as they were a generation ago in the homelands. The American Church has inherited these and other modes of worship, common to all of which is the rite which has become a sacred drama, a sung dialogue between priest and choir, with the role of the laity relegated to passive attendance. Very simple people through the centuries have found this worship quite satisfactory, and millions presumably do today, simply by a kind of meditative participation, in which a harmony of sound and vision, motion and fragrance serve as a background for occasional concentration on sacred words or phrases which obtrude from time to time with especial force from the thousands sung or uttered.

Such an atmosphere could be highly attractive to persons caught up in the tense and hurried life of our time. Historically, however, this use of the rite is by no means the original one and it is possible that it will not satisfy literate American Orthodox who may feel the need for more than a background for contemplation. If there are to be striking changes in our liturgical practice, the first one will be in the direction of increased congregational participation. This has begun in many quarters with the congregational recitation of the Creed and the Our Father. Probably it will continue until the choir is replaced for all but the most complicated settings.

Congregational participation becomes a live option only when the vernacular is used. Orthodoxy is historically committed to this policy of vernacular offices, and America can be no exception, but the problem is not simple. As the rite is now celebrated, the language used is not of great importance, and there can, of course, be no question of a substitution of languages before the need is obvious. What, too, is the theological significance of a mysterious language in worship? A large part of the believing world preserves the sacred rites in substantially unknown tongues. In the Church, the Russians, lesser Slavs, Greeks and Arabs use archaic forms of their languages. Rome still uses Latin universally;[3] the great religions of Asia, including the non-Arabic speaking Muslims, employ dead languages or obsolete forms of the vernacular in sacred books and rites. Are ecclesiastical conservatism and cultural degeneration the only explanations?

If the Church could dominate the whole culture, as it does in monastic communities, and nowhere else on a broad front, the tempo of life could be adjusted to the rhythm of the rite. If, on the other hand, it is to adopt externals to serve its children in changing conditions, the rite must be abbreviated, the congregation must be integrated into the action, and some would suggest an eventual revision of the texts in order to present the

[3][Shortly after the publication of this article, on December 4, 1963, Pope Paul VI promulgated *Sacrosantum Concilium* (Constitution on the Sacred Liturgy, see especially §36), a conciliar document that inaugurated the set of liturgical reforms, changing the previously rigid position of the Vatican regarding the use of vernacular languages in the Latin rite.—*Ed.*]

eternal message in language more comprehensible to modern man. The rite enshrines the truth of the incarnation, but we cannot assume that all of its ancient forms are beyond enrichment in the continuing experience of the life in Christ.

Monasticism

A century ago John Mason Neale remarked that "the genius of the Eastern Church is one which dispenses marks of honor till they cease to be valuable." He would readily recognize this trait in the contemporary American Church, where the dignitaries are disproportionately numerous in relation to the baptized population. One cause originally operative was the jurisdictional feuds which tempted hierarchs and party leaders to seek prestige by bestowing dignities in their tiny missionary dioceses with an abandon unknown to the great national churches of the homelands.

Security, maturity, and good taste will bring an end to these abuses, which are after all as harmless as the children's games they resemble. But these empty decorations are superficial symptoms of what will certainly prove to have been a disease of the infancy of the American Church.

A series of very general speculations on probable currents in American Orthodoxy is not the appropriate place for a consideration of the selective principles governing advancement to the episcopate, since one canon law binds the universal Church. The quandary into which the canons have led the Church has its local extensions, however, and the jurisdictions in the United States may be the principal sufferers because of the dislocations of the Orthodox norms native to the American scene.

Simply stated, the difficulty is rooted in the canonical procedure requiring bishops to be celibate, and the custom of the majority of the churches prescribing that they be monks. In its best period this process enabled the dioceses to draw on a large reserve of religious whose theological background was rather higher than the general clerical standard. With the decline of a vigorous monasticism, available candidates were restricted to widowed secular priests, who at least had the advantage of some parish experience, or to what might be called "professional archimandrites."

These were men who elected somewhere in their early career to remain celibate and offer themselves as candidates for the episcopate. They formally assumed the monastic habit, or were simply ordained honorary archimandrites, and began what they hoped would be a short wait until some episcopal see beckoned.

Since hierarchs have not been generally retired except by divine mandate, the Church frequently finds itself administered by men of more than mature years, while the only eligible candidates for replacement are those who have chosen themselves for promotion. The selection presented to the electors is limited to celibates, and these are often men whose celibacy is evidently practical rather than mystical. Few of them elect to follow a serious monastic program, and fewer still produce any literary or other fruits of monasticism. They are simply self-appointed administrators and current canonical procedure almost assures their eventual consideration for an episcopal see. The system works quite well, of course, as any casual observer of church life is aware, but is it not time that the norm be re-approached if not restored?

The suggestion that married priests be advanced to the episcopate as a remedy is unthinkable even on practical grounds. In the loosely decentralized structure of the Church, this would mean that many men who are now quite content to spend their lives as priests would be tempted to the higher office, and the Church, especially in America, lacks the disciplinary organs necessary to impose control. The tendency to fragmentation is already sufficiently well developed without adding this stimulus. Such a canonical change would need ecumenical action, but even speculation about it is unrealistic and dangerous.

The remedy must be found in the tradition: a healthy monasticism. The institution has outlived both the persecution of irreligious governments and the paternal "care" of Orthodox states, but it survives in a weakened condition. The ideal must be presented to children in their formative years, and the necessary material basis provided by administrative action if necessary. Princely patrons no longer exist to endow new foundations, and the atmosphere of church life is out of touch with the monastic spirit, in America as nowhere else. Certainly, the institution has been close to the heart of Orthodoxy, has even dominated the Church, and its extension must be a primary care of the hierarchs. Aside from its important role as a seed-bed for the episcopate, monasticism has a greater value in its program of uninterrupted prayer and example. The influence of a monastery extends far beyond its walls. A monastic revival will not simply happen. It must be prepared for, by teaching, by publicity, by prayer, and by the encouragement of those who may have the vision. In America the contemplative orders in the Roman Church, and even in Protestantism, are increasing in size and vitality: must we confess that the ancient mother of monasticism has become barren?

The Clergy Shortage

If the Orthodox priest is only a "minister of the cult," as some Protestant observers have supposed him to be, then a man with a good voice, just short of professional quality and the opportunity for better pay, and unlimited patience is all that is needed. This is not an ideal to challenge the aspirations of any vigorous adolescent candidate. Unless he is invited to sacrifice himself for the Church, with freedom to express his gifts of leadership in the parish, no self-respecting and independent youngster will prefer the priesthood. The priest in the American churches is expected to be a leader, but the parish, diocesan, and social framework of his profession is designed to stifle any initiative he may have. Many pastors are leaders, but only because they have defeated the system at one or more points, or because they have the love and respect of their people to a degree that no other executive is required to approach. Not only may the circumstances of the priesthood's existence discourage candidates, what are they calculated to do to the character of the priest who must learn to succeed, or survive, by them?

A central concern of the Church will be recruiting for the priesthood of the future, and here the jurisdictions could use a definition of aims and policy and a definite program. The matter is today in the hands of hierarchs and pastors who act without common purpose. The theological schools are prepared to train applicants, but they now do very little to enlist them. In the schools themselves the ideal objective is understood in a wide range of ways. At one extreme, certainly the lower, are those who evidently feel that fleeting exposure to professional techniques joined to a brief acquaintance with nineteenth-century manuals of dogma is enough preparation for a priest. At the other extreme is a famous theologian who would make specialized scholars of our seminarians in blissful indifference to the practical needs of the Church in the parishes. If one must choose between extremes, the latter viewpoint is obviously superior and surely graduate faculties of theology are not a luxury even in a mission field, but if the seminaries are not to train the clergy for their total task, then the Church needs institutions that will. This is not to hint that even the seminaries may be disinterested in the parish priest per se, but they are the logical agencies of recruitment, inspiration, and ultimately of the support needed for the men in the parishes who are the cutting edge of the Church and its only hope of effective survival.

There are additional factors which augur ill for the priesthood in the years ahead. Every jurisdiction in the United States has an insufficient number of candidates, many do not have enough men to fill present vacancies, none has enough in preparation. Recourse will be had to old remedies: the importation of priests from the homelands and the ordination of inadequately trained American-born men. The first expedient draws some of the more adaptable men from a useful service for which they are fitted by background in churches themselves not overstaffed, and injects them into an American environment to which they can offer nothing for many years but the fruits of experience in a vastly different world. The second alternative may have had some merit where it was a necessity against a soundly Orthodox background abroad; it has nothing to commend it in the United States; at the very least the priesthood thus loses the respect of the younger generation.

Why is there an insufficient number of candidates? It has been noted above that the compensation is minimal and so are the potential satisfactions, and these are reasons enough. But basic to them is undoubtedly the parochial system already outlined in which the priest is understood to be a hired laborer who must conform to the felt needs of his flock. Ultimately the solution to this problem will be with those who control the support of the priest, be they hierarchs or lay trustees. If the Church is an agency for domesticating God and employing his power to obtain the material and spiritual well-being of nominal Christians, the present parish structure is admirably adapted to accomplish that end. If the Church is to stand in prophetic judgement on society, creating the new race in grace by traditional standards administered by men with a divine commission, then a major reorientation is demanded in the constitution of every American diocese.

Many will continue to offer themselves, hopeful that this is a "transitional" period, rationalizing that America is "still a missionary area," and that the great improvements of the past twenty years promise much more for the immediate future. But if any observer will compare the quality of our candidates with the type of men who enter the other professions or business, he will conclude that those who love the Church should bestir themselves if its altars are to be well served.

Problems of Orthodoxy in America[1]
The Canonical Problem

Alexander Schmemann

St Vladimir's Seminary Quarterly 8.2 (1964): 67–85

1. An Uncanonical Situation

NO TERM IS USED—and misused—among the Orthodox people in America more often than the term *canonical*. One hears endless discussions about the "canonicity" or the "uncanonicity" of this or that bishop, jurisdiction, priest, parish. Is it not in itself an indication that something is wrong or, at least, questionable from the canonical point of view in America, that there exists a canonical problem which requires an overall analysis and solution? Unfortunately, the existence of such a problem is seldom admitted. Everyone simply claims the fullness of canonicity for his own position and, in the name of it, condemns and denounces as uncanonical the ecclesiastical status of others. And one is amazed by the low level and cynicism of these "canonical" fights in which any insinuation, any distortion is permitted as long as it harms the "enemy." The concern here is not for truth, but for victories in the form of parishes, bishops, priests "shifting" jurisdictions and joining the "canonical" one. It does not matter that the same bishop or priest was condemning yesterday what today he praises as canonical, that the real motivations behind all these transfers seldom have anything to do with canonical convictions; what matters is victory. We live in the poisoned atmosphere of anathemas and excommunications, court cases and litigations, dubious consecrations of

---

[1] This is the first in a series of articles dealing with several urgent problems of the Orthodox Church in America. The next article will deal with the Liturgical Problem. [Two more articles were published in this series: "Problems of Orthodoxy in America: II. The Liturgical Problem," *St Vladimir's Seminary Quarterly* 8 (1964): 164–85; "Problems of Orthodoxy in America: III. The Spiritual Problem," *St Vladimir's Seminary Quarterly* 9 (1965): 171–93.—Ed.]

dubious bishops, hatred, calumny, lies! But do we think about the irreparable moral damage all this inflicts on our people? How can they respect the hierarchy and its decisions? What meaning can the very concept of canonicity have for them? Are we not encouraging them to consider all norms, all regulations, all rules as purely relative? One wonders sometimes whether our bishops realize the scandal of this situation, whether they ever think about the cynicism all this provokes and feeds in the hearts of Orthodox people. Three Russian jurisdictions, two Serbian, two Romanian, two Albanian, two Bulgarian . . . A split among the Syrians . . . The animosity between the Russians and the Carpatho-Russians . . . The Ukrainian problem! And all this at a time when Orthodoxy in America is coming of age, when truly wonderful possibilities exist for its growth, expansion, creative progress. We teach our children to be "proud" of Orthodoxy, we constantly congratulate ourselves about all kinds of historic events and achievements, our church publications distill an almost unbearable triumphalism and optimism, yet, if we were true to the spirit of our faith we ought to repent in "sackcloth and ashes," we ought to cry day and night about the sad, the tragic state of our church. If "canonicity" is anything but a pharisaic and legalistic self-righteousness, if it has anything to do with the spirit of Christ and the tradition of his Body, the Church, we must openly proclaim that the situation in which we all live is utterly uncanonical regardless of all the justifications and sanctions that everyone finds for his "position." For nothing can justify the bare fact: Our Church is divided. To be sure, there have always been divisions and conflicts among Christians. But for the first time in history division belongs to the very structure of the Church, for the first time canonicity seems strangely disconnected from its fundamental "content" and purpose—to assure, express, defend, and fulfill the Church as divinely given unity—for the first time, in other terms, one seems to find normal a multiplicity of "jurisdictions." Truly we must wake up and be horrified by this situation. We must find in ourselves the courage to face it and to re-think it in the light of the genuine Orthodox doctrine and tradition, no matter what it will cost our petty human likes and dislikes. For unless we, first, openly admit the existence of the canonical problem, and, second, put all our thoughts and energies into finding its solution, the decadence of Orthodoxy will begin—in spite of the million-dollar churches and other magnificent "facilities" of which we are so justly proud. "For the time is come that judgment must begin at the house of God: and if it first begin at us, what shall the end be of them that obey not the gospel of God"? (1 Pet 4.17).

2. False Ideas of Canonicity

We must begin with a clarification of the seemingly simple notion of canonicity. I say "seemingly simple" because it is indeed simple enough to give a formal definition: "canonical is that which complies with the canons of the Church." It is much more difficult, however, to understand what this "compliance" is and how to achieve it. And nothing illustrates better this difficulty than certain assumptions on which the whole canonical controversy in America seems to be grounded and which are in fact a very serious distortion of the Orthodox canonical tradition.

There are those, for example, who solve the complex and tragic canonical problem of Orthodoxy in America by one simple rule, which to them seems a self-evident one: to be "canonical" one has to be under some patriarch, or, in general, under some established autocephalous church in the old world. Canonicity is thus reduced to *subordination*, which is declared to constitute the fundamental principle of church organization. Implied here is the idea that a "high ecclesiastical power" (patriarch, synod, etc.) is in itself and by itself the *source* of canonicity: whatever it decides is *ipso facto* canonical and the criterion of canonicity. But in the genuine Orthodox tradition the ecclesiastical power is itself *under* the canons and its decisions are valid and compulsory only inasmuch as they comply with the canons. In other terms, it is not the decision of a patriarch or his synod that creates and guarantees "canonicity," but, on the contrary, it is the canonicity of the decision that gives it its true authority and power. Truth, and not power, is the criterion, and the canons, not different in this from the dogmas, express the *truth* of the Church. And just as no power, no authority can transform heresy into orthodoxy and to make white what is black, no power can make canonical a situation which is not canonical. When told that all patriarchs have agreed with the patriarch of Constantinople that Monotheletism is an Orthodox doctrine, St Maximus the Confessor refused to accept this argument as a decisive criterion of truth. The Church ultimately canonized St Maximus and condemned the patriarchs. Likewise, if tomorrow all patriarchs agree and proclaim in a solemn "tomos" that the best solution for Orthodoxy in America is to remain divided into fourteen jurisdictions, this decision will not make our situation canonical and this for the simple reason that it does not comply with the canonical tradition or the *truth* of the Church. For the purpose and the function of the hierarchy is precisely to keep pure and undistorted the tradition in its fullness, and if and when it sanctions or even tolerates anything contrary to the truth of the Church, it puts itself under the condemnation of canons.[2] And it is indeed ironic that in America the canonical subordinationism, exalted by so many as the only source and guarantee of "canonicity," is being used to justify the most uncanonical situation one can imagine: the simultaneous jurisdiction of several bishops in the same territory, which is a betrayal of both the letter and the spirit of the whole canonical tradition. For this situation destroys the fundamental "note" of the Church: the hierarchical and structural unity as the foundation and the expression of the spiritual unity of the Church as "unity of faith and love." If there exists a clear and universal canonical principle it is certainly that of jurisdictional unity[3] and, therefore, if a peculiar "reduction" of canonicity leads to the *de facto* destruction of that principle, one can apply to it the words of the Gospel: "Ye shall know them by their fruits" (Mt 7.16). "Canonical subordinationism" is the best indication of how deeply "westernized" we have become in our canonical thinking. Canonicity has been identified not with truth, but with "security." And nothing short of a real canonical revival can bring us back to the glorious certitude that in Orthodoxy there is no substitute for Truth.

---

[2] "The duty of obedience ceases when the bishop deviates from the Catholic norm, and the people have the right to accuse and even to depose him," George Florovsky, "Sobornost—The Catholicity of the Church," *The Church of God* (London, 1934), 72.

[3] Cf. John Meyendorff, "'One Bishop in One City' (Canon 8, First Ecumenical Council)," *St Vladimir's Seminary Quarterly* 5.1–2 (1961): 54–62. [In the present volume, pp. 11–20.—*Ed.*]

Destructive of the Church's unity, "canonical subordinationism" leads necessarily to the destruction of the Church's *continuity*. There is no need to prove here that the continuity in faith, doctrine, and life constitutes the very basis of Orthodox ecclesiology and that the focal principle of that continuity is the apostolic succession of the episcopate; through it each local church manifests and maintains her organic unity and identity with the one, holy, catholic, and apostolic Church, the *catholicity* of her life and faith. But whereas in the genuine Orthodox tradition the "subject" of continuity is the Church, i.e., the *real* continuity of a living and concrete community with the whole tradition and order of the Church, continuity of which the succession of the episcopate is the witness and the bearer, here in the theory of "canonical subordinationism" the reality of the Church is reduced to the formal principle of "jurisdiction," i.e., subordination to a central ecclesiastical power. But then the meaning of the apostolic succession is deeply changed as is also that of the bishop and his function within the Church. In the original tradition, a bishop through his consecration by other bishops, becomes the "successor" not to his consecrators but, first of all, to the unbroken continuity of his own Church.[4]

The "Church is in the bishop" because the "bishop is in the Church," in the "organic unity with a particular body of church people."[5] In the system of canonical subordination, however, the bishop becomes a simple representative of a higher jurisdiction, important not in himself, not as the charismatic bearer and guardian of his Church's *continuity* and *catholicity*, but as means of this Church's subordination to a "jurisdiction." It is difficult to imagine a more serious distortion and, indeed, destruction of

---

[4] In all early documents the lists of bishops show their succession on the same "cathedra" and not through their consecrators: cf. for example, Eusebius, *Ecclesiastical History* 5.6.1–2; Irenaeus, *Adversus Haereses.* 3.3.3. On the meaning of episcopal consecration by several bishops, cf. my essay, "The Idea of Primacy in Orthodox Ecclesiology" in *The Primacy of Peter* (London, 1963 [republished by St Vladimir's Seminary Press, 1992]), 40ff., and also George Florovsky, "The Sacrament of Pentecost: A Russian View on Apostolic Succession," *Sobornost* (March 1934): 29–35: "Under normal conditions of Church life, apostolic succession should never become reduced to an abstract enumeration of successive ordainers. In ancient times apostolic succession usually implied first of all a succession to a definite *cathedra*, again in a particular local *sobornost*. Apostolic Succession does not represent a self-sufficient chain, or order of bishops."

[5] Florovsky, "The Sacrament of Pentecost," 32.

the Orthodox conception of continuity and apostolic succession. For the Church cannot be reduced to "jurisdiction." She is a living organism and her continuity is precisely that of life. The function of the episcopate and of "power" in general is to preserve, defend, and express this continuity and fullness of life, but it is a function *within* and not *above* the Church. The ministry of power does not *create* the Church but is created by God within the Church, which is ontologically prior to all functions, charisms, and ministries.[6] And "jurisdiction," when it is divorced from the real continuity of the Church, can become, and in fact often becomes, a principle of discontinuity and schism.

A sad but typical illustration of this is the painful story of the Russian ecclesiastical conflicts in America. Orthodoxy was planted in Alaska in the 18th century, by Russian missionaries. Since then the Church here grew organically: from a mission into a diocese, and then into a group of dioceses, or a local church. The normal jurisdictional link between the American Church and the Moscow Patriarchate was broken de facto by the tragic events of the Russian Revolution. There was no schism, no quarrel, no conflict. The bishop appointed from Moscow went to Russia and did not return. Deprived of material support from the mother church, poisoned by revolutionary propaganda, the Church in America was in a great spiritual danger. In this tragic situation[7] the decision of the Sobor of Detroit in 1924 to proclaim the temporary autonomy was not only fully justified, it was indeed an act of real continuity, i.e., of the Church's faithfulness to

---

[6]"On the day of Pentecost, the Spirit descends not only on the apostles, but also on those who were present with them; not only on the Twelve, but on the entire multitude (compare Chrysostom's *Discourses* and his *Interpretation of Acts*). This means that the Spirit descends on the whole of the Primitive Church, then present in Jerusalem. But though the Spirit is one, the gifts and ministries of the Church are very varied, so that while in the sacrament of Pentecost the Spirit descends on all, it is on the Twelve alone that He bestows the power and the rank of priesthood promised to them by our Lord in the days of His flesh. The distinctive features of priesthood do not become blurred in the all-embracing fullness of Pentecost. But the simultaneity of this catholic outpouring of the Spirit on the entire Church witnesses to the fact that priesthood was founded within the *sobornost* of the church," Florovsky, "The Sacrament of Pentecost," 31.

[7]For a description of that situation, see Dmitry Grigorieff, "The Historical Background of Orthodoxy in America," *St Vladimir's Seminary Quarterly* 5.1–2 (1961): 3–53. [An expanded version of the article appears in the present volume, pp. 119–146.—*Ed.*].

her organic growth. It was moreover an act of the whole Church: bishops[8], clergy, and laity; and its motivation was profoundly and exclusively ecclesiastical: to assure, under new circumstances, the continuity of life, faith, and order.[9] But the Moscow Patriarchate condemned the American Church as "schismatic," and in 1933 established here its own "jurisdiction" in the form of the Exarchate.[10]

We have here a clear-cut clash between the two kinds of "canonical logic." On the one hand, there is the logic of organic continuity in a Church which knows herself to be a reality, a body, a living continuity and which, for the very sake of that continuity and growth, dares to take steps best suited to that purpose. And there is, on the other hand, the legalistic logic in which the whole church life is nothing but a system of jurisdictional subordination. The creation of the Patriarchal Exarchate is, from this point of view, a very interesting phenomenon. It implies that a Church can be created, so to speak, *ex nihilo*, by the simple fact of the arrival in the USA of Bishop Benjamin. It implies also, that in the Muscovite thinking the *continuity* of the Church in America lies not in her long and organic development, but *exclusively* in her jurisdictional dependence on Moscow. And it is really astonishing how many people, even those who claim to "understand" and "justify" the Metropolia, but mainly for non-ecclesiastical reasons, fail to realize that by the standards of a genuinely Orthodox canonical and ecclesiastical tradition, the only real *schism* was originated by the declaration of Metropolitan Sergius of Moscow that Archbishop Benjamin had "organized in New York a Diocesan Council and that our North American Diocese has begun official existence."[11] This act broke the real continuity of the American Church, introduced division among Orthodox people, weakened the discipline which was restored with such pain after Detroit, opened the door to endless controversies and accusations and, in general, contributed to the canonical chaos in which we live

[8]There were three bishops at the Sobor of Detroit.
[9]Cf. Grigorieff, "The Historical Background," 19ff., and Alexander Bogolepov, *Toward an American Orthodox Church* (New York 1963), 78ff.
[10]Cf. Bogolepov, *Toward an American Church,* 81 and especially Grigorieff, "The Historical Background," 29–32.
[11]Quoted in Grigorieff, "The Historical Background," 32.

today. And if apostolic succession has been established for the sake of unity and *sobornost*, and must never become the vehicle of exclusiveness and division, if, in other terms, a schism is an act of division, a break in the *real* continuity of the Church, it was the establishment of the Exarchate that provoked a schism, and a rupture of canonicity.

We mention the Russian tragedy because, as the time goes on, it becomes more and more obviously a kind of "pattern" for the whole canonical tragedy of American Orthodoxy. What happened to the Russians is happening *mutatis mutandis* to the others, the Serbians, the Romanians, the Bulgarians, the Syrians, and for the same fundamental reason: the growing discrepancy between the real situation, the real continuity, the real needs of Orthodoxy here and the various "situations" in Bucharest or Damascus, Istanbul or Moscow. If the jurisdictional dependence of American churches on these centers in the early, formative period of Orthodoxy here was a self-evident form of its *continuity*, it has become today, paradoxically as it sounds, the cause of discontinuity and division. It is a significant fact that, with some very few exceptions, the schisms and conflicts which poison our life here and obstruct all real progress, are rooted not in the American situation itself, but precisely in this formal "dependence" on ecclesiastical centers located thousands of miles away from America and radically alienated from the real needs of the Church in America. A bishop virtually without parishes is recognized as "canonical" because he is "recognized" by his patriarch, but a bishop of the same Church with a flourishing diocese and with organic roots in the real continuity of the Church here is declared "un-canonical" for lack of such recognition. An unnecessary and vicious split in a relatively small archdiocese is declared "canonical," because ten bishops in the Middle East have decided so. A priest in trouble in his own diocese is always welcome in some other jurisdiction... We are constantly told that something is "canonical," because it is "recognized" as canonical by such or such patriarch or synod. But, once more, in the Orthodox teaching canonical is that which complies with the canons and the canons express the *truth* of the Church. We must openly reject the "romanizing" theory that something is true because some infallible authority has decreed that it is true. In the Orthodox Church truth itself is the supreme authority and criterion. At one time the patriarch of Constantinople "recognized" as Orthodox and canonical the so-called "Living Church" in Russia. This did not make it either Orthodox or canonical.

No patriarch, no synod—be it in Moscow or Belgrade or in any other place—has the infallible charisma to understand the needs and the *truth* of the American situation better than the Orthodox people who constitute the Church here. In fact, it is their lack of genuine pastoral interest in the real needs of the Church in America, it is their "recognitions" and "excommunications" that made the Orthodox Church here a pitiful chaos. Obviously, as long as we believe that the Holy Spirit acts in America only *via* Damascus or Sofia, Bucharest, or Moscow, as long as our bishops, forgetting the real content of the doctrine of apostolic succession which makes them the representatives of God and not of patriarchs, think of themselves as caretakers of interests having nothing to do with the interests of Orthodoxy in America, as long, in other terms, as we reduce the Church, her life, her unity, her continuity to blind and legalistic subordination, the canonical chaos will continue, bearing with it the fatal deterioration of Orthodoxy.

Finally, all this leads to (and also in part proceeds from) the harmful and un-Orthodox reduction of canonicity to an almost abstract principle of *validity*. When a man has been consecrated bishop by at least two other bishops, he is considered as a "valid" bishop regardless of the ecclesiastical and ecclesiological content of his consecration. But Orthodox tradition has never isolated validity into a "principle in itself," i.e., disconnected from truth, authenticity, and, in general, the whole faith and order of the Church. It would not be difficult to show that the canonical tradition, when dealing with holy orders and sacraments, always stresses that they are valid because they are acts *of*, and *within*, the Church, which means that it is their authenticity as acts of the Church that make them valid and not vice versa. To consider validity as a self-contained principle leads to a magical understanding of the Church and to a dangerous distortion of ecclesiology. Yet in America, under the impact of the multi-jurisdictional chaos this idea of validity *per se* appears more and more as the only criterion. There grows around us a peculiar indifference to *authenticity*, to elementary moral considerations. A bishop, a priest, a layman can be accused of all sorts of moral and canonical sins: the day when he "shifts" to the "canonical" jurisdictions all these accusations become irrelevant; he is "valid" and one can entrust to him the salvation of human souls! Have we completely forgotten that all the "notae" of the Church are not only equally important but also interdependent, and what is not *holy*—i.e., right, moral, just, canonical, cannot be "*apostolic*"? In our opinion nothing has harmed more the spiritual and moral foundations of Church life than the really *immoral* idea that a man, an act, a situation are "valid" only in function of a purely formal "validity in itself." It is this immoral doctrine that poisons the Church, makes parishes and individuals think of any jurisdictional shift as justified as long as they "go under a valid bishop" and makes the Church cynical about, and indifferent to, considerations of truth and morals.

3. The Meaning of Canonicity

The canonical chaos in America is not a specifically "American" phenomenon. Rather, Orthodoxy here is the victim of a long, indeed a multi-secular disease. It was a latent disease as long as the Church was living in the old traditional situation characterized primarily by an organic unity of the state, the ethnic factor, and the ecclesiastical organization. Up to quite recently, in fact up to the appearance of the massive Orthodox *diaspora*, ecclesiastical stability and order were preserved not so much by the canonical "consciousness," but by state regulations and control. Ironically enough it made not much difference whether the state was Orthodox (the Russian Empire, the Kingdom of Greece), Roman Catholic (Austro-Hungary) or Muslim (the Ottoman Empire). Members of the Church could be persecuted in non-Orthodox states, but Church organization—and this is the crux of the matter—was *sanctioned* by the state and could not be altered without this sanction. This situation was, of course, the result of the initial Byzantine "symphony" between Church and state, but after the fall of Byzantium it was progressively deprived of that mutual interdependence of Church and state which was at the very heart of the

Byzantine theocratic ideology.[12] What is important for us here and what constitutes the "disease" mentioned above is that this organic blend of state regulations, ethnic solidarity, and church organization led little by little to a divorce of the canonical consciousness from its dogmatic and spiritual context. Canonical tradition, understood at first as an organic part of the dogmatic tradition, as the latter's application to the empirical life of the Church, became canon *law*: a system of rules and regulations, juridical—and not primarily doctrinal and spiritual—in their nature and interpreted as such within categories alien to the spiritual essence of the Church. Just as a lawyer is the one who can find all possible precedents and arguments that favor his "case," a canonist, in this system of thought, is the one who, in the huge mass of canonical texts, can find that one which justifies his "case," even if the latter seems to contradict the spirit of the Church. And once such "text" is found, "canonicity" is established. There appeared, in other terms, a divorce between the Church as spiritual, sacramental *essence* and the Church as *organization*, so that the latter ceased in fact to be considered as the expression of the first, fully dependent on it. If today in America so many of our laymen are sincerely convinced that the parish *organization* is an exclusively legal or "material" problem and ought to be handled apart from the "spiritual," the root of this conviction is not only in the specifically American ethos, but also in the progressive secularization of canon law itself. And yet the whole point is that canons are not mere laws, but laws whose authority is rooted precisely in the spiritual essence of the Church. Canons do not constitute or create the Church, their function is to defend, clarify, and regulate the life of the Church, to make it comply with the essence of the Church. This means that in order to be properly understood, interpreted, and applied, canonical texts must be always referred to that *truth* of, and about, the Church, which they express sometimes for a very particular situation and which is not necessarily explicit in the canonical text itself.

If we take the canonical area which interests us more particularly in this essay, that of ecclesiastical organization and episcopal power, it is evident

---

[12] Alexander Schmemann, "Byzantine Theocracy and the Orthodox Church," *St Vladimir's Seminary Quarterly* 1.2 (1953), 5–22.

that the basic reality or truth to which all canons dealing with bishops, their consecration, and their jurisdiction point and refer, is the reality of *unity*, as the very essence of the Church. The Church is unity of men with God in Christ and unity of men one with another *in Christ*. Of this new, divinely given and divine unity the Church is the gift, the manifestation, the growth, and the fulfillment. And, therefore, everything in her organization, order, and life is in some way or another related to unity, and is to be understood, evaluated, and, if necessary, judged by it. The dogmatic or spiritual essence of the Church as unity is thus the criterion for the proper understanding of canons concerning Church organization and also for their proper application. If the canons prescribe that a bishop must be consecrated by all bishops of the province (cf. Apostolic Canon 1; First Ecumenical Council, Canon 4) and only in case of "some special reason or owing to the distance" by two or three, the meaning of the canon is obviously not that any two or three bishops can "make" another bishop, but that the consecration of a bishop is the very sacrament of the Church as unity and oneness.[13] To reduce this canon to a formal principle that there must be at least two bishops for a "valid" episcopal consecration is simply nonsensical. The canon both reveals and safeguards an essential truth about the Church, and its proper application is possible, therefore, only within the full context of that truth. And only this context explains why canons which apparently are anachronistic and have nothing to do with our time and situations are not considered as obsolete but remain an integral part of Tradition. To be sure the Meletian schism which divided Egypt at the beginning of the fourth century has in itself no great importance for us. Yet the canons of the First Ecumenical Council which defined the norms for its solution keep all their significance precisely because they

---

[13]"In the ordination of a bishop no separate bishop can act for himself as a bishop of a definite and particular local church.... He acts as a representative of the *sobornost* of co-bishops, as a member, and shares of this *sobornost*.... In addition to this it is implied that these bishops are not separated and indeed are inseparable from their flocks. Every co-ordainer acts in the name of Catholic *sobornost* and fullness.... Again, these are not only canonical, or administrative, or disciplinary measures. One feels that there is a mystical depth in them. No realization or extension of apostolic succession is otherwise possible apart from the unbreakable *sobornost* of the whole Church." George Florovsky, "The Sacrament of Pentecost," 31.

reveal that truth of the Church in the light of which, and for the preservation of which, that schism was solved. All this means that the search for canonicity consists not in an accumulation of "texts," but in the effort, first, to understand the ecclesiological meaning of a given text, and then, to relate it to a particular and concrete situation.

The necessity for such an effort is especially obvious here in America. The American ecclesiastical situation is unprecedented in more than one respect. Enough time and energy have been spent in sterile attempts simply to "reduce" it to some pattern of the past, i.e., to ignore the real challenge it presents to the canonical conscience of the Church.

4. National Pluralism and Canonical Unity

The unprecedented situation of American Orthodoxy is that the Church here, different in this from all other parts of the Orthodox world, is *multinational* in its origins. Since the Byzantine era, Orthodoxy was always brought to and accepted by whole nations. The only familiar pattern of the past, therefore, is not the creation of mere local churches, but a total integration and incarnation of Orthodoxy in national cultures; so that these cultures themselves cannot be separated from Orthodoxy but, in their depth, are genuine expressions of Orthodoxy. This organic unity of the national and religious is not a historical accident, much less a defect of Orthodoxy. In its positive expression it is the fruit of the Orthodox concept and experience of the Church as embracing the whole life. Catholicity means for an Orthodox more than geographic universality; it is, above everything else, the wholeness, the totality of life as belonging to Christ and sanctified by the Church. In this respect, the situation in America is radically different from the whole historical experience of Orthodoxy. Not only the Orthodox Church was brought here by representatives of various Orthodox nations, but it was brought as precisely the continuation of their national existence. Hence the problem of canonical or ecclesiological unity, which as we have seen is a self-evident requirement of the very truth of the Church, encounters here difficulties that cannot be simply reduced to the solutions of the past. And yet, this is precisely what happens much too often.

On the one hand, there are those who believe that the old pattern of national and religious unity can be simply applied to America. The Church is Greek in Greece, Russian in Russia, *therefore* it must be American in America—such is their reasoning. We are no longer Russians or Greeks, let us translate services in English, eliminate all "nationalism" from the Church and be one. Logical as it sounds, this solution is deeply wrong and, in fact, impossible. For what, in their cheerful but superficial "Americanism," the partisans of this view seem completely to overlook is that the rapport between Orthodoxy and Russia, or Orthodoxy and Greece, is fundamentally different from, if not opposed to, the rapport between Orthodoxy and America. There is not and there cannot be a religion *of* America in the sense in which Orthodoxy is the religion of Greece or Russia and this, in spite of all possible and actual betrayals and apostasies. And, for this reason, Orthodoxy cannot be *American* in the sense in which it certainly is Greek, Russian, or Serbian. Whereas there, in the old world, Orthodoxy is coextensive with national culture, and to some extent, *is* the national culture (so that the only alternative is the escape into a "cosmopolitan," viz., "Western" culture), in America, religious pluralism and therefore, a basic religious "neutrality," belongs to the very essence of culture and prevents religion from a total "integration" in culture. Americans may be more religious people than Russians or Serbs, religion in America may have privileges, prestige, and status it has not had in the "organic" Orthodox countries, all this does not alter the fundamentally secular nature of contemporary American culture; and yet it is precisely this dichotomy of culture and religion that Orthodoxy has never known or experienced and that is totally alien to Orthodoxy. For the first time in its whole history, Orthodoxy must live within a secular culture. This presents enormous spiritual problems with which I hope to deal in a special article. What is important for us here, however, is that the concept of "Americanization" and "American" Orthodoxy is thus far from being a simple one. It is a great error to think that all problems are solved by the use of English in services, essential as it is. For the real problem (and we will probably only begin to realize and to face it when "everything" is translated into English) is that of culture, of the "way of life." It belongs to the very essence of Orthodoxy not only to "accept" a culture, but to permeate and to transform it, or, in other terms, to consider it an integral part and object of the Orthodox vision of life. Deprived of this living interrelation with culture, of this claim to the *whole* of life, Orthodoxy, in spite of all formal rectitude of dogma and liturgy, betrays and loses something absolutely essential. And this explains the instinctive attachment of so many Orthodox, even American born, to the "national" forms of Orthodoxy, their resistance, however narrow-minded and "nationalistic" to a complete divorce between Orthodoxy and its various national expressions. In these forms and expressions Orthodoxy preserves something of its existential wholeness, of its link with life in its totality, and is not reduced to a "rite," a clearly delineated number of credal statements and a set of "minimal rules." One cannot by a surgical operation called "Americanization" distill a pure "Orthodoxy in itself," without disconnecting it from its flesh and blood, making it a lifeless form. There can be no doubt, therefore, that in view of all this, a living continuity with national traditions will remain for a long time not only a "compromise" meant to satisfy the "old-timers," but an essential condition for the very life of the Orthodox Church. And any attempt to build the unity of Orthodoxy here by opposing the "American" to the traditional national connotations and terms will lead neither to a real unity nor to real Orthodoxy.

But equally wrong are those who from this interdependence of the national and the ecclesiastical within Orthodoxy draw the conclusion that, therefore, the ecclesiastical, i.e., "jurisdictional" unity of the Orthodox Church in America is impossible and ought not even to be sought. This view implies a very narrow and obviously distorted idea of the Church as a simple *function* of national identity, values, and self-preservation. "National" becomes here "nationalistic" and the Church becomes an instrument of nationalism. One must confess that one gets tired of the frequent exhortation to "keep the faith of our fathers." By the same reasoning a man of Protestant descent should remain Protestant and a Jew a Jew, regardless of their religious convictions. Orthodoxy should be kept and preserved not because it is the "faith of our fathers," but because it is the *true faith* and as such is universal, all-embracing, and truly *catholic*. A convert, for example, embraces Orthodoxy not because it is somebody's "father's faith," but because he recognizes in it the Church of Christ, the fullness of faith and catholicity. Yet it is impossible to manifest and communicate that fullness if the Church is simply identified with an ethnic group and its natural exclusiveness. It is not the task or the purpose of Orthodoxy to perpetuate and "preserve" the Russian or the Greek national identity, but the function of Greek and Russian "expressions" of Orthodoxy is to perpetuate the "catholic" values of Orthodoxy which otherwise would be lost. "National" here has value not in itself, but only inasmuch as it is "catholic," i.e., capable of conveying and communicating the living truth of Orthodoxy, of assuring the organic continuity of the Church. Orthodoxy, if it is to remain the vehicle and the expression of a national "subculture" (and in America every exclusive ethnic nationalism is, by definition, a subculture), will share the latter's inescapable disintegration and dissolution. Orthodoxy as the natural solidarity and affinity of people coming from the same island, village, geographical area, or nation (and we have, in fact, "jurisdictional" expressions of all these categories) cannot indefinitely resist and survive the pressure of the sociological law which condemns such solidarities to a sooner or later death. What is required, therefore, is not only unity and cooperation *among* various national "jurisdictions," but a return to the real idea of *unity* as expressing the *unity* of the Church and the catholicity of her faith and tradition. Not a "united" Church, but the *Church*.

The unprecedented character of the American Orthodox situation results thus in a double requirement. The Church here must preserve, at least for a foreseeable period of time, its organic continuity with the national cultures in which she has expressed the catholicity of her faith and life. And she must, in order to fulfill this catholicity, achieve its canonical unity as truly one Church. Is this possible?

5. The Solution: *Episcopatus unus est*

The answer to this question is in the doctrinal and canonical tradition, but only if we look for its depth and truth, and not for petty and legalistic "precedents" of a situation that has none.

The canonical solution of which, in these concluding paragraphs, we can give only a very general and preliminary sketch, presents itself on three levels, which although they are levels or aspects of the same ecclesiastical structure must nevertheless be kept distinct.

There can be no doubt that the unity of the Church, expressed in her canonical structure, is expressed, first of all, in and through the unity of the episcopate. *Episcopatus unus est*, wrote St Cyprian of Carthage in the third century. This means that each local or particular church is united to all other churches, reveals her ontological identity with them, in its bishop. Just as every bishop receives the fullness of his episcopate from the oneness of the episcopate expressed in the plurality of the consecrators, this fullness includes, as its very essence, his unity with the whole episcopate. In the preceding pages we have spoken enough of the distortions implied in canonical subordinationism. It must be strongly emphasized, however, that it is the distortion of a fundamental truth: the unity and the interdependence of the bishops as the form of the Church's unity. The error of canonical subordinationism is that it understands unity only in terms of subordination (of a bishop to his "superiors") whereas, in Orthodox ecclesiology, subordination or obedience is derived from the unity of bishops. There is indeed no power above the episcopal power, but this power itself implies the bishop's agreement and unity with the whole episcopate, so that a bishop separated from the unity of bishops loses *ipso facto* his "power."[14] In this sense a bishop is obedient and even *subordinated* to the unity and unanimity of bishops, but because he himself is a vital member of that unity. His subordination is not to a "superior," but to the very reality of the Church's unity and unanimity of which the synod of bishops is the gracious organ: "The bishops of every nation must acknowledge him

---

[14]Cf. my essay "The Idea of Primacy in Orthodox Ecclesiology," cited above, and also my essay "Towards a Theology of Councils," *St Vladimir's Seminary Quarterly* 6.4 (1962): 170–84.

who is first among them and account him as their head, and do nothing of consequence without his consent . . . but neither let him . . . do anything without the consent of all; *for so there will be unanimity*" (Apostolic Canon 34).

The fundamental form and expression of episcopal unity is the *synod of bishops* and it would not be difficult to show that all subsequent forms of ecclesiastical and canonical structure (provinces, metropolitan districts, autocephalous churches) grew from this fundamental form and requirements of the canonical tradition. The various modes of groupings of local churches may have varied. Thus, the present structure of Orthodoxy as a family of "autocephalous churches" is by no means the original one. Yet what cannot change is the "synod of bishops" as the *expression* of the Church's unity. It is very significant, however, that whenever and wherever the spirit of "canonical subordinationism" triumphs, the idea of the episcopate's unity and, therefore, of the synod of bishops becomes dormant (without, of course, disappearing completely). When, for example, the Russian Church under Peter the Great was given the status of a "Department of Orthodox Confession" with, as its result, a bureaucratic system of administration through subordination, the Russian episcopate did not have a plenary synod for more than two hundred years! And, in general, since "canonical subordinationism" became more or less the working system of the Church's government, the bishops themselves felt no need of synods and "*sobornost*." They were satisfied with "patriarchal" or "governing" synods, which, although retaining something of the original ecclesiological idea, were in fact, the products of the secular principle of "centralized administration" rather than of the ecclesiastical norm of episcopal unity. But it is very important that we understand the difference between a "central administration," even if it is called "synod," and the true ecclesiological nature of an episcopal synod. A central administration may consist of bishops (as the Russian Holy Synod, or the Patriarchal Synod of Constantinople), but its very function and nature is to supply the Church with a "high power" not only not derived from the unity of bishops, but meant to be a power *above* them. Not only is it not the expression of the power of the bishops but, on the contrary, it is understood as the *source* of their power. But this is a deep distortion of the very nature of power in the Church, which is the power of the bishops united among themselves and united with their respective churches as their priests, patrons and teachers. In the synod of bishops, properly understood, all churches are truly *represented* in the person of their bishops and, in the early tradition, a bishop without a church, i.e., without the reality of his episcopacy, is not a member of the synod. The synod of bishops is the "higher power" because it speaks and acts *in* and *for* the Church and takes from the real, living Church the *truth* of its decisions.

In the canonical tradition the normal context of the synod of bishops is a "province," i.e., a geographical, territorial group of churches, forming a self-evident "whole." While the ecumenical, universal synod remains an "extraordinary" event, made necessary by a major crisis, local provincial synods are to be held at regular intervals (cf. Apostolic Canon 37; First Nicaea, Canon 5; Chalcedon, Canon 19; Antioch, Canon 20; Second Nicaea, Canon 6; Carthage, Canon 27). And again, if the precise definition of a "province" has greatly changed in Church history and, by its very nature, depends on a great variety of factors, the idea implied in these canons, i.e., that of a group of churches forming a local church, united by territory and common concerns, is quite clear. It is that part of the Church universal, which has all the necessary and sufficient conditions for a truly *catholic* existence, in which all churches are in a real interdependence and share in the same historical "situation."

All this brings us to the first "dimension" of the American canonical solution: the unity of the Orthodox Church of America is to be achieved and expressed, first of all, on the level of the episcopate. There hardly can be any doubt that America is a "province" in the canonical sense of this term, that all Orthodox churches here, regardless of their national origin, share in the same empirical, spiritual and cultural situation, that the life and the progress of each one of them depends on the life and the progress of the whole. So much has been already acknowledged by our bishops when they established their *Standing Conference*. But this Conference is a purely consultative body, it has no canonical status whatsoever, and useful and efficient as it is, it cannot solve any of the real problems because it reflects the division of Orthodoxy here, as much as its unity. The bishops must constitute the *Synod of the Orthodox Church of America* and this, prior to any other "unification." For this synod will reveal and manifest in itself the unity of the Church which up to now exists in the defective multitude of mutually independent "jurisdictions." And they must and can do it simply in virtue of their episcopate which already unites them. It is, in other words, not something new that is required from them, but the self-evident manifestation of the truth that *episcopatus unus est*, of the very essence of the episcopate which cannot belong to "churches," but always belongs to the Church in her indivisibility and oneness. One can almost visualize the glorious and blessed day when some forty Orthodox Bishops of America will open their first Synod—in New York, or Chicago, or Pittsburgh—with the hymn "Today hath the grace of the Holy Spirit assembled us together . . ." and will appear to us not as "representatives" of Greek, Russian, or any other "jurisdictions" and interests, but as the very icon, the very "epiphany" of our unity within the Body of Christ; when each of them and all together will think and deliberate only in terms of the whole, putting aside for a while all particular or national problems, real and important as they may be. On that day we shall "taste and see" (Ps 33.8) the oneness of the Orthodox Church in America even if nothing else is changed and the various national ecclesiastical structures remain for a while in operation.

But, in fact, much will be changed. Orthodoxy in America will acquire a center of unity, of cooperation, a sense of direction, a "term of reference." We do not have to enumerate here all problems that face us and which, at present, cannot be solved because no "jurisdiction" is strong enough to do it by itself. What is even more important, this center of hierarchical unity will eliminate the numberless frictions among "jurisdictions" which result in consecrations of new and sometimes very dubious bishops. If the duty of the synod, according to canon law, is to approve all episcopal consecrations (". . . and let those who are absent signify their acquiescence in writing"; First Ecumenical Council, Canon 4), the very existence of a synod will bring order into our "jurisdictional" chaos, transform it into a truly canonical structure.

6. The Solution: *Ecclesia in episcopo*

The first stage described above is so self-evident that it requires no lengthy elaboration. The next one has never been really discussed and yet, if given some thought, appears to be as obvious. It deals with the second level of unity, which is that of the *diocese*. At this point, some statistical data may be quite relevant: in the state of Ohio, to take but one example, there exist at present 86 Orthodox parishes. They belong to 14 different jurisdictions, which means that every group is very small and, of necessity, extremely limited in its educational, charitable, and any other "extra-parish" activities. There is no Orthodox bishop in Ohio, no center of unity except the local "clergy fellowships." It is not difficult to imagine what could be the possibilities of all these parishes if they belonged to one local ecclesiastical structure. Deprived of it, each parish lives "in-itself," without any real vision of the whole. And yet there are scores of colleges in Ohio with an urgent need for Orthodox programs, there are obvious educational, and charitable needs, and there is, above everything else, the need for a common Orthodox witness in a non-Orthodox world. But is it not the very purpose and function of a diocese to keep the parishes together, to make them living parts of a greater whole, indeed, the Church? A parish, left to itself, can never be truly *catholic*, for it is of necessity limited by the concerns and interests of its people. And it is maybe one of the greatest and the deepest tragedies of American Orthodoxy that the parishes have been, in fact, left to themselves and have become selfish and self-centered institutions. But how can a bishop living in New York be a living *center* of unity and leadership in Ohio, especially if his power is limited to a group of scattered parishes? No wonder our people grow in an almost complete ignorance of a bishop's function in the Church and think of him as a "guest speaker" at a parish celebration. But suppose we have a bishop of Ohio. Suppose a diocesan center is established which guides and centralizes all common concerns of the Orthodox Church in Ohio, which—instead of being, as it is today, a principle of *division*—becomes a principle of *unity* and common life. Is it really necessary to even argue in favor of such a solution? Is it not a self-evident one? To be sure there are difficulties. The

Church is multinational: to what nationality will the bishop belong? But is it an absolute difficulty? Can it not be solved if some goodwill, some patience, and, above all, some desire for unity is shown? Is it very difficult to work out a diocesan constitution which will incorporate and foresee these difficulties? There could be provisions for a multinational council to assist the bishop, a system of rotation of "nationalities," a set of checks and balances. The experience of *Orthodox clergy fellowships* which have almost spontaneously mushroomed all over the country shows that a basis already exists for such a common structure, both spiritually and materially, and that it needs only to be crowned with its logical, canonical consequence.

7. The Solution: The Parish

Finally, the third level: the *parish*. It is here that the national cultural unity, which, whether we like it or not, still constitutes a vital necessity for American Orthodoxy, fulfills its ecclesiastical function. It is probable that for quite a while the parishes will remain predominantly, if not exclusively, colored by their national background. This, of course, does not exclude the establishment of "pan-Orthodox" parishes wherever a national group is too weak to maintain its own (in new suburbs, for example). But, as a general rule, a parish cannot live by an "abstract" Orthodoxy. In reality it is always shaped by this or that liturgical tradition and piety, belongs to a definite "expression" of Orthodoxy. And it is good that it be so. At this stage of the history of Orthodoxy in America it would be spiritually dangerous—and we have explained why—to break this organic continuity of piety and culture, of memory and custom. There are some among us who dream of "uniformity" in everything, thinking that uniformity and unity are identical. But this is wrong, and it reflects a very formal and not a spiritual understanding of unity. It may be the source of many blessings for the growing Orthodox Church in America that it will profit by the best in each national culture, will "appropriate" the whole heritage of the Orthodox Church. For through its unity with parishes of all the other national backgrounds within the diocesan framework, each national parish will share its "riches" with the others and, in turn, receive from the others their gifts—and this is indeed the real catholicity! The national culture of one group will cease to be a principle of separation, of exclusiveness, of self-centeredness and, will cease, thus, to deteriorate into a psychological and spiritual "isolationism." And maybe it is in America that God wants us to heal the multi-secular national isolation of Orthodox churches, one from another, and this not by abandoning all that made the spiritual beauty and meaning of Greek, Russian, Serbian and all other "Orthodoxies," but by giving each of them finally their catholic and universal significance. It is here that we can all share and consider as truly ours the spiritual legacies of the Greek fathers, the paschal joy of St Seraphim of Sarov, the warm piety hidden for centuries in the Carpathian Mountains. Then and only then Orthodoxy will be ready for a real encounter with America, for its *mission* to America.

In the last analysis the requirements of our Orthodox canonical tradition, the solution of our canonical problem coincides, strange as it may seem, with the most practical solution, with common sense. But it is not strange. For Tradition is not a dead conformity with the past. Tradition is life and truth and the source of life. "Ye shall know the Truth and the Truth shall make you free" (Jn 8.32)—free to follow the glorious Truth and to fulfill in this great country the mission of Orthodoxy.

The Orthodox Church in America
From the Alaska Mission to Autocephaly[1]

Dmitry Grigorieff

St Vladimir's Theological Quarterly 14.4 (1970): 196–218

ON APRIL 14, 1970, Metropolitan Ireney of New York received a telegram from Patriarch Alexis of Moscow (who died a few days later) stating that the Russian Orthodox Greek Catholic Church in America, with about 850,000 members and 175 years of history, had been granted autocephaly (independence) under the title of "Orthodox Church in America," with exclusive ecclesiastical jurisdiction in North America, including Hawaii.

The universal Orthodox Church, today with an estimated 126 million faithful, consists of fifteen autocephalous churches: the patriarchates of Constantinople, Alexandria, Antioch, Jerusalem, Moscow, Georgia, Serbia, Romania, and Bulgaria; the archbishoprics of Cyprus, Greece, and Albania; and the metropolitanates of Poland, Czechoslovakia, and now of North America.

Although all autocephalous churches have equal rights, prestige among them is determined by tradition rather than by the number of their faithful. For example, the primate of Constantinople still retains the honorary title of ecumenical patriarch, which was given to him when Constantinople was the real center of the Eastern Christian world, even though the number of his immediate constituents in Turkey has been reduced in recent years to a few thousand. In addition to prestige, however, those churches with an enlightened and vigorous leadership exercise a very practical influence in pan-Orthodox and ecumenical affairs.

---

[1] The present article expands and updates Father Grigorieff's former study, "Historical Background of Orthodoxy in America," *St Vladimir's Seminary Quarterly* 5.1–2 (1961): 3–53.

In all, there are about two million Orthodox faithful in North America (although larger, but less realistic figures are sometimes circulated), distributed among eighteen different national jurisdictions which are subordinate to their respective headquarters in foreign countries or in exile for political reasons. The Greek Orthodox Archdiocese in North and South America, for example, is subordinate to the patriarch of Constantinople in Turkey. The Syrian Antiochian Archdiocese in the USA depends upon the patriarch of Antioch in Syria. The Serbian Orthodox Church in the USA is subordinate to the patriarch of Serbia in Yugoslavia. However, there is also a Serbian Orthodox Diocese in the USA which is in schism with the ecclesiastical authorities in Belgrade; the "Russian Orthodox Church in Exile" has its headquarters in New York. Other similar church organizations, established for political or ethnic reasons, exist in a state of *de facto* independence, without official canonical ties with recognized Orthodox centers.

The newly created Orthodox Church in America is dedicated exclusively to the growth and development of Orthodoxy in America. Having received an official release from its mother church, it will strive to build Orthodox unity in America with full respect for, but in full independence from ethnic or political interests of the various immigrant groups.

1

The Orthodox faith first came to the North American continent in 1794 via a church mission from Russia to the Alaskan territory which was then governed by the Russo-American Trade Company.[2] The Aleutian Islands and Alaska had been discovered by Bering and Chirikov, captains of the Russian Imperial Navy, in 1741. They were followed by Russian merchants interested in the skins of the young ursine seals. In 1784 Gregory Shelehov, a merchant trader who laid the foundations of the famous Russo-American

[2]*Ocherk iz istorii amerikanskoy pravoslavnoy duchovnoy missii: Kadyakskoy missii, 1794–1837* [Notes from a History of the American Orthodox Spiritual Mission: Kodiak Mission, 1794–1837] (St Petersburg, 1894), 4–9. The following information about the Kodiak Mission and Elder Herman has been taken from the same source. See also F. A. Golder, *Father Herman: Alaska's Saint* (San Francisco: Orthodox Christian Books and Icons, 1968).

Company, landed on Kodiak Island. Besides pursuing his fur-seal business, he became deeply devoted to the task of bringing Christianity to the natives of the newly acquired lands. He built a church on Kodiak, founded a school, and personally baptized many Aleuts. Later, together with his partner, Ivan Golikov, he petitioned the Empress Catherine II and the Holy Synod to send missionaries. The petition was granted and a mission of eight monks, under the leadership of Archimandrite Joasaph Bolotov, reached Kodiak Island on September 24, 1794.

The mission was composed of volunteers from the monks of two well-known monasteries situated in the Northwest of Russia, where geographic conditions somewhat resembled those in Alaska. There were six members in the mission from the Valaam monastery (now in Finland) and two members from the Konevtsy monastery. Four missionaries (Joasaph, Juvenaly, Athanasy and Makary) were priests; two missionaries (Nektary and Stephan) were deacons and two (Herman and Joasaph) were ordinary monks. The head of the mission, Archimandrite Joasaph (1761–1799), was from a priest's family. He had received a theological education at the Seminary of Uglich before entering the Valaam monastery. Before they took their monastic vows at Valaam and Konevtsy, Hieromonk Juvenaly had been a mining engineer, and Hierodeacon Stephan an army officer.

During the first two years the missionaries baptized 12,000 natives and built several chapels. But this initial success of the mission was marked by the martyrdom of one of its priests: Father Juvenaly was killed by the natives on the Alaska mainland in 1795. He had urged the people of a village there to send their children to the mission school on Kodiak Island. They agreed, and Father Juvenaly led a group of children to the sea shore. On the way he was overtaken and killed by villagers who had changed their mind.

The Holy Synod, having decided to establish a missionary bishopric in the Aleutian Islands and Alaska, called Archimandrite Joasaph back to Russia and consecrated him bishop of Kodiak in the cathedral of Irkutsk in Siberia on April 10, 1799. However, he never reached his see, for in May of the same year the boat of the Russo-American Company, the Phoenix, perished in stormy waters near Unalaska with Bishop Joasaph, his companions

Hieromonk Makary and Hierodeacon Stephan, and seventy other passengers. There was no new episcopal appointment for forty years.

The missionary work was carried on by the remaining monks who had come with Archimandrite Joasaph: Hieromonk Athanasy, Hierodeacon Nektary, and the monk Herman. The last on the list, St Herman, the blessed elder of Alaska (1756–1837), is an image of holiness and spirituality shining through 175 years of Orthodox growth and development in this part of the world.

Like St Seraphim of Sarov, to whom he is very closely akin, St Herman was born in a modest merchant family of a little town near Moscow. From his youth he aspired to the service of God. At the age of sixteen he entered one of the daughter houses of the famous Holy Trinity monastery founded by St Sergius of Radonezh. The community was situated near the Gulf of Finland. Seeking a quieter and even more secluded place of monastic life, he entered the Valaam monastery; and then, some years later, joined the Alaskan mission of Archimandrite Joasaph. An extremely simple man, who nevertheless was well read and eloquent, he emanated love and understanding. For the natives, Father Herman was the very symbol of Christianity.

We owe much to a certain administrator of the Russian colonies in North America, Simeon Yanovsky, a well-educated man and a ranking naval officer, for our information about Father Herman. (Yanovsky was so deeply influenced by Father Herman that he ended his life as a monk, and Yanovsky's son, who as a baby had sat in Father Herman's lap, became a hieromonk.) Pleading for the natives who were exploited mercilessly by the Trade Company, Father Herman wrote to Yanovsky: "I, the lowest servant of these poor people, with tears in my eyes ask this favor: be our father and protector. I have no fine speeches to make, but from the bottom of my heart I pray you to wipe the tears from the eyes of the defenseless orphans, relieve the suffering of the oppressed people, and show them what it means to be merciful."

On a different occasion a group of naval officers in the course of a conversation with Father Herman assured him that they loved God. "How could anyone not love him?" they said. Hearing these words, Father Herman replied: "I, a poor sinner, for forty years have tried to love God and I cannot say that I love him as I should. To love God is to think of him always, to serve him day and night, and to do his will. Do you, gentlemen, love God in this manner, do you often pray to him, do you always do his will?"

Not all administrators and merchants in the Russian colonies here were as noble and pious as Yanovsky and Shelehov. Yanovsky's successor, Baranov, and his lieutenants did not care for the missionary work. In fact, they were much annoyed by the interference of the missionaries and especially of Father Herman in their cruel use of the natives' labor. But Father Herman taught the natives at the missionary school, organized an orphanage, nursed the sick, fed the hungry, and was the administrator of the mission for a while. In his humility he always refused to be ordained a priest. Having outlived all other members of the first missionary team, he finished his life in 1837 in semi-seclusion on a small island off Kodiak, "Elovy," or Spruce Island, which he called, "New Valaam."

In its first important historical act the newly created Orthodox Church in America canonized its first saint and heavenly patron, the Blessed Elder Herman, in solemn services presided over by His Beatitude Metropolitan Ireney in Kodiak, on August 8–9, 1970. The archbishop of Karelia and all Finland, Paul—himself a former monk at Valaam—was the guest of honor and co-celebrant.[3]

New impetus was given to the missionary work by the arrival of a young priest, John Veniaminov, to Unalaska Island in 1824. He remained there for ten years, living among the Aleuts and studying their language and customs. He wrote the first grammar of the Aleut language and translated the Divine Liturgy, a catechism, and the Gospel according to St Matthew into that language. His linguistic work has been well recognized by Russian and foreign scholars.[4] He also built a church with his own hands and baptized practically the whole population of the island. After ten years of tedious missionary work at Unalaska and nearby islands, Father Veniaminov went

---

[3] The Orthodox Church in Finland in an autonomous archdiocese in the jurisdiction of the patriarch of Constantinople.

[4] *Puteshestviya i issledovaniya Leitenanta Lavrentiya Zagoskina v russkoy Amerike v 1842–1844* [Travels and Researches of Lieutenant Lavrenty Zagoskin in Russian America in 1842–1844] (Moscow, 1956), 422.

to Sitka, where he continued his missionary activities among the local Indians, the Kaloshi. In 1839, he left for St Petersburg to arrange for the publication of his works in the Aleut language.

During his stay in St Petersburg, Father Veniaminov's wife passed away. His missionary work was well appreciated in Russia, and as a result he was appointed and consecrated bishop of the missionary diocese of Kamchatka, Alaska, and the Kurile Islands. His monastic name was Innocent, after the eighteenth-century apostle of Siberia. Bishop Innocent returned to Sitka and continued his missionary activities both on the Asiatic and North American continents. He founded a seminary in Sitka, as well as various schools and orphanages. In 1848 St Michael's Cathedral was erected there; it is being rebuilt now after having been devastated in a fire several years ago. After 1852 Bishop Innocent divided his time between Alaska and the Asiatic mainland because of the expansion of missionary work among natives of the Russian Far East. From 1858 to 1870, Sitka was designated as the see of a suffragan bishop. Bishops Peter (1859–1867) and Paul (1867–1870) occupied this see. In 1868 Bishop Innocent was elevated to the highest office in the Russian Orthodox Church, that of Metropolitan of Moscow. Much of his time and energy in this office he devoted to the expansion of the work of the Russian Imperial Missionary Society, of which he became the president. He died in 1879.[5]

In 1867, the Russian government sold Alaska to the United States. Provisions were made in the second and third clauses of the bill of sale and in the Declaration of 1867 that the United States would recognize the property and the rights of the Russian Orthodox Church.[6]

On the suggestion of Metropolitan Innocent, a separate diocese was created in 1870 by the Holy Synod in the American part of the former Kamchatka diocese. Bishop John was appointed Bishop of Alaska and the Aleutian Islands.

---

[5]S. Bolshakoff, *The Foreign Mission of the Russian Orthodox Church* (London: MacMillan, 1943), 87. See also I. Barsukov, *Innokentiy* [Innocent] (St Petersburg: Synod Press, 1883).

[6]B. M. Bensin, *History of the Russian Greek Catholic Church of North America* (New York, 1941), 10.

Thus ends the early history of the Orthodox Church in America. Actually, the first Russian missionary endeavors among the natives of Alaska and the Aleutian Islands represent only the most eastern penetration of the vast missionary work of the Russian Church among various native tribes in the underdeveloped regions of Siberia and the Far East. However, an organized and separate Orthodox ecclesiastical structure was brought to the threshold of the New World as soon as Alaska was politically separated from the Russian Empire.

2

The first three Orthodox parishes in the United States proper (the Greek parish in New Orleans and the Russian parishes in San Francisco and New York), came into being almost simultaneously and independently of each other in the late 1860s. Actually, these parishes were "international." The church committee of the Greek parish in New Orleans included Slavs and Syrians, although the minutes of the meetings were written in English.[7] The Russian parishes in San Francisco and New York, supported by the Russian consulates, included many Serbians and Greeks.

These churches tended to the spiritual needs of various Orthodox nationals who happened to have come to the New World. There were members of the diplomatic corps and runaway sailors, solid Mediterranean merchants and penniless adventurers. For them the church was not just a house of prayer but also a place where they could meet their own people, have a chat about the old country, or inquire about a job.

The Orthodox churches, especially the one in New York, attracted much attention on the part of the American press and society. Orthodoxy was most often seen as a curiosity, something oriental and exotic. In spite of the efforts of the rector of the New York parish, Father Nicholas Biering, a convert from Roman Catholicism and a former professor of canon law at the Roman Catholic Seminary in Baltimore, the religious life of the parish

---

[7]B. Zoustis, *Hē Historia tēs Ellēnikēs Archiepiskopēs Amerikēs* [The History of the Greek Archdiocese of America] (New York, 1954), 45. More picturesque details about the early life of this pan-Orthodox community are found in A. Doumouras, "Greek Orthodox Communities in America before World War I," *St Vladimir's Seminary Quarterly* 11.4 (1967): 177–79.

was rather limited. From 1870 to 1880 there were only fifty-five baptisms of children, twelve weddings, fourteen funerals, and four conversions, two of these being the wife and daughter of Father Biering.[8] The Orthodox Church was not yet ready to meet the challenge of the West, especially in the setting of the New World.

In 1872 Bishop John unofficially moved the episcopal see from Sitka, Alaska to San Francisco, making his cathedral the parish church which had existed there since 1868. During the time of his successor, Bishop Nestor (1879–1882), the Russian Church authorities officially sanctioned the transfer of the episcopal see to San Francisco and thus recognized the potentialities of Orthodoxy in the United States.

The real growth of the diocese in the United States began with a mass return of Uniates to Orthodoxy and the increase of Greek, Syrian, and Slavic immigration. Toward the end of the nineteenth century many Carpatho-Russians and Galicians from Russia Rubra in the Austro-Hungarian Empire emigrated to America. They settled around the industrial centers of the Eastern states, especially in the Pennsylvania mining districts. By religious affiliation they were Roman Catholics of the Eastern Rite or, more precisely, Uniates. Their ancestors were Eastern Orthodox who lived under the Polish and Austrian Roman Catholic governments. At the unions of Brest (1596), Uzhgorod (1646), and Mukachevo (1664), over ten million people were received into the fold of the Roman Catholic Church while retaining the Eastern Orthodox liturgy and customs, including that of the married parish clergy.

A large colony of Uniates settled in Minneapolis, Minnesota, where they organized a parish and engaged a priest from their native country, Father Alexis Toth. However, the Roman Catholic Archbishop of St Paul, John Ireland, who had jurisdiction over Minneapolis, refused to grant the local Uniates permission to have their own parish and also refused to recognize Father Toth as a valid priest on account of his marriage (although Father Toth was a widower at that time). Having found themselves in such a difficult situation, Father Toth and his parishioners petitioned the Russian Orthodox Bishop in San Francisco, Vladimir, to accept them into the

[8]A. Lopuchin, *Zhizn za Okeanom* [Life beyond the Ocean] (St Petersburg, 1882), 179–206.

fold of the Orthodox Church.⁹ In 1891 Father Toth and his parishioners, numbering 361 members, were reunited to the Russian Orthodox Church. This event laid the foundation for a mass return of the Uniates in America to Orthodoxy. In the following decades, over 225,000 Carpatho-Russian and Galician Uniates became Orthodox.

It must be noted that the incident of the non-recognition of Father Toth by a Roman bishop because of his marital status was by no means the only reason for the return of former Austro-Hungarian subjects to Orthodoxy. Many of them resented oppression by a Roman Catholic state and longed for Moscow as the symbol of the Orthodox faith of their forefathers.

Since the end of the nineteenth century there also had been an increasing flow of immigrants from Imperial Russia. These were of three kinds: peasants from the poorer western regions of Russia who had the dream of making money in America and then returning to buy a farm in their native country, conscripts who illegally left Russia to avoid military service, and people who were involved, directly or indirectly, in the revolutionary movement in Russia and escaped to avoid the consequences. The last category of immigrants increased after the political disturbances of 1905 in Russia.

The Greek immigration to this country also increased considerably in the eighties and nineties of the last century. By 1893 there were already two Greek parishes in New York City: Holy Trinity, whose priests came from Athens, and Annunciation, whose priests were sent from Constantinople. Relations between the two parishes were strained. Besides the early community of New Orleans, mentioned previously, Greek parishes were formed in Chicago, Lowell, Massachusetts, and in the next decade in many other American cities.

At first all Greek parishes recognized the jurisdiction of the Russian bishop, and the Russian Church was the only recognized Orthodox Church in America. However, nationalistic feelings led to an early violation of the basic Orthodox canonical concept of one bishop and one church on one territory. In 1903–04 the Holy Trinity Greek parish in New York became

---

⁹P. Kochanik, *Yubileyniy sbornik soyuza pravoslavnych sviashchennikov v Amerike* [Anniversary collection of the Union of Orthodox Priests in America] (New York, 1936), 84–103.

legally the private property of three Greek residents in order to avoid being under the jurisdiction of the Russian Church. In 1905 it was incorporated as the "Hellenic Eastern Christian Orthodox Church" in the state of New York, as distinct from the "Greek Orthodox Church" whose head was the Russian Archbishop Tikhon. Thus, as one of the Greek church historians points out, "The Greek Church in America was saved from the Russian Jurisdiction."[10]

However, until the upheavals caused by the Russian revolution of 1917, the jurisdictional situation of the Greek parishes in America was not quite clear. On the West Coast there seems to be no question about their recognizing the canonical authority of the Russian bishop, but in the East and the Midwest many of them actually had double loyalty, recognizing the authority of the Church of Greece or of Constantinople and that of the Russian bishop at the same time. Until 1918 there were no Greek bishops in America (although negotiations in that direction were taking place between the Russians and the ecumenical patriarch Joachim III), and the Russian bishop tended to the needs of all Orthodox people in the United States.

After the Greek and Slavic Church organizations, the Syrian was next in size and chronology. The immigration from Syria and Lebanon also began toward the end of the nineteenth century and intensified around 1913–14. The first church for Arabic-speaking Orthodox Christians in the United States was founded in 1895 in New York. Archimandrite Raphael Hawaweeny, who received his higher theological education in Russia, was placed in charge of the Church's work for Syrians. In 1904 he was consecrated as vicar bishop to the Russian archbishop and became the first Orthodox bishop of any nationality to be consecrated in the United States.[11]

From 1898 to 1907 the head of the American diocese was Archbishop Tikhon, who became later Patriarch of Moscow, Primate of all the Russian Orthodox Church. During his administration in 1900, the Diocese of

---

[10]Zoustis, *Hē Historia*, 93. On the episode, see A. Doumouras, "Greek Orthodox Communities" 184–85.

[11]S. H. R. Upson, *Orthodox Church History* (Brooklyn, 1953), 92.

the Aleutian Islands and Alaska was renamed the Diocese of the Aleutian Islands and North America. The decree of the Holy Synod making this change thus acknowledged the continent-wide expansion of Orthodoxy. In February of 1907 the first All-American Church Convention, or "Sobor," convened in Mayfield, Pennsylvania.

In his convocation address, Archbishop Tikhon stressed the necessity of finding means for financial independence of the diocese as a step towards strengthening and spreading the work of the Church on this continent.[12] That was a hint of impending autonomy for the local church. A year before, in 1906, Archbishop Tikhon in his memorandum to the "Pre-Sobor Commission" of the Church of Russia, recommended a wider autonomy and even autocephaly for the American diocese,[13] justifying his suggestion by referring to the multinational character of the Church. In 1916 the same recommendation to the Pre-Sobor Commission in Russia was given by Archbishop Evdokim, the diocesan bishop at that time. However, the dream of Archbishop Tikhon and his successors had to be postponed for more than half a century because of the historical and political upheavals that followed.

Also, in Archbishop Tikhon's time the diocesan see was transferred from San Francisco to New York (1903), where a new cathedral church was built at 15 East 97th Street. The first theological seminary to train Orthodox priests for America was opened at Minneapolis in 1905. It was transferred to Tenafly, NJ in 1912 and closed for lack of funds in 1923.[14]

Thus, the Church of Russia, which first introduced Orthodoxy to North America and created the Diocese of the Aleutian Islands and North America, exercised symbolic, if not always practical, jurisdiction there among Orthodox immigrants of various national and ethnic backgrounds. Orthodox bishops in North America were appointed or confirmed only by the Holy Synod in St Petersburg. Moreover, the diocesan administration received annual financial support from the Russian government.

[12] J. Chepeleff, "American Sobors," *Russian Orthodox Calendar* (New York, 1955), 155.
[13] *Otzyvy eparkhialnych arkhiereev* . . . , part 1 [Opinions of Diocesan Bishops . . .] (St. Petersburg, 1906), 531; English translation in St *Vladimir's Seminary Quarterly* 5 (1961): 114–15.
[14] Cf. Metropolitan Leonty, "Theological Education in America," St *Vladimir's Seminary Quarterly* 9 (1965): 59–67.

3

After World War I and the Russian Revolution, the life of the Orthodox Church in America changed radically. Various non-Russian national churches sent their bishops there and established their own jurisdictions in North America in complete independence of each other. Greek, Syrian, Serbian, Bulgarian, Ukrainian, Romanian, Albanian and other national churches made their appearance. The majority of the Russian and Carpatho-Russian parishes, however, remained loyal to their diocesan administration which had been completely out off from the mother church as the result of political events in Russia.

In 1921 Archbishop Meletios, who had just consolidated various Greek factions in America into one diocese, was elected to the dignity of ecumenical patriarch as Meletios IV. In his new position Patriarch Meletios placed all Greek churches abroad under the control of the Ecumenical Patriarchate. This decree was directed not just to the Greeks in the diaspora, but to all Orthodox people. It was based on Canon 28 of the Ecumenical Council of Chalcedon, which stated that all Orthodox people in the "barbarian lands" should be under the jurisdiction of the patriarch of Constantinople; the new decree therefore placed all Orthodox parishes in Europe, America, and elsewhere outside the local autocephalous churches under the authority of the ecumenical patriarch. According to the definition of the patriarch, all Orthodox churches in the United States were to be united into an "Orthodox Archdiocese in America."[15]

Much can be said against the ecclesiastical policies of Patriarch Meletios Metaxakis. His interpretation of Canon 28 of Chalcedon is, of course, questionable, and his activity in America disregarded completely the territorial canonical rights of the Russian Church. However, Patriarch Meletios was free of narrow nationalistic aspirations. He had an inspiring and broad vision of Orthodoxy. In his enthronement address in Constantinople, he said in reference to America:

---

[15]Zoustis, *Hē Historia*, 147–51. See also, Constantin Callinicos, *The History of the Orthodox Church,* 2nd edition (Los Angeles, 1957), 114–17.

I saw the largest and best part of the Orthodox Church in the diaspora, and I understood how exalted the name of Orthodoxy could be, especially in the great country of the United States, if more than two million Orthodox people there were limited into one church organization, an American Orthodox Church.[16]

These words must ring in all Orthodox ears. Unfortunately, most of the Church leaders, Greek and Russian alike, had not grown beyond their narrow provincial prejudices; and the patriarchal project of one church in America did not succeed. The newly created Greek Archdiocese itself was plunged into years of controversies and disturbances.

Part of the Greek parishes did not recognize Archbishop Alexander, the exarch of the ecumenical patriarch, and remained "independent." The situation worsened soon after, for Patriarch Meletios was deposed by the Turks in 1923 and strife in America between the Venizelists and Royalists deepened. Bishop Basil, formerly of Methymna, arrived in America and organized the Royalist faction into an independent diocese, and by 1929 there were 133 parishes under Archbishop Alexander and 50 parishes under Bishop Basil. This bitter split continued until 1930, when Archbishop Damaskinos of Corinth, future archbishop of Athens and regent of the Kingdom of Greece, was appointed exarch of the ecumenical patriarch in America. Archbishop Damaskinos, upon his arrival, sent Archbishop Alexander and Bishop Basil back to Greece and restored order in the Greek Archdiocese. Having accomplished his task, Archbishop Damaskinos returned to Greece and was succeeded by Archbishop Athenagoras, the present ecumenical patriarch.

In 1930 the lofty concept of the Greek Archdiocese, as defined by Patriarch Meletios, was drastically changed. The new bylaws adopted in that year defined the Archdiocese as distinctively Greek, embracing those Orthodox people in America who use Greek as their liturgical language and by implication excluding all other Orthodox Christians in America.[17]

---

[16]Zoustis, *Hē Historia*, 147.
[17]*Ibid.*, 216.

The Syrian Orthodox people in this country also had their share of troubles. Bishop Raphael, head of the Syrian Mission within the framework of the Russian Diocese, died in 1915. His successor was Bishop Aftimios Ofeish, consecrated in 1917. There were twenty-eight parishes and one mission under his authority. In 1914 Germanos Shehadi, former Bishop of Zehle, Lebanon, came to this country. He was well known to many Syrians in America, many of whom had emigrated from his diocese in Lebanon. He started to organize new parishes, and by 1924 had a diocese consisting of about twenty-five churches and congregations.

These two parallel Syrian church organizations existed until 1933, when Bishop Aftimios resigned for personal reasons and Bishop Germanos returned to Beirut. At that time the majority of the Syrian parishes of both factions recognized the authority of Bishop Victor Abo-Assaley, who represented the Patriarch of Antioch in the United States. The transfer of jurisdiction was done with the knowledge and approval of Russian church authorities. In 1934 Bishop Victor died, and from 1936 to 1968 the Syrian Antiochian Orthodox Archdiocese was headed by Metropolitan Archbishop Anthony Bashir, who was succeeded by the present Metropolitan, Philip. The Archdiocese includes more than eighty parishes in the United States, Canada and Mexico. Its cathedral is located in Brooklyn, NY.[18]

Meanwhile, as a result of the Bolshevik revolution the Russian-American diocese was plunged into years of troubles, which explains the *de facto* recognition of emerging parallel jurisdictions. The diocese was torn apart by internal strife, financial difficulties, and claims by the schismatic group established in Soviet Russia and known as the "Living Church" or "Renovated Church," which had some followers in America. This group succeeded in taking over the diocesan cathedral of St Nicholas in New York and threatened other church properties.

The grave situation was alleviated by the return in 1921 to America of one of the highest hierarchs of the Russian Church, Metropolitan Platon (Rozhdestvensky). Born in 1866, former rector of the Kiev graduate school of theology, consecrated bishop in 1902, former exarch of Georgia, then Metropolitan of Kherson and Odessa, a member of the Duma (Russian

---

[18]Upson, *Orthodox Church History,* 147.

Parliament), he had ruled the American diocese from 1907 to 1914, and consequently was well known to his people. He succeeded in restoring peace and order in the diocese, and prominent churchmen urgently petitioned Patriarch Tikhon to reappoint him formally as head of the American Church. Communications with the Patriarch at that time were extremely difficult. They could be carried through indirect, illegal channels only. Communication thus received from the patriarch indicated his willingness to relieve Metropolitan Platon of his see of Kherson and Odessa and to confirm him as the ruling bishop of America.

The third All-American Sobor, held in Pittsburgh, PA, on November 25–27, 1922, requested the metropolitan to rule the diocese, but at the same time decided to postpone final confirmation of its decision to the next Sobor in hope of better contact with the patriarch.[19]

Meanwhile, Patriarch Tikhon made the appointment of Metropolitan Platon orally through a Mr Colton, a representative of the YMCA, who was in Moscow, in the presence of Fr Theodore Pashkovsky (who later became Bishop of Chicago with the name of Theophilus, and after the death of Metropolitan Platon succeeded him as the ruling archbishop). After his release from prison, Patriarch Tikhon confirmed this oral appointment by the decree dated September 29, 1923. The authenticity of this decree has been questioned; it was, however, confirmed in an article by A. Kazem-Bek concerning the court case of St Nicholas Cathedral in New York and printed in the *Journal of the Moscow Patriarchate* 6 (1957).[20]

The normalization and further development of life in the Russian-American Diocese was based on decisions taken at the All-American Sobor in Detroit in 1924. In complete accordance with the proposals of the historical Moscow Sobor of 1917–18 and the decrees of Patriarch Tikhon regarding dioceses severed from the highest church administration, the American Diocese of the Russian Church was reorganized as a temporarily autonomous Metropolitan District (Metropolia) and incorporated as the Russian Orthodox Greek Catholic Church in America. At its head there was to be an elected Archbishop-Metropolitan, a Council of Bishops, and

---

[19] *Russian Orthodox Calendar-Almanac*, 1955, p. 158.
[20] *Zhurnal Moskovskoy Patriarchii* [Journal of Moscow Patriarchate] 6 (1957): 67.

a Council made up of representatives from the clergy and laity, as well as periodic All-American Sobors.[21] This reorganization, as we can see now, actually paved the way for the autocephalous Orthodox Church in America, to be established forty-six years later.

During these years of natural growth and development, the American-Russian Metropolitanate acquired the prerequisites of an autocephalous church: maturity, its own territory, a sufficient number of parishes and parishioners, a hierarchy canonically capable of making subsequent appointments of new bishops, and the means by which to train new clergymen.[22]

4

In regard to the Russian Orthodox Church in the Soviet Union headed by the patriarch, the Metropolitanate never questioned its canonical authenticity or spiritual authority; but it always insisted on its own administrative self-government and independence as the only reasonable and ecclesiastically correct arrangement in view of the political situation.

However, not all Russian Orthodox people in America shared these feelings and convictions. A substantial number of Russian immigrants who came to America after the Russian Revolution or following the Second World War joined the jurisdiction of the "Russian Orthodox Church Outside Russia," which has about one hundred parishes in North and South America, with a total membership of approximately 70,000. The higher church administration of this group was organized in Constantinople in 1920 by a group of *émigré* bishops headed by Metropolitan Anthony of Kiev and Galicia, who left southern Russia at the end of the Civil War with the remnants of the White Russian Army. Soon they had to move from Constantinople, the seat of the ecumenical patriarch, to Yugoslavia,

---

[21] Postanovleniya osviaschennago sobora (official minutes) [Decisions of the Holy Synod], (New York, 1924). See also V. Rev. A. Schmemann, "The Canonical Position of the Russian Orthodox Church of North America," *1953 Year Book of Russian Orthodox Greek Catholic Church of North America* (New York, 1953).

[22] Alexander A. Bogolepov, *Towards an American Orthodox Church* (New York: Morehouse-Barlow, 1963), chapter 2.

where they settled in Sremski-Karlovtsy, proclaiming themselves to be the supreme ecclesiastical authority for all Russian churches outside Russia and to be the source of their "canonicity."

This ecclesiastical group adhered to a political program which was extremely conservative. Among the resolutions of its first convention held in Yugoslavia in November, 1921, are found the following: "And may the Lord God return to the All Russian throne his anointed, strong in the love of the nation, the lawful Orthodox tsar of the House of Romanov."[23] This resolution aggravated the extremely difficult situation of the Church in Russia and of the patriarch. On May 3, 1922, Patriarch Tikhon officially ruled that refugee hierarchs had no right to speak on behalf of the Russian Orthodox Church; their pronouncement did not "represent the official voice of the Russian Orthodox Church and, in view of their political character, did not possess ecclesio-canonical character."[24] Furthermore, in the same ruling, he formally dissolved the church administration which had been set up in Karlovtsy and transferred the administration of all Russian Orthodox churches in Western Europe to Metropolitan Eulogius, who had his headquarters in Paris.[25] Under the auspices of the metropolitan, the Karlovtsy group was then re-named "Synod of Bishops."

On his way to America, Metropolitan Platon himself participated in the organization of the church center in Karlovtsy for the Russian refugees, considering it, of course, to be only a temporary institution for the masses of refugees who needed church guidance. The Synod in Karlovtsy did not, however, consider itself a temporary administration, or as a communication center, but assumed all prerogatives of an autocephalous Orthodox church. Metropolitans Platon and Eulogius could not agree on such broad authorities of the Synod; as a consequence, many rifts arose between them

---

[23] M. Spinka, *The Church in Soviet Russia* (New York, 1956), 25.

[24] *Ibid.*, 26. See also *Put moyey zhizni* [The Way of my Life] (Paris: YMCA Press, 1947), 402. [In English: Metropolitan Evlogy (Georgievsky), *My Life's Journey: The Memoirs of Metropolitan Evlogy*, vols. 1 and 2, Orthodox Christian Profiles 5 (Yonkers, NY: St Vladimir's Seminary Press, 2014).—*Ed.*]

[25] *Ibid.*, 402–03. See also *Russkaya pravoslavnaya tserkov v Severnoy Amerike: Istoricheskaya spravka* [The Russian Orthodox Church in North America: historical background] (Jordanville, NY: Holy Trinity Monastery Press, 1955), 5.

and the Synod, and finally a complete break occurred between the two metropolitans Platon and Eulogius, who had been appointed to their sees directly by Patriarch Tikhon, and the Synod of Karlovtsy. In March of 1927, the Synod suspended Metropolitan Platon and appointed Bishop Apollinarius in his place, thus establishing another parallel church in America. Although in the beginning very few parishes joined Archbishop Apollinarius, their number increased with the coming to America of displaced persons after World War II.

In the early twenties the Karlovtsy group assembled people who had just left their motherland. Hatred of the Communists, despair of defeat, hopes for eventual revenge were their dominant feelings. In the Church they sought strength and inspiration, a symbol of unity, and a victorious banner for the fulfillment of their patriotic task. Bishops who had abandoned their dioceses in Russia found themselves amidst great political and historical upheaval, surrounded by the White Russian generals, former imperial ministers and politicians, and princes of the royal house of Russia. They wholeheartedly plunged into *émigré* politics and aspirations. From that time on the church organization of the bishops' Synod Abroad was strongly patriotic and nationalistic. Its main concern was to preserve Russian Orthodoxy and Russian nationality in the non-Orthodox, non-Russian world, until the day when "the rule of the antichrist" will end in Russia. Even now, it regards the present official Orthodox Church in Russia as a sacrilegious institution which serves Satan and his power.

In 1935 on the initiative of the Patriarch of Serbia, Barnabas, heads and representatives of major Russian church groups outside the Russian borders assembled in Sremski-Karlovtsy in an attempt to reach an accord. Metropolitan Theophilus, who had succeeded the late Metropolitan Platon as the ruling Russian primate in North America, attended the meeting. At this meeting a "Temporary Statute" of the Russian Church Abroad was adopted. According to this document, the American Russian Metropolitanate entered into union with three other Russian Metropolitanates outside Russia. Bishops, clergy, and parishes of the American diocese of the Synod of Bishops Abroad under Bishop Apollinarius accepted the authority of Metropolitan Theophilus. It was understood that all parts of the agreement would recognize in the Moscow Patriarchate the ultimate source of their canonicity. The name of the patriarchal locum tenens, Metropolitan Peter of Krutitsa, was to be commemorated liturgically by all, although Metropolitan Peter was then exiled in Siberia and could not exercise his functions.

In October 1937, the sixth All-American Church Sobor convened in New York and the Sobor reluctantly confirmed the Temporary Statute. The reluctance was a consequence of the feeling that the American Church did not really need any formalities with such temporary émigré groups as the Synod of Karlovtsy. The results of the open balloting were: 105 for the Statute, 9 against, and 122 abstaining. "The Temporary Statute," Metropolitan Theophilus said at the Sobor, "has a moral and not administrative significance; it shows our agreement and our unity, but it does not bind us."[26] This temporary accord between the American Metropolitanate and the Russian Synod of Bishops Abroad was terminated at the end of World War II.

In the 1930s another Church group, the Russian Patriarchal Exarchate (a diocese headed by a bishop appointed by the Moscow patriarchal authorities), was established in North America. In 1933, a former military ordinary of the White Russian Army and one of the founders of the Russian Synod of Bishops Abroad, Archbishop Benjamin Fedchenkoff, arrived in New York from Paris. His express purpose for coming to this country was a lecture tour, and he was received by Metropolitan Platon and other church officials with due respect and sincerity. However, it soon became known that he was assigned by the acting locum tenens of the Moscow patriarchal throne, Metropolitan Sergius, to demand from Metropolitan Platon and his clergy a written pledge of loyalty to the Soviet power.[27]

Metropolitan Platon categorically refused to give any pledge of loyalty to the Soviet state. Furthermore, in his epistle to the faithful of America, June 3, 1933, he reaffirmed the principles accepted in Detroit in 1924,

---

[26] *Official Minutes of Sixth All-American Sobor*, 21–24.
[27] *Nasha tserkov v Amerike i trebovaniya patriarshego prestola* [Our Church in America and the demands of the patriarchal throne], a pamphlet by Fathers P. Kohanik and A. Kukulevsky (New York, 1945), 12.

rejecting administrative submission to the Moscow Patriarchate as long as it was dependent upon a communist anti-religious government, and declaring the autonomous status of the diocese in America, pending establishment of normal church life within Russia. The epistle emphasized that this branch of the Russian Church had the intention of remembering its Russian religious heritage, but no intention of remaining politically connected with Russia, still less with the Soviet regime, "which is saturated with communistic and atheistic principles."

In view of Metropolitan Platon's refusal to be subordinated to the Moscow Patriarchate, Archbishop Benjamin proclaimed himself the new head of the Russian diocese in America and urged all the faithful to unite around him. He also sent a detailed report and a copy of Metropolitan Platon's epistle to Moscow. In 1934, Metropolitan Sergius appointed Benjamin as his exarch and permanent ruling bishop of the Russian North American diocese. By 1945, the number of parishes which recognized him was only thirteen.[28] His headquarters were located at 38 Halsey Street, Brooklyn, where he had a small chapel in his apartment.

Metropolitan Platon died on April 20, 1934. On November 20–23 of the same year, the fifth All-American Church Sobor of the Russian Orthodox Church in North America was held in Cleveland, Ohio. The Sobor elected Bishop Theophilus (Pashkovsky) of San Francisco as successor to Metropolitan Platon with the title "Archbishop of San Francisco and Metropolitan of All America and Canada." The Sobor upheld the autonomous path chosen by the late Metropolitan Platon and defined its relation to the Church in the Soviet Union accordingly. The Sobor reaffirmed the spiritual bond with the mother church, but emphatically refuted any possibility of administrative connection.[29]

5

The war between Germany and the Soviet Union which broke out in June, 1941, made a great impact on church life in America. The majority

---

[28] *New York Supreme Court*, p. 78 [sic].
[29] *Official Minutes of Fifth All-American Sobor.*

of Russian Orthodox people were deeply touched by the tragic events in the land of their fathers. Their feelings were expressed in the words of the epistle issued by the Sobor of Bishops of the Metropolitanate on October 9, 1941:

> Having been separated from our motherland by a great distance, but being always close to it spiritually, we cannot be silent witnesses and passive spectators of the bloody Golgotha of our much suffering people. As our flesh and blood, we have to carry them in our hearts, suffer with their sufferings, weep with their bloody tears and use all our efforts and means to save them.[30]

From that time on national and political considerations constituted the predominant factor in all subsequent church events. Three distinctively different approaches to the monumental crisis in Eastern Europe manifested themselves:

1. A burning desire to see communism in Russia destroyed by all means and at any cost, and a dream of the restoration of old imperial Orthodox Russia.

2. Indiscriminate patriotism which drove many Russian Orthodox people into the pro-Soviet camp.

3. Careful differentiation between the struggle of Russian people for national and spiritual freedom on the one hand and the Soviet communist aims on the other, without swaying either towards the Axis powers or towards Moscow.

The election of the patriarch in 1943 and a new seemingly favorable Soviet policy towards the Church made a great impression not only in Russian circles, but in the whole free world. The Synod of Bishops Abroad, at a meeting in Vienna held under the Nazis on October 21 of the same year, condemned the patriarchal election in Moscow as unlawful and issued a statement of non-recognition of the new patriarch.[31] Metropolitan

---

[30]*Russian American Orthodox Messenger* 10 (1941).
[31]*Russkaya pravoslavnaya tserkov v Severnoy Amerike* [The Russian Orthodox Church in North America], 94.

Theophilus of North America and Canada, in a cautious interview with the Russian-American press, called the patriarchal election "beneficial for the welfare of the Russian Church and people, provided the election was free and canonically correct."[32] Metropolitan Benjamin burst into unrestrained glorification of the election and the new Soviet policy:

> It should be made clear that this does not place any degree of control or restraint upon the Church such as was exercised by the tsar. On the contrary, it guarantees the complete independence of the church in that separation of church and state established by the Soviet Constitution. It was the fulfilment of the constitutional guarantee of religious freedom as regards the Orthodox Church.[33]

The election of the patriarch was acclaimed in the British Commonwealth and the United States as a dramatic turning point in Soviet policies, internal and external, and the manifestation of religious freedom in Russia. A majority of Russian Orthodox people in America also wholeheartedly accepted the election of the patriarch. This event, which received so much publicity, only strengthened the patriotic feelings kindled by the heroic struggle of the Russian people against the Nazis. Most of them were not political immigrants, and they did not experience that innate deep revulsion at everything "Soviet." But there were also those who started to raise their voices in favor of bringing the local church under patriarchal authority.

Another group of Russians did not recognize the Patriarch of Moscow, or any other member of the official hierarchy in the USSR, and regarded them simply as communist agents dressed in clerical garb. The elevation of the patriarch's name at divine services in the churches of the Metropolia struck them as a gross sacrilege. They condemned all other Eastern Orthodox churches for their recognition of the Moscow Patriarchate. They regarded the Synod of Russian Bishops Abroad, with its head, Metropolitan Anastassy, as the only bulwark of unspoiled Orthodoxy in the

---

[32] *Russian American Orthodox Messenger* 10 (1943).
[33] *Christian Register* (October, 1943): 348.

world. Others charged Metropolitan Anastassy and the Bishops Synod with collaboration with the Nazis.

Such was the psychological situation in which Metropolitan Theophilus and his administration had to lead one of the largest groups of Eastern Orthodoxy in this country. Several important objectives governed their subsequent actions:

1. The preservation and continuity of the American-Russian ecclesiastical tradition, as laid down 150 years ago by the first Russian missionaries in Alaska and embodied in the Russian Missionary Diocese in North America.

2. The preservation of the spiritual tie with the mother church in Russia. At all times, the Church in Russia, regardless of political conditions there, and not the émigré Synod, was regarded as the source of canonicity by the Metropolia.

3. The preservation of the full internal autonomy proclaimed by the Detroit Sobor of 1924 and rejection of any Soviet political interference with local church life as incompatible with loyal American citizenship.

4. The preservation of all people and parishes entrusted to their spiritual care by a long line of predecessors. There was serious apprehension that many parishes might break off from the Metropolitanate and join the jurisdiction of Metropolitan Benjamin. In this extremely complicated political and psychological situation, the Metropolia became entangled in tedious and futile negotiations with the Moscow Patriarchate. The Patriarchate invited the Metropolitanate to send its representatives to the local Sobor of the Russian Church held in Moscow from January 31 to February 2, 1945. The American delegates, having failed to receive appropriate visas on time, arrived in Moscow after the closing of the Sobor.[34]

---

[34] Very Rev. Joseph Dzvonchik, "My Journey to Moscow," *The Russian Orthodox Journal* (June 1945).

A special envoy of the patriarch, Archbishop Alexei of Yaroslavl and Rostov, was sent to the United States to begin the negotiations. But when, on November 26, 1945, the All-American Sobor met in Cleveland, Ohio, it recognized the spiritual, but not the administrative authority of the patriarch of Moscow; it advised the bishops to carry on negotiations and reaffirmed the administrative autonomy of the American Church. It also officially broke relations with the Synod of Bishops Abroad.[35] Since then the Synodal group has become a distinctly separated church organization in America once again.

At that time the Patriarchal Exarchate in America, established in 1933, reached the numerical peak of its success and attained to the size of fifty parishes through defections from the Metropolitanate and elsewhere.

In the summer of 1947 another envoy of the patriarch, Metropolitan Gregory of Leningrad and Novgorod, arrived in New York to continue the negotiations. Neither side was willing to make final concessions. The Patriarchate was willing to grant ecclesiastical autonomy to the local church but insisted on its right to approve the ruling bishop elected by the American Sobor and to maintain appellate jurisdiction over the American bishops in the system of ecclesiastical courts. On the other side, the American negotiators insisted on autonomy which was virtually complete independence, preserving just a token of connection with the mother church in the recognition of the purely spiritual leadership of the patriarch. A stalemate was reached, and Metropolitan Gregory left the United States without accomplishing his mission.[36]

The answer to the proposals of Metropolitan Gregory and an explanation of the stand taken by the American hierarchy came in the middle of November of the same year, when the bishops of the Metropolitanate convened in San Francisco. The resolution of the bishops officially announced their decision, "to put off the formulation of any canonical tie of the North American Orthodox Church with the Church and Patriarchate of Moscow until a more propitious time" because it was impossible "at the present

---

[35] *Official Minutes of the Seventh All-American Church Sobor.*
[36] Russian Orthodox Greek Catholic Church of North America, *Documents bearing on relations with the Patriarchate of Moscow* (New York, 1947).

time" to reconcile the project of autonomy proposed by Metropolitan Gregory with the one adopted by the Metropolitan Council.[37]

A pastoral epistle issued by the same Bishops' Council gave the reasons for this decision:

> The difficult conditions of the times and the special governmental control over all the foreign contacts of the Patriarchate of Moscow exclude, on our part, at the present time, any administrative, judicial or material allegiance to Moscow. . . . The only possibility at present, both for the Russian Church itself and for us, is the strengthening of one another in prayer, while remaining upon the paths given us by God. In this spiritual recognition of the contemporary Russian Church and of her heroic stand on the Russian Land, we call upon our flock to pray constantly for all Russia and her First Hierarch.[38]

Soon a patriarchal decree dated December 26, 1947, reached America. By this decree Metropolitan Theophilus and the bishops in his jurisdiction were put under interdict.

6

In 1961 representatives of the mother church and the Metropolitanate unofficially reestablished communications at the General Assembly of the World Council of Churches in New Delhi, India. In 1963, a delegation of Christian churches from the Soviet Union, led by Metropolitan Nikodim (who was then Archbishop of Yaroslavl), head of the Department of External Affairs of the Russian Orthodox Church, came to the United States at the invitation of the National Council of churches. The Metropolitan visited Metropolitan Leonty, head of the Metropolia, and conversed with other officials of the local church. The illness and death of Metropolitan Leonty interrupted further attempts to improve relations between the two churches. In 1967, during a visit of Metropolitan Nikodim to the United States, and in 1968, during the General Assembly of the World Council of

---

[37] *The Russian American Orthodox Messenger* 11 (1947); also, *Documents*.
[38] *Ibid.*

Churches in Uppsala, Sweden, unofficial meetings produced a platform and a procedure for negotiations. It was agreed that the Moscow Patriarchate would exercise its canonical right to grant autocephaly to the American Church on the grounds that the Russian Church first planted Orthodoxy in North America and established an Orthodox diocese here.

Another unofficial meeting of representatives of the Metropolitanate with Metropolitan Nikodim occurred in January 1969, in New York. Official meetings were convened in Geneva, Switzerland, in August, and in Tokyo, Japan, in November. At these meetings, a final draft of agreement between the Moscow Patriarchate and the American Church was prepared. It was ratified by the American bishops at their meeting in December and signed by both Metropolitan Ireney and Metropolitan Nikodim in March 1970, in New York. The Patriarchal and Synodal Tomos granting autocephaly to the Russian Orthodox Greek Catholic Church in America was signed by Patriarch Alexis of Moscow on April 10 of that year, a few days before his death. On May 18, 1970, it was solemnly handed to the delegation of the Orthodox Church in America, led by Bishop Theodosius of Alaska, by the locum tenens, Metropolitan Pimen, at his headquarters in Moscow. The ceremony was attended by the US ambassador to the USSR, Jacob D. Beam.

According to the terms of agreement and of the Patriarchal Tomos, the former Metropolia was declared to be the "Autocephalous Orthodox Church in America," absolutely independent and self-governing with an exclusive ecclesiastical jurisdiction in North America, including the state of Hawaii.[39] As to Central and South America, the parties agreed that neither of them now possesses or claims to have exclusive jurisdiction, and the canonical status quo is to be preserved there.

As a result of the agreement, the patriarchate has agreed to dissolve its exarchate in North America and to recall the patriarchal exarch from the territory of the American Church. The parishes of the exarchate have been advised by the patriarchal authorities to join the newly created autocephalous church. Those which refuse for the time being to join the new church will be administered by one of the vicar bishops of the Patriarch

---

[39] The Orthodox Church 6.6 (June–July, 1970).

of Moscow. The Moscow Patriarchate will continue to be represented in America by a delegate of the priestly rank, residing at St Nicholas Cathedral in New York.

As a part of the agreement the American Church terminated its special position in Japan, which had existed there since the American occupation following the Second World War, and the Moscow Patriarchate elevated the Orthodox Church in Japan, historically the Russian Mission, to the rank of an autonomous church. Simultaneously, the diocese of the Moscow jurisdiction created in 1967 was officially dissolved. The American born Bishop Vladimir of Tokyo and Japan was elevated by the Moscow Patriarchate to the rank of Metropolitan. The newly reorganized statute of the Orthodox Church of Japan admits no external interference in its affairs.[40]

It is the hope of most Orthodox Americans that the decision of the Patriarchate in Moscow to give up its rights in America may pave the way for the other Orthodox national churches to join the new autocephalous church. The encyclical letter of the Great Council of Bishops of the new church to the Orthodox faithful expresses the following attitudes:

> Having acquired freedom and independence from all external influences, our church life will no longer be based on the principle of temporary self-government, but will be in conformity with a permanent, canonical "autocephalous" status, according to the holy canons of the Orthodox Church and to our own Statute, adopted by our All-American council of bishops, clergy, and laity.
>
> Conscious of being a local American church, our Metropolitanate has often and publicly stated its belief that Orthodoxy cannot develop in America except in unity, and independence, in conformity with the project of Patriarch Tikhon. Today, as the mother church, which established its Mission in America 175 years ago, solemnly recognizes our autocephaly, a threefold task opens up for us:
>
> - the task of uniting all the Orthodox Christians of America into one Church,

[40] *Ibid.*

- the task of witnessing freely to the true Christian faith in the whole world,
- the task of growing spiritually, from strength to strength, through the prayers of the holy Father Herman of Alaska.

The unity of Orthodoxy in America is possible only by free consent and in conformity with the canonical order of the Church. We believe that all local autocephalous Orthodox churches, which have branches in America, will recognize that that which is good for a united Orthodoxy in America, is good for them also, and that canonical unity does not mean suppression of particular national traditions. The unity of Orthodoxy is not based on the predominance of one national tradition over the others, but on the cooperation of all in love for the good of the One Church. If some autocephalous churches should prefer to preserve their jurisdictions on the American continent and control them directly, the Autocephalous Orthodox Church in America would always be ready for full cooperation, communion in prayer and Christian action, in expectation of that day when the necessity for full unity will become evident to all.[41]

"There should not be any illusions that this event will, *ipso facto*, resolve all difficulties in moving toward inclusive administrative unity," said an editorial in *The Logos*. What is important, however, "is the fact that with the explicit or implicit approval of the other jurisdictions, the foundation for total jurisdictional unity has been laid!"[42]

---

[41] *The Orthodox Church* 6.4 (April, 1970).
[42] *The Logos* 3.5 (May, 1970): 8.

PART II

And Beyond... (1970–2016)

A Meaningful Storm
Some Reflections on Autocephaly, Tradition, and Ecclesiology[1]

Alexander Schmemann

St Vladimir's Theological Quarterly 15.1–2 (1971): 3–27

"Wherefore putting away lying, speak every man truth with his neighbor; for we are members one of another" (Eph 4.25).

1

THE STORM PROVOKED by the autocephaly of the Orthodox Church in America is probably one of the most meaningful crises in several centuries of Orthodox ecclesiastical history. Or rather it could become meaningful if those who are involved in it were to accept it as a unique opportunity for facing and solving an ecclesiastical confusion which for too long a time was simply ignored by the Orthodox. For if America has all of a sudden become the focus of Orthodox attention and passions, it is because the situation of Orthodoxy here, being the most obvious result of that confusion, was bound to reveal sooner or later the true nature and scope of, indeed, a pan-Orthodox crisis.

Not many words are needed to describe the American situation; by 1970, Orthodoxy in America existed in the form of: one Greek jurisdiction, three Russian, two Serbian, two Antiochian, two Romanian, two Bulgarian, two Albanian, three Ukrainian, one Carpatho-Russian and some smaller groups which we omit here for the sake of simplicity. Within every national subdivision each group claimed to be the only canonical one and denied recognition to others. As to criteria of this canonicity, they were

---

[1] [This text was reprinted in Alexander Schmemann, *Church, World, Mission: Reflections on Orthodoxy in the West* (Crestwood, NY: St Vladimir's Seminary Press, 1979), 85–116.—*Ed.*]

also quite diversified. Some groups saw it in their jurisdictional dependence on their mother churches, some, which—like the Carpatho-Russian Diocese—could not claim any identifiable mother church, on their recognition by the ecumenical patriarch, some on some other kind of continuity and validity. Several of these jurisdictions did—while others did not—belong to the Standing Conference of Orthodox Bishops, a non-official voluntary association established to promote the unification of Orthodoxy in the New World, but which in ten years of its existence could not agree even on general principles of such a unification. This unique and quite unprecedented situation existed for many decades. But what makes it even more appalling is the fact that at no time did it provoke any noticeable alarm in the Church at large, at least in her officialdom. Indeed, no one seemed either to see or to admit that American Orthodoxy had in fact become a blatant denial of all that which learned Orthodox delegates to ecumenical gatherings were at the same time proclaiming to be the essence of Orthodoxy as the true Church and the *una sancta*. I am convinced that to future historians this American situation, made up of progressive fragmentation, court trials, passionate polemics and mutual suspicion, will be a source of endless amazement.

The storm began early in 1970 when one of the largest and oldest jurisdictions brought to an end its long quarrel with its mother church by asking for and receiving a status of total administrative independence (autocephaly), dropped from her name a qualification ("Russian"), which after 175 years of unbroken continuity on this continent was obviously obsolete, and adopted a geographical definition ("in America") corresponding both to its location and vocation. Yet if some fifty years of chaos and divisions, confusion, and progressive deterioration, left the Church at large perfectly indifferent, this simple fact—the emergence of an Orthodox Church in America based on equally simple and empirical presuppositions, that the Church here, after almost two centuries of existence, might be *independent* and could be *American*—raised a storm which keeps gaining momentum and has by now involved the entire Orthodox Church.

The purpose of this article is not to defend the autocephaly. It is rather to investigate the nature and the causes of the storm it ignited, the deep and probably almost unconscious motivations behind these passionate reactions. That autocephaly was met at first with insults, innuendos, and interpretations *ad malem partem* was probably to be expected. But insults never prove or solve anything. And I am convinced that beneath them there is an immense and truly tragic misunderstanding. My only goal in writing this article is to try to locate and to assess it. Above all we need today a clarification. Only then may a more constructive and meaningful discussion, a search for common solutions, become possible.

2

The natural and essential term of reference in Orthodoxy is always *Tradition*. That the present controversy takes the form of appeals to Tradition, of argumentation *ex traditione*, is therefore perfectly normal. What is less normal but deeply revealing of the present state of Orthodoxy is the fact that these appeals and arguments seem to result in openly contradicting and mutually exclusive claims and affirmations. It is as if we were either reading different Traditions or the same one differently. It certainly would be unfair to explain these contradictions merely by ill-will, ignorance, or emotions. If to some the coming into existence of an Orthodox Church in America is a first step towards genuine Tradition, while to some others it is the beginning of a canonical collapse, the reason for this must be a deeper one; not only, indeed, do we differently read the same Tradition, but we also appeal to different traditions. And it is this fact that we have to understand and to explain.

Let us remember first of all that the Orthodox concept of Tradition cannot be reduced to that of texts and regulations which everyone who wants to prove anything has merely to quote. Thus the holy canons, i.e., that collection of canonical texts which is common to all Orthodox churches, does not exhaust the canonical tradition. This observation is especially important in view of the fact that the key words of our present debates—*autocephaly, jurisdiction*, etc.—are virtually absent from the holy canons, and current appeals and references are made almost exclusively to various precedents of the past. Now, such appeals to the past and to precedents have always been considered as perfectly legitimate from the Orthodox point of view, for Tradition most certainly includes *facts* as well as *texts*. It is also clear, however, that not all past, in virtue of being past, is to be identified with Tradition. In the 18th century the ecumenical throne abolished the Serbian autocephaly. More recently it recognized the heretical "Living Church" in Russia. Muscovite bishops used to reconsecrate the bishop elected to the patriarchal office. At some time or another virtually all Orthodox churches established their jurisdictions in America. Are all these facts canonical precedents simply because they occurred in the past and were institutionalized? Is it not obvious, therefore, that past itself always needs evaluation, and that the criterion of such an evaluation is not factual ("it happened") but *ecclesiological*, that, in other words, it consists in a reference to the permanent and unchanging doctrine of the Church, to her *essence*? If the forms of the Church's life and organization change, it is in order precisely to preserve unchanged the essence of the Church; for otherwise the Church would cease to be a divine institution and become a mere product of historical forces and developments. And the function of Tradition is always to assure and to reveal this essential and unchanging identity of the Church, her sameness in space and time. To read Tradition is therefore not to *quote* but to *refer* all facts, texts, institutions and forms to the ultimate essence of the Church, to understand their meaning and value in the light of the Church's unchanging *esse*. But then the question is: What is the basic principle and the inner criterion of such a reading, of our appeals to Tradition?

3

All Orthodox canonists and theologians have always agreed that for the canonical tradition such an inner criterion is to be found in the holy canons, i.e., that corpus which includes the Apostolic Canons, the decisions of ecumenical and some local councils, and rules extracted from various patristic writings. This corpus has been always and everywhere considered as *normative*, not only because it constitutes the earliest layer of our canonical tradition, but because its primary content and term of reference is precisely the essence of the Church, her basic structure and constitution, rather than the historically contingent forms of her existence. This layer is thus the norm of any subsequent canonical development, the inner measure of its canonicity, the very context within which everything else in the history of the Church, be it past, present, or future, is to be evaluated.

If this is true, and until now it has always been held as true by the consensus of Orthodox canonists and theologians, we have a first methodological clue to our present controversy, one principle by which to evaluate the various appeals to Tradition. It is indeed quite significant then that references to this essential canonical tradition are very scarce, not to say non-existent, in the storm originated by autocephaly. The reason for this is simple, and I have already mentioned it: the holy canons virtually ignore the terms which are at the heart of the debate: *autocephaly, jurisdiction*, etc. One is naturally tempted then to refer directly to those layers of the past and to those traditions which seem to be of greater help in providing proofs and precedents. But it is here precisely that we must locate the initial weakness and the fundamental deficiency of this entire method of arguing. For on the one hand, it is probably possible with some know-how to find a precedent and a canonical justification for almost anything. Yet on the other hand, the whole point is that no precedent as such constitutes a sufficient canonical justification. If the notion of autocephaly came into existence after the fixing of the *normative* tradition, this does not mean that the former does not need to be referred to the latter, understood and evaluated in its ecclesiological context. One cannot meaningfully debate the question of who has the right to grant autocephaly unless one first agrees on the basic ecclesiological meaning of that *right* and of *autocephaly*. One cannot speak of autocephaly as canonical or uncanonical unless one first sees and understands it in the light of the canons, i.e., the essential and universal canonical tradition. If autocephaly—and here everyone will agree—is one particular mode or expression of the churches' relationship to one another, where, if not in the *essential* tradition, is the fundamental nature of that relationship to be found?

4

My first conclusion is a simple one. If notions such as *autocephaly* or *jurisdiction* are absent from the canonical tradition which everyone accepts as normative, this very absence is a tremendously important factor for the proper understanding and evaluation of these notions. In the first place this absence cannot be termed accidental; if it were accidental, we would of necessity have been able to find an equivalent notion. It cannot furthermore be ascribed to, let us say, the underdeveloped character of earlier ecclesiology, for it would mean that for several centuries the Church existed without something essential for her very life. But then this absence can be explained by only one fact: a significant difference in the very approach to the Church between the *essential* tradition and the one which appeared at a later date. It is this difference that we must understand if we are to grasp the true ecclesiological meaning of *autocephaly*.

Even a superficial reading of the canons shows that the Church they depict is not, as it is today for us, a network of sovereign and independent entities called *patriarchates* or *autocephalous* or *autonomous* churches each having under itself (in its jurisdiction) smaller and subordinated units such as dioceses, exarchates, parishes, etc. This jurisdictional or subordinationist dimension is absent here because, when dealing with the Church, the early ecclesiological tradition has its starting point and its basic term of reference in the *local church*. This early tradition has been analyzed and studied so many times in recent years that no detailed elaboration is needed here. What is important for us is that this local church, i.e., a community gathered around its bishop and clerus, is a *full* Church. It is the manifestation and the presence in a given place of the Church of Christ. And thus the main aim and purpose of the canonical tradition is precisely to protect this fullness, to guarantee, so to speak, that this local church fully manifests the oneness, holiness, apostolicity, and catholicity of the Church of Christ. It is in function of this fullness, therefore, that the canonical tradition regulates the relation of each Church with other churches, their unity and interdependence. The fullness of the local church, its very nature as the Church of Christ in a particular place, depends primarily on her unity in faith, tradition, and life, with the Church everywhere; on her being ultimately the *same* Church. This unity is assured essentially by the bishop whose office or *leitourgia* is to maintain and to preserve, in constant union with other bishops, the continuity and the identity in space and time of the universal and catholic faith and life of the one Church of Christ. For us the main point, however, is that although *dependent* on all other churches, the local church is not subordinate to any of them. No Church is under any other Church and no bishop is under any other bishop. The very nature of this dependence and, therefore, of unity among churches, is not jurisdictional. It is the unity of faith and life, the unbroken continuity of Tradition, of the gifts of the Holy Spirit, that is expressed, fulfilled, and preserved in the consecration of one bishop by other bishops, in their regular synods, and, in brief, in the organic unity of the episcopate which all bishops hold in *solidum* (St Cyprian).

The absence of jurisdictional subordination of one Church to another, of one bishop to another, does not mean absence of hierarchy and order. This order in the early canonical tradition is maintained by the various levels of *primacies*, i.e., episcopal and ecclesiastical centers or focuses of unity. But again primacy is not a jurisdictional principle. If, according to the famous Apostolic Canon 34, the bishops everywhere must know the *first* among them—the same canon refers this primacy to the Holy Trinity, which has order but certainly no subordination. The function of primacy is to express the unity of all, to be its organ and mouthpiece. The first level of primacy is usually that of a province, i.e., a region in which all bishops, together with the metropolitan, take part in the consecration of the bishop of that region, and meet twice a year as synod. If we had to apply the notion of autocephaly to the early Church it should be properly applied to this provincial level, for the main mark of autocephaly is precisely the right to elect and to consecrate bishops within a given region. The second level of primacy is that of a wider geographical area: Orient with Antioch, Asia with Ephesus, Gaul with Lyons, etc. The content of this primacy is primarily doctrinal and moral. The churches of any given area usually look up to the Church from which they received their tradition and in times of crisis and uncertainty gather around her in order to find under her leadership a common solution to their problems. Finally, there is also from the very beginning a universal center of unity, a universal primacy: that of the mother church of Jerusalem at first, then that of the Church of Rome, a primacy which even modern Roman theologians define, at least in that early period, in terms of solicitude rather than in those of any formal power or jurisdiction.

Such is the *essential* canonical tradition of the Church. And it is only in its light that we can understand the real significance of those subsequent layers which were added to it and complicated it during the long earthly pilgrimage of the Church.

5

The early structure of the Church was substantially changed and complicated, as everyone knows, by the event which still remains the most important single event in the history of the Church: the Church's reconciliation with the Empire, and an alliance between them within the framework of a Christian *oikoumenē*, a Christian universe. Ecclesiologically this event meant, above all, a progressive organizational integration of the Church's structures into the administrative system of the Empire.

Let me stress immediately that this integration, and the entire second layer of our canonical tradition which is derived from it and which can be termed *imperial*, cannot be considered from an Orthodox point of view as a passing accident, or, as some Western historians think, a result of a surrender of the Church to the Empire. No, it is an integral part of our tradition and the Orthodox Church cannot reject Byzantium without rejecting something belonging to her very substance. But it must be understood that this layer is a *different* one, based on different presuppositions and having therefore different implications for Orthodox ecclesiology. For if the first layer is both the expression and the norm of the unchanging *essence* of the Church, the fundamental meaning of this second, imperial level is that it expresses and regulates the *historicity* of the Church, i.e., her equally essential relation to the world in which she is called to fulfill her vocation and mission. It belongs indeed to the very nature of the

Church that she is always and everywhere *not of this world* and receives her being and life from above, not from beneath, and that, at the same time, she always *accepts* the world to which she is sent and adjusts herself to its forms, needs, and structures. If the first layer of our canonical tradition refers to the Church in herself, to those structures which, expressing her essence, do not depend on the world, the second one has as its very object her acceptance of the world, the norms by which she is related to it. The first deals with the unchanging, the second with the changing. Thus, for example, the Church is a permanent reality of the Christian faith and experience whereas the Christian Empire is not. But inasmuch and as long as this Empire, this Christian world, is a reality, the Church not only accepts it *de facto* but enters into a positive and in a sense even an organic relationship with it. The essential aspect, the canonical meaning of that relationship, however, is that it does not bestow on anything in this world the same essential value as the one the Church possesses. For the Church the "image of the world always fades away" (1 Cor 7.31), and this applies to all forms and institutions of the world. Within the framework of the Christian *oikoumenē* the Church may easily accept the right of the Christian *basileus* to convoke ecumenical councils or to nominate bishops or even to change the territorial boundaries and privileges of the churches. All this does not make the emperor an essential category of the Church's life. In this sense the second canonical layer is essentially *relative*, for its very object is precisely the Church's life within relative realities of *this* world. Its function is to *relate* the unchanging essence of the Church to an ever-changing world.

Now it is obvious that what could be termed the *jurisdictional* dimension of the Church and of her life had its roots precisely in this second, imperial layer of our tradition. But it must be stressed immediately that this jurisdictional level neither *replaced* nor merely *developed* the earlier, essential one. Even today, after centuries of an almost complete triumph of jurisdictional ecclesiology, we say, for example, that all bishops are equal in grace, denying thus that distinctions in rank (e.g., patriarch, archbishop, bishop) have any ontological content. It is absolutely important to understand that this jurisdictional layer, although perfectly justified and even necessary in its own sphere of application, is a *different* layer, not to be confused with the essential one. The source of that difference lies in the fact that the jurisdictional power comes to the Church not from her *essence*, which is not of this world, and is, therefore, beyond any *jus*, but from her being in the world and thus in a mutual relationship with it. Essentially the Church is the Body of Christ, the Temple of the Holy Spirit, the Bride of Christ; but empirically she is also a *society* and as such a part of this world and in relation with it. And if any attempt to separate and to oppose to one another those two realities leads to a heretical disincarnation of the Church, her reduction to a human, all too human institution, a confusion between the two is equally heretical for it ultimately subordinates grace to *jus*, making Christ, in the terms of St Paul "die in vain" [Gal 2.21]. The heart of the matter is that the essence of the Church—which is not jurisdictional—can and even must have in this world an inevitable jurisdictional projection and expression. Thus, for example, when the canon says that a bishop is to be consecrated by "two or three" bishops, this in itself is not a juridical norm but the expression of the very essence of the Church as an organic unity of faith and life. The full reading and understanding of this canon implies, therefore, of necessity, its reference to the essential ecclesiology. Yet at the same time this canon is obviously a rule, a practical and objective norm, a first and essential criterion for discerning a canonical from a non-canonical consecration. As rule, as *jus* it is neither self-sufficient nor self-explanatory, and the essence of the episcopate cannot evidently be reduced to it. Yet it is that rule which—properly understood within the context of ecclesiology—maintains precisely the identity of the Church's essence in space and in time.

During the first centuries of her existence the Church was denied any legal status and jurisdiction by this world which persecuted her. But within the new situation—that of a Christian *oikoumenē*—it was normal and inevitable for the Church to receive and to acquire such a status. Remaining essentially what she was, what she always is and always will be—in any situation, society and culture—the Church received within a given situation a jurisdiction which she did not possess before and which is not essential, although beneficial, for her to possess. The state, even a Christian state, is entirely of this world, i.e., of the order of *jus*, and it cannot express its relationship with the Church in any but a jurisdictional manner. In the world's categories the Church is also primarily a jurisdiction—a society, a structure, an institution with rights and obligations, privileges, and rules, etc. All that the Church can require from the state is that this jurisdictional understanding not mutilate and reform her essential being, that it be not contrary to her essential ecclesiology. It is therefore within this new situation and, in fact, *from* the Christian Empire that the Church received in addition, so to speak, to her essential structure a *jurisdictional* one, meant to express primarily her place and function within the Byzantine *symphony*: the organic alliance in one *oikoumenē* of the state and Church. The most important aspect of that jurisdictional aspect is that organizationally, institutionally, the Church followed the state, i.e., integrated itself into its own organizational structure.

The best example, indeed the focus of that integration and of the new jurisdictional order is, without any doubt, the place and function of the patriarch of Constantinople within the Byzantine *oikoumenē*. No historian would deny today that the quick rise of the see of Constantinople was due exclusively to the new imperial situation of the Church. The ideal of *symphony* between the *imperium* and the *sacerdotium*—the very basis of Byzantine ideology—required an ecclesiastical counterpart to the emperor, a personal focus of the Church corresponding to the personal focus of the empire. In this sense the jurisdiction of the bishop of Constantinople as the ecumenical (i.e., imperial) patriarch is an *imperial* jurisdiction, whose true context and term of reference is, above all, the Byzantine theocratic ideology. And it is very interesting to note that there is an obvious difference between the imperial legislation concerning the role and the function of the patriarch and the canonical tradition of the same period. Canonically, i.e., in reference to essential ecclesiology, the patriarch of Constantinople, in spite of his unique imperial position, remained the primate of the Eastern Church, although even this primacy was given him because his city was that of the "emperor and the senate" (Fourth Ecumenical Council, Canon 28), and also the primate of his own diocese. Imperially, however, he became the head of the Church, her spokesman to the empire and her link to it, the focus not only of the Church's unity and agreement, but also of her jurisdictional government.

We know also that this imperial logic was not accepted easily and without resistance by the Church: the fight against Constantinople of the old centers of unity or primacies—those of Alexandria and Antioch—is here to witness it. The historical tragedy which transformed these once flourishing churches into mere remnants put an end to that resistance; and for several centuries the New Rome became the center, the heart and the head of one imperial Church—the religious projection of the one universal Christian empire. The jurisdictional principle, although in theory still distinct from the essential ecclesiology, occupied the center of the stage. local bishops, like civil governors, became more and more the representatives and even the delegates of a central power: the patriarch and his by now permanent synod. Psychologically, in virtue of the same imperial and jurisdictional logic, they became even his subordinates, as well as the subordinates of the emperor. What was primarily a *mode* of the Church's relationship to a particular world began to permeate the Church's mentality itself and to be confused with the Church's essence. And this, as we shall see later, is the main source of our present confusion and disagreements.

6

We are coming now to the third historical layer of our tradition, a layer whose formative principle and content is neither the local church, as in the early tradition, nor the empire, as in the imperial tradition, but a new reality which emerged from the progressive dislocation of Byzantium: the *Christian nation*. Accordingly we shall define this third layer as *national*. Its appearance added a new dimension, but also a new complexity, to Orthodox ecclesiology.

Byzantium thought of itself, at least in theory, in universal and not national terms. Even on the eve of its final collapse a Byzantine Patriarch wrote to a Russian prince a long letter explaining to him that there can be but one emperor and one empire under heaven, just as there is but one

God in heaven.² Ideologically and ideally the empire was *universal* (incidentally *Roman* and not *Greek* according to official imperial language), and it was this universality that was the main basis for its acceptance by and alliance with the Church.

But we know today that this Byzantine universalism began, and this at a relatively early date, to dissolve itself into a rather narrow nationalism and exclusivism which were naturally fed by the tragic events of Byzantine history: the Arab conquest of its provinces, the unceasing advance of the Turks, the Latin invasion of 1204, the appearance of the Slavic challenge in the North, etc. In theory nothing changed; in practice Byzantium was becoming a relatively small and weak *Greek* state whose universal claims were less and less comprehensible to the nations brought into her political, religious, and cultural orbit: Bulgars, Serbs, and later, Russians. Or rather, these very claims, this very Byzantine ideology was to become, in a truly paradoxical fashion, the main source of a new Orthodox nationalism. (The second source was the later transformation of this nationalism under the influence of the secular nationalism of 1789.) Less and less impressed by the ailing empire, more and more impatient with its religio-political claims, these nations which were born of Byzantine ideology, began to apply this very ideology to themselves. From that complex process there emerged the idea of a *Christian nation*—with a national vocation, a kind of corporate identity before God. What is important for us here is that only at this stage in the history of the Eastern Church did there appear the notion of *autocephaly*—which, if not in its origin (it was used in various senses before but always *occasionally*), at least in its application, is a product not of ecclesiology, but of a *national* phenomenon. Its fundamental historical connotation is thus neither purely ecclesiological, nor jurisdictional, but *national*. To a universal Empire corresponds an imperial Church with its

---

²[The author refers to the famous letter sent by the Patriarch of Constantinople, Anthony IV (1389–1390, 1391–1397), to the Grand Prince of Moscow, Vasily I Dmitriyevich (1389–1425), in September-October 1393. For more details see: J. Darrouzès, *Les Regestes des actes du Patriarcat de Constantinople* (vol. I, fasc. VI) (Paris, 1979), no. 2931; P. Guran, "Frontières géographiques et liturgiques dans la lettre d'Antoine IV au Grand Prince de Moscou," in M.-H. Blanchet, et al., eds., *Le Patriarcat Œcuménique de Constantinople et Byzance hors-frontières (1204–1586)*, Dossiers byzantins 15 (Paris, 2014), 81–97.—*Ed.*]

center in Constantinople: such is the axiom of the Byzantine imperial ideology. There can therefore be no political independence from the empire without its ecclesiastical counterpart or autocephaly: such becomes the axiom of the new Orthodox theocracies. Autocephaly, i.e., ecclesiastical independence, becomes thus the very basis of national and political independence, the very status symbol of a new Christian nation. And it is very significant that all negotiations concerning the various autocephalies were conducted not by churches, but by states: the most typical example here is the process of negotiating the autocephaly of the Russian Church in the sixteenth century, a process in which the Russian Church herself took virtually no part.

We must stress once more that this new autocephalous Church, as it appears in Bulgaria and later in Russia and in Serbia, is not a mere jurisdictional entity. Its main implication is not so much independence (for in fact it is usually totally dependent on the state) but precisely the *national* Church, or, in other words, the Church as the religious expression and projection of a nation, as indeed the bearer of a *national identity*. And again there is no need to think of this as a deviation—in merely negative and disparaging terms. In the history of the Orthodox East, the Orthodox nation is not only a reality, but in many ways a success; for in spite of all their deficiencies, tragedies, and betrayals, there indeed were such realities as Holy Serbia or Holy Russia, there truly took place a national birth in Christ, there appeared a national Christian vocation—and, historically, the emergence of the national church, at a time when the ideal and the reality of the universal Christian empire and its counterpart, the imperial Church, were wearing themselves off, was perfectly justified. What is not justified, however, is to confuse this historical development with the essential ecclesiology and, in fact, to subordinate the latter to the former. It is when the very essence of the Church began to be viewed in terms of this nationalism and to be reduced to it, that something which in itself was quite compatible with that essence became the beginning of an alarming ecclesiological deterioration.

7

It may be clearer now what I meant when, at the beginning of this article, I stated that in our present canonical and ecclesiastical controversies we appeal in fact to different traditions. It is an obvious fact indeed that these appeals are made to one of the three layers briefly analyzed above as if each one of them were a self-sufficient embodiment of the entire canonical tradition. And it is another obvious fact that at no time was an effort made within the Orthodox theological and canonical consciousness to give these three layers, and especially their interrelation inside Tradition, a serious ecclesiological evaluation. It is this strange fact that constitutes the main source of our present tragic misunderstandings. Now, the historical reason for that total lack of ecclesiological reflection and clarification is again a rather simple one. Virtually until our very time and in spite of the progressive disappearance of the various Orthodox worlds, the Orthodox churches lived within the spiritual, structural, and psychological context of these organic worlds—and this means by the logic of either the imperial or the national traditions, or else a combination of both. And the plain fact is that for several centuries there was in Orthodoxy an almost total atrophy of ecclesiological thinking, of any real interest in ecclesiology.

The collapse of Byzantium in 1453 provoked no such ecclesiological reaction and we know why: the Islamic concept of a "religion-nation" (*millet*) assured for the entire Byzantine world, now under Turkish domination, the continuity of the imperial tradition. In virtue of this principle the ecumenical patriarch assumed not only *de facto*, but even *de jure*, the function of the *head* of all Christians; he became, so to speak, their emperor. This even led at one time to the liquidation of former autocephalies (Serbian, Bulgarian), which had never really become an integral part of the Byzantine system (the Greeks even today rarely use the term *autocephaly* as a clearly defined ecclesiastical concept) and were always granted reluctantly and under political pressure. One can say that this Byzantine imperial system was indeed reinforced by the Turkish religious system, for it made the Greek imperio-ethnic self-consciousness even greater. As to the Church-nations born before the downfall of the empire, they were either absorbed by the monarchy of the ecumenical throne or, as in the case of Russia, made this very downfall the basis of a new national and religious ideology with messianic overtones ("the Third Rome"). Both developments clearly excluded any serious ecclesiological reflection, a common reevaluation of the universal structures in the light of the radically new situation. Finally the impact on post-patristic Orthodox theology of Western thought forms and categories shifted the ecclesiological attention from the Church as the Body of Christ to the Church as means of sanctification, from the canonical Tradition to the various systems of canon law, or, more sharply, from the *Church* to ecclesiastical *government*.

All this explains why for many centuries the Orthodox churches lived in a variety of *status quos* without even trying to relate these to one another or to evaluate them within a consistent ecclesiological Tradition. One must add that these centuries were also the time of an almost total lack of communications between the churches, of their mutual alienation from one another, and, consequently, of growth of mutual mistrust, suspicion, and—let us admit it—sometimes even hatred! The Greeks, weakened and humiliated by the Turkish dominion, became accustomed—and not always without reason—to see in every Russian move a threat to their ecclesiastical independence, a Slavic threat to Hellenism; the various Slavic groups, while antagonistic to one another, developed a common hatred for the Greek ecclesiastical dominion. The fate of Orthodoxy became an integral part of the famous "oriental question" in which, as everyone knows, the Western powers and their Christian establishments took a great and by no means a disinterested part. Where, in all this, was any place left for an ecclesiological reflection, for a serious and common search for canonical clarification? There are not many darker pages in pan-Orthodox history than the ones dealing with the modern age, the age which for Orthodoxy was—with a few remarkable exceptions—that of divisions, provincialism, theological sclerosis, and, last but not least—a *nationalism* which by then was almost completely secularized and therefore paganized. It is not surprising then that any challenge to the *status quo*, to the tragically unnoticed and normalized fragmentation, was inescapably to take the form of an explosion.

8

That America became both the cause and the focal point of such an explosion is only too natural. Chances for an open crisis were indeed very small as long as Orthodox churches lived in their respective worlds in almost total isolation from one another. What happened to one Church hardly mattered to others. Thus the peculiar Greek autocephaly of 1850 was viewed as an internal Greek affair, not as an event with ecclesiological implications for all churches. The same attitude prevailed towards the complex ecclesiastical developments within the Austro-Hungarian Empire, the "Bulgarian Schism," the purely administrative liquidation by the Russian government—not the Church—of the venerable Georgian autocephaly, etc. All this was politics, not ecclesiology. And indeed the Russian Foreign Office, the Western embassies in Istanbul and Athens, the imperial court of Vienna, the obscure interests and intrigues of the Phanariot families, were at that time a greater factor in the life of the Orthodox Church than the lonely meditations on her nature and essence by a Khomiakov.

In America, however, this situation was bound to reach a moment of truth. Here in the main center of Orthodox *diaspora*, of Orthodox mission and witness to the West, the ecclesiological question—that of the *nature* and *unity* of the Church, that of the relationship within her between her canonical order and her life, that ultimately of the true meaning and true implications of the very term *Orthodox* was finally revealed as an existential, not academic, question. Here the tragic discrepancy between the various layers of the Orthodox past, the multisecular lack of any serious ecclesiological reflection, the absence of a common mind, were revealed in their truly tragic evidence.

In the first place the American situation revealed the hypertrophy of the *national* principle, its virtually total disconnection from the essential ecclesiology. The national principle which, in a different ecclesiological context and in continuity with the genuine canonical tradition, had been indeed a principle of unity and thus a valid form of the Church's self-fulfillment (one Church in one place), became in America exactly the opposite: a principle of division, the very expression of the Church's subordination to the divisions of this world. If in the past the Church *united* and even *made* a nation, here nationalism *divided* the Church and became thus a real denial, a caricature of its own initial function. This *reductio ad absurdum* of a formerly positive and acceptable principle can best be shown by the example of churches which in the old world were virtually free from nationalism. Take, for instance, the Patriarchate of Antioch, which never had any nationalistic identity comparable to that of the Russian or Serbian churches. Paradoxically enough it is this patriarchate's almost sporadic extension into new worlds that created little by little a nationalism *sui generis*, that at least of a jurisdictional identity.

In America the national principle resulted in something totally new and unprecedented: each national Church claimed now a *de facto* universal jurisdiction on the basis of national belonging. In the old world even at the height of ecclesiastical nationalism, the rich and powerful Russian monasteries on Mount Athos never questioned the jurisdiction of the ecumenical patriarch, or the very numerous Greek parishes in southern Russia that of the Russian Church; and as to the Russian parish in Athens, it is still in the jurisdiction of the Church of Greece. Whatever their inner nationalism, all churches knew their *boundaries*. The idea that these boundaries are exclusively national, that each Russian, Greek, Serb, or Romanian *belongs* to his Church wherever he may live, and that *ipso facto* each national Church has canonical rights everywhere, is therefore a new idea, truly the result of a *reductio ad absurdum*. There appeared even "churches-in-Exile" with territorial titles of their bishop and diocese; there appeared national extensions of non-existent churches; there appeared finally a hierarchy, a theology, even a spirituality, defending all this as something perfectly normal, positive, and desirable.

If in the early and essential tradition the territorial principle of the Church's organization (one Church, one bishop in one place) was so central and so important, it is because it was indeed the essential condition for the Church's freedom from this world, from everything temporary, accidental, and non-essential. The Church knew herself to be simultaneously at home and in exile everywhere, she knew that she was primarily and essentially a new people and that her very structure was the expression of all this. The rejection of this principle in the diaspora inescapably led to a progressive enslavement of the Church to, and her identification with, that which is precisely accidental—be it politics or nationalism.

The incompatibility between this mentality and the very idea of an American autocephaly is so evident that it does not need to be explained or elaborated. It is thus in the national layer of our tradition, a layer, however, almost completely detached from the essential tradition of the Church and even self-sufficient, that we find the first *locus*, cause and expression of our present ecclesiastical crisis.

9

The first but not the only one. If nearly all Orthodox churches are in various degrees victims of hypertrophied nationalism and appeal almost exclusively to the national precedent in the Orthodox past, the moment of truth which descended upon us concerns also the layer which we termed *imperial*. It is here indeed that we find the deep root of the syndrome which is at the very heart of the specifically *Greek* reaction to the present storm.

It is not a mere accident, of course, that the most violently negative reaction to autocephaly has been that of the Ecumenical Patriarchate. This reaction, however, is at such variance with the entire personal image of Patriarch Athenagoras, an image made up of ecumenical generosity, universal understanding and compassion, opposition to narrow-mindedness in all its forms, openness to dialogues and reevaluations, that it certainly cannot be explained by anything petty and personal. Neither can this reaction be ascribed to a lust for power, a desire to rule the Orthodox Church in the "papist" fashion, to subjugate *under* Constantinople all Orthodox Christians in the diaspora. Indeed, during several decades of jurisdictional and national pluralism in America and elsewhere, the ecumenical patriarch neither condemned it as uncanonical, nor made any direct and consistent claims on all these lands as belonging to his jurisdiction. Even in the most recent documents issued by the patriarchate the main theme is the defense of the *status quo* and not a direct jurisdictional claim. The idea to charge the ecumenical throne with the solution of the canonical problems of the *diaspora* was in fact developed some twenty years ago by a group of Russian theologians (including this writer) but met, on the part of the Greek and Phanariot circles, with total indifference. All this means that the real motivations behind the Greek reaction must be sought elsewhere. But where?

The answer to this question lies, I am convinced, in the developments analyzed in the preceding pages. It is indeed in the *imperial* layer of that development that we must seek the explanation of something essential in the Greek religious mentality: its almost total inability to understand and therefore to *accept* the post-Byzantine development of the Orthodox world. If for virtually all other Orthodox the basic term of reference of their ecclesiastical mentality is simply national, the nationalism of the Greek mentality is precisely *not simple*. The roots of this nationalism are not, as in the case of other Orthodox, in the reality and experience of Church-nation, but primarily in those of the Byzantine *oikoumenē*, and this means in that layer of the past which we termed *imperial*. Thus, for example, the churches of Greece or of Cyprus or even the Patriarchate of Alexandria and Jerusalem are, technically speaking, *autocephalous* churches; but to them this autocephaly has a meaning deeply different from the one attached to it by Russians, Bulgarians, or Romanians and, in fact, they very seldom, if at all, use that term. For whatever their jurisdictional status or arrangement, in their consciousness, or shall we rather say, subconsciousness, they are still organic parts of a greater whole; and this whole is not the Church Universal but precisely the Byzantine world with Constantinople as its sacred center and focus.

Indeed, the central and the decisive fact in the post-Byzantine religious history of the Greeks is this almost unconscious yet obvious *transformation* of the imperial layer of the Orthodox tradition into an *essential* one, the transformation of Byzantium into a permanent, essential, and normative dimension or *nota* of Orthodoxy itself. The reasons for that paradoxical process are too numerous and too complex to be even enumerated here. Some have their roots in Byzantium itself, some in the long Turkish captivity, some in more recent layers of Greek history. But the fact is here: the tradition which we described earlier as conditioned by the fundamental *historicity* of the Church, i.e., the acceptance of the contingent and relative worlds to which she is related during her long earthly pilgrimage, resulted in its very opposite: the equally fundamental *anti-historical* or *a-historical* character of the Greek religious world view. Byzantium for the Greek is not a chapter, however central, important, and in many ways decisive, in the history of the Church in her unending pilgrimage, but the fulfillment of this history, its permanent *terminus ad quem* beyond which nothing significant can happen and which therefore can only be preserved. The *reality* of this unique and ultimate world does not depend on history. The historical collapse of the Empire in 1453 not only did not destroy it but, on the contrary, by depriving it of all that which is merely historical, i.e., temporary and contingent, transformed in a truly supra-historical reality, an essence no longer subject to historical contingencies. Historically the Imperial City may have been called Istanbul for half a millennium, for the Greek it is Constantinople, the New Rome, the heart, the center, and the symbol of a reality which is beyond all history.

But the truly paradoxical character of that reality is that it cannot be easily identified with either a form or a content. It is certainly not the Byzantine Empire as such, not the political dream of its eventual restoration. Greeks are too practical not to understand the illusory nature of such a dream. In fact, they expatriate themselves more easily than many other Orthodox, their adjustment to any new situation is usually more successful, and they certainly have not transferred any Byzantine and theocratic mystique to the modern Greek state. But it is not content either—in the sense, for example, of a particular faithfullness to or interest in the doctrinal, theological, spiritual, and cultural traditions of Byzantium, that "Orthodox Byzantinism" which constitutes indeed an essential part of the Orthodox tradition. Greek academic theology has been not less "Westernized" than the theology of other Orthodox churches, perhaps more so; and the great patristic, liturgical, iconographic revival of our time, the new and passionate rediscovery of the Byzantine sources of Orthodoxy, did not originate in Greece or among Greeks. Thus the Byzantine world which consciously or mainly unconsciously constitutes the essential term of reference for the Greek religious mentality is neither the *historical* Byzantium nor the *spiritual* Byzantium. But then what is it? The answer—of decisive importance for the understanding of the Greek religious and ecclesiastical world view—is: Byzantium as both the foundation and the justification of Greek *religious nationalism*. It is indeed this unique and truly paradoxical amalgamation of two distinct, if not contradictory, layers in the historical development of the Orthodox world that is at the very heart of that immense and tragic misunderstanding which, in turn, determines in many ways our present ecclesiastical crisis.

I call it paradoxical because, as I have said already, the very essence of the Byzantine imperial tradition was not national, but *universal*. And it is only this *universality*, however theoretical and imperfect, that made it possible for the Church to accept the empire itself and to make it her earthly habitation. The Byzantines called themselves Romans, not Greeks; because Rome, not Greece, was the symbol of universality, and for this reason the new capital could only be a "new Rome." Until the seventh century the official language of the Byzantine chanceries was Latin, not Greek, and finally the Church Fathers would have been horrified if someone were to call them Greeks. It is here indeed that lies the first and deepest misunderstanding. For when a Fr Florovsky speaks of Christian Hellenism as a permanent and essential dimension of Christianity, when a Philaret of Moscow puts in his *Catechism* the definition of the Orthodox Church as "Greek-Catholic," they obviously do not refer to something ethnic or national. For them this Christian Hellenism—that of theology, liturgy, iconography—is not only not identical with the Greek but, in fact, is in many ways its very antidote, the fruit of a long and sometimes painful and critical transformation of the Greek categories. The fight between the "Greek" and the "Christian" is indeed the very content of the great and eternally normative patristic age, its real theme. And it is the Greek revival, the appearance of a Greek nationalism, no longer referred to Christian Hellenism, which, in the last years of Byzantium, was one of the essential factors in the tragedy of Florence.

What happened in the Greek mentality was the result thus not of an evolution or development but of a metamorphosis. The tragic events in the history of the empire, the bitter experience of the Turkish domination, the fight for survival and liberation, transformed the Byzantine imperial tradition, gave it a meaning exactly opposite to the one it had at the beginning and which justified its acceptance by the Church. The universal was replaced with the national, Christian Hellenism with Hellenism, Byzantium with Greece. The unique and universal Christian value of Byzantium was transferred onto the Greeks themselves, onto the Greek nation, which, because of its exclusive identification with Hellenism, acquired now a new and unique value. It is very characteristic, however, that when even Greek hierarchs speak of Hellenism they refer not so much to the Christian Hellenism of Byzantium, but to ancient Greek civilization, to Plato and Pythagoras, to Homer and the Athenian democracy, as if being Greek makes one in an almost exclusive sense an heir and a bearer of that Hellenism.

But in reality, this Hellenism is the Greek expression of the secular nationalism common to all modern nations, whose roots are in the French Revolution of 1789 and in European Romanticism. As every nationalism of that type, it is built upon a mythology partly secular and partly religious. On the secular level the myth is that of a unique relationship between the Greeks and that Hellenism which constitutes the common source and foundation of the entire Western civilization. On the religious level the myth is that of a unique relationship to Byzantium, the Christian *oikoumenē*, which is the common foundation of all Orthodox churches. And it is this double mythology—or rather its impact on Greek ecclesiastical thinking—that makes the ecclesiological dialogue with the Greeks so difficult.

10

The first difficulty lies in the different understanding of the place and function within the Orthodox Church of the ecumenical patriarch. All Orthodox churches without any exception assent to his primacy. There is, however, a substantial difference in the understanding of that primacy between the Greek churches and all others.

For the non-Greek churches the basic term of reference for this primacy is the essential ecclesiology which has always and from the very beginning known a universal center of unity and agreement and therefore a *taxis*, an order of seniority and honor among churches. This universal primacy is thus both *essential*, in the sense that it always exists in the Church, and *historical*, in the sense that its location may vary and indeed has varied; for it depends on the historical situation of the Church at a given time. The primacy of Constantinople was established by ecumenical councils, by the consensus of all churches; this makes it essential, for it is truly the expression of the churches' agreement, of their unity. It is equally true, however, that it was established within a particular historical context, as an ecclesiological response to a particular situation—the emergence of a universal Christian Empire. And although no one today in the whole Orthodox Church feels and expresses the need for any change in the churches' *taxis*, such changes took place before and, at least theoretically, may happen tomorrow. Thus, for example, in the case of a conversion to Orthodoxy of the Roman Catholic Church, the universal primacy may—or may not—return to the first Rome. Such is, in its simplest form, the ecclesiological stand of all non-Greek Orthodox churches. The fully accepted primacy of the patriarch of Constantinople does not imply here either any national implication, nor that of some divinely instituted and therefore eternal *taxis* of the churches. The consensus of the churches expressed through an ecumenical council may, if necessary, change this *taxis*, as it has before—in the case of Antioch and Jerusalem, of Ephesus and Cyprus, and of Constantinople itself.

This theory, however, is anathema to the Greeks, and it is here that the fundamental ambiguity of contemporary Orthodox ecclesiology becomes obvious. For the Greeks the term of reference for the primacy of the ecumenical throne lies not in any particular ecclesiological tradition, be it essential or imperial, but in the unique position held by the ecumenical patriarch within that Hellenism which, as we have just seen, constitutes the essence of their religious world view. For if the secular center of that Hellenism is in Athens, its religious focus and symbol is most certainly in Constantinople. For the long centuries of the Turkish dominion the patriarch was the *religious ethnarch* of the Greek nation, the focus and the symbol of its survival and identity. And thus the ecumenical throne remains for the Greeks today a reality not so much of an ecclesiological and canonical, but primarily of a spiritual and psychological order. Canonically, the Greeks may or may not belong to the patriarchate. Thus the Church of Greece is independent from the patriarchate, whereas every Greek in Australia or Latin America is in the latter's jurisdiction. But whatever their jurisdictional status they are all *under* Constantinople. Here it is not Constantinople as the universal center of unity and agreement that is essential, it is Constantinople as such, the ecumenical throne as the bearer and guardian of Hellenism. The primacy of Constantinople is ascribed now to the very *esse* of the Church, becomes in itself a *nota Ecclesiae*. The ecclesiological formula: "there *is* Constantinople, to which the Church has entrusted the universal primacy" becomes: "there *must* be Constantinople." But the tragic ambiguity of this situation is precisely that the primate, whose function is to assure the *universality of the Church*, to be guardian of that Christian Hellenism which preserves every Church from a total identification with nationalism, is at the same time for one particular nation the bearer and the symbol of its very *nationalism*. The ecumenical primacy becomes the primacy of the Greek.

It is this ambiguity in the Greek religious and national mentality that made it—and still makes it—so difficult for Greeks to understand the true meaning of the post-Byzantine Orthodox world, of its real problems, of its unity as well as diversity. Essentially they failed to understand that the collapse of the Byzantine Empire was not necessarily the end of Orthodox unity based on the common acceptance of Orthodox Byzantium, i.e., Christian Hellenism. For the whole point is that the Slavs, for example, who sought their independence from the empire were, in fact, not less Byzantine than the Greeks, and were seeking independence from the Greeks but not from Christian Hellenism. The first Bulgarian Empire—that of Boris and Symeon—was truly Byzantine in its entire ethos, culture, and, of course, religious tradition. Father Florovsky in his *Ways of Russian Theology* speaks of the "early Russian Byzantinism." All these new nations had no cultural tradition comparable to the one the Greeks had in ancient

Greece and their initial and formative tradition, the one that gave them their national birth and made them into Orthodox nations was the Christian Byzantine tradition. And in spite of all conflicts, misunderstandings and mutual isolation, this unity in the Byzantine tradition has been never really broken or forgotten, but has always constituted the common foundation, the very form of unity, of the entire Orthodox East.

But for the Greeks, imprisoned as they progressively became by the identification of the Byzantine with the Greek, of the national and even ethnic reduction of Byzantinism, any attempt to establish political and ecclesiastical independence from the empire—on the part of Slavs, or Arabs, or Romanians—meant almost automatically a threat to Hellenism, an attempt to destroy the Greeks and their birthright within Orthodoxy. They never understood that the essential unity of the Orthodox world is neither national nor political nor even jurisdictional, but the unity precisely of Christian Hellenism, the Orthodox embodiment of the essential Christian tradition. And they did not understand it because they identified this Christian Hellenism with Hellenism, i.e., with the Greek national and ethnic identity. The Slavs in this perspective were viewed as an alien and essentially "barbarian" force aimed at the destruction of Hellenism. And since the Slavs were strong and the Greeks weak this view took sometimes almost paranoic forms. After the liberation of Greece in the 19th century and the emergence of new Western Greek nationalism, Pan-slavism became—not without the help of Western powers—a real catchword, the synonym of *the* Threat and *the* Enemy. One must add here that the Russian imperial policy in the "Oriental question" was not always of great help in alleviating these fears, and was certainly guilty of many a tasteless tactic, but it is equally true that at the very height of Russia's own messianic and imperialistic nationalism, never did the Russian Orthodox consciousness question the primacy of Constantinople and of the venerable Eastern patriarchates or press for a change in the *taxis* of Orthodox churches. On the contrary, the 19th century in Russia was marked by a revival of precisely Byzantine interests, by a return to Christian Hellenism as the source of Orthodoxy, by a return to a truly universal Orthodox ecclesiology, by the progressive liberation from the narrow, pseudo-messianic nationalism of the "Third Rome." Whatever the various diplomatic difficulties, ecclesiologically the real obstacle to a recovery by the Orthodox Church of her essential unity lay, at that time, not in any mythological Pan-slavism but in the narrowly nationalistic reduction, by the Greeks, of Christian Hellenism to Hellenism.

All this explains why the Greek ecclesiastical officialdom (we do not speak here of the popular feelings which have always somehow preserved the intuition of Orthodox unity) never really *accepted* the post-Byzantine ecclesiological development, never integrated it into its own world view. The various autocephalies granted during and after the Byzantine period were concessions and accommodations, not the acknowledgement of something normal, something as adequate to the new situation as the acknowledgement of the imperial Church was adequate to the previous situation—that of a Christian empire. For that new situation had really no room within the Greek religious mentality, and was viewed indeed as accidental and temporary. For this reason no autocephaly has ever been granted freely but has always been the result of fight and negotiation. For this reason also, even today the principle of autocephaly, which constitutes the basic principle of the Church's present organization, is never quite understood by the Greek officialdom, whether in its *principium* (the "right to grant autocephaly") or in its *modality* (its implications for inter-Church relations).

One thing is clear, however, and constitutes probably the ultimate paradox of this entire development. Having reluctantly recognized this principle *de facto*, the Greek officialdom seems to justify it by that very reasoning which in the past made the Greeks reject and fight it: the idea of an *essential* difference between the Hellenic and the various non-Hellenic "Orthodoxies." If in the past they fought autocephalies because they rejected the idea that Christian Hellenism—as the essence of Orthodoxy—may have any other ecclesiological expression than that of one imperial Church which is Greek, today they accept them because, having in fact replaced Christian Hellenism with Hellenism, they believe that the other Orthodoxies must necessarily be the expression of some other essences: Russian Orthodoxy, Serbian Orthodoxy, etc. And just as the vocation of Greek

Orthodoxy is to preserve Hellenism, the vocation of other churches is to preserve their own—ultimately national—essences. Having completed thus its full circle, the imperial mentality joined the national one. And this was inevitable if one remembers that the real source of modern nationalism lies not in Christianity but in the ideas of the French Revolution of 1789, the true mother of the petty, fanatical, and negative nationalisms of the 19th and 20th centuries. But what makes this new (not Byzantine but *modern*) Greek nationalism distinct from other Orthodox nationalisms is the certitude, surviving in it from its imperial antecedents, that within all these Orthodox essences the Greek essence has a primacy, occupies, *jure divino*, the first place. Having forgotten that it is not Hellenism as such but Christian Hellenism that constitutes the real unity of Orthodoxy and truly has a spiritual and eternal primacy over all other expressions, having identified this Hellenism with themselves, the Greeks claim a primacy which indeed might have been theirs but on entirely different presuppositions. This is today the fundamental ambiguity of the universal primacy in the Orthodox Church. Does it belong to the first among bishops, the one whom the consensus of all churches respects, loves, and venerates in the person of the ecumenical patriarch, or does it belong to the spiritual head and bearer of Hellenism, whose Christian value and affiliation is as questionable as that of any modern and half-pagan nationalism?

11

We can interrupt here our reflections on the true nature and causes of our present ecclesiastical storm. I am convinced that as long as the questions raised in this article are not answered, all our polemics and controversies about the new autocephaly will remain superficial, non-essential, and ultimately meaningless. To answer them, however, means necessarily to achieve a deep and constructive clarification of Orthodox ecclesiology itself.

What happened—or rather what happens—in America can indeed be reduced to a simple formula: it is an almost *forced* return to the *essential* Orthodox ecclesiology, to its very roots, to those fundamental norms and presuppositions to which the Church always *returns* when she finds herself in a new situation in this world whose fashion is passing (1 Cor 7.31). I use the term *forced* because this return is the fruit not of abstract academic thinking but of life itself, of the circumstances in which the Church discovers—painfully and not without torments and sufferings—that the only way of survival for her is precisely to be the *Church*, to be that which eternally shines and illumines us in the primordial and essential ecclesiology in which the unique and eternal experience, form, and consciousness—the very being—of the Church, have found their expression.

That only one part of the Orthodox Church in America has up to now been forced into that return because its own situation made it inevitable; that this has provoked passions, fears, suspicions; that some of the external factors make some of these fears understandable—all this is natural, all this was probably inevitable. Fear, however, is a bad counselor. Only if we are able to raise our questions to that level which alone can make them answerable and which is that of essential ecclesiology, only if we are able to see and to evaluate facts in this essential perspective, will the storm be revealed as meaningful, will it lead to a common victory.

Sooner or later it will become clear to all that it is not by concentrating on the preservation of Hellenism, Russianism, or Serbianism that we will preserve Orthodoxy; but, on the contrary, by preserving and fulfilling the demands of the Church we will salvage all that which is essential in all incarnations of the Christian faith and life. If Father Florovsky, a Russian theologian living and working in exile, had the courage (in his *Ways of Russian Theology*) to denounce and to condemn the deviations of Russianism from the Christian Hellenism and to liberate thus an entire generation of Russian theologians from the last "hang-ups" of any pseudo-messianism and religious nationalism, is it not time for a Greek, be it only one, to perform the same painful yet necessary and liberating operation with the ambiguities of Hellenism?

Sooner or later it will become clear to all that the ecumenical patriarch, if he is to fulfill his universal primacy, will achieve it not by defensive and negative reactions, not by questionable appeals to equally questionable and inapplicable precedents and traditions, but by constructive leadership towards the fulfillment by the Church of her essence in every place of God's dominion. Personally I have spent too much of my theological life defending the universal primacy of the patriarch of Constantinople to be accused of any anti-Constantinopolitanism. This primacy, its necessity for the Church, its tremendous potential for Orthodoxy, I once more solemnly confess and affirm here. This primacy, however, to become again what it is, must be purified of all ambiguities, of all non-essential contexts, of all nationalistic connotations, of the dependence on anything—in the past, present, and future—which is not the Church and only the Church. It is maybe the most urgent task of the universal primacy today—to liberate us from pagan and heretical nationalisms which choke the universal and saving vocation of the Orthodox Church. We should cease to speak of our "glories." For *glory*—in the essential tradition of the Church—belongs to God alone, and it is for the glorification of God, not of herself, that the Church was established. Once we have realized this, things impossible with men become possible with God.

Forgiveness Sunday, 1971.

Autocephaly in Orthodox Canonical Literature to the Thirteenth Century[1]

John H. Erickson

St Vladimir's Theological Quarterly 15.1 (1971): 28–41

THE PROLIFERATION OF autocephalous churches in the 19th and 20th centuries has made the question of what constitutes and establishes such a church a central one among modern Orthodox canonists. There exists, consequently, a considerable literature on the subject.[2] Yet, perhaps because of the very urgency of the question, this literature has dealt largely with the foundations and antecedents of our current constellation of autocephalous local churches. As a result, discussion concerning autocephaly has been virtually limited to the late medieval and modern periods in Church history and has been colored by various nationalistic considerations. For example, we are comparatively well-informed about the establishment of a Serbian national church in the 13th century, or about the circumstances surrounding the establishment of an autocephalous Russian church in the 15th century. At the same time, we know comparatively little about the term "autocephalous" and the reality behind it during the ancient and early medieval periods in Church history. This is particularly unfortunate since the period in question saw the formation and finest flowering of the Orthodox canonical tradition. Therefore, if we are to make historically sound applications of the Church's canons to our modern situation, further attention to the problem of autocephaly in these earlier periods would be desirable.

---

[1] [A slightly expanded and updated version of this article was published in John H. Erickson, *The Challenge of Our Past* (Yonkers, NY: St Vladimir's Seminary Press, 1991), 91–113 (Chapter 7: "The 'Autocephalous Church'").—*Ed.*]

[2] The most convenient introduction in English to the subject is A. Bogolepov, *Toward an American Orthodox Church* (New York, 1963).

In current Orthodox usage, a church is termed "autocephalous" if it possesses (1) the right to resolve all internal problems on its own authority, independently of all other churches, and (2) the right to appoint its own bishops, among them the head of the church, without any obligatory expression of dependence on another church.[3] The reality behind this term "autocephalous church" is an ancient one. The Orthodox Church has always regarded itself as a union of sister churches, bound together more by a common faith than by a juridical structure. However, the adjective "autocephalous" itself over the centuries has had—and still has—a variety of meanings. While in the Orthodox canonical tradition, at least through its 12th century golden age, it is not difficult to distinguish between these various meanings, potential for confusion has always existed. Hopefully a brief examination of the term "autocephalous" will provide a measure of clarity.

Αὐτοκέφαλος ([*autokephalos*] "self-headed") is used occasionally by Byzantine historical writers in the non-technical meaning of "politically independent." Constantine Porphyrogenitos (†959), for example, uses this term freely to designate the independent cities of Dalmatia.[4] More frequent is the use of the ecclesiastical term αὐτοκέφαλος ἀρχιεπίσκοπος [*autokephalos archiepiskopos*], referring to a bishop without suffragants, subject directly to a patriarch rather than to the provincial metropolitan. Thus, the earliest known *Notitia episcopatuum*, probably dating from the reign of Heraclius (610–41), already distinguishes between αὐτοκέφαλοι ἀρχιεπίσκοποι ([*autokephaloi archiepiskopoi*] autocephalous archbishops) and ἐπίσκοποι ἐπερχόμενοι ([*episkopoi eperchomenoi*] dependent bishops).[5] Finally, αὐτοκέφαλος [*autokephalos*] is sometimes used in its current technical meaning, to describe a self-governing, independent local church. The earliest such use of the word occurs in the *Church History* of Theodore Lector (*c.* 540), where the metropolis of Cyprus is referred to as

---

[3]Bogolepov, *Toward an American Church*, 15.

[4]*De administrando imperio* 29, ed. Gy. Moravcsik (Washington, 1967), 126.

[5]*Expositio praesessionum patriarcharum et metropolitarum* PG 86/1:798–92, where it is mistakenly ascribed to Epiphanius. On this work, and on the origin of "autocephalous archbishoprics," see most recently E. Chrysos, "Zur Entstehung der Institution der autokephalen Erzbistümer," *Byzantinische Zeitschrift* 62 (1959): 263–86.

αὐτοκέφαλος [*autokephalos*] and no longer subject to Antioch.[6] However, the reality of autocephalous churches existed much earlier.

As is well known, even before the establishment of Christianity as the favored religion of the state, ecclesiastical organization in the Roman Empire was modeled along the lines of civil administration. Roughly speaking and with several important exceptions, each provincial church, with a metropolitan and his bishops, constituted what in effect was an autocephalous church.[7] Custom, however, had somewhat modified this arrangement. Thus, I Nicaea, Canon 6 begins:

> Let the ancient customs in Egypt, Libya and Pentapolis prevail, that the Bishop of Alexandria have jurisdiction in all these, since the like is customary for the Bishop of Rome also. Likewise, in Antioch and the other provinces, let the churches retain their privileges.[8]

Often interpretations of this canon emphasize the prerogatives of Alexandria, Rome, and Antioch as supra-metropolitan powers; but it is important to notice the context of these words. The two preceding canons both deal with provincial organization and with the prerogatives of metropolitans in particular; and after its initial acknowledgement of certain exceptions arising from "ancient custom," this canon itself immediately continues with a further problem of metropolitan organization:

> And this is to be universally understood, that if anyone be made bishop without the consent of the metropolitan, the great synod has declared that such a man ought not to be a bishop . . .[9]

It is also important to recognize the circumstances which produced these "ancient customs." Ecclesiastical organization in Egypt and Italy

---

[6] *Excerpta ex ecclesiastica historia* 2.2; PG 86/1:183–84.
[7] See particularly Antioch, Canons 8, 9, 11, 13, 15, 19, 20, and I Constantinople, Canon 2. On this subject of "accommodation" to patterns of civil administration see F. Dvornik, *The Idea of Apostolicity in Byzantium and the Legend of the Apostle Andrew*, Dumbarton Oaks Studies 4 (Cambridge, MA: Harvard University Press, 1958), 3–38, and his *Byzantium and the Roman Primacy* (New York: Fordham University Press, 1966), esp. pp. 27–39.
[8] NPNF² 14:15.
[9] *Ibid.*

had not kept pace with the changes in civil administration introduced by Diocletian toward the end of the third century. As a result, the bishops of Alexandria and Rome were, in effect, metropolitans over several provinces—an anomaly which the council felt obliged to justify. On the other hand, "ancient customs" arising from more strictly religious considerations were not sufficient in the eyes of the council to permit an exception to their general rule of accommodation to the patterns of civil administration. Thus, while the bishop of Jerusalem is to be honored on account of "custom and ancient tradition," he still remains subject to the metropolitan of Caesarea, the civil administrative center.[10]

Concern for maintaining the integrity of metropolitan organization and authority against encroachment is expressed even more forcefully in Canon 8 of the Council of Ephesus (431):

> Our brother bishop Rheginus, the beloved of God, and his fellow beloved of God bishops, Zeno and Evagrius, of the Province of Cyprus, have reported to us an innovation which has been introduced contrary to the ecclesiastical constitutions and the Canons of the Holy Apostles [Canon 35], and which touches the liberties of all. Wherefore, since injuries affecting all require the more attention, as they cause the greater damage, and particularly when they are transgressions of an ancient custom; and since those excellent men, who have petitioned the synod, have told us in writing and by word of mouth that the bishop of Antioch has in this way held ordinations in Cyprus; therefore the rulers of the holy churches in Cyprus shall enjoy, without dispute or injury, according to the canons of the blessed fathers and ancient custom, the right of performing for themselves the ordination of their excellent bishops. The same rule shall be observed in the other dioceses and provinces everywhere, so that none of the God-beloved bishops shall assume control of any province which has not heretofore, from the very beginning, been under his own hand or that of his predecessors. . . . Wherefore, this holy and ecumenical synod has decreed that in every province the rights which heretofore, from the beginning,

---

[10] I Nicaea, Canon 7; NPNF² 14:17.

have belonged to it, shall be preserved to it, according to the old prevailing custom, unchanged and uninjured: every metropolitan having permission to take, for his own security, a copy of these acts. And if any one shall bring forward a rule contrary to what is here determined, this holy and ecumenical synod unanimously decrees that it shall be of no effect.[11]

This canon, quoted here at length because of its singular interest, often has been interpreted as granting independence to the Church of Cyprus, as though Cyprus formerly had been legitimately subject to Antioch.[12] The actual wording of the canon, however, makes it obvious that the council was not *granting* independence to Cyprus but rather was *confirming* and *preserving* Cyprus' independence against the illegitimate intrusion of Antioch. Indeed, the canon expressly attempts to preserve the liberties of all metropolitans and their provincial churches against innovations introduced by the supra-metropolitan powers.

While the Council of Ephesus did succeed in preserving the independence of the Church of Cyprus, it did not check the growth of supra-metropolitan organization. The nascent patriarchates, already outlined in Nicaea's Canon 6, had been strengthened by Canon 2 of the Council of Constantinople (381), which gave official sanction to supra-metropolitan organization in the three "minor" civil dioceses of Thrace, Pontus, and Asia as well as in Egypt and the East. Canon 28 of the Council of Chalcedon (451) carried this process further by placing Thrace, Pontus, and Asia under the bishop of Constantinople, specifying that metropolitans in these dioceses be ordained by him. Since Jerusalem, under its ambitious and unscrupulous bishop Juvenal (†458), already had gained supra-metropolitan status, organization of the imperial Church into five centralized patriarchates—Rome, Constantinople, Alexandria, Antioch, and Jerusalem—was virtually complete.

With the rise of Monophysitism and the Arab conquests, the see of Constantinople easily eclipsed Alexandria, Antioch, and Jerusalem,

---

[11]NPNF² 14:234–5.
[12]*E.g.*, Balsamon. See below at n. 23.

weakening whatever pragmatic basis this pentarchy of patriarchates might have possessed. Nevertheless, particularly in the course of the iconoclastic controversy, the theory of the pentarchy gained new strength. To combat imperial interference in dogmatic matters, iconodules like St Theodore of Studios argued that dogmatic decisions rested not with the emperor but with the Church as represented by all five patriarchs.[13] With time this theory of the pentarchy acquired a quasi-theological status. Typical is a letter of Peter of Antioch (1054), chiding Peter of Grado for employing the title of patriarch:

> The body of a man is ruled by one head, but in it there are many members, all of which are governed by only five senses. . . . So also, the Body of Christ—that is, the Church of the faithful—made up of diverse nations or members and governed in the same way by five senses—by the five great sees mentioned earlier—is ruled by one head, Christ himself. And just as no senses other than the five senses exist, so also no patriarch of any sort other than the five patriarchs is allowed.[14]

Despite this ascendance of the pentarchy as a theory of ecclesiastical government, in practice there were already several exceptions—local churches other than the five patriarchates with the right to appoint all their own bishops and resolve all their internal problems. The exceptional status of one such church, that of Cyprus, might be justified by a "pentarchist" on the grounds that an ecumenical council's decision had been needed for its approval. However, several other such exceptions exist. Foundations for the autocephaly of Georgia, for example, were laid in the 5th

---

[13]E.g. Theodore of Studios, *Epist.* 124; PG 99:1417: "There is no discussion about secular things. To judge them is the right of the emperor and the secular tribunal. But [there is discussion] about divine and celestial decisions, and these are not committed to others than those to whom God the Word himself said, 'Whatsoever you shall bind. . . . ' Who are the men to whom this order was given? He who holds the throne of Rome, which is the first; he who holds the throne of Constantinople, the second; and after them they who hold those of Alexandria, Antioch, and Jerusalem. This is the pentarchic authority of the Church; these have jurisprudence over divine dogmas. To the emperor and to the secular authority belong the giving of assistance and the confirming of what has been decided." Trans. Dvornik, in *The Idea of Apostolicity,* 169.

[14]*Acta et Scripta quae de controversiis ecclesiae graecae et latinae saeculo undecimo composita extant,* ed. C. Will (Leipzig, 1861) 211–12.

century, when, in exchange for a political alliance and acceptance of his pro-Monophysite *Henotikon*, the emperor Zeno recognized the catholicos of the Georgian Church as autocephalous, though still vaguely dependent on Antioch. At the beginning of the 7th century the Georgian Church returned to Orthodoxy but retained its exceptional status, and by the 8th century it was fully independent.[15]

Imperial commands effected the creation of two additional autocephalous churches. In 666 Emperor Constans II issued a *privilegium* to the archbishop of Ravenna and to the appropriate civil authorities declaring the Church of Ravenna autocephalous. By 677, however, Ravenna's metropolitans again were obliged to seek consecration at Rome; and, because of the ephemeral character of Ravenna's autocephaly, the case did not enter into the "memory" of the Church.[16] Of far greater consequence to the Orthodox canonical tradition is the case of Justiniana Prima. To honor the place of his birth, the Emperor Justinian in 535 issued a *novella* granting to the archbishop of Justiniana Prima virtually patriarchal jurisdiction over much of the Balkan peninsula,

> So that the present most holy head of our native place, Justiniana Prima, might be not just a metropolitan ... but an archbishop and that other provinces might be under his authority ... that your beatitude and all the heads of the church of Justiniana Prima shall have the rank of archbishop and enjoy the prerogatives, the power, and the authority over other bishops which that title gives: that your holiness shall ordain them; that you shall have the highest sacerdotal dignity in the above mentioned provinces; that this high dignity and these great honors shall be inherent in your see; that these provinces shall have no other archbishop; and that you in no way shall be dependent upon the archbishop of Thessalonika. . . . When, however, your holiness departs

---

[15] On the Georgian church see esp. M. Tarehnishvili, "Die Entstehung und Entwicklung der kirchlichen Autokephalie Georgiens," *Le Muséon* 73 (1960): 107–26.

[16] F. Dölger, *Regesten* (Corpus der griechischen Urkunden des Mittelalters und der neueren Zeit, Reihe A, Abt. 1) nos. 233, 238. [see the second edition of this invaluable collection: F. Dölger, A.E. Müller, et al., *Regesten*, Zweite Auflage (1. Teil, 1. Hanbband) (München, 2009) nos. 233, 238.—*Ed.*].

from this life, your successor shall be ordained by the venerable council of the metropolitans of your see.[17]

The terms of this novella, reiterated in Novella 131, clearly describe what today would be termed an autocephalous church, even though the word "autocephalous" itself is not used; and although the very location of Justiniana Prima was soon forgotten as a result of the 7th century Slavic invasions of the Balkan peninsula, this legislation concerning Justiniana Prima continued to play an important role in the ecclesiastical politics of the Balkan peninsula throughout the Middle Ages.

During the period of the first Bulgarian Empire, Byzantium occasionally recognized the existence of an independent Bulgarian patriarchate, but this was due to sheer expediency rather than to an application of the terms of Justinian's *novellae*. However, the situation changed following the destruction of the Bulgar state (1014) by Emperor Basil II. Although the Bulgarian primate, John of Ochrid, was compelled to exchange the title of patriarch for that of archbishop, a series of imperial *novellae* confirmed to him the same jurisdiction which he formerly had possessed.[18] On the death of Basil (1025) John was replaced by a Greek, and increasingly Greeks came to dominate the higher clergy. Yet, almost paradoxically, a chief pursuit of the Greek archbishops of Ochrid was the defense of the ancient privileges of their see against the encroachments of Constantinople. For example, Theophylact of Ochrid (c. 1075)—a former cleric of Haghia Sophia—at one point complains:

> Why is the patriarch of Constantinople participating in the affairs of the Bulgars, since he does not have the right to select or ordain their autocephalous archbishop nor does he have any other privileges among them?[19]

Similarly, John Comnenos, nephew of Alexius I, resurrected for himself the title of Archbishop of Justiniana Prima (c. 1143).[20]

---

[17] Novella 11.
[18] Dölger, *Regesten* nos. 806–8.
[19] *Epist.* 27; PG 126:428.
[20] Mansi 21:837.

Ochrid's vigorous defense of the privileges of Justiniana Prima, along with the continuing existence of autocephalous churches in Cyprus and Georgia, is significant for Byzantium's 12th-century golden age of canonical thought, if only because commentators on ecclesiastical organization felt obliged at least to mention such anomalies. Sometimes these autocephalous churches receive only grudging attention. For example, Nilus Doxopatres, who in 1143 dedicated a treatise on ecclesiastical geography to King Roger of Sicily, devotes one paragraph each to Cyprus and Bulgaria, both of which are described as "autocephalous, not subject to any of the greater sees, governing themselves on their own authority, and ordaining their own bishops."[21] Then with a note of impatience he announces: "And so much for these," and immediately he continues with an exposition of the theological significance of the pentarchy, the five senses of the Church's single head, instituted by the Holy Spirit himself.[22] Professional canonists, on the other hand, devote somewhat more attention to these exceptional cases. For example, Balsamon, perhaps the greatest Byzantine canonist, offers a stimulating account of the origins of the churches of Cyprus, Georgia, and Bulgaria. In his commentary on I Constantinople, Canon 2 he writes:

> Note from the present canon that once all metropolitans of the provinces were autocephalous and were ordained by their local synods. This, however, has been changed by Canon 28 of the Council of Chalcedon, which determined that the metropolitans of the dioceses of Pontus, Asia, and Thrace along with a few others mentioned in that canon were to be ordained by the patriarch of Constantinople and subject to him. But if you find yet other autocephalous churches, like that of Bulgaria, that of Cyprus, and that of Iberia [i.e., Georgia], do not be surprised. For Emperor Justinian honored the archbishop of Bulgaria.... The third synod [i.e., the Council of Ephesus] honored the archbishop of Cyprus.... Likewise a decision of an Antiochene synod honored the archbishop of Iberia. For it is said that at the time of the

---

[21]*Notitia thronorum patriarchalium*; PG 132:1097.
[22]*Ibid.*

most holy patriarch of the city of God great Antioch, lord Peter, there was a synodal dispensation that the church of Iberia, then subject to the patriarch of Antioch, should be free and autocephalous.[23]

While Balsamon's account does not entirely accord with the results of subsequent historical scholarship,[24] his basic position is clear: that churches become autocephalous in a variety of ways, whether by decision of an ecumenical council, by action of the mother church, or by imperial fiat.

This pragmatic view of ecclesiastical organization is found in Balsamon's discussion of the patriarchates as well. The Church of Jerusalem, for example, had been founded by St James;[25] nevertheless it was subject to the metropolitan of Caesarea, until I Nicaea, Canon 7 honored it on account of Christ's death and resurrection.[26] Even the Church of Rome, though founded by St Peter,[27] owed its prerogatives and privileges to the decisions of ecumenical councils (e.g., I Nicaea canon 6) and above all to the so-called *Donation of Constantine*.[28] Constantinople, on the other hand, could claim no illustrious founder;[29] but because it was the imperial city, I Constantinople canon 3 and Chalcedon canon 28 had conferred on it all the privileges possessed by Old Rome, including those conveyed by the *Donation of Constantine*.[30] Balsamon's position leaves little room for pentarchic theory, at least in its more metaphysical aspects. While Balsamon devotes an entire treatise to describing and defining the powers and prerogatives of the five patriarchates, he does not attribute their

---

[23]PG 137:317–20.

[24]On the question of Georgia's autocephaly see above at n. 15. Balsamon's "lord Peter" perhaps is Peter the Fuller, monophysite Patriarch of Antioch; thus Tarchnishvili, "Die Entstehung und Entwicklung."

[25]*Meditatum de patriarcharum privilegiis*; PG 138:1013.

[26]Commentary on I Nicaea, Canon 6; PG 137:252–53.

[27]*Meditatum*; PG 138:1013.

[28]E.g., commentaries on I Constantinople, Canon 3 (PG 137:321) and Antioch, Canon 12 (PG 137:1312).

[29]*Meditatum*; PG 138:1013. Though Balsamon at this point links St Andrew with Thrace, he does not claim him as founder of the church of Constantinople, nor does he account St Andrew's disciple Stachys as first bishop of Constantinople. On the legend of the Apostle Andrew see Dvornik, *The Idea of Apostolocity*, esp. pp. 138–64.

[30]Thus, the passages cited n. 28 above.

existence to some cosmic necessity or to a special revelation of the Holy Spirit. Rather, for Balsamon, patriarchates, primacies, special prerogatives, and other such aspects of supra-episcopal organization are established by means of essentially juridical acts, like conciliar canons and imperial decrees. These juridical acts, in turn, have been framed in order to express certain special circumstances. These circumstances may involve religious considerations, though no particular regard is paid to circumstances surrounding the foundation of a given church (e.g., apostolic origin). Thus, Jerusalem is honored as the site of Christ's passion, not because it was founded by St James. But far more important are political circumstances: Constantinople, like Rome before it, is honored because it is the imperial city.

This awareness of the importance of political circumstances for ecclesiastical organization is very much in the tradition of the early canons' emphasis on accommodation to patterns of civil administration and enables Balsamon to account for the existence of a variety of autocephalous churches. At the same time there are obvious dangers in too closely linking ecclesiastical organization to the whims of secular politics. Balsamon, for one, is aware of the problem and tries to provide a greater measure of stability by stressing the juridical acts requisite for effecting any changes in a church's status and, more specifically, by invoking Canon 37 of the Synod in Trullo, which preserves the rights and status of bishops unable to enter their dioceses on account of barbarian incursions. It is principally on these grounds that he defends the prerogatives of the patriarchates which have fallen into the hostile hands of the Latins, his own see of Antioch among them.[31] Unfortunately for the history of Orthodox canon law, Balsamon did not live long enough to comment on the full range of ecclesiastical problems which can arise from complete disruption of political circumstances. In 1204, within a decade of Balsamon's death, a western crusading army captured Constantinople itself, making it the capital of a Latin empire; and hard upon political collapse followed ecclesiastical chaos.

With the Latin conquest, the remnants of Byzantine ecclesiastical and political organization were placed in an awkward position. On the one

[31] *Meditatum*; PG 138:1032.

hand, the importance of the imperial will and presence for ecclesiastical organization had always been recognized in Byzantium. But where was the empire now? Several Greek successor states had been established on former imperial territory, but none possessed unquestioned legitimacy of dynasty, preponderance of physical power, or (most importantly) the imperial city of Constantinople. On the other hand, crowning and anointing by the patriarch had come to be considered essential to the making of the emperor.[32] But now a Latin was enthroned as patriarch in Constantinople, and the pre-1204 patriarch, John X Camateros, had taken refuge in Bulgaria, pointedly ignoring invitations to the court of Nicaea, the leading Greek successor state. Byzantium's delicate balance of Church and empire now had degenerated into a frustrating state of paralysis. Disputes over ecclesiastical jurisdiction raged but achieved no definitive resolution, at least on the level of theory. Many central canonical questions were raised but left unanswered—or else left with too many answers. A detailed discussion of the ecclesiastical politics of this period would be out of place at this point,[33] but a brief sketch of some of the canonical issues involved perhaps will suggest some of the reasons why autocephaly, comparatively clearly understood in earlier periods, now comes to be a subject for debate and confusion.

The lead in restoring the forms of the old Byzantine court was taken by Theodore I Lascaris of Nicaea. Patriarch John Camateros, who had rejected Lascaris' overtures, died in 1206, and the patriarchal throne remained vacant until 1208 when, after winning the support of most

---

[32]On Byzantine imperial coronation see the brief bibliographical orientation in G. Ostrogorsky, *History of the Byzantine State* (New Brunswick, NJ: Rutgers University Press, 1957), 56 n.2. On anointing of emperors, most of the relevant texts are assembled by A. Michel, "Die Kaisermacht in der Ostkirche (843–1204)," *Ostkirchliche Studien* 2 (1953): 10–13. [See the monograph by the same author published only few years later: A. Michel, *Die Kaisermacht in der Ostkirche (843–1204)* (Darmstadt: H. Gentner, 1959).—*Ed.*]

[33]The subject will soon be treated in a Yale University PhD dissertation by Mr Apostolos Karpozilos, who kindly provided the present writer with many helpful suggestions concerning the problem of autocephaly in this period. [See the published version of this dissertation in: A. Karpozilos, *The Ecclesiastical Controversy between the Kingdom of Nicaea and the Principality of Epiros (1217–1233)*, Byzantine Keimena kai Meletai 7 (Thessaloniki/Athens: Kentron Byzantinon Ereunon/Grigoris, 1973).—*Ed.*]. For the historical narrative which follows and additional bibliography see Ostrogorsky, *History of the Byzantine State*, 371–91.

of the Anatolian metropolitans, Lascaris arranged for the appointment of Michael Autoreianos as patriarch. Immediately thereafter Autoreianos crowned Lascaris emperor. Thus, by a kind of *allelogenesis*, a Greek emperor and patriarch now held court in Nicaea. Needless to say, the other Greek states were not quick to accept these new arrangements.

In distant Trebizond, where David and Alexius Comnenos, grandsons of Emperor Andronicus I, had established a little empire, the local metropolitan became in practice autocephalous. Ecclesiastical relations with the patriarch at Nicaea were restored only in 1260, when Patriarch Nicephorus II, to assure Trebizond's cooperation in Emperor Michael Palaeologos' coming campaign to recapture Constantinople, recognized the church of Trebizond's right to handle all its own internal affairs and to appoint its own bishops and metropolitans on the condition that a representative of the patriarch of Constantinople be present at the consecration of the metropolitan of Trebizond.[34] A similar pattern was followed in Epirus, where the Angeloi were proving worthy rivals of Nicaea's Lascarids. Metropolitans like John Apokaukos of Naupactos, ignoring the claims of Nicaea's patriarchs, assumed control of stauropegial monasteries (monasteries subject directly to the patriarch rather than to the local bishop) and proceeded with the ordination of bishops and fellow-metropolitans.

The protracted ecclesiastical and political duel between Nicaea and Epirus took a new turn in 1211, when Nicaea's Patriarch Germanus II consecrated Sava, saintly son of the King of Serbia, as autocephalous archbishop of Serbia. Since the six ecclesiastical provinces comprising the Serbian church until this point had been under the jurisdiction of the autocephalous archbishop of Ochrid, the canonicity of the patriarch's action was immediately questioned. In a letter of reprimand to the new Serbian primate, Demetrius Chomatianos—archbishop of Ochrid, distinguished canonist, and partisan of the Despotate of Epirus—claimed that by ordaining Sava the patriarch had violated I Constantinople Canon 2, Apostolic Canon 35, and Antioch Canon 13 (all directed against bishops performing

[34]On this episode see L. Petit, "Acte synodal du patriarche Nicéphore II sur les privilèges du métropolitain de Trébizonde (1er janvier 1260)," *Izvestia Russkago Arkheologicheskago Instituta v Konstantinopole* [Proceedings of the Russian Archeological Institute in Constantinople] 8 (1902): 163–71.

ordinations outside their own jurisdiction), Chalcedon canon 12 (against setting up two metropolitans within a province by recourse to the civil powers) and Ephesus Canon 8 (defense of the Church of Cyprus against interference by the Patriarch of Antioch).[35]

Needless to say, the canonical merits of Chomatianos' position were ignored both in Serbia and in Nicaea. However, Chomatianos soon was able to even the score somewhat. In 1224 Theodore Angelos, Despot of Epirus, captured Thessalonika from the Latins, proving that his state was a serious contender in the race to recapture Constantinople and restore the empire. Theodore's ambitions were literally crowned by Chomatianos, who crowned and anointed him emperor, in direct opposition to the claims of Nicaea's Lascarids. As one might expect, Patriarch Germanus II questioned the legality of Chomatianos' act, chiefly on the grounds that only a patriarch could bless the μύρον (chrism) used for anointing the emperor.[36] In reply, Chomatianos argued that as head of the autocephalous church of Justiniana Prima he certainly could bless the chrism.[37] In addition he suggested that, in view of the radically changed circumstances brought about by the Latin conquest, Patriarch Germanus should confine himself to Anatolian affairs and that he, Demetrius, would handle Balkan matters. Not without sarcasm he bemoans the fact that old Constantinopolitan customs must now be continued in distant Bithynia and asks, "Whenever has one heard of shepherding the metropolitan of Nicaea himself and at the same time being called patriarch of Constantinople?"[38]

Epirus' triumph was short-lived. In 1230 Theodore Angelos was decisively defeated in battle, captured, and blinded by the Bulgarian tsar, John Asen II. Though the Epirote state survived, it no longer was a serious contender for Constantinople, and in its place Nicaea was able to assert its authority in ecclesiastical as well as political matters. As a sign of the changing times, a patriarchal exarch visited Epirus in 1232, and Metropolitan John Apokaukos, one of the leaders of Epirote ecclesiastical separatism, was

---

[35]Edit. J.-B. Pitra, *Analecta sacra et classica spicilegio solesmense parata* 7 (Rome, 1891), 381–90.
[36]*Ibid.*, 484–85.
[37]*Ibid.*, 493–94.
[38]*Ibid.*, 489–90.

forced to retire to a monastery. Chomatianos retained his see, and Ochrid remained autocephalous; however, its importance and geographic extent was considerably diminished. Even before the Serbian Church withdrew from Ochrid's jurisdiction, the church of the revived Bulgarian empire, likewise made up of provinces formerly under Ochrid's jurisdiction, had become *de facto* autocephalous under its own patriarch at Trnovo; and in 1235, ignoring Ochrid's claims, the patriarch of Constantinople at Nicaea, along with the other eastern patriarchs, had granted official recognition to this new patriarchate.

After the fall of Epirus, Nicaea's emperors and patriarchs had no serious rivals in the Greek world. The jurisdictional chaos of the period 1204–30 effectively came to an end; and after Constantinople was recaptured from the Latins (1261), emperor and patriarch moved from Nicaea back to the imperial city, restoring some semblance of the *status quo ante*. However, since 1204 changes had taken place in ecclesiastical organization, seriously affecting the term "autocephalous." If nothing else, ecclesiastical geography was different. In addition to the autocephalous churches described by Balsamon—Ochrid, Cyprus, and Georgia—there now existed an autocephalous Serbian Church under the Archbishop of Pec and an autocephalous Bulgarian Church under the patriarch of Trnovo.

These two churches possessed a number of features in common, distinguishing them from earlier autocephalous churches. At least at the time of their establishment, the autocephalous churches of Justiniana Prima and Cyprus—and indeed the five ancient patriarchates as well—were part of one empire and achieved juridical confirmation of their status by the unilateral decree of an emperor or an ecumenical council. The new foundations, on the other hand, came into existence as one facet of bilateral treaties between two civil governments. This reflects a tendency to regard autocephaly chiefly as the sign of an independent national state. Formerly autocephaly had meant independence on a more strictly ecclesiastical level from interference from an outside ecclesiastical authority. Now autocephaly meant above all the capacity for consecrating the μύρον [*myron*] needed for anointing an emperor. As one curious result of this virtual redefinition of terms, autocephaly increasingly became (at least by the standards of previous centuries) conditional and partial, limited by treaty. Thus, in exchange for autocephaly (i.e., permission to consecrate the μύρον [*myron*]) the Serbian and Bulgarian churches both agreed to commemorate the patriarch of Constantinople first in the liturgy and to pay him an annual tax.

Another feature peculiar to these new autocephalous churches is that ecclesiastical recognition of their status came in the first instance from the patriarch of Constantinople. Balsamon, at this point representative of the earlier canonical tradition, had recognized that churches can become autocephalous in a variety of ways—by the decree of an ecumenical council, of the mother church, or of the emperor—but attributed no special prerogatives in this regard to Constantinople. Now, however, because the question of autocephaly had become so deeply entangled in the immediate political situation of rivalry between Epirus and Nicaea, the claims of the mother church were ignored and the authority of the Patriarchate of Constantinople was extended. Autocephaly assumes an ad hoc quality, less affected by the Church's canonical tradition than by the political exigencies of the hour. In part this is because virtually all parties involved were not above juggling canons to suit their own private ends; but it partly is because the canons themselves, predicated for the most part upon the existence of one Christian empire, failed to provide consistent and unequivocal answers to the problems of the day. The political and military triumph of Nicaea, by restoring the empire, provided a respite from jurisdictional chaos and assured continuation—and indeed expansion—of the authority of the patriarch of Constantinople, the New Rome. However, the canonical problems raised by the collapse of the empire remained, and still remain, unresolved.

With the 13th century, the problem of what constitutes and establishes an autocephalous church takes on much of the complexity and confusion that characterizes modern discussions of the subject. The ancient church had been well acquainted with the reality of the autocephalous local church, sacramentally and juridically self-sufficient. With the rise of suprametropolitan imperial forms of ecclesiastical organization, local churches were integrated in wider "patriarchal" structures. Churches like Cyprus and Justiniana Prima survived as remnants of the past, overshadowed on the theoretical level by the idea of a pentarchy of patriarchs and on the practical level by the growing power of the Patriarchate of Constantinople. However, with the turmoil following the fall of Constantinople to the Latins, new "autocephalies" immediately arose, challenging the imperial "pentarchic" system. We today are heirs not only to the canonical riches of the earlier centuries but also to this canonical chaos of the 13th. There is no empire able to impose its own solution. Shall we regret it, or rather look for the original norms of church organization, which our canonical tradition, with its wise pragmatism, has learned to adapt to the changing streams of historical development?

The Quest for Orthodox Church Unity in America[1]

John E. Rexine

St Vladimir's Theological Quarterly 19.1 (1975): 57–64

NOBEL PRIZE WINNER Alexander Solzhenitsyn, who has not hesitated to challenge the leadership of the Russian Orthodox Church, particularly its patriarch and bishops, recently responded to a request by Metropolitan Philaret of the Russian Orthodox Church-in-Exile to give his opinion of Russian Orthodox Church life outside the Soviet Union, on the occasion of a sobor of that group in Jordanville, New York, by stressing the dangers inherent in division: "What is more dangerous for Russian Orthodoxy? Violent internal oppression, or internal division through discord? I will speak for myself: under oppression I never lost courage, while division leads me here to despair" (quoted in *The Orthodox Church* 10. 9 [November 1974]). It is precisely this division which is plaguing not only the Russian Orthodox Church throughout the world, including the United States, but is also the principal scandal of the Orthodox Church in the United States. In his recently translated diatribe entitled *The Autocephaly of the Metropolia in America*, Professor Panagiotes N. Trembelas of the School of Theology of the University of Athens, fully cognizant of the fact that there are in the United States, in his own words: "one Greek jurisdiction, three Russian, two Serbian, two Antiochian, two Romanian, two Bulgarian, two Albanian, three Ukrainian, one Carpatho-Russian and some

---

[1] A review of Panagiotes N. Trembelas, *The Autocephaly of the Metropolia in America*, trans. and ed. by George S. Bebis, Robert G. Stephanopoulos, and N. M. Vaporis (Brookline, Massachusetts: Holy Cross Theological School Press, 1974); and Archimandrite Serafim, *The Quest for Orthodox Unity in America: A History of the Orthodox Church in North America in the Twentieth Century* (New York: Saints Boris and Gleb Press, 1973).

smaller groups,"² deplores the proclamation of the "Metropolia" (formerly the Russian Orthodox Greek Catholic Church of America) as an autocephalous Church because he argues that such autocephaly was unilaterally declared by the Patriarchate of Moscow, even though three months earlier the late Patriarch Athenagoras I had warned that such a granting of autocephaly was uncanonical and could have dire consequences. His little book is, in effect, an attack on the persons and arguments of Fathers Alexander Schmemann and John Meyendorff, the principal theoreticians of American Orthodox autocephaly and two of the most outstanding Orthodox theologians in the United States. A great deal of this invective is spent on attacking the scholarship and even the Christian integrity of these two clergymen who have unquestionably served the cause of Orthodox Christianity to a far greater degree than Professor Trembelas (the correct transliteration of modern Greek *mp* is *mb*, not as the translators have done) would ever give them credit for. In fact, the future of Orthodox Christianity in America will depend much more on the work and words of these two than on any theologian pontificating from Athens! The editors and translators of Professor Trembelas's little opus are cautiously generous when they describe it as a "careful and well-reasoned survey of this action (i.e., the autocephaly), its historical background, and its canonical and other ramifications and consequences for all Orthodox Christians in the United States" and as a study that will provide "a much broader and clearer understanding of the problem than has been hitherto available."³ It is true that Professor Trembelas surveys the problem of the many ecclesiastical jurisdictions in America and its cause; the events which immediately preceded the proclamation of the autocephaly; territorial jurisdiction, its foundation and evolution; the canonical evidence, as he sees it, regarding the autocephaly of the Metropolia; and he comes to the conclusion that "the existing pluralism of jurisdictions of the Orthodox Church in America was created from the confusion resulting after the Russian Revolution in 1917 and the subsequent domination of the Soviet regime. The autocephaly granted by the late Patriarch Alexis, instead of contributing to the more

²Trempelas, *The Autocephaly of the Metropolia*, 7.
³*Ibid.*, 3.

canonical normalization of ecclesiastical conditions in America, on the contrary gave official status to this pluralism by retaining under his own jurisdiction numerous parishes which are under the administration of the patriarchal exarch resident in Canada."[4]

It would not be appropriate to give such a short treatise an extended review, but certain general comments need to be made. The critique is not without value in certain particulars but it is hardly irenic or constructive. Though it bemoans the divisions in American Orthodoxy, it would do nothing to promote union or unification. Though it sees inconsistency in the granting of autocephaly to the Russian Metropolia, citing the Patriarchate of Jerusalem's *Tomos* that "the Holy Synod of Moscow badly contradicts itself by granting with one hand the autocephaly to the Russian Metropolia in America and by preserving with the other their own authority and jurisdiction over parishes within the very same ecclesiastical area—this being contrary to fundamental canonical regulations—they disclaim and invalidate the autocephaly they previously granted,"[5] what would have been Professor Trembelas's canonical reaction if the Russian Patriarch had forced all Russian churches of its jurisdiction to join the newly declared Orthodox Church in America? The inconsistency is there, but has Professor Trembelas, who belongs to the Church of Greece, considered the scandalous canonical irregularities in his own Church? How many of his colleagues were prepared to correct these irregularities under the trying days of the military junta or are making progress in this direction even now under the democracy? Inconsistency here hardly compares to the situation in practice with the Church of Greece and its leaders and theoreticians. It is true, I believe, that it would have been much more tactful for the negotiations leading to the declaration of autocephaly to have been shared with other Orthodox churches so that the negotiating parties could "have avoided hasty and secretive activities, averting thus any suspicions about their meaning."[6] I have elsewhere[7] in my review of *The*

---

[4]*Ibid.*, 65.
[5]Cited *ibid.*, 18.
[6]*Ibid.*, 20.
[7]*The Logos* 6.6 (November-December 1973), 19.

Russian Autocephaly and Orthodoxy in America: An Appraisal (New York: The Orthodox Observer Press, 1972) indicated that the Russians were tactless and inconsiderate in the unilateral nature of their declaration, but the Greeks are demonstrating, as does Professor Trembelas and others, that they can surpass any Roman lawyer in legalistic argumentation. Professor Trembelas would do well to keep in mind Archbishop Iakovos's statement in the aforementioned publication[8] that "[i]t seems that we tend to forget that ecclesiastical jurisdictions always coincided with provincial or national boundaries and the Church, in both the Byzantine and Russian empires, was the established Church, a state religion, and as such her administrative structure was closely bound with that of the state. The situation here is, of course, fundamentally different; no particular Orthodox Church can claim to be the established Church not only because no one was nationally established when the others began to form into ecclesiastical communities, but simply because the state does not establish or disestablish any Church whatsoever." Professor Trembelas would even push the argument *ad absurdum* so that "it is not permissible to the Patriarch of Moscow to jurisdictionally invade the United States or any other territory elsewhere and under any pretext whatsoever. Even if it may appear to some that these territories are under the jurisdiction of no one, *one thing is certain, that they are not under the jurisdiction of the Patriarchal throne of Moscow.*"[9] What an incredibly unhelpful argument, as ridiculous as continuing to describe the United States as one of "the barbaric nations"! This term, by the way, should be properly translated, and the use of this "barbaric" term should cease by all parties. What an insult to American Orthodox! Since there are now no ecumenical councils recognized beyond the seventh, and since the principle that "the ecumenical councils, as the highest authority exercised in the entire Church, guarantee perpetually the autocephality of whichever ecclesiastical territory they thus recognize by vote, this being a fact attested by ancient and time-honored tradition,"[10] how are

---

[8] *The Russian Autocephaly and Orthodoxy in America* (New York: The Orthodox Observer Press, 1972), 11.
[9] Trempelas, *The Autocephaly of the Metropolia*, 56–57. Italics mine.
[10] *Ibid.*, 10

we canonically to explain the existence of autocephalous churches after this date? History provides the answers which every student of Orthodox Church history knows only too well.[11] But one obvious thing does emerge from Trembelas's survey that any objective observer will be able to extract almost immediately. The fundamental argument as to why there cannot be an autocephalous Church in the United States is because the Greeks—not the Russians—constitute the majority; and so we come back to the argument cited early in this study,[12] which betrays the nationalistic fear that there could not possibly be a viable situation in which a single American Orthodox Church could emerge under Russian initiative and leadership. Nationalism, reinforced by theologians from the mother countries, proves to be a very formidable obstacle to Christian understanding, inter-Orthodox cooperation, and a solution to a pressing problem that even Alexander Solzhenitsyn sees as scandalous. (Because Solzhenitsyn is Orthodox, even Archbishop Iakovos has been quick to claim him in public pronouncements as "one of our own"!)

To sum up, Professor Trembelas's piece contributes a survey of a troublesome problem with some interesting, if narrowly perceived, information but in no way offers a solution to the problem of Orthodox unity in America. It is, instead, a judgmental piece that castigates Fathers Meyendorff and Schmemann in particular, and the Russian Metropolia and the Moscow Patriarchate in general. It betrays an unhappiness with the present situation in the Russian Church and presumably looks to the ecumenical throne for a solution.

The Quest for Orthodox Church Unity in America was reviewed in a curiously unrevealing way by the Rev. Gino K. Piovesana, S.J., in *Diakonia*[13] under the title of "Toward a History of the Russian Orthodox Church in the USA—Apropos of Serafim Surrency's Book." Either Father Piovesana was being very charitable or he completely missed the whole point

---

[11] Archbishop Michael (Constantinides), *The Orthodox Church* (Brookline, MA: Theological Institute Press, 1952), 106, 107; R. M. French, *The Eastern Orthodox Church* (London: Hutchinson's University Library, 1951), 75; John Meyendorff, *The Orthodox Church* (London: Darton, Longman, & Todd, 1962), 172 [3rd rev. ed. St Vladimir's Seminary Press, 1981—*Ed.*].

[12] Trempelas, *The Autocephaly of the Metropolia*, 23–27.

[13] Diakonia 9.1 (1974): 83–86.

of Archimandrite Surrency's book. Anyone who knows Father Serafim knows that the insertion of "Russian" before "Orthodox Church Unity in America" by the reviewer has changed the intended orientation. There is no need to rehearse here what has already been noted by Father Piovesana in his review. It should be noted for the record that Archimandrite Serafim was awarded the graduate degree of Candidate of Theology by the Orthodox Theological Academy of Leningrad [Saint Petersburg—*Ed.*] in 1971 for this work and that he has been the Secretary of the American Exarchate of the Moscow Patriarchate as well as editor of *One Church*, the official journal of the Exarchate, and a consultant to the Standing Conference of Canonical Orthodox Bishops (SCOBA), and is currently on the staff of St Nicholas Cathedral in New York City. The author himself best expresses his purpose in writing this book: "It will be seen that this thesis is primarily concerned with the efforts of the Orthodox Hierarchy in North America to achieve a unity among themselves while attempting to maintain canonical ties with the mother church, having in mind the ultimate goal of establishing a canonical local Orthodox Church which would be recognized by the entire Ecumenical Orthodox Church. To put it another way, the primary emphasis of this thesis will be on the efforts toward organizational unity of Orthodoxy in America, primarily on the hierarchical and jurisdictional levels,"[14] and this is precisely what the author does in his eight full chapters, which cover a chronological period that extends from 1794 to 1970. Though obviously written from a Russian Orthodox point of view, Father Serafim is knowledgeable about the interactive role of the Greek and Syrian churches in the total history of American Orthodoxy and devotes an entire chapter to the Albanians, Bulgarians, Belorussians, Carpatho-Russians, Estonians, Greeks, Macedonians, Romanians, Serbians, Syrians, and Ukrainians, and deals intimately with SCOBA, its history and role in bringing the various "canonical" Orthodox churches together under the aegis of the exarch of the ecumenical patriarch, Archbishop Iakovos. For the independent observer, the most important part of the book may very well be the appendix, which has conveniently gathered the following documents into one place: a list of the ruling hierarchs of the North

---

[14] Archimandrite Serafim, *The Autocephaly of the Metropolia*, 11.

American Diocese of the Russian Orthodox Church; a table of statistics for Orthodox churches in the United States and Canada; a list of religious bodies in the United States and Canada which purport to be a part of the Orthodox Church; the alleged *ukaz* of Patriarch Tikhon to Metropolitan Platon; the 1924 *ukaz* of Patriarch Tikhon to Metropolitan Platon; texts of decisions of the 1924 Detroit Sobor; an extract from the *ukaz* of the acting Patriarchal locum tenens and his temporary patriarchal Holy Synod; an extract from the pastoral letter of the Acting Patriarchal locum tenens to the ruling bishop, Archbishop Benjamin, and the clergy and laity of the American diocese; an open letter of Archbishop-Exarch Benjamin to the clergy and faithful assembled or represented in the Cleveland Convention (1934); an extract from the *ukaz* of the Patriarchal locum tenens Sergius, Metropolitan of Moscow, dated January 4, 1935; excerpts from an act to amend the religious corporations law, in relation to the Federated Orthodox Greek Catholic Primary Jurisdictions in America, and renumbering certain articles thereof (major extracts); the complete text of the "Bayonne Resolutions"; the *ukaz* of Patriarch of Moscow and All Russia Alexis, and of the Sacred Synod of the Russian Orthodox Church, February 14, 1945, regarding Metropolia; memorandum of five professors on the status of the Russian Orthodox in America dated October 18, 1946; resolution of the Seventh All-American Sobor, held in Cleveland, Ohio, on November 26–28, 1946; the Constitution of the Standing Conference of Canonical Orthodox Bishops of the Americas adopted on August 8, 1961; the letter of Bishop Dositheus to the member-hierarchs of SCOBA, dated May 16, 1962; the SCOBA resolution concerning the Ukrainian Autocephalous Church; the SCOBA report of the ad hoc Commission on Unity; the appeal of the Standing Conference of Canonical Orthodox Bishops in the Americas to the forthcoming Pan-Orthodox Conference to be held in Geneva; texts of letters by Archbishop Iakovos to the churches of Constantinople, Cyprus, Moscow, Greece, Bulgaria, Romania, Yugoslavia, and to all Patriarchs (May 26, 1970); complete text of the agreement of March 31, 1970; the Tomos of Alexis, Patriarch of Moscow and All Russia (April 10, 1970); John Meyendorff's "The Problem of the Autocephaly of the Orthodox Church in America" (October 17, 1970); the Constitution of the Orthodox Church in America; a statement adopted unanimously by the First Council of the Orthodox Church in America on October 22, 1970; the resolution unanimously adopted by the First Council of the Orthodox Church in America concerning the ecumenical movement; the complete text of the decree issued in December 1970 by Patriarch Athenagoras to Archbishop Iakovos naming the latter patriarchal exarch plenipotentiary. In addition to a general bibliography and bibliographies for each chapter of the book, there is a Russian-language bibliography and a name index.

Father Serafim is a patient realist and cautiously optimistic. The declaration of the Metropolia as the autocephalous Orthodox Church in America may have healed the schism between itself and the mother Russian Church, but in the words of Archimandrite Serafim, "the events of the last two years (1971 and 1972) have not seemed to justify the optimism of those who welcomed the autocephaly as a major step in the unification of Orthodoxy in America in the immediate future nor has it justified the fears of those who opposed the autocephaly on the grounds that it would bring about a greater fragmentation of an already fragmented American Orthodoxy."[15] The author believes that full unification will take more time, perhaps as much as two generations. In the meantime, the Orthodox Church in America (O.C.A.) has insisted that "autocephaly is not: the submission of the Orthodox Church in America to any church or nation; the submission of any Church jurisdiction in America to the Orthodox Church in America; the cause of any formal or structural changes in parish life; the depreciation of any valuable cultural heritages and traditions; the rejection of continued cooperation and progress on the pan-Orthodox level; the concern and possession solely of the members of the Orthodox Church in America."[16] It would seem only reasonable that the ecumenical Patriarchate of Constantinople should rise to the challenge and in the spirit of ecumenism and brotherly love take the appropriate and vigorous measures necessary to clarify and set in proper order the relations of the Orthodox churches in America to each other and to work assiduously to bring about a unification of those churches under the aegis of the Ecumenical

---

[15] *Ibid.*, 9.
[16] Cf. Serafim, *The Autocephaly of the Metropolia*, A173.

Patriarchate in a way that will bring about peace and harmony among those churches. For, as was noted recently in an article on "Our faith" in *The Orthodox Weekly Bulletin*,[17] "The Scriptures call the Church the 'Body of Christ,' and when you cut off a member of the body it bleeds. But the Church has become so mutilated." That mutilation should not be allowed to continue.

---

[17] *The Orthodox Weekly Bulletin* (Cliffwood, NJ: Vestal, January 12, 1974).

Concrete Structural Organization of the Local Church
The 1971 Statute of the Orthodox Church in America[1]

John H. Erickson

St Vladimir's Theological Quarterly 20.1–2 (1976): 9–18

WHEN I WAS AN UNDERGRADUATE, I heard an Orthodox monk speak on the subject of "The Church: An Orthodox Perspective." His lecture, though inspiring, was also rather perplexing: roughly half of it was devoted to the Garden of Eden and the other half to the New Jerusalem of Revelation.

His approach to ecclesiology is not unusual among Orthodox. A wealth of biblical allusions, emphasis on the Church as Mystery, appreciation of wider theological concerns—all this has characterized much of Orthodox discussion of ecclesiology, both past and present: the many excellent modern Orthodox studies of the christological, pneumatological, trinitarian, etc., dimensions of the Church are very much part of a tradition going back to Nicholas Cabasilas, Maximus the Confessor, and beyond.

Perhaps a measure of the value of such an approach is its revival in recent years in Roman Catholic statements on the Church—in the first chapters of *Lumen gentium*, for example. Yet it has been the experience of this Consultation—and of many involved in ecumenical discussion—that such an approach at times can lead to misunderstanding, that behind the same words can lie considerable differences of meaning. Like undergraduates, we would like to find out about the Church not only as she truly *is* in

---

[1] A paper originally prepared for the Eleventh Orthodox/Roman Catholic Bilateral Consultation. Washington, D.C., May 19–20, 1975. [The 1971 Statute has been replaced by the new 2015 Statute, adopted at the 18th All-American Council meeting in Atlanta. For a Report on the 2015 Statute see: "Documentation: Report on the Statute Revision for the Orthodox Church in America," *St Vladimir's Theological Quarterly* 61 (2017): 453–82.—*Ed.*]

Genesis and Revelation, at the beginning and at the end of history, but also as she meets us in our own limited everyday experience. Hence the present topic assignment: "Concrete Structural Organization of the local church." We wish to look at the institutional features and the concrete patterns of organization of the local church, in the pious hope that they will tell us something about our understanding of the Church.[2]

With this assignment I intend to comply. But attention first must be called to at least one potential source of confusion: What is meant by "local church?" In books on Orthodoxy, particularly of a popular sort, there is some ambiguity, probably unconscious, at this point. (1) The term sometimes refers to the several autocephalous churches—the Patriarchate of Constantinople, the Patriarchate of Antioch, the Church of Greece, the Church of Russia, etc.; (2) but it is also used for the congregation of the faithful gathered around their bishop and celebrating the Eucharist.[3] This is perhaps a philological quibble; the immediate verbal problem is obviated if we adopt a distinction regularly employed in some other languages between "particular" (= 1) and "local" (= 2).[4] However, this ambiguity is of some significance because two distinct approaches to the Church can lie behind it. Is the particular church the fundamental ecclesiastical organism, of which all lesser bodies are but parts? (Thus the 1917–18 Council of Moscow: "The Diocese is a *part* of the Russian Church.") Or is the local church—the Body of Christ, the temple of the Holy Spirit, possessing all the *notae ecclesiae*—the basic unit, on which all subsequent speculation must be based?

The former approach is implicit in the institutions and patterns of organization of much of present-day Orthodoxy, though it finds its most complete expression in the Church of Russia. Its genealogy can be traced

---

[2] Attention might be called at this point to Fr M. Fahey's analysis of the term *structure*, in the opening pages of his "Continuity in the Church amid Structural Changes," *Theological Studies* 35.3 (September 1974): 415–40.

[3] Thus the English language edition of John Meyendorff, *The Orthodox Church* (London: Darton, Longman, & Todd, 1962) [3rd rev. ed. St Vladimir's Seminary Press, 1981—*Ed.*] uses "local" in its first acceptation on p. 143 and in its second pp. 212–13. Examples could be multiplied.

[4] For such a distinction Fr H. de Lubac has pleaded, *Les églises particulières dans l'église universelle* (Paris, 1971); noted by Fahey, "Continuity in the Church," 433.

to efforts in the later Middle Ages to establish in the emerging Slavic lands national counterparts to the imperial church.[5] But while the Byzantine church and its Slavic analogues tended to imitate medieval imperial monarchy, the autocephalous church since the eighteenth century has imitated—in organization and vocabulary—the modern sovereign state.[6] Hence the preoccupation of older textbooks in canon law with locating the Highest Authority in the church—be it holy synod, council, patriarch or what have you[7]—and the general assumption that this Highest Authority has the right to govern the church as it sees fit: As Highest Authority it *could* erect or suppress dioceses, change their boundaries, transfer bishops and other clergy, etc., though in actual practice the degree of such centralization may vary from one church to another. Above this Highest Authority, there is none save Jesus Christ; below this Authority, church structure is a matter of indifference, the only important question being: "Under whose jurisdiction are you?"

The weaknesses of this approach have become more and more apparent. Like the pre-World War I system of sovereign states, the system of autocephalous churches has failed to meet the demands made on it in our tragic century. The result: alternation of confrontation and paralysis. But the defects of this approach to ecclesiology are not only on the pragmatic level. Though Orthodox responses to Vatican I argued that the existence of these sister autocephalous churches is an alternative to papalism,[8] in

---

[5] I trace the beginnings of this development more closely in "Autocephaly in Orthodox Canonical Literature to the Thirteenth Century," St *Vladimir's Theological Quarterly* 15 (1971): 28–41 [in this volume, pp. 179–195.—*Ed.*]. See also Alexander Schmemann, "A Meaningful Storm: Some Reflections on Autocephaly, Tradition, and Ecclesiology," St *Vladimir's Theological Quarterly* 15 (1971): 3–27 [in the present volume, pp. 149–78.—*Ed.*].

[6] Striking are similarities between political science textbook discussions of external and internal sovereignty and canon law textbook presentations of the two characteristics of the autocephalous church: the right to resolve all internal problems on its own authority, independently of all other churches, and the right to appoint its own bishops, including the head of the church.

[7] "Highest Authority": the expression is A. Bogolepov's, *Toward an American Orthodox Church* (New York: Morehouse-Barlow Co., 1963), *passim*. The approach is followed above all by Milash and by Russian canonists of the last century.

[8] P. Evdokimov, "Les principaux courants de l'écclésiologie orthodoxe au XIXe siécle," *Revue des sciences religieuses* 34 (1960): 70–72.

fact the search for the Highest Authority in the Church cannot stop at the level of the particular church. Inevitably this approach to ecclesiology demands a pope.[9] From time to time the Patriarchate of Constantinople has made gestures in this direction,[10] and more frequently appeals are made to the supreme authority of the ecumenical council. But surely the ecumenical council—in an Orthodox understanding—is more a charismatic event than it is a permanent institution for church government.[11] Like the appeals of the iconophiles in the eighth and ninth centuries to the pentarchy of patriarchs, appeals to the ecumenical council represent a call for consensus, not the recognition of a Highest Authority.

This ecclesiology of the Highest Authority (or "universal ecclesiology," as it is often denominated[12]) is now largely discredited in Orthodox theological circles, though its continuing influence can still be seen in the official utterances of the particular churches. Its reliance on the language and thought-patterns of law and diplomacy has given way to a more "churchly" approach, with emphasis on the liturgy and the fathers.

The main lines of this more recent approach are well known and need only to be sketched here:[13]

(1) The point of departure is the Ignatian vision of the local church: the faithful coming together as Church, becoming the Body of Christ in the

---

[9] This point is pursued by Alexander Schmemann, "The Idea of Primacy in Orthodox Ecclesiology," in *The Primacy of Peter* (London, 1963 [republished by St Vladimir's Seminary Press, 1992]), 35–36.

[10] "I have in mind the language of patriarchal acta especially of the fourteenth century, in which the patriarch becomes "the shepherd and teacher of the whole *oikoumene*," "the common father of all Christians to be found on earth," etc., and in which metropolitans even in distant Russia become his vicars, needed only because the patriarch himself is not ubiquitous. Some examples in H.-G. Beck, *Kirche und Theologische Literatur im byzantinischen Reich* (= Handbuch der Altertumswissenschaft XII.1.1, Munich, 1959), 35.

[11] See J. Meyendorff, "What is an ecumenical council?" St *Vladimir's Theological Quarterly* 17 (1973): 259–73. The East has never had a *frequens*, and the attempt in the decade following I Nicaea at church government by "ecumenical council" can hardly be considered a success.

[12] The term is Afanassieff's, "The Church which Presides in Love," *The Primacy of Peter*, 57–110.

[13] Afanassieff's often one-sided "eucharistic ecclesiology" has been given a sounder foundation especially by J. Zizioulas. The title of Zizioulas' major book on the subject, *The Unity of the Church in the Eucharist and the Bishop during the First Three Centuries* (in Greek, Athens, 1965), suggests the main lines followed in recent versions of this approach to ecclesiology.

Eucharist, becoming one Body out of many ("As this piece of bread was scattered over the hills and then was brought together and made one . . ." [Didache 9]); with the bishop personifying this unity, summing up the local church in himself ("I received your large congregation in the person of Onesimus, your bishop in this world . . ." [Ephesians 1]), standing—like Christ—before God in the place of all the faithful, standing—again like Christ—before the faithful in the place of God ("Let the bishop preside in God's place . . ." [Magnesians 6]).

(2) This Eucharistic assembly under the presidency of the bishop is the Church in all its fullness, not just a part of the Church. But the Church that dwells in Corinth has the same unity, the same fullness as the Church that dwells in Jerusalem, Antioch, Rome. This essential unity of the local churches means the essential unity and equality of their bishops. Hence episcopal consecration, with its plurality of consecrators: "It is not the transfer of a gift by those who possess it, but the manifestation of the fact that the *same* gift, which they have received in the Church from God, has now been given to this bishop in this Church."[14] Hence the council of bishops, with its emphasis on unanimity, with each bishop subscribing, giving his own testimony to the truth held by all: Here we have an expression of the common mind of the episcopate, an expression of the authority of all, not a Highest Authority over all.[15]

(3) But this equality of local churches and of bishops does not mean uniformity, just as unity of essence does not exclude plurality of utterly unique hypostases. Each local church is unique; and of these, some may "preside in love," some may more completely and perfectly express the common faith because they do not try to possess it for themselves alone but share all that they are with the others. Many factors may contribute to the potential for presidency: antiquity and apostolicity of foundation, the glory of martyrdom and suffering for Christ, geopolitical advantages, size, wealth. But the presidency itself consists not in *having* any or all of these elements but in *sharing* them, making the patrimony of one church—of

---

[14] A. Schmemann, "The Idea of Primacy," 41.
[15] On this point see I. Zizioulas, "The Development of Conciliar Structures to the Time of the First Ecumenical Council," in *Councils and the Ecumenical Movement*, World Council of Churches Studies 5 (Geneva, 1968), 34–51.

the first church—the patrimony of all. A favorite comparison at this point: God the Father, who shares all that he is with the Son, the image of the person of the Father, coequal and consubstantial with the Father.[16]

This ecclesiology of the local church, at least in its broad outlines, is widely accepted among Orthodox theologians. But sometimes there is an air of unreality in literature on the subject, so far removed is it from everyday church life. Sometimes the more we look to the fathers and to the structures of church life in the first centuries the less application we find to our own situation. We note with satisfaction the understanding of conciliarity and primacy expressed in Apostolic Canon 34:

> The bishops of every nation must acknowledge him who is first among them and account him as their head, and do nothing of consequence without his consent; but each may do those things only which concern his own parish, and the country places which belong to it. But neither let him who is the first do anything without the consent of all. For so there will be unanimity, and God will be glorified through the Lord in the Holy Spirit.

With this trinitarian doxology, our mind's eye turns to the divine council of Genesis, to God the Trinity saying "let us make man in our image, after our likeness." And in pursuing this approach we would appear to have returned to the old Garden of Eden/New Jerusalem syndrome, to an unbridgeable gap between the theory of church structures and the "concrete structural organization of the local church."

Such a verdict would not be wholly justified. A gap may exist, but it is not absolute. For one thing, the organization of most of the particular churches maintains a careful balance between conciliarity and primacy (though the place of the local church in all this often is ambiguous). Further, there is also a widespread desire that this gap be narrowed, even if it cannot be completely eliminated. Very few would be willing to say that ecclesiology is just a matter for theologians and historians. But unfortunately the caesaropapism of circumstances often limits our ability to translate our

---

[16]Thus O. Clement, "Orthodox Ecclesiology as an Ecclesiology of Communion," *One Church* 6 (1970): 114–15.

ecclesiology into concrete forms. No one can doubt that the pressures of life under the Soviet regime have contributed greatly to the extreme centralization of the Russian Church today. So also, the ecclesiological witness of the Patriarchate of Constantinople has been adversely affected by restrictions placed by the Turkish civil authorities on the assembly of its bishops; and in Greece, constant political changes have replaced systematic efforts at renewal of church structure—the 1967 plan for reorganization, for example—by canonical chaos. In short, the diversity that a systematic examination of "concrete structural organization" would reveal, would be less a sign of the richness of our ecclesiological tradition than a reflection of the chaos of current events.

Such considerations have led me to treat in detail only the 1971 Statute of the Orthodox Church in America (OCA). I do so not to be chauvinistic, nor because I regard the document as altogether perfect and exemplary, but because in America Orthodoxy is free at least from the overt and grossly palpable varieties of outside interference in church life and organization. But there are additional points of interest: Regardless of how one views its status, the OCA at least claims to be an autocephalous church, a "particular church"; she is the daughter of the Russian Church, one of the great exponents of an ecclesiology of the Highest Authority; but at the same time many of her most influential theologians are leading exponents of an ecclesiology based on the local church. Hence the significance of the OCA Statute is greater than numbers or age of that body would suggest.

Of the text of the 1971 Statute, perhaps two thirds comes from the Statute of 1955, as amended several times in the interval. Therefore a few words about the 1955 Statute are necessary.

The 1924 Detroit Sobor (or Convention) of the American metropolitanate decided on a course of "temporary autonomy" in view of the changed situation in Russia. For the organization of the metropolitanate, the sobor determined to follow the principles laid down by the 1917–18 Moscow Council and that a detailed statute should be prepared. The result, the 1955 Statute, though adopted some thirty years later, faithfully reflected this original goal.[17] This accounts for some of the strengths and weaknesses of

---

[17] Bogolepov, *op. cit.*, 90–95, provides a brief analysis.

the 1955 document, and in turn for some of the features of the 1971 Statute. On the positive side, the 1917–18 Council represents the culmination of more than ten years of careful planning and study of possible church reform and renewal by what at the time was by far the largest, richest, and best educated of the Orthodox particular churches. At the same time, the Council's peculiar way of combining the idea of *sobornost*, an infatuation with schemes for representative democracy, and an ecclesiology of the Highest Authority makes its ecclesiology slightly ambiguous.[18] This ambiguity is reflected in the main points of emphasis in the 1955 Statute: (1) A desire for conciliarity and lay participation on all levels, but (2) in fact a preoccupation with the central authority in the church and relative neglect of "lower" levels. One further characteristic might also be noted: a sometimes oppressive legalese, emphasizing "rights," "obligations," etc., and a tendency to get bogged down in details, to provide for the least contingency. All this is epitomized by Article I of the 1955 Statute: After an initial section dealing briefly with the name of the Church (the counterpart to Article I of the 1971 Statute), section 2 reads: "Supreme Authority. The supreme legislative, administrative, and judicial authority within the Church is the All-American Sobor. The Metropolitan and the organs of church administration report to the All-American Sobor"; and sections 3–20, going on for 13 pages, discuss the Sobor in great detail.

The 1971 Statute modifies the 1955 Statute in a number of ways. For example, there is an effort to soften the prevailing legal tone, to encourage a more theological approach to church membership and life. Hence occasional words of exhortation, like "The delegates [to the Diocesan Assembly] are encouraged to receive the Holy Mysteries of the Church, manifesting their membership in the One Body of Christ and their commitment to live and act accordingly" (Article VII Sec. 1). This continues a process already

[18]The dilemma is pointed out by J. Meyendorff, "What is an Ecumenical Council?" 270–71: "But were the principles of democratic 'representation' of the episcopate, the clergy, and the laity, as distinct 'classes' of Christians, truly adequate from the ecclesiological point of view? Does not the early Christian church structure—small dioceses, *local* eucharistic conciliarity of the bishop and the presbyterium, full lay responsibility in the life of the local eucharistic community—imply that provincial and 'ecumenical' councils are councils of bishops alone? However, since 'local conciliarity' does not exist, is not *sobornost* at the higher level—provincial or ecumenical—a valid (though possibly temporary) substitute?"

underway in the 1960s, when the original 1955 article on the parish was completely rewritten, putting it into its present form. But there are also important changes in emphasis:

(1) The All-American Sobor, now the All-American Council, remains an important element in church structure, but it has been shorn of its former pre-eminence. It has been shifted from Article I to Article III, after discussion of the Holy Synod of Bishops, and its initial description is relatively modest: "The highest legislative and administrative authority within the Church is the All-American Council. (Cf. Article III, Section 12)." (The article in question deals with approval by the hierarchy of all resolutions.)

(2) While conciliarity/*sobonost*—lay and presbyteral representation, participation and coresponsibility—continues, with some modification, on this "highest" level, the emphasis of the 1971 Statute has shifted to conciliarity on the diocesan level. While the 1955 Statute had provided for a diocesan assembly and a diocesan council, it devoted little attention to them (less than two pages for the diocesan assembly), and their role in actual church affairs was often minimal. This has changed in the 1971 Statute. The structure and workings of both bodies are more clearly delineated, and their important role in the management of diocesan affairs (e.g., nomination by the diocesan assembly of candidates for election as diocesan bishop—Article VI, Section 10) is stressed.

(3) This interest in diocesan assembly and council is part of a larger effort to restore the diocese as the fundamental unit of church structure. In the 1955 Statute, the diocese "is a part of the Church"; now it is "the basic church body." This verbal shift is accompanied by a number of concrete provisions intended to restore the integrity of the diocese as *local church*. This is seen above all in the role assigned to the diocesan bishop. Formerly the diocesan bishop, though defined as "the head of the diocese," in fact had little authority in his diocese. Candidates for holy orders had to be presented to the metropolitan; likewise applications for establishment and dissolution of parishes. Appointment of priests to parishes in the diocese was subject to the approval of the metropolitan.[19] And in cases

---

[19] On all these points compare the 1971 Statute's Article VI, Section 4, which places no such restrictions by the metropolitan on the diocesan bishop.

of disagreement with decisions of the diocesan assembly, the matter was referred to the Bishops' Sobor. All these limitations, typical byproducts of the old ecclesiology of Highest Authority, arise ultimately from a separation of the power of orders and the power of jurisdiction. According to the 1955 Statute, the diocesan bishop "has the fullest hierarchical power in matters of doctrine, morals, worship, and pastoral care," i.e., in magisterial and sacramental matters.[20] But he obviously has no such *plenitudo potestatis* in matters of jurisdiction, for that depends on the Highest Authority. Now this distinction between the sacramental and the juridical, though axiomatic for the West and for the westernized East, is foreign to the eastern canonical tradition. The government of the Church and the worship and sanctification of the faithful are linked so intimately that at times a change of the one has had as its natural corollary a change of the other. In Muscovite Russia, for example, a new patriarch would be consecrated *even if he already was a bishop*: superior jurisdiction demanded what amounted to a new sacrament. On the other hand, a bishop without jurisdiction was a grave anomaly which, though tolerated at times, was given no theoretical justification. The 1971 Statute tries to restore this traditional unitary understanding of authority in the Church by concrete measures designed to make the bishop truly the head of the diocese in all aspects of its life, including the juridical. "By virtue of his episcopal consecration and canonical appointment to his diocese, the diocesan bishop possesses full hierarchical authority within his diocese" (Article VI, Section 4). Period. And by restoring the bishop to his place in the diocese, the 1971 Statute has helped to restore the diocese to something more closely approximating the Ignatian vision of the local church, to make it at least "the basic church body" and not just a "part."

(4) In line with this emphasis on the integrity of the bishop and his diocese is a corresponding re-evaluation of the place of the metropolitan. "Among the bishops of the Church, the Metropolitan enjoys primacy, being the first among equals. He is the diocesan bishop of one of the dioceses of the Church and bears the title, 'Metropolitan of All America and Canada'" (Article IV, Section 1). His primacy consists in part in providing

---

[20]Compare the 1971 Statute's Article VII, Section 15, which drops this provision.

a focus for the unity of the particular church[21] and in part in initiating and presiding over activities affecting the whole.[22] Excluded is interference in the internal affairs of another bishop's diocese; i.e., his former rights of approval and of visitation of other dioceses have been eliminated.

(5) A final word is in order concerning the Holy Synod. While its description—"the supreme canonical authority in the Church"—suggests the ecclesiology of Highest Authority, the Holy Synod's competence is roughly that of the provincial synod of bishops in fourth-century canonical texts, i.e., limited to appeals and to matters affecting the whole. Thus the synod is intended to be less an authority *over* the bishops than an expression of the authority *of* the bishops. It is also important to note that this authority of the bishops in synod is tied not to their membership in a certain *ordo* but to their position as heads of local churches. "The Holy Synod includes, as voting members, all the diocesan bishops of the Church" (Article 11, Section 2); auxiliary and titular bishops, admitted as voting members to the Bishops' Sobor under the 1955 Statute, are excluded. Again, the intimate link between the juridical order and the sacramental order is stressed.

Such are the leading tendencies of the 1971 Statute of the OCA. They indicate a deliberate effort to remodel the concrete structures of a particular church along the lines suggested by an ecclesiology of the local church, to recapture something of the vision of the Church that one finds in the fathers and the early canons. To be sure, this effort has not been uniformly successful. At points there are inconsistencies, born of hesitancy to discard the familiar old ecclesiology of the Highest Authority too abruptly.[23] But even though the Statute may not be a definitive expression of Orthodox ecclesiology, it at least demonstrates that "the concrete

---

[21]E.g., by consecrating and distributing the Holy Chrism and by providing the diocesan bishops with the relics necessary for consecration of altars and antimensia (Article IV, Section 2a, b).

[22]E.g., convening the All-American Council, presiding over it, and promulgating its decisions, and convening and presiding over meetings of the Holy Synod of Bishops and the Metropolitan Council (Article IV, Section c, d). This compares closely to the canons of the Council of Antioch dealing with provincial organization.

[23]For example, the metropolitan is elected by the All-American Council (Article IV, Section 4). Procedure would more closely correspond to that of the early church were he elected in the same manner as the other diocesan bishops (described in Article VI, Section 10).

structural organization of the local church," as we meet it here and now in twentieth-century America, need not be hopelessly at variance with the Church of Genesis and Revelation.

Orthodox Unity in America
New Beginnings?

John Meyendorff

St Vladimir's Theological Quarterly 35.1 (1991): 5–19

WRITING TO POPE DAMASUS a few short years before his death, St Basil the Great describes the sadly chaotic state of the Church a few decades after the "Constantinian peace," i.e., the recognition of the Church by the Roman empire, which gave Christians all the opportunities to pray, to teach, to bear witness to society at large, and to organize Church life as they saw fit. Freedom came in AD 312; but by AD 375, although the Arian heresy was largely overcome by the work of St Athanasius and the Cappadocian fathers, bishops were still fighting bishops; the churches of Alexandria and Rome were supporting—against the Cappadocian fathers—a "super-Orthodox" (so-called "Old Nicaean") group, which pretended alone to preserve the true faith of St Athanasius; and all were soliciting state intervention in Church affairs to aid their cause. Yet it is precisely that period in Church history that we Orthodox consider as the "classic" period, the period of the fathers, the time when our faith in the Holy Trinity was formulated in a definitive way, precisely by St Basil, who expressed his despair of ever seeing ecclesiastical peace and who, indeed, died in 379, before seeing the fruits of his efforts.

The comforting side of all this is that the Church of God is obviously not kept alive by Church politics, but by the power of the Spirit, and that if there is a Church today, in spite of all the scandals of history, this is obvious prior proof of the Church's *divine* origin, which cannot be destroyed by human weakness, not even by the "gates of hell . . ." (Mt 16.18). But the example of the fathers, who were the instruments of the Spirit, shows that the Spirit works through human efforts (this is the meaning of the Orthodox doctrine of "synergy" between divine grace and human freedom), and that it is not futile to keep struggling within the boundaries of the historical Church, which—as an institution—always remains "human," i.e., limited, but also *sent into the world* for its salvation. There would be no hope without the divine promise that, at the end, God will be "all in all," i.e., without eschatology, which we experience each time we celebrate the Eucharist. But precisely because we *are being given* that experience—in the world and for the world—we are also called to make it visible and real in the empirical existence of the Christian community, i.e., in the Church *as it is historically*, rejecting the temptation of pride, of sectarian or individualistic separatism and fragmentation, knowing that the ultimate victory will not be ours, but the Lord's.

There are many reasons for "human" despair, when one considers the state of affairs of Orthodoxy in America, especially in terms of canonical unity. In 1905—i.e., 86 years ago—Archbishop Tikhon took that unity for granted, and publicly defined the principles which should preside over its realization: unity of the Church and pluralism of immigrant national traditions. More sweepingly still, in 1921, Ecumenical Patriarch Meletios, in his enthronement address, spoke of an "American Orthodox Church" in the making. Today, our hierarchs are generally much more reserved on that matter than their predecessors. The Standing Conference of Bishops, created in 1960, never even succeeded (although it tried!) to have Orthodox unity placed on the agenda of pan-Orthodox meetings! It remained itself an *ad hoc* consultative body with many illogical aspects in its structure and activity. In 1970, one Church—the Russian—finally took canonical action, and established the Autocephalous Orthodox Church in America, which basically followed the model proposed by archbishop Tikhon in 1905. There was now a Church in America, for Americans, but national traditions were preserved wherever needed. Russian, Ukrainian, and other Slavic traditions were maintained in many parishes, and Romanians, Bulgarians, and Albanians were organized into distinct dioceses, with their bishops having full voting rights in the Holy Synod.

I will not speak here of the substance of the debate between the patriarchates of Constantinople and Moscow which followed the establishment of autocephaly,[1] except to say that the autocephaly was defined as the *beginning*, and not the end of a process; that the Russian Church, although it possessed canonical priority in America, as having been in charge of territorial dioceses existing here from 1840 to 1921, could not and did not challenge other churches, but required from the newly established autocephaly to respect their rights; that those who criticized and rejected the autocephaly did not propose any alternative plan for Orthodox unity, insisting simply on the *status quo*, claiming that Orthodox Americans, particularly Greek Americans, were not "ready" or "mature" enough for either autocephaly or unity. There was also the debate as to who has the right to establish new autocephalous churches.

After twenty years, it may be time for a new beginning. Indeed, if some of the positions taken in 1970 remain the same, many elements of the problem are being modified by the historical developments of our time. This seems to justify a new look at the *norms* which belong to the holy Tradition of the Church, at the *obstacles* standing in the way of their implementation, and at concrete—and possibly innovative—*solutions* which must be considered, if one seeks concrete results.

1. The Norms

The norms are so well known that there is no—actually there cannot be any—disagreement within Orthodoxy as to their substance. The problem lies in the implementation.

The holy Church is a new unity of people in Christ. Divided by sin and by the "powers of this world," human beings are offered to enter through baptism—i.e., through death and resurrection in Christ—into one Church, as anticipation of the kingdom of God. The New Testament teaches us that salvation is a matter of personal decision and free choice—one is baptized upon a profession of personal faith in Christ—but also that life in Christ is

---

[1] The full text of the letters exchanged on that occasion as well as the *Tomos* of Autocephaly itself, have been published, in English translation, in *St Vladimir's Theological Quarterly* 15.1–2 (1971): 42–80 (and in a separate booklet entitled *Autocephaly*). This is the only publication including *both sides'* views. Other publications were deliberately one sided. [The *dossier* that the author is referring to is reprinted in the *Appendix* of this volume.—*Ed.*]

communion and *community*, or *ekklēsia*: a gathering of people called *from* the world to share a new life, where there is "neither Jew nor Greek, neither slave nor free, neither male nor female," but where "all are one in Christ Jesus" (Gal 3.28). To become a Christian does not mean simply to adopt some ethical norms, or to acquire new personal convictions, or to become spiritually or esoterically initiated into some private club. Such alternatives all existed at the time of Christ and the apostles, but they were not accepted as valid. We learn that "all the faithful were together and had all things in common; they sold their properties and their belongings and divided the proceeds among all, according to each person's need; they remained daily together in the temple breaking bread at home . . ." (Acts 2.45–46).

Although this description of the early Christian community can be realized literally today only in monastic communities, the model itself points to the nature of the Christian faith, which always implied that those who accepted it became "members of each other" (Eph 4.25; cf. St Paul's comments on the body of Christ in 1 Cor 12.12–27), and that this "corporal" unity was not simply a psychological or moral state of mind, but a *gift of God*, implied in baptism and realized in the Eucharist. It is because this basic teaching of the New Testament is not taken seriously, that it is often so difficult to make people understand why the concrete realization of Church unity is so crucial both for our own salvation and for a consistent witness to those outside.

But our baptism does not imply only that we are taken "out of the world." The community, forming Christ's body, does not require physical withdrawal from reality, from history, from human society at large. Although the particular monastic path of withdrawal has been blessed and acknowledged as fully legitimate *for some*, the Church as a whole is being sent into the world to perform a *mission*; Christ was *sent* into the world by the Father, and he also *sends* his disciples; and their unity in Christ is what makes their mission believable (Jn 17.18, 21). So disunity is sin indeed, and also a betrayal of Christ and of his mission.

Do we know how to go about concretely securing unity? The New Testament contains few practical guidelines, because the early Christian community was supposed to understand and live up to the norms spontaneously. Did it always in reality? Certainly not. St Paul is indignant at the community in Corinth, where Christians of Jewish origin would not share the Eucharist with converts from paganism, and created their own separate community (we would say "jurisdiction"). "Each one of you say," he writes, "I belong to Paul, and I belong to Apollos, and I belong to Cephas, and I belong to Christ. Is Christ divided? Was Paul crucified for you, or were you baptized in the name of Paul?" (1 Cor 1.12–13).

So there is no need to idealize the early church. It faced some of the problems we face today in realizing concretely the unity of the Christian community *in each place*. But we can learn much by considering the means which were used to overcome the temptation of divisiveness. Indeed, if we believe in *Tradition*—as we say we do—the experience of the apostles and the fathers is obligatory for us. We simply have no right to reject it, although we can and we must see how the guidelines which they provided can and must be applicable to *our* conditions, in *our* time. Our link with Tradition, in this respect, is the *canons*.

Taken as a whole, the Orthodox canonical tradition is not a "juridical system" or a code. It contains texts which today are inapplicable, or in contradiction with others. Those who attempt to use canons as Protestant fundamentalists use Scriptures, ignore how much they themselves are influenced by Western approaches which absolutize legalism and institutional structures. Canons need interpretation in the light of Tradition as a whole, and their interpreters must first of all acquire that mind of the Church, without which individual canonical texts are often meaningless. It remains, however, that with regard to some basic theological, ecclesiological, and moral principles there is clear canonical consensus, and it is possible to understand why this consensus exists.

Such a consensus exists on two points which are of crucial importance for our problem: 1) the Church must be one in each place; 2) the office of the episcopate is particularly responsible for realizing and witnessing to the unity of the true Church locally, regionally, and universally. Both of these points are obviously not only "canonical," but theological, ecclesiological, and spiritual.

"Unity in each place" is, of course, a flexible concept. A "place" can be a house, a village, a city area, a country. With modern means of transportation and communication, with communities organized at workplaces, etc., there are various ways in which one can define a "place." What is involved here is the desire, the readiness and the ability of Orthodox Christians to share a *common* sacramental and community life with their *neighbors* on the basis of no other criterion and principle than a common faith, belonging to the same Church, hoping for the same salvation, sharing in the same anticipation of the Kingdom of God. This is, after all, exactly what St Paul meant when he was wondering, writing to the Corinthians, whether "Christ was divided" in Corinth. If the readiness and desire to share one's faith exists, practical accommodations are always possible to meet difficulties, such as the absence of a common language (on that, see the section below on "obstacles").

But the canons are unanimous in requiring local unity, and place particular responsibility on the bishops. In each place, the local church is headed by a bishop, originally the only celebrant of the Eucharist, image of Christ, and center of unity. "There may not be two bishops in a city," proclaims the First Ecumenical Council of Nicaea (Canon 8). And, quite logically, the bishops (who were elected for life by the clergy and laity of their particular church) "are not to go beyond their own diocese to churches lying outside of their bounds, nor bring confusion on the churches. . . . And let not bishops go beyond their diocese for ordinations and any other ecclesiastical ministrations, unless they be invited" (Second Ecumenical Council, Canon 2).

But the "one bishop in each place" principle does not mean that each local church is isolated and self-sufficient. Canons require that bishops of each province meet in synod twice a year (First Ecumenical Council, Canons 4 and 5). The regular meetings are necessary for solving common problems, but particularly to fill vacant sees; for no bishop can ordain another bishop alone, particularly not his own successor. Conciliarity is therefore a basic principle. Within each church, the bishop heads the community together with his presbyters (who are compared to the apostles by St Ignatius of Antioch), and the affairs of the province are directed by the bishops together. Among the bishops of a province, one is a "primate," often designated as "metropolitan." His personal approval is necessary for the election of all new bishops, and the bishops are forbidden to act without his knowledge, just as he too does not act without theirs (Apostolic Canon 34). He therefore coordinates and sanctions episcopal conciliarity on the level of the province.

On the universal level, the emperor (at least in the early Byzantine period) acted as coordinator, not by himself, but together with five "patriarchs" (the so-called "pentarchy"). With the disappearance of the Western empire, the bishop of Rome, always recognized as the first among patriarchs, developed a self-sufficiency which would eventually lead to schism. The ecumenical patriarch of Constantinople, who had been granted "privileges of honor after the bishop of Rome" (Second Ecumenical Council, Canon 3), became the recognized coordinator, as "first bishop" within Orthodoxy. His actual powers, however, varied from period to period. Before the fall of Byzantium (1453), he acted in close coordination with the emperor. Under the Turkish regime, he became the political head of the entire Christian *millet* of the Ottoman empire, which gave him a *de facto* control over the other Eastern patriarchs. Russia developed quite independently, as did the independent kingdom of Georgia and its ancient patriarchate.

Responsible for unity locally, a bishop also shares in the universal episcopate: he is not bishop by himself, but only because he is in communion and conciliar cooperation with the world episcopate of the Church. All this is symbolized by the so-called "diptychs": at the liturgy a local bishop mentions the head of the province or of the autocephalous church to which he belongs, while the head of the church mentions all the other heads by order of precedence.

2. The Obstacles

There is no doubt that the strange and utterly abnormal situation of Orthodoxy in America today is, first of all, rooted in ecclesiastical nationalism—a relatively recent phenomenon in Orthodoxy and a legacy of modern secularism.

By "nationalism" I do not mean the fully legitimate development of national cultures which characterized the expansion of Christianity in the Middle East, and later from Orthodox Byzantium, throughout Eastern Europe. The use of vernacular languages in worship—a contrast with the linguistically uniform Latin church of the West—created "national churches." The Christian faith became part of culture, and neither Islam nor modern Communism were able to uproot it. However, modern nationalism, resulting from the French Revolution and the "revival of nations," has provoked a very subtle but decisive reversal of priorities. Instead of the previous situation, when the Church made use of culture to instill its influence on society, secular states, secular societies, and secular politicians began making use of the Church for their own purposes. This was the case in Russia following the reforms of Peter the Great; in Greece, after the Greek Revolution of 1821, and in the other Balkan countries, as they liberated themselves from the Turkish yoke.

In the past, innumerable wars, political changes and competition between kingdoms and empires divided the Balkans, but the unity of the Church in each place was never destroyed. In 1860–70, however, the truly shameful tribal struggle between Greeks and Bulgarians led to the establishment of two competing churches, divided on the same territories along ethnic and linguistic lines. Fortunately—and although the responsibilities of the schism were obviously split—the new heresy of "phyletism" was formally defined as "the establishment of particular churches, accepting members of the same nationality and refusing the members of other nationalities, being administered by pastors of the same nationality," and as "*a coexistence of nationally defined churches* (italics mine—J.M.) of the same faith, but independent from each other, in the same city and village."[2]

This clearly defined and condemned "heresy" is, of course, precisely what exists in America today. And what is even more deplorable is that this situation is considered by many—many Orthodox included—as normal. Eastern Christianity is an "ethnic" faith of Greeks, Russians, Serbians

---

[2] Greek text of the decrees quoted in Maximos of Sardis, *Τὸ Οἰκουμενικὸν Πατριαρχεῖον ἐν τῇ Ὀρθοδόξῳ Ἐκκλησίᾳ* [The Ecumenical Patriarchate in the Orthodox Church] (Thessaloniki, 1972), 323–35.

and others. Each of these nationalities has "its own" church, which may be "in communion" with the other Orthodox churches, just as, today, the various Protestant denominations are "in communion" with each other. Many believe that, with Americanization, these will be integrated into mainstream Protestant denominationalism.

The mass media emphasize the most exotic, the most foreign and, to most Americans, most unusual aspects of Orthodox public behavior. Thus, the main obstacle to unity is the ecclesiastical nationalism which—although it is originally rooted in a positive and holy concern for integration of Christianity into culture—has *de facto* become a form of unenlightened and careless tribalism, incompatible with the Orthodox and catholic understanding of the Church.

Curiously—but perhaps fortunately—the Orthodox actually look much worse in the public image they present than they are in reality. There are so many mission-oriented parishes, so many areas where Orthodox communities are really acting together as one church, and—even more importantly—so many Orthodox in America who share the same truly catholic vision of the faith and experience of the Eucharist, that the caricature which has become familiar to outsiders is very often quite wrong.

Related to these facts is one approach to the problem, which is often being used by the mother churches, when they condescend to discuss the American situation: multiplicities of jurisdictions and ethnicity are expressions of what is called the Orthodox *diaspora*. One is told therefore to look for solutions of a "diaspora problem." I strongly believe that, although this approach might be applicable temporarily to some immigrant groups for empirical reasons, the overall situation in America lies much beyond an "immigrant" or diaspora problem. Furthermore, and quite importantly, it is *theologically wrong* to apply the concept of "diaspora" to the Church.

Diaspora is a biblical concept applied to Jews living outside the promised land of Israel. It appears in the New Testament (Jn 7.35; Jas 1.1; 1 Pet 1.1) with exactly that sense, but is it *never* used—or ever could be used—in canonical texts or any Christian ecclesiological context. Indeed, for the people of the New Testament, the promised land is the New Jerusalem on high. This is precisely why the members of the Church of Christ are "at home" and in no "diaspora," in every time and place where they celebrate the divine liturgy, because the New Jerusalem is manifested everywhere. Living out of one's own country might be painful, but political or economic emigration is not, as such, an ecclesiological dimension. In the canonical tradition, there is actually one precedent: the Orthodox inhabitants of Cyprus—an autocephalous church of ancient times— had to be relocated in the Hellespont, near the sea of Marmara, following the invasion of their island by the Arabs. The Council in Trullo (or Sixth Ecumenical, Canon 39) made a special provision in order to avoid destroying the territorial principle and to respect the rights of Cyprus: the local metropolitan (of Cyzicus) was submitted to the Cypriot archbishop who received the title of Justinianopolis, and who was also given "the rights of Constantinople," i.e., the right to ordain metropolitans within his new territory (a right which in the Hellespont previously belonged to the ecumenical patriarch in accordance with Canon 28 of Chalcedon). So there were still no overlapping jurisdictions.

Shall we make the intellectual and spiritual effort to get out of our truly intolerable American situation, where competing Orthodox metropolitans and archbishops, acting as ethnarchs, are in fact betraying their divinely-established duty and right to be the guardian of. Church unity?

But the application of the notion of *diaspora* to America does not always imply theological and canonical meaning. It simply implies that the Orthodox of America are away from their natural "home" and should therefore organize their church life on a temporary basis, until they return to "their" country. Such an approach truly verges on the ridiculous, except, of course, for an always present minority of recent immigrants, who do, indeed, need pastoral care and respect for their needs and customs. But, for the vast majority of the Orthodox in America, America is their permanent country. Most of them are children, grandchildren, or great-grandchildren of immigrants who came here of their own free will and in order to stay. In any case, when the Russian Church was establishing its diocese before 1921, first in Alaska, then in San Francisco, New York, and Canada, the idea was to organize a permanent canonical Church life for the citizens of this country and of Canada. Furthermore and most importantly, the Church

Orthodox Unity in America

is missionary. Today it includes a very large proportion of converts—more than half of the bishops of the OCA, many priests, half of the student body at St Vladimir's Seminary, and innumerable laity in many parishes of all jurisdictions. How can they possibly be considered as *diaspora*?

Overcoming all the psychological, intellectual, pseudo-canonical, and political obstacles, we need to establish our united Church on a solid, permanent, and truly canonical basis.

3. The Solutions

In order to establish the Orthodox Church on this continent as a canonically united body, two procedures are "on the table," officially or unofficially.

The first one was spelled out by archbishop Tikhon in 1905 and formally proposed in 1970—for those who wanted it, solicited it, and accepted it—by the Church of Russia: an autocephalous Church in America, canonically headed by a synod of bishops, where various national groups and traditions are represented, and an inner structure which 1) meets the needs of these ethnic groups, and 2) follows Orthodox principles of conciliarity, and clergy-laity responsibility, including participation in the nomination of candidates for the episcopacy, to be canonically elected by the synod. As a churchman and a theologian, I do believe that this solution is canonically correct and pastorally logical. The experience of the autocephalous Orthodox Church in America during the past twenty years shows that it is also practical, although I do not claim that all things within the OCA are always done in a consistent way. The major problem is that only part of the Orthodox leadership in America supported the autocephaly and that the Ecumenical Patriarchate opposed it.

The second procedure would consist in canonical unity under the Ecumenical Patriarchate. Ecumenical Patriarch Dimitrios seems to have publicly proposed it. Speaking in Washington last summer, he mentioned that America belongs to the patriarchate's "ecclesiastical jurisdiction." Obviously there is a matter of principle, not a historical fact, which is implied here, since before 1921, the only ecclesiastical jurisdiction represented by bishops in North America was that of the Church of Russia.

The existence of these two points of view suggest (to me, at least) the following observations:

1. There is the eminently positive fact that unity is the avowed goal on both sides, and that—as could also be noted in the exchange of letters between Moscow and Constantinople following the autocephaly of 1970—the most eminent authorities in Orthodoxy are not happy with the present situation and consider the return to territorial unity as a necessity. They would cease to be Orthodox if they believed otherwise.

2. Although they follow different policies, these same authorities show flexibility (and charity). The autocephalous Orthodox Church intends to remain in full sacramental communion and canonical relations with all the other autocephalous churches (as required by the Tomos of 1970). It recognizes—and even solicits—a leadership of the Ecumenical Patriarchate in pan-Orthodox affairs. It participates in the Standing Conference of Bishops, presided by the exarch of the Ecumenical Patriarchate. The latter, on the other hand, also maintains communion and canonical relations, not only with the OCA, but also with the other jurisdictions (Antiochian, Serbian, Romanian, Bulgarian), which should clearly be seen as uncanonical also, if Constantinople's claims for jurisdiction in America are taken seriously. It is obvious, therefore, that all sides recognize that a solution requires pan-Orthodox agreement and cannot be reached unilaterally. World Orthodoxy does not know an authority, which, like the papacy, would be entitled to impose a solution by decree.

Taking for granted, therefore, that the procedure to follow should involve pan-Orthodox consensus, the goal to be reached is a Church *united and American*. United—for the obvious reasons discussed above. *American*—not in a neo-nationalistic or neo-ethnic sense, but a church for Americans and in America, necessarily reflecting the pluralism and the diversity of American society, offering Orthodoxy not only to Greeks or Russians, but to all Americans, including Hispanics, African-Americans, Amerindians, and others. The Ecumenical Patriarchate, particularly, should realize this challenge fully, if it wants to play the role which belongs to it by tradition and by right, and not present the image of being only "Greek." Some new attitudes and emphasis in that positive direction were fortunately apparent during the recent visit of Patriarch Dimitrios. Movement in that direction by Constantinople would imply change in style and structures. At present, the patriarchate is already willing to accept non-Greek ethnic groups into its jurisdiction, but without the establishment of regional canonical unity. Within the OCA, the bishops heading Bulgarian, Romanian and Albanian groups are voting members of the Holy Synod. Within the Ecumenical Patriarchate, such bishops (like the heads of Carpatho-Russian and Ukrainian dioceses in the USA) are given Greek episcopal titles *in partibus infidelium* (i.e., of non-existing ancient sees) as is the practice in the Greek church for auxiliary bishops (and they are indeed listed as auxiliaries in Greek reference books), without becoming members of the synod of the [Greek] Archdiocese of America. This gives them great latitude and independence; but it is canonically quite irregular, because in a sense it is the same old "phyletism" with the ecumenical patriarch's endorsement.

I mention this fact not by way of any negative criticism, but for the sake of discussion, and also in order to suggest that one of the most essential features of Orthodox unity must be an episcopal synod including *all* bishops, as well as other organs of administration, with participation of clergy and laity of all groups. We must follow Orthodox canonical models, and not the papal model, which allows—as we all know—parallel jurisdictions everywhere (e.g., the Uniate diocese in America), with coordination *only* in Rome, because Rome and not the local church is the criterion of unity in Roman Catholicism. For us Orthodox, there must be *one* Church in America—not many churches, each controlled by a faraway foreign center, which, in the case of Constantinople (unlike Rome), can only be rather nominal and uninvolved.

There is no doubt that the American situation is historically unprecedented. It is therefore impossible to find in the canonical tradition specific texts giving specific solutions. We must therefore look for new ways to realize what is absolute, permanent, and unchangeable in the nature of the Church: Her conciliar unity in each place. For instance, it might be of great help if we could stop using terms and categories which had meaning—sometimes different meanings—at other times, and look for practical solutions which are in conformity with the need for regional and universal unity, and are not to be identified in somewhat outdated and ambiguous categories (like "diaspora," "autocephaly," "dependence," etc.).

Let us consider, for instance, the role of the Ecumenical Patriarchate. On the one hand, it possesses a territory (which, besides Turkey, includes northern Greece, Crete, and the Greek islands); but, in some of this territory (northern Greece) it has, for practical reasons, transmitted its right to the Church of Greece. On the other hand, the patriarchate has its universal "primacy" and functions of pan-Orthodox leadership, whose exact definition is quite vague. All this shows that the institution of the patriarchate exercises its canonical and moral powers in a variety of ways. Can there not be a special and new way in which it would play a role in securing order in America, without giving the impression of a simple transfer of jurisdiction from one ethnic patriarchate to another over the various groups of American Orthodoxy?

Furthermore, the term "autocephaly" also has a variety of meanings. In Byzantine times, archbishops, who were not dependent on any metropolitan but were appointed directly by Constantinople, were called "autocephalous." On the other hand, in a well-known text by the canonist Balsamon, all metropolitans were "autocephalous" inasmuch as they were canonically elected by their own synods. Eventually, the term became—quite unfortunately—identified with national independence, and served to justify nationalism and "phyletism." Even today the distinction between an "autonomous" and an "autocephalous" church is a very fine one: thus, the church of Czechoslovakia is termed "autocephalous" by some and "autonomous" by others.

Why not think of a "United Orthodox Church of America," canonically governed by a synod of all its ruling bishops, electing its own chairman (cf. the proceedings existing in the Roman Catholic Conference of Bishops) and confirming elections of bishops with, however, an exarch of the Ecumenical Patriarchate (who might or might not be a bishop) exercising a measure of control and coordination? If they so desire, other patriarchs could also have such "exarchs" in charge of their mother churches' interests and projects in America.

Of course, the simple establishment of a joint, fully independent church for all Americans—as the existing OCA, and on the basis of the *Tomos* of 1970—would be simpler; but it does also require pan-Orthodox consensus, which so far is lacking. Furthermore, involvement of the Ecumenical Patriarchate in securing Orthodox unity is indeed needed. The system suggested above would secure it. The consultation leading to such a decision might be a difficult process because our ecclesiastical procedures are cumbersome. But I am convinced that the vast majority of our priests and laity—once they become aware of the issue—would support it enthusiastically.

Let us not lose faith, hope, and love.

Accession to Autocephaly

Archbishop Peter L'Huillier

St Vladimir's Theological Quarterly 37.4 (1993): 267–304

1

THE LEGITIMATE WAY for a church entity to become canonically emancipated from the tutelage of a primatial see is a topic which, from the fourth century onward, has often raised controversies. Now more than ever, it appears at first glance that opposite standpoints on this issue can hardly be reconciled. Beyond any doubt, if such a problem has never been clearly elicited in the past and remains a source of disagreement, it is because neither ecclesiological presuppositions nor historical evidence provides an incontrovertible answer. Stating this fact, however, is not tantamount to admitting the impossibility of a solution based on canonical principles, Actually, this is not the only problem in the area of church order for which our written canon law does not provide a clearly articulated answer.[1] If the problem of autocephaly is so controversial, undoubtedly this stems from its emotional connotations and almost always involves extrinsic factors.

Why have we mentioned the fourth century as when, in an embryonic form, problems about what would later be called "autocephaly" started looming into sight? Doubtless, this phenomenon ought to be related to the evolution in the administrative structures of the Roman Empire during the reign of Emperor Diocletian (284–305).[2] Such a process had an impact on Church organization. Already in early Christianity one can discern a trend favoring close relationships among the churches of the same province.[3]

---

[1] For example, this is the case with matrimonial legislation.
[2] A. H. M. Jones, *The Later Roman Empire*, vol. 1 (Baltimore, MD: Johns Hopkins University Press, 1986), 42–52.
[3] Fr Dvornik, *Byzantium and the Roman Primacy* (New York: Fordham University Press, 1979), 27–39.

One must, however, avoid taking an anachronistic approach to the pre-Constantinian period. On this issue, the actual situation toward the middle of the third century is accurately described by St Cyprian of Carthage:

> Inasmuch as the bond of concord exists and the indissoluble fidelity to the unity of the catholic Church is maintained, each bishop determines himself his action and management according to his will, but he will be accountable to the Lord.[4]

This statement does not express the particular standpoint of St Cyprian; it reflects an understanding shared throughout the catholic Church at that time.[5] The thinking of Cyprian, however, should not be misinterpreted. The bishop of Carthage did not support the total independence of each local church. He conceived this internal autonomy within the framework of the catholic Church. Moreover, he strongly favored episcopal collegiality realized by bishops' synods.[6]

For church organization, the most consequential administrative reform initiated by Emperor Diocletian was the multiplication of provincial entities. In their reduced territorial format, communications became much easier, Thus, insofar as persecution did not prevent such a move, bishops' meetings in a civil province started taking place on a regular schedule. The Council of Nicaea (325) took for granted the coincidence between Church units and civil provinces, albeit with a few exceptions based on ancient customs (ἀρχαῖα ἔθη).[7] The acceptance of the principle of territorial accommodation implied the preeminence of the bishop of each provincial capital. According to Nicene legislation, this personage has the exclusive right to confirm the election of the bishops in the province.[8] Nevertheless, it is likely that already at that time the leading bishop held other

---

[4]Epist. 60.21.2, Saint Cyprien, *Correspondence*, Texte établi et traduit par le chanoine Bayard, tome 2, deuxième édition (Paris : Les Belles Lettres, 1961), 144.

[5]Othmar Heggelbacher, *Geschichte des frühchristlichen Kirchenrechts* (Freiburg/Schweiz: Universitätsverlag, 1974), 36–56.

[6]S. M. Walker, *The Churchmanship of St Cyprian* (Richmond, VA: John Knox Press, 1969), 336–60.

[7]Canon 6.

[8]Canons 4 and 6.

responsibilities. These are spelled out by the council of Antioch which, in all probability, took place about AD 330, i.e., five years after Nicaea.⁹ Mentioning the prerogatives of the bishop of the metropolis, the Fathers of Antioch referred to "the ancient rule" (τὸν ἀρχαῖον . . . κανόνα).¹⁰ This specified that this bishop undertakes the care (φροντίδα) of the whole province. He has precedence of honor and coordinates the activities of the bishops of the province but without interfering with their jurisdictional authority (ἐξουσίαν).¹¹ Bishops cannot be elected without his presence.¹² He also presides over the provincial synod.¹³ Furthermore, allowing clerics to appeal to the emperor falls within his competency.¹⁴ In the eastern part of the Roman Empire, this primate was called either "the bishop of the metropolis" or "metropolitan bishop" or simply "metropolitan." In the West, during the fourth and fifth centuries, terminology remained in flux because provincial organization was less developed than in the East.¹⁵

According to the oft-quoted remark of Balsamon in his commentary on Canon 2 of the Second Ecumenical Council (381), by that time every ecclesiastical province was autocephalous.¹⁶ Autocephalous status denotes only the right for a church entity freely to elect its leading bishop. Such an election and consecration (χειροτονία [*cheirotonia*]) does not need further confirmation by any higher authority.¹⁷ As we have seen above, the Council of Nicaea had taken for granted the principle of territorial accommodation, save for the case of Alexandria in reference to the situation of Rome and Antioch. Both exceptions are justified by the existence of ancient customs. Undoubtedly in the original intent of the lawgiver,

---

⁹See our article, "Origines et développement de l'ancienne collection canonique grecque," *Messager de l'Exarchat* 93–96 (1976): 59.

¹⁰This phrasing suggests that the Fathers of Antioch traced the origin of this customary rule to long before the enactment of the Nicene canons.

¹¹Canon 9.

¹²Canon 19.

¹³Canon 20.

¹⁴Canon 11.

¹⁵W. M. Plöchl, "Geschichte des Kirchenrechts," Band 1, *Zweite erweiterte Auflage* (Wien-München: Verlag Herold, 1960), 157–59.

¹⁶Rhallis and Potlis, II, 171.

¹⁷See our article, "Problems Concerning Autocephaly," *The Greek Orthodox Theological Review* 24 (1979): 167–68.

those exceptions do not imply any kind of supra-metropolitan rights. They indicated only that the metropolitan prerogatives of the bishops of Rome and of Alexandria went beyond the boundaries of a single civil province.[18] Under such conditions the issue of acceding to autocephaly had nothing to do with what would happen later on since, as a general rule, civil provinces and metropolitanates overlapped. To be sure, the strict implementation of the principle of accommodation occasionally brought about controversies when, for example, a civil province was cut in two. That is what happened in 372 with Cappadocia when the province of Cappadocia Secunda was formed. Immediately, Anthimos the Bishop of Tyana, the new metropolis, stopped regarding himself as a suffragan of St Basil of Caesarea. Thenceforth he considered himself a metropolitan. St Basil did not accept the new situation because, in his mind, that partition had been made intentionally to downgrade his authority.[19] Problems sometimes arose in connection with the status of churches beyond the limits of the Roman Empire. This was mostly the result of two factors, i.e., the consolidation of the provincial system of church government and the new kind of relationship between Church and state inaugurated under the reign of Constantine. The churches located outside the Roman Empire were unable to fit in with the metropolitan system delineated by the Council of Nicaea. Furthermore, the above-mentioned new kind of relationship between Church and state in the Roman Empire tended to blur the distinction between *Christianitas* and *Romanitas*. This situation could create problems for the Christians living in other countries, especially in Persia.[20]

The case of Armenia is the oldest example of such a conflictual situation. Gregory the Illuminator had been consecrated at Caesarea in Cappadocia around 314. The Bishops of Caesarea thought that thereby a precedent had been firmly established, more especially as the five successors of St Gregory were also consecrated at Caesarea. In the second half of the fourth

---

[18] Vl. Phidas, Προϋποθέσεις Διαμορφώσεως τοῦ Θεσμοῦ τῆς Πενταρχίας τῶν Πατριαρχῶν [*Proypotheseis Diamorphōseōs tou Thesmou tēs Pentarchias tōn Patriarchōn*], I, (Athens, 1965), 51–95.

[19] "Problems Concerning Autocephaly," 171.

[20] A. H. M. Jones, *Constantine and the Conversion of Europe* (Toronto: University of Toronto Press, 1978), 169–81.

century, this situation became a source of embarrassment for the Armenians because of the growing influence of Persia in their country. Then in 373, King Pap appointed a certain Shahak as Catholicos without the approval of the see of Caesarea. St Basil reacted strongly against this innovation.[21] Canonical relations with Caesarea were soon resumed. Nonetheless, given the political context, those relations more and more tended to be loose. As noted by Bishop Garabed Amadouni, the autocephaly of the Armenian Church took form slowly, based on customary law and in no way by a spirit of separatism.[22] Was the Church of Armenia considered by Caesarea and Constantinople as fully independent or as merely autonomous? This question cannot be clearly answered because, first and foremost, such an approach is anachronistic. By that time, as will be shown below, the difference between those two sorts of status was not so clearly delimited as is the case nowadays. Besides, regarding territories beyond the boundaries of the empire, Byzantine authorities were ready to be flexible and to resort to a policy marked by expediency. It is noteworthy that toward the end of the fourth century, church law was vague on this issue. Canon 2 of of the Second Ecumenical Council states: "But the churches of God among the barbarian nations should be administered according to the custom which has prevailed from the times of the fathers."[23]

Thinking of the Church universal in the fourth century as composed of metropolitanates highly centralized and maintaining among themselves loose relations would be a distorted view of reality. Above all, one must keep in mind that still at that time the basic ecclesiastical unit was the local church headed by its bishop. The translation of a bishop from one see to another remained infrequent, at least among the Orthodox, and canon law made this point explicit. Exceptions to the rule were barely regarded as acceptable.[24] Furthermore, the canons clearly delineate the jurisdictional authority of the local bishop and the rights of the metropolitan within the framework

---

[21] Faustus of Byzantium, 5, 29, *Fragmenta historicorum Graecorum* 5 (Paris, 1938), 293–94.

[22] Garabed Amadouni, "L'autocéphalie du katholicat arménien," *Orientalia Christiana Analecta* 181 (1968): 164–65.

[23] The vagueness of this statement reflects a situation prior to the delimitation of the Church into five patriarchates.

[24] See our article, "Les translations épiscopales," *Messager de l'Echarchat* 57 (1967): 24–38.

of episcopal collegiality.²⁵ The ecclesiastical province was not viewed as a close administrative entity, as can be shown by regulations regarding "larger synods" which included bishops of a neighboring province.²⁶

A decline in provincial autocephaly took place from about the end of the fourth century to the middle of the fifth. This dramatically altered the canonical structures of the Church. Amazingly enough, evidential materials on this mutation are relatively scarce. Nevertheless, discovering the reasons underlying this structural evolution is not difficult. Actually, several factors were simultaneously at work. As seen above, in Eastern Christendom, the principle of territorial coincidence between civil provinces and church metropolitanates was usually carried out. Since the split of the former was a continuous process, it had an impact on the latter. In many cases, this tended to lessen the prestige and authority of metropolitans.²⁷ Doubtless, the legislation issued by the Councils of Nicaea, Antioch, and Constantinople took for granted the autocephaly of the ecclesiastical provinces. This meant that the election of the metropolitan bishop did not need confirmation by some higher authority. However, this point was never explicitly articulated. In the intent of the lawmakers it probably appeared to have been self-evident. Furthermore, the real significance of Canon 6 of Nicaea was soon forgotten and misleading interpretations began to surface. To be sure, such misinterpretations were inevitable when one was unaware of the precise historical context which led to the drafting of that canon. In the original intent of the Nicene fathers, the purpose of that canon was to affirm the right of the bishop of Alexandria to supervise all episcopal cheirotonies in Egypt, Libya, and Pentapolis. This privilege was based on "the ancient customs," i.e., on the situation prevailing prior to the reform of Diocletian. The reference to Rome is made only to show that such a situation also existed in Italy.²⁸ For obvious reasons, the growth of the Roman see's authority throughout the times and therefore during the fourth and fifth centuries has been carefully scrutinized by Church

---

[25] Antioch, Canon 9; cf. Apostolic Canon 34.

[26] Antioch, Canon 12, 14. Sardica, Canons 3, 4, 5 (Greek numbering system). Constantinople, Canon 6.

[27] A. H. M. Jones, *The Later Roman Empire*, 42–43.

[28] Vl. Phidas, Προϋποθέσεις [*Proypotheseis*], 51–95.

historians. Dealing with this issue would lie far beyond the scope of the present study. Suffice it to say that addressing the problem of universal primacy claimed by the Roman see is irrelevant to the purpose of our enquiry. The expansion, however, of the supra-metropolitan jurisdiction of Rome in Western Christendom deserves, at least, some consideration. On the process of regional centralization one can discern both similarities and differences between East and West.

We have no reliable sources on the organization of the Church in Egypt up to the middle of the third century and, even from that time to the beginning of the fourth, evidential materials are scarce. Be that as it may, we can assume with certainty that the administrative reform of Emperor Diocletian had no impact on Church organization. As in the past, the bishop of Alexandria continued to consecrate or confirm all the bishops in his territory including Thebaid and Pentapolis. At the time of the Nicene Council, however, he seems to have met some opposition in the above-mentioned remote areas, as indirectly attested by canon 6 of Nicaea.[29]

The same canon also mentions the see of Antioch as an example of a derogation to the principle of accommodation. Actually, this reference is confusing because it seems to suppose a strict parallelism between the position of Alexandria and Antioch. In contrast with the former, Antioch at most extended its jurisdictional rights only to Coele-Syria and to some adjacent areas. This does not imply that the prestige and influence of Antioch did not go farther. They encompassed not only the civil diocese of "Oriens" but also the "barbarian" territories beyond the eastern boundaries of the Roman Empire. Otherwise the alteration of the status quo which began to take place in the last two decades of the fourth century would be unexplainable. From that time onward the bishop of Antioch tried to oversee the election of the metropolitans in the whole diocese of "Oriens." This expansionism, of course, was legitimized by an inaccurate understanding of Canon 6 of Nicaea. It is noteworthy that Pope Innocent I (402–417) and St Jerome (d. 420) supported this stand.[30] Be that as it may, if we use the

---

[29] H. Chadwick, "Faith and Order at the Council of Nicaea: A Note on the Background of the Sixth Canon," *Harvard Theological Review* 52 (1960): 171–95.

[30] Pope Innocent, Epist. 24, PL 20:547–51; St Jerome, *Liber ad Pammachium* 37, PL 23:40A.

terminology of our time, we can state that, within the approximate span of half a century, several provinces lost their "autocephaly" and became "autonomous." By and large, the process was achieved in such a quiet way that to trace the details of this evolution is almost impossible.³¹ The bishops of Antioch, however, did not fully succeed in their attempt to control all the metropolitanates of the diocese of "Oriens." The Church in Cyprus fiercely opposed the interference of Antioch. The Cypriots vehemently claimed that they had always elected their bishops without any confirmation by Antioch. The Council of Ephesus (431) gave a qualified answer: Insofar as the claims of the Cypriots were well grounded, they could continue to elect their bishops without higher confirmation.³² For Antioch, however, the main challenge to its control over the whole civil diocese of "Oriens" came from the South. Historical evidence shows that from the middle of the fourth century, Aelia Capitolina retrieved its ancient name of Jerusalem and, on the basis of its indisputable apostolicity, freed itself from any control of the metropolitan see of Caesarea. In this case also, the wording of the Nicene legislation was used in a way that did not reflect the original intent of the lawgiver.³³ At all events, in the fifth century, the problematic changed. The issue at stake was not the subordination of Jerusalem to Caesarea but the geographical limits between the respective supra-metropolitan rights of Antioch and Jerusalem. This question was eventually solved by mutual agreement during the Council of Chalcedon and ratified by imperial authority.³⁴ In both cases, viz., the settlement regarding the respective spheres of influence of Antioch and Jerusalem, and the definitive recognition of the autocephaly of Cyprus, the decision fell to the imperial authority.³⁵ As we shall see below, in the East the decisive role of the

---

³¹A. H. M. Jones, *Constantine and the Conversion of Europe*, 885. As rightly pointed out by Bréhier, geopolitical factors did not favor Antiochian hegemonism over the entire diocese of Oriens, *Les institutions de l'empire byzantin* (Paris: Albin Michel,), 451.

³²Motion (ψῆφος) = Canon 8 of the later Byzantine collections.

³³In Canon 7 of Nicaea, the lawgiver does not specify what the "sequence of honor" (τὴν ἀκολουθίαν τῆς τιμῆς [*tēn akolouthian tēs timēs*]) practically implied for the see of Aelia.

³⁴The agreement was reached on October 23; *ACO* II, ii, 2, 20–21 [112–13]. It was confirmed on October 26; ibid. II, i, 3, 4–7 [362–66].

³⁵John Hackett, *A History of the Orthodox Church of Cyprus* (London: Methuen and

basileis in this area was seldom questioned. According to the principle of harmony (συμφωνία [*symphōnia*]) between *sacerdotium* and *imperium*, problems related to the formation, abolishment, and adjustment of boundaries of large Church entities necessarily needed imperial involvement. In fact, this is understandable because such actions usually had political implications. Yet, a point should be underlined: In those matters, imperial government could hardly make an arbitrary decision. It had to take into account the ancient customs of the Church, especially when they had been confirmed by nomocanonical legislation.[36]

Compared to what we know about the jurisdictional expansion of other major sees, in the case of Constantinople we have good documentation at our disposal. Since historical evidence on this subject has been carefully analyzed, it would be pointless to deal at length with such a topic.[37] Let us observe that, for Constantinople, the process of jurisdictional expansion did not fundamentally differ from what happened in the case of Rome, Antioch, and Jerusalem. In the canonical statement issued by the Council of 381, we read as a tersely worded appendix to the second part of this text: "The bishop of Constantinople, however, shall have the priorities of honor (τὰ πρεσβεῖα τῆς τιμῆς [*ta presbeia tēs timēs*]) after the bishop of Rome because [this city] is the New Rome."[38] In all probability, the fathers of that council were mainly anxious to affirm the position of the bishop of Constantinople in order to oppose the meddling of Alexandria in the ecclesiastical affairs of the new capital. Thus, they do not allude to the practical implications of their decision with respect to the territorial jurisdiction of Constantinople. Precisely because the statement on the position of the bishop of Constantinople is very short, it can be understood in different ways. At all events, two extreme interpretations should be rejected; neither bears up under critical scrutiny. On the one hand, it would be wrong to understand the phrase "τὰ πρεσβεῖα τῆς τιμῆς [*ta presbeia tēs timēs*]" as

Company, 1901), 23–28. It seems that this event took place in 488, under the reign of Emperor Zeno.

[36]This principle fully applied to the Patriarchal pentarchy, *CJC* III (Berlin 1959), Nov. CXIII, 3, p. 597; Nov. CXXXI, 2, 655.

[37]G. Dagron, *Naissance d'une capitale* (Paris: P.U.F., 1974), 461–87.

[38]G. Dagron, 454–61.

denoting a merely honorary position. Actually, this prerogative implied that Constantinople was thenceforth ranked among the major sees of Christendom and had to be considered as the most important center of communion in the East. On the other hand, an inference from that text of the acknowledgement of jurisdictional rights over the Thracian, Pontic, and Asian dioceses would be exaggerated. Were it so, the fact that such rights were several times questioned until the last session of the Council of Chalcedon would be incomprehensible. The motion passed at the last session of that Council, later reckoned as "Canon 28" of Chalcedon, was the result of a compromise about the respective prerogatives of the archbishop of Constantinople and of the metropolitans in the three above-mentioned civil dioceses.[39] The rule issued by the Fourth Ecumenical Council confirmed the existing trend and finally gave a legitimacy to the protracted process altering the status of the metropolitan in those regions, Then it was clear that the provinces could no longer claim to be "autocephalous" but, at least in principle, they kept their autonomy since the election of the local bishops had merely to be confirmed by their own metropolitans.[40]

Meanwhile in the West, the formation of the Roman patriarchate was achieved in a different way, reflecting other political and societal circumstances. Insofar as this issue presents only a peripheral interest for the object of our enquiry, we will not address the complex problem of the relationship between Rome and the other churches in the West during late Antiquity. Moreover, a great many scholarly works have been published on this topic. Suffice it to mention very briefly the case of Illyricum. From the end of the fourth century onward, this huge territory constituted a bone of contention between Rome and Constantinople.[41] About 379 Pope Damasus instituted the vicarate of Thessalonica. The main prerogatives of

---

[39]See our article, "Un aspect estompé du 28e canon de Chalcédoine," *Revue de droit canonique* 29 (1979): 12–22.

[40]The respective competencies of the ecumenical patriarch and of the Metropolitans remained a controversial issue during the entire Middle Ages. See J. Darrouzès, *Documents inédits d'ecclésiologie byzantine* (Paris: Institut français d'études byzantines, 1966), 21–29 and 116–59.

[41]Fr Dvornik, *The Idea of Apostolicity in Byzantium and the Legend of the Apostle Andrew* (Cambridge, MA: Harvard University Press, 1958), 25–29

the vicars consisted in confirming the election of the bishops and in solving possible conflicts. In 421, Emperor Theodosius II issued a constitution ordering that all ecclesiastical controversies in Illyricum should be referred to the bishop of Constantinople.[42] Pope Boniface strongly disagreed and got the support of Honorius, the emperor of the West, and eventually this law was withdrawn.[43] During the "Acacian Schism" (482–519), a part of the episcopate of Illyricum switched its loyalty to the see of Constantinople. What remained of Christian Illyricum after the great *Völkerwanderung* of the early Middle Ages was eventually integrated into the Byzantine patriarchate by an imperial decision made in the mid-eighth century.[44] It is noteworthy that, in spite of papal complaints, this decision was never rescinded, neither during the temporary reestablishment of ecclesiastical relations between Rome and Constantinople (787–815), nor after the definitive restoration of Orthodoxy (842).

If we look at the evolution of canonical praxis from late Antiquity to the early Middle Ages, we can observe a process of erosion of the provincial structure and simultaneously the continuous strengthening of patriarchal authority. In fact, this situation reflected the decreasing importance of the province as a fundamental civil unit. This was a consequence of the administrative reform initiated by Emperor Heraclius (610–641).[45] The Fourth Ecumenical Council unambiguously states that the civil promotion of a city to the honorific rank of "metropolis" by imperial favor does not affect church order, so the rights of the real "metropolis" (τῇ κατ' ἀλήθειαν μητροπόλει [*tē kat' alētheian mētropolei*]) must be preserved.[46] This ordinance, however, was not observed for a long time. The newly created *metropoleis* of that kind were placed under the direct jurisdiction of the patriarchal see. The heads of those exempt bishoprics were called,

---

[42]*CTh* XVI, 2, 45, ed. Th. Mommsen (Berlin 1905), 352.

[43]Mansi VII, 759–760.

[44]Given the lack of precise data, it is impossible to determine with certainty whether this action took place in 732–33 or 752–53. See J. M. Hussey, *The Orthodox Church in the Byzantine Empire* (Oxford: Clarendon Press, 1986), 46, n. 36.

[45]George Ostrogorsky, *History of the Byzantine State*, rev. ed. (New Brunswick, NJ: Rutgers University Press, 1969), 132–33.

[46]Canon 12.

until the thirteenth century, "autocephalous" archbishops.⁴⁷ Such phrasing appears confusing in our time. Presumably, it started to look so during the high Middle Ages, resulting in the disappearance of that appellation. Thenceforth the term "autocephalous" was only applied either to a self-governing body or to its primate.

On the organizational level, at the end of Justinian's reign, the pattern of church units was shaped in the following manner:

- The Patriarchate of Rome comprised the whole of Western Christendom. This unit was far from being homogeneous; it included several church entities. Some of them were under the close control of Rome; others were autonomous or semi-autonomous. Doubtless, Africa remained a self-governing unit. Eastward the Roman see extended its jurisdiction beyond the linguistic and cultural boundaries of the Latin-speaking world throughout all of Illyricum. By a personal decision of Emperor Justinian, who intended to honor his birthplace, a separate unit comprising seven provinces was subtracted from the authority of Thessalonica. The center of this new unit was Justiniana Prima, presumably near present-day Skopje.⁴⁸ In 545, Pope Vigilius conferred the title of Vicar Apostolic on the archbishop of that city. This Archdiocese practically disappeared as a consequence of the invasions of the Avars and Slavs in the Balkan peninsula; however, the title of Justiniana Prima resurfaced in connection with a Church entity during the high Middle Ages.

- The see of Constantinople exercised its jurisdiction over the metropolitans of the three civil dioceses, viz., Thracia, Pontus, and Asia. Furthermore, it extended its direct jurisdiction over the bishops in the parts of the aforesaid dioceses which were "among the Barbarians" (ἐν τοῖς βαρβαρικοῖς [*en tois barbarikois*]). The Byzantine commentators of the canons, Aristene, Zonaras, and Balsamon, have accurately indicated what territories "among the Barbarians" the lawgivers had in mind.⁴⁹

⁴⁷H. Gelzer, *Text der Notitiae Episcopatuum* (Munich, 1901), 551.
⁴⁸*CJC* III, 2, Nov. CXXXI, iii, 655–656.
⁴⁹Rhallis and Potlis, II, 282–286.

- On the basis of "ancient customs," the archbishop of Alexandria either himself consecrated or gave his previous assent for all the episcopal consecrations in Egypt and Libya.[50] Southward beyond the borders of the empire, he extended his authority over the Nilotic World.
- The patriarch of Antioch exercised a supra-metropolitan jurisdiction over the greater part of the civil diocese of "Oriens." Eastward, the patriarch extended a very loose authority over the Christians in the Persian Empire; however, even before the beginning of the Christological controversies, the Council of Dadisho (424) asserted the complete independence of the Church in Persia.[51]

The territory on which the Bishop of Jerusalem exercised supra-metropolitan rights had been carved out of the civil diocese of "Oriens." Until the Council of Chalcedon, however, the limits between the respective jurisdictional areas of Antioch and Jerusalem were not clearly marked and this situation caused recurrent conflicts. During the Council of Chalcedon, a solution was found on the basis of mutual agreement (*non decreto iudiciario sed ex communi consensu*)[52] between Maximus of Antioch and Juvenal of Jerusalem. Yet, to take effect, this agreement had to be confirmed by the imperial authority. This happened at the eighth synodal session. Thus, the Bishop of Jerusalem extended his suprametropolitan prerogatives only on the three provinces of Palestine, viz., Prima, Secunda, and Salutaris.[53]

A century later, this segmentation of the whole *Reichskirche* was affirmed in the Justinianic legislation.[54] It must be noted that, henceforth, the title of "patriarch" was restricted to those five archbishops. Previously, it had been broadly used to characterize prominent hierarchs.[55] As we will see below, the acknowledgement of such a title to

[50] A. H. M. Jones, *Constantine and the Conversion of Europe*, 883–84.
[51] W. F. Macomber, "The Authority of the Catholicos Patriarch of Seleucia-Ctesiphon," *Or. Chr. An.* 181 (1968): 179–200.
[52] *ACO* II, ii, 2, p. 20 [112].
[53] Those provinces are approximately coterminous with the present-day state of Israel, the "Occupied Territories," a part of Jordan and the Sinai Peninsula.
[54] Cf. supra note 36.
[55] Article "Patriarch," *Encyclopedia of Early Christianity* (New York and London: Garland Publishing, 1990), 698–99.

primates of the Bulgarian Church during the high and late Middle Ages does not actually invalidate this assertion.

Finally, besides the pentarchical order, as "lonely survivor of the old provincial system,"[56] we should mention the autocephalous Church of Cyprus.

Having come to the end of the historical survey on late Antiquity and the early Middle Ages, and keeping in mind the purpose of our enquiry, we can at least draw some conclusions: First and foremost, we ought to observe that there is a huge difference between the concept of autocephaly as perceived in olden times and the widespread contemporary understanding of what this status supposedly implies. For example, at that time, being autocephalous did not necessarily preclude belonging to a larger regional entity. This fact is clearly evidenced by Canons 2 and 6 of the Second Ecumenical Council.

For a province, the fact of becoming and remaining autocephalous or of losing this status could result from various factors. By virtue of the aforementioned principle of accommodation, the division or merger of two civil provinces could have a direct impact on this matter. In many occurrences also, the progressive weakening of the metropolitan authority, from the end of the fourth century onward, frequently favored intervention by the major sees. Occasionally such actions aroused hostile reactions. We can say, however, that generally speaking this trend did not meet consistent opposition. For this reason, in the majority of cases, no comprehensive records of this evolution toward centralization have been kept. As we can infer from the minutes of the Council of Chalcedon, the real issue at stake was the rights of the metropolitans to consecrate their suffragan bishops. In the East, at the time of Chalcedon, the Nicene system of provincial autocephaly had almost fallen into abeyance.

Finally, the question of the role of the ecumenical councils with respect to the granting and abolishment of autocephaly must be addressed. This has not only a purely historical interest but is also relevant for our time,

---

[56]John Meyendorff, *Imperial Unity and Christian Divisions* (Crestwood, NY: St Vladimir's Seminary Press, 1989), 57.

since, nowadays, a theory is gaining acceptance in some Orthodox milieus. According to its exponents, the only organ, on a strict canonical level (κατ' ἀκρίβειαν [*kat' akribeian*]), fully entitled to establish definitively an autocephalous church would be an ecumenical council.[57] Actually, this theory does not bear up under scrutiny. A critical examination of historical evidence does not corroborate it. In fact, an enquiry into this issue shows that, with one exception, the input of ecumenical councils was somewhat marginal.

The First Nicene Council took for granted the principle of territorial accommodation. This implied the "autocephaly" of every province. The council indicated the metropolitan prerogative to confirm the bishop's cheirotonies. Surely this rule could hardly be viewed as a bold innovation. The council underlined that the exceptional rights of the Alexandrian see were grounded in a long-existing custom; furthermore, this was also the case for Rome and Antioch. The Council of Constantinople produced a canonical statement that later on was divided into three or four canons, depending on the collections.[58] Among other matters bearing on church order, the council insisted on the preservation of the Nicene legislation (κατὰ τὰ ἐν Νικαίᾳ [*kata ta en Nikaia*]) regarding the provincial system. At the end of this second part we find a short declaration concerning the position of the bishop of the "New Rome." This declaration takes into account a factual situation based on the principle of accommodation. In civil law at that time, the newly founded second capital had a particular status that was not completely equal to that of the "Ancient Rome." Nonetheless, the imperial city of Constantine lay outside the standard system of the administrative division of the Roman Empire into prefectures, dioceses, and provinces.[59] As such, the bishop of the new city had to be ranked immediately after the Roman pontiff. Given the legal status of Constantinople at that stage, however, it would have been difficult to attribute officially to its bishop a direct jurisdiction over the neighboring provinces. This situation

---

[57]John H. Erickson, *The Challenge of Our Past* (Crestwood, NY: St Vladimir's Seminary Press, 1991), 91–114, esp. 91.

[58]See our article, "Faits et fiction à propos du deuxième concile Œcuménique," *Église et Théologie* 13 (1982): 135–56, esp. 144–45.

[59]G. Dagron, *Naissance d'une capitale*, 48–76.

is accurately reflected in the conciliar statement.[60] This council, which in its membership was actually an interdiocesan synod of the Eastern part of the Roman Empire, did not intend to alter the existing church order. As already mentioned, the declaration on the rank of Constantinople had a specific purpose, viz., to oppose the intrusion of the see of Alexandria beyond the boundaries of its territorial jurisdiction.

What was the involvement of the Ecumenical Council of Ephesus in the issue of autocephaly? It is commonly assumed that this council established the autocephaly of Cyprus. This view does not wholly correspond to reality: Two irreconcilable positions existed at that time. The bishop of Antioch pretended to extend legitimately his supra-metropolitan rights on the island. The bishops of Cyprus considered this claim as unfounded. Both parts tried to justify their stand on the basis of precedent. The Council of Ephesus prudently decided that the province of Cyprus should enjoy in the future the status it had in the past. Thereby, the independence of the Cypriot Church was conditionally recognized insofar as it could be clearly proved that she had never been under the jurisdiction of Antioch.[61] The motion (ψῆφος) passed at the Council, however, did not put the controversy to an end. The autocephaly was definitively recognized later on, probably in 488 by a decision of Emperor Zeno, when the relics of St Barnaby were found.[62] Therefore, as shown by historical evidence, the role of the Council of Ephesus was limited in the process that led to the full recognition of Cyprus' autocephaly.

The Council of Chalcedon dealt with two issues relevant to our present enquiry, viz., the territorial extent of the supra-metropolitan rights of the see of Jerusalem, and the legitimacy of the jurisdictional claims set forth by the Church of Constantinople. With regard to Jerusalem, the problem at stake was not the status of Jerusalem, but the conflict between Antioch and Jerusalem over some territories. The problem, as seen above, was solved by an amicable arrangement between the two primates.

---

[60]Vl. Phidas, Ἐνδημοῦσα Σύνοδος [Standing synod] (Athens, 1971): 21–38.
[61]The Antiochians being absent were unable to present their position.
[62]Cf. supra note 35.

The second issue was far more problematic because the claims of Constantinople over the provinces in the dioceses of Thracia, Pontus, and Asia could not be unquestionably supported by "ancient customs." Moreover, those claims were adamantly opposed by the Roman legates who affirmed the permanent validity of the Nicene order. Nevertheless, there were enough precedents to prop up the claims of Constantinople. Besides, the representatives of Emperor Marcian at the council expressed clearly their support for Archbishop Anatolius of Constantinople and, ignoring the protest voiced by the Roman legates, eventually declared that the discussion was closed.[63] In fact, the adopted motion was shaped as a synodal decree: "... ἡμεῖς ὁρίζομεν καὶ ψηφιζόμεθα [ēmeis horizomen kai psēphizometha]." Hence the legitimacy of the jurisdictional rights of Constantinople does formally rest on written law; however, as shown by the debates preceding the adoption of the motion, the fathers took account of some precedents. Surely, those precedents could not be considered as "ancient customs." They did, however, reflect an ongoing process that had started several decades before. Under such circumstances, we cannot see this decision as a complete novelty but rather as an approval and confirmation of a powerful current.

The Fifth and Sixth Ecumenical Councils focused their attention only on doctrinal matters. Then about ten years after the end of the latter, Emperor Justinian II deemed it necessary to summon a general council dealing with issues of church order. This assembly took place at Constantinople in 692. It would lie far beyond the scope of the present study to discuss the ecumenical character of that synod. Suffice it to say that in the Byzantine East, its authority remained unchallenged.[64] Two canons are relevant to the purpose of our enquiry. Canon 36 indicates the hierarchical order (τάξις [taxis]) of the five major sees of the Church universal. This had been already set up in the *Corpus Juris Civilis* and therefore the lawgivers did not introduce anything new in the Byzantine nomocanonical legislation.

[63] *ACO* II, i, 3, 99.
[64] V. Laurent, "L'Œuvre canonique du concile in Trullo (691–92), source primaire du droit de l'Église orientale," *Revue des études byzantines* 22 (1965): 7–41.

Another decision by this council addressed a very specific issue. Emperor Justinian II (685–95 and 705–11), within the framework of his colonization program, transferred a very large part of the population of Cyprus to Hellespont. John, the head of the Church of Cyprus, conferred with the emperor on the matter.[65] Canon 39 deals with the issue of the status of that autocephalous metropolitan. The council declared that this metropolitan residing in the newly founded city of Justinianopolis is entitled to consecrate the Bishop of Cyzicus.[66] This ruling enters into the category of canons solving particular situations. Doubtless the emperor himself suggested this decision. About 699, the Cypriots came back to their homeland and this ruling became pointless.

The second Council of Nicaea (787), the last Council received by the Orthodox Church as "ecumenical," did not treat questions related to the matter under scrutiny. Indeed, Pope Hadrian I (772–95) asked the council to return the territories of the Western patriarchate which had been taken from the Roman jurisdiction during the time of Iconoclasm, but this demand was completely ignored.[67]

In late Antiquity and the early Middle Ages, i.e., approximately during the period of the seven ecumenical councils, it appears that, in the making of the patriarchal areas, the modification of ecclesiastical borders, and the change of status of bishoprics, the role of the imperial government became continuously more prominent. Since this period is also that of the elaboration of the bulk of written church law, the significance of that factor must not be overlooked. Furthermore, during the following period, i.e., the high and late Middle Ages, this policy was carried out in a consistent way. From the time of Justinian onward, the Byzantine East considered the pentarchical system as *an immutable order independent of*

[65]Constance Head, *Justinian II of Byzantium* (Madison, Milwaukee, and London: University of Wisconsin Press, 1972), 45–47.

[66]In its original draft the canon states that "new Justinianopolis shall have the rights of the city of the Constantinians." In the *textus receptus*, instead of Constantia (the metropolis of Cyprus) we find "Constantinople." The first reading is attested in the best manuscript tradition. See Fonti, fasc. IX, t. I, i, 174. Moreover, this reading is confirmed by the text cited by Constantine Porphyrogenitus, *De Administrando Imperio*, ed. Gyula Moravcsic, Dumbarton Oaks Texts 1 (Washington, DC: Dumbarton Oaks Research Library and Collection, 1967), 227.

[67]Letter of Hadrian, Mansi XII, col. 1073 CD.

the factual reality.⁶⁸ Within the framework of the present study, going into all the details concerning the formation and suppression of autocephalous church entities in the high and late Middle Ages is not possible. Suffice it to focus our attention on salient facts evidencing our assertion; but first we shall try to set forth the political philosophy underlying the position of the Byzantines toward autocephaly during that period.

A major problem started surfacing in the seventh century.⁶⁹ Thenceforth, a discrepancy arose between the claims of universality of the Byzantine state and the fact of the dramatic reduction of its territory. On the one hand, the Byzantines consistently refused to recognize *de jure* this new situation. On the other hand, for obvious reasons, they could not completely close their eyes to reality. They therefore had to make adjustments that were seen as concessions based on "economia." A typical statement made by the Trullan Council provides good insight into the theoretical position of the Byzantines at that time. Canon 37 specifies that barbarian inroads should not cast a slur on the honor and rights of the bishops suffering such a predicament.⁷⁰ Incidentally, let us note the use of the term "inroads" (ἔφοδοι [*ephodoi*]) which suggests something merely temporary. Be that as it may, the lost territories continued to be formally considered as part and parcel of the Empire. From about the ninth century, the various tribes, by that time permanently established in Greece and in the peninsula of Haemus (now called the Balkans), started looking at the Christian religion. Boris, kniaz of Bulgaria, intended to enter the family of "civilized nations." Thus in 865, he accepted Christianity.⁷¹ Byzantine missionaries baptized him with his subjects. A little more than a century later (988?), Vladimir the Great, prince of Kiev, was baptized by the Bishop of Kherson,

---

⁶⁸For example, this ideological stand can be easily detected in Balsamon's treatise "On the Privileges of the Patriarchs," Rhallis and Potlis, IV, 542–55.

⁶⁹Ostrogorsky, *History of the Byzantine State*, 123–46.

⁷⁰Notice the final sentence of that canon: "οὐ γὰρ ὑπὸ τοῦ τῆς ἀνάγκης καιροῦ καὶ ἀκριβείας περιγραφείσης, ὁ τῆς οἰκονομίας ὅρος περιορισθήσεται [*ou gar hypo tou tēs anangkēs kairou kai akribeias perigrapheisēs, ho tēs oikonomias horos perioristhēsetai*]." This very idiomatic Greek sentence can be rendered: "For, if the circumstances of necessity constitute an obstacle to the strict observance [of the law], it shall not restrict the limit of flexibility."

⁷¹Dimitri Obolensky, *The Byzantine Commonwealth* (London: Sphere Books, 1974), 117.

a suffragan of the ecumenical patriarch. Thereafter many "Rus" followed his example willingly or unwillingly.[72]

2

The Byzantines did not go so far as to blur completely the distinction between Church (ἐκκλησία [*ekklēsia*]) and *Christian Orthodox society* (πολιτεία or πολίτευμα [*politeia* or *politeuma*]). Yet, on a practical level they had a tendency to identify the visible Church with the Roman Byzantine *Commonwealth*.[73] In contrast with what happened in medieval Western Christendom, the concept of the earthly Church as an independent corporation was totally foreign to the ecclesiological approach of the Easterners.[74] In the mainstream of the Church, the rights of the emperor to make decisions pertaining to the sphere of doctrine were never acknowledged. With regard to church order, imperial interference was usually accepted insofar as such initiatives remained within the limits of legality and canonicity.[75] If there was any area of church order in which imperial involvement was considered normal, it was in matters concerning the modification of the higher ecclesiastical circumscriptions.[76] In the same area, imperial involvement included the granting, confirmation, or cancelation of autocephalous status for the churches regarded by the Byzantines as parts of the "commonwealth." That was, of course, the viewpoint of the imperial authorities and of the ecclesiastical milieus in Constantinople. Given those ideological presuppositions, a double standard affecting the concept of autocephaly was inevitable. On the one hand stood the five ancient patriarchates and the Church of Cyprus, while on the other hand stood the recent autocephalous bodies. The statute of the latter was considered neither as complete nor as necessarily permanent. Although this principle was not clearly articulated before the late Middle Ages, it was,

---

[72]Ibid., 256.
[73]This tendency is abundantly evidenced in the hymnography of the Byzantine Church.
[74]Yves Congar, *L'ecclésiologie du haut Moyen-Age* (Paris: Cerf, 1968), 344–57.
[75]Demetrius Chomatianos, "Answers to Constantine Cabasilas," Rhallis and Potlis, V, 429.
[76]Second letter of Patriarch Photios to Pope Nicholas (Γ'– 3), I.N. Valetta, Φωτίου Ἐπιστολαί [Photios' letters] (London: D. Nutt, 1864), 162.

in fact, applied from the ninth century onward. Indeed, from that time the Byzantines tried to instill this ideology into the mind of the recently converted people, and to a certain extent they were successful. More often than not, however, the result was not what was expected. The heads of the newly formed states had a tendency to appropriate for themselves the imperial privileges, including those concerning autocephaly and the title of the primates of their state churches. Some contemporary canonists oppose this idea of a double standard for autocephaly because it does not fit in with ecclesiological premises.[77] Doubtless that objection cannot be easily brushed aside. Actually, taking a stand on this issue is more complex than it might look at first sight. The answer depends on the understanding of autocephaly. If autocephaly simply means that the episcopacy of a determined area elects its first hierarch without further confirmation by a higher authority, the aforementioned distinction does not constitute an *articulus stantis vel cadentis Ecclesiae* ["the article by which the Church stands or falls"—*Ed.*]. If, however, the emphasis is put on the "sovereignty" of each autocephalous entity, the medieval distinction made by the Byzantines is not relevant.[78]

To be sure, nowadays there is no more Christian Polity headed by a "very religious Emperor." Nevertheless, the Byzantine theory has not totally fallen into abeyance, but has survived in a modified form. Moreover, the disappearance of a Christian Polity does not automatically justify the validity of the opposite theory about autocephaly.

Before going further, we should take a brief glimpse at the appearing and vanishing of autocephalous bodies in the Middle Ages. We suppose the general historical background to be known, and will therefore concentrate our attention on those facts that are directly related to the scope of the present study.

At the Constantinopolitan Council of 879–80, as a token of good will towards the papacy, the Byzantines agreed on the transfer of Bulgaria to the patriarchal jurisdiction of Rome. Kniaz Boris, albeit voicing

---

[77]S. Troitzky, "De l'autocéphalie dans l'Église," *Messager de l'Exarchat* 12 (1952): 34–35.
[78]Pr. Liviu Stan, "Autocefalia şi Autonomia în Ortodoxie," *Mitropolia Olteniei* 13.5–6 (1961): 278–316, esp. 283.

no objection, quietly decided to maintain the ecclesiastical status quo in his state. Thus, the Byzantines ceased to consider the Church of Bulgaria as a part of the Patriarchate of Constantinople, while Rome was unable to set up a new hierarchy. Thereby, the Bulgarian Church became de facto independent but continued to keep close cultural and religious links with Byzantium.[79] This situation was not contrary to the interests of the empire and therefore was tacitly accepted by the Byzantines. In spite of continual conflicts between Byzantium and Bulgaria under the reign of Tzar Symeon (893–927), the ecclesiastical status quo was not altered, as shown by the correspondence between Patriarch Nicholas and the archbishop of Bulgaria.[80] In the last period of his reign, i.e., after the fall of 924, Tzar Symeon decided to bestow the title of patriarch on the archbishop of his capital, Preslav. As far as we know, the Byzantines did not take any stand concerning this honorary promotion. When, under the reign of Peter (927–969), the relations between the two states were normalized, the Bulgarian ruler was officially recognized as "*basileus*" and his primate as "patriarch." The Byzantines considered those titles as merely temporary concessions which altered neither the concept of the unicity of the empire nor of the pentarchical church order. After the death of Tzar Peter, the Bulgarian Empire fell into rapid decline. The Russian prince Svyatoslav occupied and ransacked Western Bulgaria. Soon after, the Byzantine Emperor John Tsimiskes completely defeated Svyatoslav (971) and annexed Bulgaria to the Empire. Damian, the Bulgarian patriarch, having set his see in Dorostolon, was deposed (καθῃρέθη), and the independence of the Bulgarian Church was suppressed.[81] Interestingly enough, the notice which informs us of those ecclesiastical events does not mention the role of the Byzantine Church authorities but only of the emperors and the senate. Understandably, the Bulgarians did not accept this demotion. Tzar Samuel (976–1014) was able to restore for a short span of time a powerful state and an independent Church, the head of which used the title of

---

[79] Fr Dvornik, *The Photian Schism* (Cambridge: Cambridge University Press, 1948), 210–15.

[80] *Izvori za Balgarskata Istoriia* [Sources for Bulgarian history] 8 (Sofia: Akademiia na Naukite), 186–297.

[81] Ibid., XIV, 109.

patriarch. Emperor Basil II (976–1025), after difficult campaigns, emerged victorious and succeeded in subjugating the whole of Bulgaria (1018). Nevertheless, he followed a wise policy in civil and ecclesiastical matters.[82] The autocephaly of the Bulgarian Church was not canceled. The primatial see remained in Akhris (Ohrid) but its holder bore simply the title of "archbishop" and had to be appointed by the emperor himself. As appears evident, the legitimacy of the autocephalous archdiocese of Akhris lay on the ordinances (σιγίλλια [*sigillia*]) issued by the emperor, who also by his own authority fixed the geographic limits of that church.[83] For the Greek Archbishops of Akhris, their position as successors of Bulgarian primates did not look prestigious enough. Thus, during the second half of the twelfth century, they claimed that the real source of their rights and privileges stemmed from those of the ancient Justiniana Prima and, consequently, included in their title the name of that city, although it had disappeared long before.[84] Under Turkish domination, the archbishop of Akhris maintained, at least theoretically, his status until 1767 when, officially under the request of the authorities of this Church, it was integrated into the Patriarchate of Constantinople.[85] Toward the end of 1185 an insurrection broke out in Bulgaria. In 1186, the rebels triumphed and this led to the formation of a new state between the Balkan Mountains and the lower Danube. The center of the second Bulgarian Empire was the city of Trnovo. The Church in Bulgaria proclaimed her independence, thereby breaking canonical relations with the see of Constantinople. They were re-established in 1235, following a treaty concluded between Emperor Theodore II Lascaris and Tzar Asen II. The Bulgarian Church was recognized as a self-governing body (αὐτόνομος, *autonomos*) and the first hierarch was honored with the title of "Patriarch." The Bulgarians understood this as the recognition of a fully independent patriarchate. For the Greeks, this agreement, concluded by expediency, involved only an internal autonomy and, with regard to the patriarchal title, was considered as something merely

[82]Ostrogorsky, *History of the Byzantine State*, 310–13.
[83]E. Dölger, *Regesten*, nrs. 806, 807, 808.
[84]Hussey, *The Orthodox Church in the Byzantine Empire*, 209.
[85]S. Runciman, *The Great Church in Captivity* (Cambridge: Cambridge University Press, 1968), 379–80.

honorary.⁸⁶ At all events, those concessions were made for political reasons.⁸⁷ The ecumenical patriarch Germanos II and the Standing Synod ("... πάντων τῶν ἐπιδημούντων ἱερωτάτων ἀρχιερέων, *panton ton epidemounton hierotaton archieron*) rubber stamped those decisions.⁸⁸ In 1393, the Turks captured and ransacked Trnovo and destroyed the Bulgarian state. No successor was appointed when Patriarch Evthymy was sent into exile. From then on, we have no more information on the life of the Bulgarian Church. It seems that about 1415 Bulgaria became ecclesiastically a province of the Patriarchate of Constantinople.⁸⁹

The Serbian Church achieved accession to full autonomy, i.e., autocephaly, in a peaceful manner. St Save, the brother of King Stephen "the First Crowned," went to Nicaea twice (1219, 1220) to deal with this matter. Allegedly, the Nicaean Authorities were initially very reluctant to bestow such a status on the Serbian Church, but finally this was granted because of the great friendship Emperor Theodore I Lascaris felt for St Sava.⁹⁰ In fact, historical evidence suggests that political factors played a major role in the benevolent attitude of the emperor. Be that as it may, this action aroused a fierce opposition from Demetrios Chomatianos, the incumbent of the see of Akhris (Justiniana Prima) and a distinguished canonist besides. He sternly denied the canonicity of the autonomy given to the Church in Serbia, arguing that the Ecumenical Patriarchate had overstepped its rights and encroached on the jurisdiction of Justiniana Prima. Undoubtedly this position reflected canonical exactness.

On the status of the Church in Georgia (Ἰβηρία [*Ibēria*]) during the first millennium, evidence is scant, and furthermore it is difficult to disentangle fact from fiction. However, there is no doubt that from the beginning of the seventh century (*c.* 608/9) the Georgian Catholicos Kirion severed

⁸⁶J. Darrouzès, *Regestes*, nr. 2442. See the complete text of the letter of Patriarch Callistus to Bulgarian monks (1361–1362) in the work of A.A. Tachiaos, *Πηγὲς Ἐκκλησιαστικῆς Ἱστορίας τῶν Ὀρθοδόξων Σλάβων* [Sources for the ecclesiastical history of the Orthodox Slavs] (Thessalonica: Aphon Kyriakides, 1984), 90–96.

⁸⁷G. Ostrogorsky, 314.

⁸⁸*Regestes*, nrs. 1278 and 1282 (end of 1234 and spring of 1235).

⁸⁹A. A. Tachiaos, "Die Aufhebung des bulgarischen Patriarchats von Tirnovo," *Balkan Studies* 4 (1962): 67–82.

⁹⁰*Regestes*, nr. 1226 (a. 1220).

Accession to Autocephaly

his allegiance with the Armenian Church for doctrinal reasons. Thus, the Georgian Church became de facto independent. The Byzantines raised no objections then or later.[91] Contacts with the empire became closer after the partial reconquest of the Caucasian regions toward the end of the reign of Emperor Basil II (976–1025). Then during the Patriarchate of Peter III of Antioch, a council held in that town recognized the Church of Georgia as independent and autocephalous (ἐλευθέραν ... καὶ αὐτοκέφαλον [*eleutheran ... kai autokephalon*]). According to Balsamon, this church was previously under the authority of the Antiochian see.[92] By the beginning of the nineteenth century, Georgia was incorporated into the Russian Empire. A decision in 1811 of Alexander I, emperor of Russia, suppressed the autocephaly of its church. This sovereign acted in a way very similar to that of the Byzantine Emperor John Tsimiskes vis-à-vis the Bulgarian Church in the tenth century. This takeover aroused no protest among the Orthodox churches.

The accession of the Russian Church to autocephaly followed a path which actually was dictated by external factors.[93] Doubtless, from the fourteenth century the Church and the Muscovite state had had a very close connection. Clearly, the Church was a national institution and the Grand Dukes preferred that a Russian metropolitan head the Church. Notwithstanding, there was no significant current opposing the appointment of that prelate by Constantinople. Then, when Metropolitan Isidore, a Greek and an ardent supporter of the Union of Florence, had, for this reason, to be expelled from the see (1441), the Russians hesitated for seven years on what had to be done. At that time, the incumbent of the Constantinopolitan see was the unionist Patriarch Gregory Mammas (1445–50). Given this situation, in December 1448, a synod held in Moscow elected Jonas of Ryazan as "Metropolitan of Kiev and All Russia." However, at that stage it does seem probable that the Russian episcopacy considered this initiative as more than a temporary expedient. The conquest of Constantinople by the Turks in 1453 brought about a new problem. Under

---

[91] J. Meyendorff, *Imperial Unity and Christian Division*, 105–09.
[92] Rhallis and Potlis, II, 172.
[93] Obolensky, *The Byzantine Commonwealth*, 346–50.

such circumstances, the majority of the Russians deemed allegiance to the Church of Constantinople as inconceivable, though for at least a generation a minority dissented from the mainstream.[94] The Council held in Moscow in 1459 went a step further. This assembly committed to the future by declaring that the successors of Jonas should be the legitimate metropolitans of All Russia.[95] Surely the ecclesiastical circles in Constantinople were not pleased by the new status of the Church in Muscovite Russia, but they were aware they had no possibility of changing the course of events. Furthermore, directly hurting the only Orthodox monarch would have been unwise. Thus, in 1561 the ecumenical patriarch Joasaph II confirmed in a very official way the legitimacy of the coronation of Ivan IV as "βασιλεὺς [*basileus*]" (tzar), made at Moscow in 1547 by Macarius, the metropolitan of Moscow.[96] Thus, the patriarch of Constantinople carefully avoided breaking canonical links with the Russian Church. At most, there were occasional reminders of the unsettled problem regarding the canonical position of the Russian Metropolitanate.[97]

The coronation of Ivan IV as tzar created an unprecedented situation which did not fit in with the political philosophy of Eastern Christianity, expressed in the axiom "*Imperium sine patriarcha non staret*."[98] Eventually, both problems were solved at once. In 1588 the Ecumenical Patriarch Jeremias II visited Russia to solicit financial help and, in January of the following year, he elevated Job, the metropolitan of Moscow, to the dignity of patriarch. This act was subsequently approved by the Synod of Constantinople (May 1591). In 1593, another synod was held in the same city at that time with the presence of the four Eastern patriarchs. The patriarchal dignity of the Muscovite see was solemnly confirmed, and it was specified that the patriarch of Moscow was to be "co-numerate" with the other patriarchs and obtain the fifth rank, i.e., after the patriarch

---

[94]Such was the case of St Paphnuty of Borovsk; G. P. Fedotov, *The Russian Religious Mind (II)* (Belmont, MA: Nordland, 1975), 291.

[95]A. V. Kartashev, *Ocherki po Istorii Russkoi Tzerkvi* [Essays on the History of the Russian Church] (Paris: YMCA Press, 1959), 364–66.

[96]A.A. Tachiaos, *Die Aufhebung des bulgarischen Patriarchats*, 156–64.

[97]A. M. Ammann, *Storia de la Chiesa Russa* (Turin: Unione Tipografico, 1948), 135–136.

[98]*Epist. Caloiohanniss ad Innocentium*, Izvori XII, 319.

of Jerusalem. It is noteworthy that in all of those decisions there was no allusion to a regularization of the status of the Russian Church between 1448 and 1589.[99]

After the final collapse of the Byzantine Empire in 1453, the Turkish authorities recognized the ecumenical patriarch as the head of all the Orthodox in the Ottoman Empire.[100] Under such circumstances, his power overshadowed that of the other Eastern patriarchs and primates of autocephalous churches within the boundaries of the Ottoman Empire. Thus, in ecclesiastical matters, the ecumenical patriarch inherited, at least to a certain extent, the position of the Byzantine emperors, especially with respect to acknowledging and suppressing autocephalous bodies. However, it became a serious issue with the weakening of the Ottoman Empire and the rise of national self-awareness among the peoples under the Turkish yoke. Those developments began to bud toward the beginning of the nineteenth century. The subsequent formation of national states to the detriment of the Ottoman Empire entailed the independence of the national church. Actually, although sometimes after a period of tension, Constantinople consented to issue a tomos of autocephaly. In the case of the Bulgarian exarchate, a conflict arose, because this self-proclaimed autocephaly antedated the formation of a state. In many places, Greek and Bulgarian populations were living together, and the two ecclesiastical jurisdictions overlapped, transgressing for the first time in history the principle of territorial jurisdiction.[101] In 1872, a council summoned in Constantinople characterized this deviation as ethnophyletism. However, as ironically pointed out by a Roman Catholic author: "Ce que les Grecs ... ont reproché au concile de Constantinople de 1872 est devenu depuis cette époque le péché mignon de beaucoup d'autocéphalies"[102] (What the Greeks found blameworthy at the Council of Constantinople in 1872 has since become the besetting sin of many autocephalies).

---

[99] A. A. Tachiaos, *Die Aufhebung des bulgarischen Patriarchats*, 210–23.

[100] Runciman, *The Great Church in Captivity*, 167–68.

[101] On the events which eventually led to the schism, see the scholarly and objective study of Patriarch Kiril of Bulgaria: *Ekzarch Antim* (Sofia: Synodal Press, 1956), 351–456.

[102] Martin Jugie, *Le schisme byzantin* (Paris: P. Lethielleux, 1941), 342.

It cannot be considered as merely accidental that from the twenties of our century, the ways of acceding to autocephaly became highly controversial within the Orthodox world. Actually, by that time, several factors were at work to bring about confusion and uncertainty. The dramatic political changes which happened in connection with the First World War had a tremendous impact on the Orthodox Church. The imperial throne of Russia fell and the Russian Church faced hard persecutions. Under such circumstances, its influence in the Orthodox world vanished for several decades. The Ottoman Empire collapsed and the new Turkish republic became officially a secular state. Within its boundaries, after the exchange of population (1923), the ecumenical patriarch was the religious head of a tiny minority. Consequently, the patriarchate became more inclined than before to emphasize its primatial authority in the entire Orthodox Church. Within the framework of the present study, we cannot deal with this historical development. Suffice it to spotlight the consequences of this new situation.

In fact, from the fall of Byzantium to the nineteen twenties, the see of Constantinople had granted all the autocephalies, and those acts raised no question since the churches which received this status had been a part of the Patriarchate of Constantinople. This situation changed when a huge number of Orthodox who previously lived in the territory of the Russian Empire became subjects of neighboring countries, the local hierarchy asked the pressure of civil authorities, the local hierarchy asked the Patriarchate of Constantinople to receive the status of autocephaly. The ecumenical patriarch Gregory VII and his synod accepted this request in November 1924. About the same time, some other churches that until the Bolshevik revolution had been part of the Russian Church obtained the status of autonomy. The Moscow Patriarchate consistently denied the validity of those actions. As a result of this disagreement, both parties produced polemical works of uneven quality. The Moscow Patriarchate not only regarded the Constantinople initiative as null and void but also took a completely different stand regarding accession to autocephaly: Any patriarchate or autocephalous church is entitled to grant full autonomy or autocephaly to any territory belonging to its jurisdictional area inasmuch as this action would be good and profitable for the newly established Church. Actually, the Moscow Patriarchate implemented this principle for Poland (1948) and Czechoslovakia (1951). Later on, the Russian Church, taking into account that it had chronological priority in missionary activities and hierarchical organization in North America, bestowed autocephaly on the *Orthodox Church in America* (1970). For various reasons, this action provoked a strong reaction from Constantinople. It provided the opportunity for both parties to reaffirm their own stand with regard to the procedure for granting autocephaly. Professor John H. Erickson has accurately summarized the two viewpoints and we cannot do better than to quote him verbatim:

> To put matters in simplest terms, according to the Russian Church, any autocephalous church has the right to grant canonical independence to one of its parts. According to Constantinople, on the other hand, only an ecumenical council can definitively establish an autocephalous church, and any interim arrangements depend upon approbation by Constantinople, acting in its capacity as the "mother church" and "first among equals."[103]

Being formulated in sharply opposed terms, the two standpoints seem to be completely irreconcilable, more especially as each side considers its position, as it were, strongly based on an existing norm (*de lege lata*). As shown above, the paradigms from the past do not provide an incontrovertible model for our time. This does not mean, however, that some perennial ecclesiological rules have lost their validity.

For logical reasons, we shall begin to examine the second standpoint because, at first sight, it sounds more consonant with the basic standards of canon law as, for example, expressed in Canons 14 and 15 of the "First-Second Council." This position was also clearly articulated by St Basil and Demetrios Chomatianos.[104] Furthermore, from his commentary on Canon

---

[103]Erickson, *The Challenge of our Past*, 91.
[104]On St Basil's stand see Faustus of Byzantium, 5, 29, *Fragmenta Historicorum Graecorum* 5 (Paris, 1938): 293–94. On the canonical position of Demetrios Chomatianos see Letters 86 and 114, J. B. Pitra, *Analecta Sacra* (Paris-Rome, 1891), cols. 381–90 and 487–98.

2 of the Constantinopolitan Council in 381, one can infer that Balsamon favored this view. Notwithstanding, we must acknowledge that historical evidence does not provide many examples with respect to the implementation of such a procedure. Surely, as rightly pointed out by Professor A. V. Kartashev: "History is not a canonical norm. It comprises a countless number of ideological deviations."[105] Be that as it may, we cannot ignore the fact that acceding to autocephalous status, from the Middle Ages onward, has never been a purely ecclesiastical event. In the overwhelming majority of cases, political factors have played a predominant role. Needless to say, this is also the case nowadays. The present tendency to envision autocephaly as a completely sovereign entity contributes to making the problem more sensitive.

Now let us take a dispassionate look at the first position. Sometimes its adversaries raised the accusation of "papism" against the Constantinopolitan stand. We think that such an accusation constitutes an oversimplification. Papacy is a unique system of church government which throughout history has taken shape and eventually reached a high level of coherence. The whole system has been included in the province of dogma. Accordingly, the pope exerts a universal and *immediate* jurisdiction over the whole Church.[106] Moreover, the Patriarchate of Constantinople has more than once sharply denounced the papal system.[107] The idea that, in the interstices between the ecumenical councils, the last of which was held in 787, the see of Constantinople is entitled "by economy" to bestow the status of autocephaly, is supposedly based on the primatial prerogatives given to that see by the Councils of Constantinople, Chalcedon, and Trullo. Actually, those canons do not deal with the matter at hand; they merely affirm the primacy of Constantinople after the see of Rome within

---

[105] *Na Putiakh k Vselenskomu Sobaru* [*On the Ways to the Ecumenical Council*] (Paris: YMCA Press, 1932), 21.

[106] Denzinger-Schönmetzer, *Enchiridion*, 3060. Analyzing the real significance of the decree issued on this matter by Vatican I is outside the scope of the present study.

[107] See, for example, the well-known "*Answer of the Orthodox Patriarchs of the East to Pope Pius IX*" in 1848, J. Karmiris, Τὰ δογματικὰ καὶ συμβολικὰ Μνημεῖα [*Ta dogmatika kai symbolika Mnēmeia*], vol. 2 (Athens, 1953), 902–25.

the framework of the *Reichskirche*, and in the case of Chalcedon "Canon 28" specifies the territorial extent of its jurisdiction.

During the Middle Ages, as already mentioned, the granting of autocephaly was mainly determined by the emperors on the basis of expediency and was considered as a concession that was always revocable. This approach, related to the concept of the permanence of the "Roman Empire," has obviously lost its relevance. Yet, nowadays, in the whole Orthodox Church, no one denies the *primacy of honor* of the Constantinopolitan see. Furthermore, there is a large agreement on the fact that doubtless the term "honor" implies more than a merely honorific position. Nevertheless, in contrast with Roman Catholic ecclesiology, in Orthodoxy the issue of primacy is not regarded as a topic pertaining to the province of doctrine. Therefore, it is no wonder that no full consensus can be reached about the content of such a primacy.

Exploring all the aspects of this problem would lead us far astray. Nevertheless, it should be noted that the very existence of another position regarding the accession to autocephaly shows that the relation between primacy and the right to grant such a status is far from being self-evident in the Orthodox world. Thus, in the present stage the two positions seem to be irreconcilable. This does not mean, however, that a solution cannot be found, provided that both parties would be ready to take a fresh approach. We have shown that, beyond any doubt, historical evidence does not furnish a perennial procedural pattern which could be regarded as compelling, especially if we take into account the interference of factors which, through the ages, have partly distorted the original concept of autocephaly. Under such conditions, it would be difficult not to concur with this statement made by the ecumenical patriarch Benjamin in 1937: "It is known . . . that concerning the manner in which the separation must occur and the manner of establishing the autocephaly of any part of the Church, none of the sacred canons provides direction or inkling."[108] Perhaps this blunt statement, albeit true, needs to be somewhat nuanced. Surely, none of the

---

[108] Answer of the ecumenical patriarch Benjamin to Patriarch Nicholas of Alexandria (December 7, 1937), Apost. Glavinas, Ὀρθόδοξη Αὐτοκέφαλη Ἐκκλησία τῆς Ἀλβανίας [*Orthodoxē Autokephalē Ekklēsia tēs Albanias*] (Thessalonica, 1985), 63.

canons addresses the question directly. Let us bear in mind that our corpus of canon law is not to be seen as an accumulation of legal texts that necessarily provide prefabricated answers to every question on church order. Nonetheless, we must have a holistic vision of canon law. This implies that specific rules on inter-hierarchical relations are not merely a question of protocol but reflect principles intended to maintain Church unity.

If we peruse our official collection of canons contained in the last recension of the *Syntagma of the XIV Titles*, we can, by and large, tabulate the rules under the following categories: 1) Rules affirming the validity of "ancient customs"; 2) canons recalling the validity of previous rules tending to be neglected; 3) decisions made in order either to meet new situations or to solve authoritatively points of uncertainty. Due to complex historical reasons, for a long time the issue of acceding to autocephaly has not been a major concern in Orthodoxy. Under the impact of dramatic changes in the political world order in our century, this has come to the fore, and the lack of consensus among the Orthodox has brought about controversies which sometimes have reached a high degree of bitterness.

What solution can be suggested to overcome this stalemate? We think that a presupposition should be admitted, namely the necessity of reconsidering the issue. As has been evidenced by our historical survey, no canonical rule directly addressing this question has been enacted in the past, and precedents do not offer an unquestionable model. Thus, it must be candidly acknowledged that this topic pertains to the sphere of the *de lege ferenda*. This implies that, within the parameters of the fundamental principles of our canonical Tradition, a new law dealing with this specific question has to be promulgated. Why do we mention those parameters? Because the new ruling must take into account the existing canonical materials bearing on inter-hierarchical relations.[109] What Church organ is entitled to formulate an authoritative statement on this issue? Indubitably,

---

[109] We must observe that the canonical documents included in the *Syntagma of the XIV Titles* do not contain many statements dealing with the relations between the major sees. Infrequent exceptions can be ranked within the category of "occasional statements," for example I Constantinople, Canon 2; the Letter of the African episcopate to Pope Celestine; Hagia Sophia, Canon 1.

to be effectively implemented, such a decision must result from an agreement among the major sees of the Orthodox Church. In principle, it would be better to have a statement issued by a Pan-Orthodox Synod. Actually, for decades the question of holding such an assembly has been in the air and documents on this topic have been already prepared, but the gathering of the "Great and Holy Council" has been continually delayed. Doubtless, with regard to the issues under review, we think that it would be the most suitable organ entitled to enact an authoritative decree, spelling out first the reasons adduced to justify the usefulness of an official statement on this matter.

If the gathering of the "Great and Holy Council" is indefinitely postponed, there is, of course, an alternative solution: an agreement can be reached between the major sees after consultations. This latter solution, however, has to be considered as makeshift because it involves drawbacks: such an agreement would lack the firmness of a *synodal determination* and would not necessarily become part of our written law.

As mentioned above, in the mainstream of Orthodoxy, only two positions concerning accession to autocephaly are worthy of examination. Other standpoints, being blatantly in opposition with the spirit and letter of canon law, do not deserve attention in connection with the area of the *de lege ferenda*. At first glance, the two positions seem to be deeply at variance. Nonetheless, if we look at the problem with a certain serenity, the two procedural ways are not irreconcilable. On the basis of canonical order, no part of the Church is allowed to separate unilaterally from the higher authority of the mother see and its Synod, except in the case of heresy. Therefore, none can question the exclusive right of the mother church to decide about the request presented by the portion of the Church that asks for autocephaly. According to the thought of the ancient Church, nothing more was required. For, at that time, the concept of autocephaly did not include the accretions that throughout the ages, and especially from the last century, it has gotten.

Albeit questionable, we cannot ignore the result of such an evolution. In any event, the emphasis on autocephaly has inevitably led to the feeling that to be admitted into the circle of autocephalous churches requires a general consensus from the churches enjoying this status. This has also created the so-called problem of the diptychs. According to written law, this order (τάξις [taxis]) is only clearly established for the ancient patriarchates and the Patriarchate of Moscow. We do not deem that this secondary problem has to be treated within the framework of the present study.[110]

3

Having now come to the final part of this study, we must try to offer concrete proposals for reconciling standpoints which at first sight appear to be mutually incompatible.

We should make one preliminary remark. As stated above, historical evidence does not provide a unique procedural pattern for obtaining autocephaly. This does not mean, however, that every way to reach such a goal is legitimate. Actually, although canon law does not deal directly with this issue, it includes rules prohibiting arbitrary rupture of communion. This is the underlying presupposition of Canons 34 of the Holy Apostles, 4 and 9 of Antioch. This is spelled out in Canons 14, 15 and 16 of the so-called First-Second Council held in 861. Unilateral withdrawal of obedience therefore is reprehensible, unless obviously justified by doctrinal or canonical reasons.

Thus, to reach a pan-Orthodox consensus on the appropriate way of obtaining autocephaly, the lawmaker first and foremost must take into account those data provided by canon law which express the principle of an ecclesiology of communion. In delineating the procedure, the lawmaker cannot ignore the present geopolitical context which doubtless is at variance with that prevailing in former stages of history.

The request for autocephaly must respond to an ecclesiastical necessity. This is the case when a canonical dependency of a primatial see represents a hindrance to regular Church life.

The part of the Church sharing such a feeling must constitute a territorial entity. The claim of autocephaly should reflect the wish of the

[110]"Problems Concerning Autocephaly," 178–79. However, Fr Justin Popovich considers that it is a serious problem which has deeper implications than it seems at first glance. "On the Summoning of the 'Great Council' of the Orthodox Church," E.T. *Orthodox Life* 1 (1978): 44.

overwhelming majority of the faithful, clergy, and episcopate. To be sure, the part of the Church wishing to become autocephalous must fulfill some *substantive requirements*. Since the subject has been appropriately treated elsewhere, we do not deem it necessary to address this issue.[111] The first step should be a formal request from the regional episcopate submitted to the Synod of the mother church. In this request, the reasons for such a status must be cogently articulated.

The answer of the synod of the mother church is to be regarded as the crucial factor. Three possibilities exist: 1) The request receives full approval; 2) Granting autocephaly is not ruled out, but the mother church considers that the issue needs further examination; 3) the request is rejected. Surely, whatever the answer may be, the reasons for the stand taken by the synod should be indicated. In the event of a negative answer, the portion of the Church having petitioned for autocephaly is not canonically allowed to sidestep the decision. This would bring about a state of schism. However, inasmuch as an unqualified negative decision can have detrimental effects, the upholders of autocephaly are entitled to voice their concerns and to draw the attention of the mother church to those detrimental effects.

Up to this point of the procedure, we cannot discern basic disagreements within the mainstream of contemporary Orthodoxy.

The picture is different regarding further procedural developments, since at first sight the two prevailing viewpoints on this matter in contemporary Orthodoxy are at variance.[112] Nevertheless, we should notice that this bipolarity is a relatively recent phenomenon which did not start surfacing prior to the end of the twenties of our century and even later. As seen above, Ecumenical Patriarch Benjamin acknowledged that on this matter there were no well-determined rules of procedure.[113] Here we would like to formulate a candid remark: In such a matter, the intricacies of procedure cannot be treated in the abstract. Undoubtedly a necessary presupposition for finding a solution lies in the existence of a genuine spirit of trust

---

[111]S. Troitsky, *L'autocéphalie ecclésiastique*, 29. Our article, "Problems Concerning Autocephaly," 186–87. Sp. Troianos, Παραδόσεις Ἐκκλησιαστικοῦ Δικαίου [*Paradoseis Ekklēsiastikou Dikaiou*], 2d ed. (Athens-Komotene: A. N. Sakkoulas, 1984), 130–32.

[112]Erickson, *The Challenge of our Past*, 91.

[113]Glavinas, Ὀρθόδοξη Αὐτοκέφαλη [*Orthodoxē Autokephalē*], 63.

among the major sees. Mutual fears of purported hegemonistic ambition have cast a gloom over inter-Orthodox relations during a large part of our century. At all events, the collapse of the communist system in the former Soviet Union and its satellites has created a new political situation. Among new data, one should mention the arising of nationalistic feelings. Such is the case in Ukraine. Thus, in April 1922, the self-governing Church of Ukraine petitioned the "Bishop's Assembly" of the Moscow Patriarchate for full autocephaly. The assembly formulated a cautious answer including the following statement: "In order to obtain autocephaly, the canonical lawful order calls for a corresponding decision [which is to be made] by the 'local Council,'[114] in agreement with all the other local Orthodox churches."[115] That the "local council" is considered as the competent organ for granting autocephaly is not a novelty in the view of the Moscow Patriarchate. Given the restrictions imposed upon the Russian Church by the Soviet government, convening local councils on a regular schedule was impossible. Therefore, autocephaly was granted to some churches by decision of the episcopate alone. Nevertheless, the matter was regularized *ex post facto* by the local council held in 1971, on the occasion of the election of a new patriarch.[116] However, in the last part of the above-mentioned statement, a supplementary condition for autocephaly is enunciated, viz., the agreement of the other churches. This requirement marks a departure from the position formerly held by the Russian Patriarchate which considered as sufficient the decision of the mother church. Thereby a major point of dissention is eliminated on the procedure regarding the accession to autocephaly. Hence, *this clause must be included in a future Pan-Orthodox "Agreed Statement."*

The last step consists in the formal proclamation of autocephaly. According to the contemporary view, the newly-acknowledged status has to be articulated in a tomos. Such a document indicates the official appellation

---

[114] *SOP*, #167, 3.

[115] About the respective composition and competency of the "bishop's assembly" and of the "local council," see *The Statute of the Government of the Russian Orthodox Church*, adopted by the local Council of the Russian Orthodox Church on June 8, 1988, chapters 2 and 3.

[116] *The Local Council of the Russian Orthodox Church*, May 30–June 2, 1971, published by the Moscow Patriarchate, Moscow 1972, 139–40.

of that church and its territorial boundaries. Usually, it includes some guidelines on canonical order. As seen above, nowadays there are two different positions regarding the competent organ entitled to issue such a tomos and subsequently communicate the decision to the other Orthodox churches.

On a merely canonical level, this last step is far from being the most important, since in the whole process the fundamental points are, first, the consent of the mother church, and immediately thereafter, the favorable opinion of the major sees. However, in the light of what happened during the last decades, and given the fact that in this span of time conflicting views have been brought to the fore, this constitutes a highly sensitive issue. Therefore, attempting to solve the problem at issue necessarily requires a fresh approach. Let us make one point clear: such a reconsideration does not imply an infringement of church order because, as already mentioned, *canon law does not provide a compelling model*. Hence, the problem belongs to the realm of *de lege ferenda*. Moreover, though the essential features of autocephaly remain immutable, one cannot ignore that the sociological and political conditions of church life are completely at variance with those prevailing in the past. Those conditions influence some peripheral components of the makeup of autocephaly. However, those peripheral components make all the more complicated the requirements for acceding to that stature.

We suggest that the last step of the process be considered as falling within the competency of the primatial see of Constantinople. Inasmuch as the previous stages of procedure would be carefully observed, and provided that such a prerogative would be based on a pan-Orthodox consensus, we do not see why this should be regarded as canonically objectionable.

If, hopefully, an agreement on this procedure can be reached, it would strengthen the canonical unity of the Orthodox Church.

Greek Orthodoxy, the Ecumenical Patriarchate, and the Church in the USA

Elpidophoros Lambriniadis

St Vladimir's Theological Quarterly 54.3–4 (2010): 421–439

Venerable hierarchs, Rev. Dr John Behr, Dean, Reverend Clergy, Brothers and sisters,

It is a particular privilege and pleasure to be among you today, in the academic halls of St Vladimir's Orthodox Theological Seminary, this nursery of theological letters and priestly vocation, which has been grounded in the Russian spirituality and intellectual thought of such great theologians and ministers of the Church as the Fathers George Florovsky, Alexander Schmemann, and John Meyendorff.

I wish to express my sincere gratitude to the successors of these extraordinary theologians for the invitation extended to me to participate in this distinguished scholarly symposium in order to enjoy the opportunity to convey to all of you the paternal greetings and patriarchal blessings of His All Holiness ecumenical patriarch Bartholomew, Primate of the Great Church of Christ, the mother church of Constantinople.

The topic that I have been asked to address today is: "Greek Orthodoxy, the Ecumenical Patriarchate, and the Church in the USA." Beginning with the content and historical development of the phrase "Greek Orthodoxy," I will endeavor to explore its relationship to the Ecumenical Patriarchate in order, finally, on this basis, to interpret the perception of the Church of Constantinople with regard to the ecclesiastical situation in the United States and present its vision for the future of Orthodoxy in this land.

From its very foundation on this earth by our Lord Jesus Christ, but especially from the outset of its organization by the local bishops, the Church of Christ was profoundly—and quite naturally—influenced by the political, administrative, and cultural context of the Roman Empire, which was in turn characterized as an empire by syncretism, multi-ethnicism, and multi-culturalism, as well as uniformity of law, government, language, currency, and so forth. From the moment that Christianity was first registered as recognized and tolerated after the period of persecution and thereafter as the official religion of the empire, the very identity of the Church was directly affected, while in turn affecting the identity of the Roman citizen. I will discuss neither the degree to which divine providence in this way prepared the political and cultural historical context for the extension and establishment of the Church of Christ, nor the scope to which the multi-ethnic and multi-cultural identity of the empire facilitated a Christianity that was based on the same external elements.

Nevertheless, I would like to draw your attention to the concept and content of the Roman citizen (or inhabitant of the Roman Empire), especially from the time that he or she began to sense the Christian faith as a characteristic feature of identity.

The Roman Christian could—at least ethnically—belong to any race and have any native language. Yet, in spite of this, the Roman Christian would be a member of the Church under the *one* bishop of a particular city that served as either temporary or permanent residence, just as he or she would be subjected to the Roman administrator or governor of the region. The identity of the Roman Christian as citizen of the Kingdom of God bore—analogically speaking—the same characteristics of identity enjoyed by every citizen of the Roman Empire, irrespective of race, language, or origin.

The same applied to one's identity within the Church of the Roman Empire: namely, the basis and criterion of organization was always geographical, with one bishop elected for every city, to whom all inhabitants of the region were submitted without any discrimination (linguistic or other), in accordance with the apostolic instruction: "There is no longer Jew or Greek, there is no longer slave or free, there is no longer male nor female; for all of you are one in Christ Jesus" (Gal 3.28).

On the basis of the same principle, the Orthodox churches today are called the "Church of Alexandria," the "Church of Antioch," the "Church of Jerusalem," the "Church of Russia," and so on—that is to say, they are defined geographically. In this respect, it is both untraditional and uncanonical from an ecclesiastical perspective for the patriarchates to be named "Russian," "Serbian," "Romanian," "Bulgarian," or "Georgian," or for their patriarchs to be addressed as "Patriarch of the Russians," "of the Serbs," "of the Romanians," "of the Bulgarians," or "of the Georgians." For these characterizations introduce—not only in the diaspora, but also in the local Orthodox churches—a criterion of ethnophyletism, thereby dividing the flock of the local bishop on the basis of ethnic origin and allowing the possibility of infringement into another eparchy or jurisdiction. This applies to both realities, in local churches and in diaspora, since the sacred canons cannot have selective or circumstantial application, but are universal.

This experience and teaching of the Church was also confirmed by the decisions of the ecumenical councils, which codified and recorded in a binding manner for all of Christianity not only the "faith once delivered" [Jude v.3] together with its doctrine, but also the principles of administration and organization. I would remind you that the ecumenical councils did not dogmatize *ex nihilo*; nor did they impose definitions and conditions of ecclesiastical organization that hitherto did not exist. Both in matters of faith and in matters of administration, they codified the apostolic teaching, the Church experience, and the patristic tradition. There is no reason here to expand on the well-substantiated refutation of the erroneous distinction of sacred canons into doctrinal (and therefore not conducive to revision) and administrative (and hence susceptible to modification).

Resuming the analysis of the terminology, I would call to mind the fact that the Church within the Roman Empire—that which Western historians in the 18th century labeled as Byzantine—was in fact originally called Roman, particularly when schismatic and heretical ecclesiastical structures appeared and required some form of distinction from a terminological perspective. This was especially evident and instituted in the Orthodox East after the Schism of 1054 and, in particular, with the capture of the Eastern Roman Empire by the Ottomans.

Henceforth, the non-Christian sultan ratified and formally instituted the phrase "Roman Nation" (*Rum Milleti*), which included all Christian Orthodox inhabitants of the occupied empire. For the sultan, just as for his

Roman predecessor, there were no distinctions according to race, but only according to religion and confession. This is precisely why the populations that embraced Islam were not called "Roman Muslims" but Turks. Those who converted to Islam became Turkish—that is to say, they changed their identity.

Therefore, the Ottoman Empire adopted and respected the existing ecclesiastical terminology, according to which the conquered Roman Christian was not distinguished on the basis of linguistic or ethnic origin, but on the basis of his or her identity as a member of the Church.

In this respect, in the eastern languages (namely, Greek, Turkish, and Arabic), the patriarchates (the Ecumenical Patriarchate, as well as those of Alexandria, Antioch, and Jerusalem) were characterized as "Rum (or Roman) Orthodox" in contradistinction to "Rum (or Roman) Catholic" or the Armenian and Syrian churches.

Problems arose when, with the rise of nationalism in the Balkans during the 19th century, the term "Rum" was translated as "Greek" in order also to determine the principle of reorganization and independence of the various Orthodox peoples from an ecclesiastical viewpoint. Meanwhile, of course, the Greek state had been established and every concept of Hellenism was understood in nationalistic terms, thereby attributing an entirely different content to the original term "Rum."

Without further expanding, I would summarize as follows: The meaning of the phrase "Greek Orthodoxy" has in our day assumed an ethnic sense which, however, distorts reality. The phrase "Greek Orthodoxy" or "Rum Orthodox" is more accurately rendered in English as "Roman Orthodox." Just as the phrase "Roman Catholic" cannot be translated as "Italian Catholic," so too the term "Rum" or "Roman" when referring to Orthodox Christians should not be translated as "Greek Orthodox" in a way that conveys an ethnic content to a purely ecclesiastical terminology.

The original sense of the term is even preserved in the Uniate churches, which unfortunately bear the inappropriate title "Greek Catholic." For their members are certainly not Greeks, but Uniates subjected to the Pope and adhering to the Byzantine (or Eastern Roman) rite.

Another characteristic fact is that all the Slavic peoples—at least in the period preceding the rise of nationalism—had no problem whatsoever with being called "Rum Orthodox" and with being under the jurisdiction of the Ecumenical Patriarchate, which—we should not forget—never endeavored to Hellenize them, since this was contrary to its principles and very identity as Ecumenical. Indeed, there was no attempt to Hellenize the Slavs even during the period of their Christianization. On the contrary, their language was enhanced—in fact engendered—with the creation of a specific alphabet and the consolidation of a cultural identity.

It is not by chance that the Church of Russia from the 18th century until the October Revolution had no difficulty being called "Greek-Russian,"[1] while even your own Church here in the United States was, until 1971, called "Russian Orthodox Greek Catholic Church of America."[2]

Thus, since I believe that we have together established sufficient evidence that the phrase "Greek Orthodox"—at least in reference to the patriarchates of the East—is not an accurate rendering of their actual reality, we may better interpret contemporary developments in diaspora as well as within the patriarchates themselves.

Ever since the creation of the independent Greek state, which terminologically was also identified with the patriarchates of the East, all of these churches underwent a period of crisis of identity.

The Ecumenical Patriarchate granted autocephaly to the churches of Greece, Serbia, Romania, Bulgaria, Georgia, Poland, Albania, as well as the Czech Lands and Slovakia during the 19th and 20th centuries; moreover, following the destruction of Asia Minor, with the signing of the Treaty of Lausanne and the exchange of populations between Greece and Turkey, it lost almost all of its flock remaining within Turkey.

The Patriarchates of Antioch and Jerusalem also underwent a period of crisis of identity inasmuch as their Greekness risked being identified with the fate of the Greek state and the policy of the Republic of Greece. And

---

[1]Metropolitan Evgenii Bolchovitinov, *Slovar' istoricheskiy o byvshikh v Rossii pisatelyakh dukhovnogo china Greko-rossiyskoy Tserkvi* [Historical dictionary about former writers of spiritual rank of the Greek-Russian Church in Russia] (St Petersburg, 1818).

[2]*Orthodox America, 1794–1976: Development of the Orthodox Church in America*, ed. Constance J. Tarasar (New York: Orthodox Church in America, 1976), 259.

the Church of Russia, having been reduced to a state organ following the dissolution of the patriarchate by Peter the Great, was compromised by the pan-Slavist direction of the Russian state's foreign policy after the 19th century, because the latter provided the possibility of promoting its own interests with the full support of the state. Thus, with the formation of the Palestinian Society on May 28, 1882, whose purpose was to offer assistance to Russian pilgrims, it also became an instrument of tsarist interests in the Middle East, while at the same time advocating its interests in this sensitive region.

The Patriarchate of Alexandria directed its attention to missionary activity among the peoples of Africa. After evolving and establishing an organized mission, in 2001 it officially sought from the Ecumenical Patriarchate the concession of jurisdiction over the entire continent. From that time, the phrase "and of all Africa" was added to the title of the patriarch of Alexandria, whereas hitherto he was only known as "and of all Egypt."

Nationalism encroached upon the Patriarchate of Jerusalem, whose Palestinian faithful could not readily understand why their church bore the title "Rum (improperly rendered as 'Greek') Orthodox," while they communicated in Arabic and enjoyed an Arabic consciousness. Nevertheless, through prudent and pastoral sensitivity to the needs of its Palestinian flock, it managed to confront the various nationalistic predicaments that appeared from time to time.

I feel that this outline was necessary in order to appreciate the contemporary situation of the Orthodox Church in the United States as well as the approach of the Ecumenical Patriarchate.

For the Ecumenical Patriarchate is not ethnic in the modern sense of the term. It is the continuation of the traditional and patristic expression of Christianity, as this was organically shaped in the historical context of a non-ethnic, ecumenical empire, and as this was recorded and codified in the decisions of the ecumenical councils.

The ecumenical councils recorded the original Christian and apostolic understanding regarding the organization of church life purely on the basis of geographical criteria and not any linguistic or ethnic origin. The jurisdiction of each church was accurately described and defined in their decisions, while the holy and inspired fathers knew very well that certain regions existed outside the boundaries of the Roman world and outside the then-known *"oikoumenē,"* which they labeled with the term "barbarian." The pastoral responsibility for these regions was assigned to the ecumenical patriarch.

The geographical jurisdictions of the churches and patriarchates that were created later—that is to say, after the ecumenical councils—were also accurately described and defined by the patriarchal and synodal tomos issued by the Ecumenical Patriarchate, assuring and expressing the pan-Orthodox conscience and consent.

It has been sufficiently proven by scholarship that the Church of Russia developed missionary activity in Alaska from the 18th century, when this region was a Russian territory, just as other imperial churches of the time were active in their colonies.

The canonical question that arises is the following: Does the territorial expansion of a state comprise a self-evident extension of the jurisdiction of that church in that particular region? And by analogy: Does the development of missionary activity in a geographical region outside a particular jurisdiction at the same time imply a claim by that jurisdiction?

The preaching of God's word and the spread of Christ's gospel are clearly praiseworthy, while the saintly and sacrificial ministry of the early missionaries is universally admired and respected; however, the geographical jurisdiction of the Church of Russia is plainly defined in its tomos of autocephaly received from the Ecumenical Patriarchate. The argument that it was first to evangelize a portion of the American continent is neither ecclesiological nor canonical, expressing instead a mentality of colonialism. At this point, we could also cite the examples of Russian missionary activity in China and Japan, lands which the Church of Russia claims to be its canonical territory. The proper response to similar circumstances, as we have already observed, is that of the Patriarchate of Alexandria, which requested and officially received jurisdiction over the entire African continent.

The later development of Orthodox Christianity in the United States around the end of the 19th and during the 20th centuries bears all the characteristics of the Orthodox diaspora throughout the world. Accordingly, Orthodox Christians organized themselves ecclesiastically on the basis primarily of ethnicity and their churches of origin.

Consequently, it is not fair to claim that "this unity was broken and then arbitrarily replaced with the unheard-of principle of 'jurisdictional multiplicity.'"[3]

The ancient patriarchates respected the 28th Canon of the Fourth Ecumenical Council and the jurisdiction of the Ecumenical Patriarchate over regions outside the geographical boundaries of the Orthodox churches. The only exception, unfortunately, was the Patriarchate of Antioch, which, in the confusion created toward the end of the 19th century with the otherwise correct rendering and accurate content of the phrase "Rum Orthodox Patriarchate," was misled by the rise of Arab nationalism, making unconventional ecclesiological choices in order to survive at the time in an environment recognized for its dangerously intensifying anti-Western mentality, at least from a geo-political perspective.

The ongoing presence of the Church of Russia in the United States was deeply influenced by the ramifications of the October Revolution of 1917 and the establishment in Russia of an atheist state. Communication with the troubled Patriarchate of Moscow became difficult, while dependence on it was regarded with suspicion and increasing reservation, because of its perceived cooperation with the atheistic state. The Cold War between the two superpowers later contributed to this attitude, rendering any ecclesiastical subjection to Moscow inconceivable for American citizens.[4]

Already in 1924, as you well know, the decision was made for the "temporarily self-governing" presence of the Church of Russia in the United

---

[3]Alexander Schmemann, "To Love is to Remember," in *Orthodox America*, 12. See also 188.

[4]See the Christmas Encyclical of Metropolitan Irinei to the Orthodox Patriarchs (1966): "Even when the political relations between the two states are normal and friendly, the Church which is under the authority of a foreign leadership is suspected of being 'alien.' What can be said then about our situation, when the relations between the two political giants of our era, the Soviet Union and the United States of America, continue to be grounded in mutual distrust and competition?" *Orthodox America*, 269.

States.⁵ Moscow questioned its canonicity,⁶ while here the patriarch of Moscow was commemorated as its ecclesiastical head by way of formality.⁷ We cannot overlook the fact that, in 1946, there was an attempt—albeit in vain—to subject the church here to the then Patriarch of Moscow, Alexei I.⁸ A similar effort again occurred in 1966, when Metropolitan Irinei communicated with all the Orthodox Primates.⁹

The events that led to granting of "autocephaly" to the Metropolia, which the Patriarchate of Moscow had renamed officially only in 1970 from "Russian Orthodox Greek Catholic Church of America" to "Orthodox Church in America," are well known.¹⁰

Beyond the issue concerning the canonicity of this "autocephaly" (which it is not by chance that only the churches of Soviet influence recognized),¹¹ the following questions arise:

- Was the pursuit of regional independence by the Metropolia from the Church of Moscow exclusively and solely dictated by ideological reasons as well as by ecclesiological principles regarding the local nature of the Church? Or was it an inevitable choice and need to divest itself of any suspicion that it is spiritually subjected to and directed by a state church, which was considered the primary threat against the United States?¹²

- Are the words of Fr John Meyendorff verified today, forty years later, that: "the criticisms which [autocephaly] encountered were

---

⁵During the 4th All American Church Sobor held in Detroit (March 20-April 2, 1924). See *Orthodox America*, 184.

⁶"... [T]he Metropolia not only had no support from its mother church but was denounced by the latter as 'schismatic' and deprived of canonical basis." *Orthodox America*, 184.

⁷*Orthodox America*, 185.

⁸*Orthodox America*, 201.

⁹*Orthodox America*, 267–69.

¹⁰This is mentioned in the same telegram dated April 13, 1970, from Patriarch Alexei to Metropolitan Irinei, where the granting of "autocephaly" is announced. See *Orthodox America*, 264.

¹¹*Orthodox America*, 201.

¹²See the opinion: "The Metropolia always experienced its separation from the mother church as forced upon it by events beyond its control, always looked forward with hope to the day of reunion and restoration of normal relations." *Orthodox America*, 261.

provoked not by any canonical or ecclesiological considerations, but by the fear that the 'phyletistic' (or ethnocentric) structure of the existing 'jurisdictions' would henceforth be decisively challenged by a canonical and healthy American Church, which, at the same time, would be fully open to the preservation of all valid national customs and traditions of the various Orthodox immigrant groups"?[13]

The efforts by the OCA to establish in the United States a concept and reality of the *local church* are welcome and admirable. As we noted earlier, this is also the vision of the Ecumenical Patriarchate. Yet, I wonder whether a jurisdiction can claim *locality*, when in fact it comprises a minority, when it overlooks all the other churches.

In reading the Encyclical of the OCA Hierarchy, whereby in 1970 the granting of "autocephaly" was officially proclaimed, I discerned a threefold goal at the time:

- "The task of uniting all the Orthodox Christians of America into one Church."

- "The task of witnessing freely to the true Christian faith in the whole world." And:

- "The task of growing spiritually from strength to strength, through the prayers of the Holy Father Herman of Alaska."

Once again, I wonder whether, today, after forty years, we could readily admit success in any of these three goals. The first goal has clearly not been achieved. With regard to the other two goals, I would simply pose the following two questions:

- Was the granting of autocephaly necessary to meet these two goals? Did not precisely the same possibilities exist prior to the granting of this "autocephaly"? And, related to this:

---

[13] The Standing Conference of Canonical Orthodox Bishops in America. *Orthodox America*, 244.

- Were the other Orthodox churches in the United States in any way deprived in these areas of "witnessing freely" and "growing spiritually from strength to strength" by not having the status of autocephaly?

Summarizing my humble reflections on the granting of "autocephaly," permit me to say that it appears that, no matter how good intentions may be in the Church, the violation of the sacred canons never produces positive results. The consequences of uncanonical actions must be addressed sooner or later, as we recently (2009) witnessed in the decisions of the Fourth Pre-Conciliar Pan-Orthodox Conference held in Chambésy (Geneva). That is to say, while the OCA commenced with all the praiseworthy optimism of uniting all the Orthodox in the USA and establishing a conscience regarding the geographical nature of the Church, today it comprises a hindrance and problem to be resolved, inasmuch as it is not a church recognized by all Orthodox. This is because, in accordance with Article 1 of the "Rules of Operation for Episcopal Assemblies in the Orthodox Diaspora," approved by the Pan-Orthodox Conference: "All Orthodox bishops of each region, from those regions defined by the Fourth Pre-Conciliar Pan-Orthodox Conference, who are in canonical communion with all the local autocephalous Orthodox churches, form each Episcopal Assembly." Moreover, in its Decision 2c) regarding "The Orthodox Diaspora," the same conference declared that "decisions on these subjects will be taken by consensus *of the churches* who are represented in the particular assembly."

The Ecumenical Patriarchate organized its own jurisdictional presence in the United States following the migration there of faithful from the regions of Thrace, Pontus, and Asia Minor after the great destruction. This was a natural historical development with a specific historical significance. Therefore, it founded the "Greek Orthodox Archdiocese of North and South America," without implying that this was created solely for Greeks. Proof of this lies in the fact that the jurisdiction of the Ecumenical Patriarchate includes Albanians, Ukrainians, Carpatho-Russians, and Palestinians, without any of these ever feeling that they have as a result been either Hellenized or in any way slighted. The very founder of the holy Archdiocese, ecumenical patriarch Meletios (Metaxakis) spoke in his enthronement address about the pastoral concern for all Orthodox Christians in the diaspora, making particular reference to the faithful in the United States.[14] The same patriarch not only resists any distinction among the faithful on the basis of ethnic origin, but also refers to the decisions of the Great Council of Constantinople in 1872 which condemned ethnophyletism. It is important to recall that this council proclaimed as heretics all those who established a "separate altar" and created "their own ethnic faction"—namely, on the basis of exclusively ethnic criteria, which were deemed "contrary to the teaching of the gospel and the sacred canons of our blessed fathers."[15]

This jurisdictional dependence of the Greek Orthodox Archdiocese thus constituted no impediment for its spiritual and administrative progress. Or, at the very least, one cannot claim that the Archdiocese is in any way lacking in anything or in any field by comparison with the "autocephalous" OCA. On the contrary, without ceasing to be in the direct jurisdiction of the Ecumenical Patriarchate, its experience and development have materialized the vision of the late Professor Anton Vladimirovich Kartashev concerning the restoration "of *sobornost* (i.e., the responsible participation of the entire people of God, clergy as well as laity, in the life of the Church) from the top to the bottom."[16]

The Ecumenical Patriarchate has always responded with prudence and understanding to the various historical challenges presented by the OCA.

---

[14]"We should also make explicit reference to the administration of the Orthodox churches in the diaspora . . . where the Great Church of Christ is canonically obliged to take swift precautions for the appearance of the Orthodox Church even in the diaspora, maintaining inviolable the canonical order, which the great Council that convened in Constantinople 50 years ago proclaimed to be essential for the preservation of spiritual unity in the bond of peace. I have, in any case, personally witnessed the far greater majority of the Orthodox Church in the Diaspora, and I have personally experienced the degree to which the name of Orthodoxy will be elevated, especially the great United States of America, if the over two million Orthodox faithful are organized into one, united Church administration as an American Orthodox Church." In *Ekklēsiastikē Alētheia Kōnstantinoupoleēs* 40.4 (January 29, 1922): 30.

[15]See A. Nanakis (Metropolitan of Arkalochorion), "The Ecumenical Patriarchate: From the Condemnation of Ethnophyletism (1872) to the Macedonian Struggle," [in Greek] in *Apostolos Titos*, III/3 (December 2005): 91–92.

[16]*Orthodox America*, 261.

When the latter was confronted with controversy regarding its canonicity in relation to the Church of Russia during the Soviet era, the Ecumenical Patriarchate maintained constructive cooperation and communion. Even when, despite every concept of canonical order, it was granted "autocephaly," the Ecumenical Patriarchate regarded this more as a settlement of a disagreement with the Patriarchate of Moscow and manifested sensitivity by practicing canonical *economia* and not rupturing communion with it, continuing to concelebrate with its hierarchs. I do not wish here to expound upon the arguments of the Ecumenical Patriarchate on the subject; after all, these are well known and documented. However, I consider it my obligation to underline our common visions and common principles, which are often undermined and overlooked in jurisdictional juxtaposition, which usually monopolizes our relations. In this respect, I would like to remind you of the words of the late Metropolitan Irinei, who in his Christmas Encyclical to the Orthodox Patriarchs in 1966, stated that "unity can be reached only through an agreement between all the national churches,"[17] and consequently not by means of unilateral actions of dubious canonicity.

The Ecumenical Patriarchate did not come to this land as an ethnic Church in order to establish an ethnic jurisdiction. This would have been incompatible with both its ecclesiological principles and its very identity, but also with its long history. The Archdiocese is "Greek" in the sense analyzed at the outset of my address, without this signifying the abolition or oppression of the ethnic origin, language and culture of the faithful that comprise its jurisdiction, whether these are Greeks or not. And I believe that we are all in agreement on this.[18]

When speaking about the Greek Archdiocese in America, it should be underlined that one encounters parishes where Greek is the liturgical

[17] *Orthodox America*, 268.

[18] See the "Message to All Orthodox Christians in America," 1970: "We firmly believe that this variety constitutes the richness of American Orthodoxy and that whatever is true, noble, inspiring and Christian in our various customs and practices ought to be fully preserved and, if possible, shared. Therefore, although we insist that the One Orthodox Church here must be the home of all, we equally stress that there must be no loss of our respective national and cultural heritages and certainly no domination of any group by any other but full equality, total trust and truly Christian brotherhood." *Orthodox America*, 277.

language primarily used and others where there is an equal emphasis on Greek and English, while still others that adopt either mostly or only English. In other words, therefore, while one may have an initial impression of the heavy Greek influence in the Church, the truth is that this is simply not the case.

Nevertheless, I would dare to advance the following argument as well: The Greek language itself became a "victim" of the prevailing nationalism, serving even in the United States as an instrument of the notion of independence from the "mother churches." This, too, is surely regretful inasmuch as Greek is not merely an ethnic language, but the language of the gospel, of the definitions and decisions of the ecumenical councils, of exceptional and influential representatives of the patristic tradition, as well as of the original texts of liturgical sources in the Orthodox Church.

Finally, I wonder why it is that the Archdiocese of the Ecumenical Patriarchate cannot constitute the expression of the entire, united Orthodox presence in the USA simply because it bears the title "Greek," while the same claim is made by the OCA despite officially bearing until 1970 the title "Russian" (and "Greek") and being administered until recently by hierarchs of Russian descent.[19]

In this regard, then, "Greekness" did not constitute any impediment for our faithful becoming genuine Americans, devoted citizens of the United States and willing supporters of its interests.

---

[19] See expressions such as ". . . Russian leadership of the North American Church. . . ." In *Orthodox America*, 191. Archbishop Eftym expressed the same in 1927; see *The Orthodox Catholic Review* 1.4–5 (April-May, 1927): "For a hundred years the Russian leadership and control over Orthodoxy in America was unquestioned. . . ." Such expressions are in agreement with the viewpoint of Patriarch Tikhon of Moscow (1905): "In North America a whole Exarchate can easily be established, uniting all Orthodox national churches, which would have their own bishops under one Exarch, the Russian Archbishop." *Orthodox America*, 268. Of course, in an encyclical dated September 1969 on the occasion of the 175th anniversary of Orthodox presence in America, Metropolitan Irinei states that the Metropolia "was never Russian in the narrow meaning of the word: everyone who confessed Holy Orthodoxy . . . was received with love in its boundaries." In: *Orthodox America*, 297. These words reflect the genuine Orthodox conscience of an Orthodox hierarch who maintains a geographical principle and not an ethnic criterion. The question that arises, however, is: Why is this possibility not recognized for the hierarch representing the Ecumenical Patriarchate, who is in any case granted this right by the Ecumenical Councils?

Moreover, the hesitation of some to accept the term "diaspora," which by definition includes an element of temporariness, is comprehensible and perhaps justifiable. Of course, for the greater majority of Orthodox faithful in the United States—and beyond—the element of temporariness with regard to their existence in these regions constitutes an anachronism. Nevertheless, we are obliged to realize that, in speaking of "Diaspora," we are not referring simply to *people* that have been "dispersed" but, above all today, to the *geographical region* where the "Diaspora" has occurred. In this sense, then, it is neither a pejorative nor anachronistic to make reference to the particularity of a *geographical region* with a specific terminology from an ecclesiastical perspective. I do not believe that anyone would refuse to accept that the pastoral concern of regions outside the geographical boundaries of the local churches is a matter that today preoccupies the entire Orthodox Church and must at the very least be claimed and named in order to be evaluated and resolved. Those formerly dispersed are today native, established Christians, who have spread roots and borne fruits in this land.

In and of itself, the American dream which you rightly invoke does not presuppose the erasure of the historical memory and culture of the people that comprise it, but promotes their creative synthesis in the remarkable mosaic called the United States of America. "We hold these truths to be self-evident, that all men are created equal, that they are endowed by their Creator with certain unalienable Rights, that among these are Life, Liberty and the pursuit of Happiness," says the American Declaration of Independence. And former US President Jimmy Carter adds: "We become not a melting pot, but a beautiful mosaic. Different people, different beliefs, different yearnings, different hopes, different dreams."[20] President Carter's words echo Vice President Hubert H. Humphrey:

> Fortunately, the time has long passed when people liked to regard the United States as some kind of melting pot, taking men and women from every part of the world and converting them into standardized, homogenized Americans. We are, I think, much more mature and

---

[20] 39th President of the United States of America (1977–81).

wise today. Just as we welcome a world of diversity, so we glory in an America of diversity—an America all the richer for the many different and distinctive strands of which it is woven.[21]

In concluding my presentation to you, I would like to state that uncanonical actions and developments—even when dictated by historical necessity—do not constitute correct choices because they will always return to haunt and hinder our journey for pan-Orthodox unity and witness. Thus, the decisions of the Fourth Pre-Conciliar Pan-Orthodox Conference provide an historic opportunity for Orthodoxy and for America to transcend the competitive mentality of the past and see that the Ecumenical Patriarchate is governed by the same trans-ethnic principles as the OCA and the USA. Respect for the decisions of the ecumenical councils, as well as for the nurturing Orthodox tradition and faith, and relating this faith to our contemporary life constitutes the only sure way toward unity and progress in Christ.

In his address to the Primates of the Orthodox churches, who convened at the Phanar in October 2008, ecumenical patriarch Bartholomew boldly declared:

> We have been deigned by our Lord to belong to the one, holy, catholic and apostolic Church, whose faithful continuation and expression in history is our holy Orthodox Church. We have received and preserved the true faith, as the holy fathers have transmitted it to us through the ecumenical councils of the one undivided Church. We commune of the same body and blood of our Lord in the divine Eucharist, and we participate in the same sacred mysteries. We basically keep the same liturgical typikon and are governed by the same sacred canons. All these safeguard our unity, granting us fundamental presuppositions for witness in the modern world.

Despite this, we must admit in all honesty that sometimes we present an image of incomplete unity, as if we were not one Church, but rather a

---

[21] 38th Vice President of the United States of America (1965–69) and US Senator from Minnesota (1949–64 and 1971–78).

confederation or a federation of churches. Of course, the response commonly proffered to this question is that, despite administrational division, Orthodoxy remains united in faith, the Sacraments, etc. But is this sufficient? When before non-Orthodox we sometimes appear divided in theological dialogues and elsewhere; when we are unable to proceed to the realization of the long-heralded Holy and Great Council of the Orthodox Church; when we lack a unified voice on contemporary issues and, instead, convoke bilateral dialogues with non-Orthodox on these issues; when we fail to constitute a single Orthodox Church in the so-called diaspora in accordance with the ecclesiological and canonical principles of our Church; how can we avoid the image of division in Orthodoxy, especially on the basis of non-theological, secular criteria?

We need, then, greater unity in order to appear to those outside not as a federation of churches but as one unified Church. Through the centuries, and especially after the Schism, when the Church of Rome ceased to be in communion with the Orthodox, this throne was called—according to canonical order—to serve the unity of the Orthodox Church as its first throne. And it fulfilled this responsibility through the ages by convoking an entire series of pan-Orthodox councils on crucial ecclesiastical matters, always prepared, whenever duly approached, to render its assistance and support to troubled Orthodox churches. In this way, a canonical order was created and, accordingly, the coordinating role of this patriarchate guaranteed the unity of the Orthodox Church, without in the least damaging or diminishing the independence of the local autocephalous churches by any interference in their internal affairs. This, in any case, is the healthy significance of the institution of autocephaly: while it assures the self-governance of each church with regard to its internal life and organization, on matters affecting the entire Orthodox Church and its relations with those outside, each autocephalous church does not act alone but in coordination with the rest of the Orthodox churches. If this coordination either disappears or diminishes, then autocephaly becomes "autocephalism" (or radical independence), namely a factor of division rather than unity for the Orthodox Church.

Therefore, dearly beloved brothers in the Lord, we are called to contribute in every possible way to the unity of the Orthodox Church, transcending every temptation of regionalism or nationalism so that we may act as a unified Church, as one canonically structured body. We do not, as during Byzantine times, have at our disposal a state factor that guaranteed—and sometimes even imposed—our unity. Nor does our ecclesiology permit any centralized authority that is able to impose unity from above. Our unity depends on our conscience. The sense of need and duty that we constitute a single canonical structure and body, one Church, is sufficient to guarantee our unity, without any external intervention.

A Response to Archimandrite Elpidophoros Lambrianidis

Paul Meyendorff

St Vladimir's Theological Quarterly 54.3–4 (2010): 441–447

PLEASE ALLOW ME TO express my gratitude for the clarity and forthrightness with which you express the position of the Ecumenical Patriarchate. Such clarity is essential if we are to move forward in resolving the tangled ecclesiastical web that is Orthodoxy in North America.

There are many elements in your presentation with which we members of the Orthodox Church in America (OCA) are in complete agreement. I am particularly grateful for your positive view of the OCA's self-understanding, which largely coincides with the Ecumenical Patriarchate's own vision.

This includes, first of all, a vision of Orthodoxy that is neither ethnic nor national, but inclusive of all Orthodox, of whatever background. This is an approach that, to a greater or lesser extent, was an aspect of the Russian mission to North America from its very inception. The Russian missionaries, in fact, sought to defend Native Americans from exploitation by representatives of the Russian-American Company in Alaska. St Innocent translated the Bible and liturgical services into the native languages. The move of the mission diocese's headquarters from Alaska to San Francisco and then to New York was fostered by a missionary perspective that saw Orthodoxy as a gift to all peoples. This vision was reflected as well in Archbishop Tikhon's move to ordain Bishop (now Saint) Raphael (Hawaweeny) to minister to Orthodox Christians from the Middle East, as well as his never-realized plans to do the same for Greek and Serbian communities in America. He commissioned Isabel Florence Hapgood, a well-known American journalist and literary critic, to translate liturgical services into

English.[1] St Tikhon, in a 1905 report to church authorities in Moscow, expressed his vision for an autocephalous church in America for Orthodox of all nationalities, including Americans![2]

Even after the Russian Revolution and the subsequent creation of multiple ethnic jurisdictions in America, the inclusive vision of Orthodoxy was not lost. St Vladimir's Seminary, founded in 1938, was from its inception intended as a school for mission in America. And even before the 1970 autocephaly, various ethnic groups found their home within the Metropolia, the successor of the pre-1917 Russian mission. Thus, significant groups of Romanians, Bulgarians, and Albanians were incorporated into it, and their bishops participated as full members of its synod. During the 20th century, as generations succeeded one another and as this church also absorbed growing numbers of converts, the Metropolia lost its predominantly Slavic character and came, more and more, to resemble that ethnic melting pot that is America (particularly the United States and Canada).

This vision, a fully united Orthodox Church for all peoples, we share with the Ecumenical Patriarchate. Our general impression of the Greek Orthodox Archdiocese (GOA), however, is that it has to a much greater extent maintained its ethnic Greek character. One result of this is that its membership consists of many fewer converts than either the OCA or the Antiochian Archdiocese. In part, this can be explained by an ongoing influx of immigrants from Greece. But there is also within the Archdiocese a much greater focus on maintaining a specifically Greek identity. Thus, for example, bishops of the ethnic dioceses under the Ecumenical Patriarchate (Carpatho-Russian, Ukrainian, Albanian) are not members of its Synod. It was even reported to me by a priest in the GOA that when the issue of including them in the Synod was brought up, one of the Greek bishops stated that their inclusion would dilute the Greek composition of

---

[1] On Isabel Hapgood, see my article, "Liturgical Translations of the Orthodox Church in America," *Logos* 41–42 (2000–01): 59–82. The book she produced (*Service Book of the Holy Orthodox-Catholic [Greco-Russian] Apostolic Church* [Boston and New York: Houghton, Mifflin, and Company, 1906]) remains in print and is still widely used in many parishes.

[2] Of course, one should not idealize the situation in this period. Not all Orthodox parishes were united under the Russian diocese: many were independent, or very loosely and flexibly connected to old-world churches, whether Constantinople, Athens, Antioch, Serbia, or others.

the Synod. Similarly, your own address delivered last year at Holy Cross Seminary was widely perceived as criticizing the GOA for failing sufficiently to maintain its Greek identity![3] Your presentation today appears to soften that position, and there are many who will be relieved to hear that the Ecumenical Patriarchate, at least in theory, rejects ethnophyletism. But the GOA is, de facto, the face of the Ecumenical Patriarchate in North America, and its strong emphasis on maintaining its Greek identity undermines the Ecumenical Patriarchate's claim that it is pan-ethnic.

The Autocephaly of the Orthodox Church in America

Not unexpectedly, you are critical of the process leading to the autocephaly of the OCA. Here, some clarification of the historical events may be in order. What you do not mention is that, already in the 1960s, representatives of the then "Metropolia" approached the Ecumenical Patriarchate in order to resolve the canonical problem that had resulted from the Metropolia's split with the Moscow Patriarchate following the tragic events of 1917. As a result of these events, as well as efforts by the Communist authorities to control it, the former Russian missionary diocese became de facto autonomous, resulting in a break in communion with Moscow. The response of the Ecumenical Patriarchate to the Metropolia's overtures was to refer them back to Moscow, because it understood the situation as a problem internal to the Church of Russia and did not therefore wish to interfere in the internal affairs of another local church.

This position of the Patriarchate raises some interesting issues. First, what about the other ethnic dioceses, including Carpatho-Russian and Ukrainian, that were accepted into the jurisdiction of Constantinople? Why were they not directed to approach their mother churches? What about Constantinople's interpretation of Canon 28 of Chalcedon, by which Constantinople claims exclusive jurisdiction over all territories outside the recognized patriarchates and churches?

---

[3] The lecture, entitled "Challenges of Orthodoxy in America and the Role of the Ecumenical Patriarchate," was delivered at that seminary's chapel on March 16, 2009.

So, rebuffed by Constantinople, representatives of the Metropolia began discussions, at first informal and secret, with the Moscow Patriarchate. These led, in 1970, to the granting of the Tomos of Autocephaly and the creation of the OCA—with the subsequent "meaningful storm," in the words of Fr Alexander Schmemann. Though communion between the OCA and all the other local churches was not broken, the position of the OCA remains ambiguous: the autocephaly is accepted by most Slavic churches (Moscow, Bulgaria, Georgia, Poland, and Czech Lands and Slovakia); it is rejected by the predominantly Greek-speaking churches (Constantinople, Greece, Cyprus, Alexandria, and Jerusalem); while other churches take a neutral position (Antioch, Serbia, Romania).

Questions of Autocephaly and Jurisdiction

The autocephaly of the OCA raised a number of issues that remain unresolved:

The first of these is the process of granting autocephaly. In your presentation, you make it seem simpler than the far messier reality. First, no canons deal explicitly with the issue. And historically, in just about every case, autocephaly occurred as a fait accompli, only gradually accepted by Constantinople and the other local churches. The Church of Russia is a case in point: Moscow was de facto autocephalous for a century and a half before 1593, when this was formally recognized by Constantinople, and only under duress. Similarly, the numerous national churches that arose in the 19th century after the collapse of the Ottoman Empire achieved their autocephaly with only grudging acceptance, often post factum, by the Ecumenical Patriarchate, which was seeing its once vast jurisdiction slip away. One could therefore question the notion that Constantinople alone can grant autocephaly. Rather, is it not more appropriate to say that the role of Constantinople is to reflect a consensus among all the Orthodox churches in recognizing a local church as autocephalous, usually some time after the autocephaly has been declared?

But there is also a deeper question, also raised by your paper, about the very nature of autocephaly. You accurately point out that many of the 19th-century autocephalous churches were created along nationalistic lines and were modeled less on the Church's canonical tradition than on the European nation state. Clearly, the very notion of autocephaly needs careful examination and correction. Surely autocephaly cannot mean absolute independence, with no accountability whatever to other local churches! In this regard, the actions of the Ecumenical Patriarchate in calling together the primates of the local churches are a welcome step.

This raises as well the acute issue of ethnophyletism which, though condemned by a pan-Orthodox council in 1872, remains a problem to this day. Indeed, recent moves by both the Patriarchates of Russia and Romania to unite all their compatriots living in "diaspora" under their jurisdiction clearly violates the principle of territoriality, even if it responds to certain pastoral needs. On this issue, I believe that the Ecumenical Patriarchate and the OCA are in full agreement.

Your presentation appeals as well to Canon 28 of Chalcedon to justify Constantinople's claims of jurisdiction over the "barbarian lands." According to this interpretation, the barbarian lands are those territories which are not part of the ancient patriarchates or any of the newer Orthodox churches—and thus include North and South America, Australia, and much of Asia. This claim, more than any other, is disputed by a number of churches, as well as church historians and canonists. We need not rehearse the arguments here, but suffice it to say that Constantinople's appeal to this canon is quite recent. In fact, when then Archbishop Meletios Metaxakis founded the GOA in 1923, he was Archbishop of Athens, and the GOA was under the jurisdiction of the Church of Greece. Only after he became ecumenical patriarch did he transfer the GOA under the ecumenical throne and begin to appeal to Canon 28. Even earlier, during the 18th and 19th centuries, when Russian missions spread eastward to Siberia, China, Japan, and Alaska, Constantinople raised no objections and made no such jurisdictional claims. Admittedly, during this period, the Ecumenical Patriarchate, still under the Ottoman yoke, was hardly in a position to do so, and it was concerned primarily with Orthodox (or "Rum") Christians within the Ottoman Empire, and not with world Orthodoxy.

The fundamental issue here concerns the interpretation of the ancient canons and their applicability today. Are the canons, including the famous Canon 28, laws that bind the Church for all time? Or are they applications of the Gospel at a given time and place, reflecting particular and limited circumstances, and thus adaptable to meet the pastoral needs of each epoch? In reading the canons, are we to read them literally, or are we to seek the theological rationale behind them? Are all canons equally important and valid, touching on the essence of the faith, or can they be broken down into disciplinary and dogmatic categories? On all these issues, there is a broad diversity of opinions among theologians and church leaders, and these questions are in need of careful examination.

The Episcopal Assemblies and the OCA

The recent creation of the episcopal assembles in the so-called "diaspora" is a welcome development, as well as a positive expression of the role of the Ecumenical Patriarchate to unify the Orthodox, who are split into multiple jurisdictions. At the same time, the structure of the episcopal assemblies to some extent reflects exactly the kind of ethnophyletism that is criticized in your paper, with jurisdictions treated as "colonies" of the mother churches. The bishops in the Americas were not involved in the discussions leading up to the formation of the assemblies, and there is no adequate place for the OCA, which has no "mother church."

Nevertheless, the OCA, as the second largest jurisdiction in North America, is absolutely committed to participate in the assembly process, which we hope will lead to a united, autocephalous church in America. We are therefore relieved that a way was found for the OCA to participate, even if our metropolitan is not seated on the executive committee. We are, of course, aware that the Ecumenical Patriarchate does not recognize the validity of our autocephaly, though we stand absolutely committed to the principle that America needs a fully autocephalous or autonomous, local church. Thus we see our autocephaly as only a first and provisional step toward unifying all the Orthodox in America.[4] In fact, were the episcopal

---

[4] The OCA's Tomos of Autocephaly itself states that it is provisional, in the sense that it is a stepping-stone toward full administrative unity.

assembly to propose such a united, territorial church, recognized by the Orthodox churches worldwide, we would willingly join such an effort—in fact, we pray for just such an outcome.

Conclusion

In theory, the solution should be simple. The ecclesiology that lies behind the Orthodox canonical tradition calls for a local, self-governing church in each place, with a council of bishops headed by a primate, and in a relationship of communion and accountability with all other local churches. However, because of the vicissitudes of history, as well as human sin, we have placed many obstacles along the way. Often, ethnophyletism or various geo-political agendas obscure our vision. The meaning of autocephaly, as well as the way to achieve it, needs to be clarified. On these issues, I believe we all fully agree.

The first step towards a solution is precisely the kind of face-to-face, frank, and open dialogue that has taken place here at this symposium. We are particularly grateful to you, Fr Elpidophoros, for agreeing to come speak, and especially for the frankness of your remarks. We hope that this, alongside the work of the episcopal assembly, will lead to a positive resolution to the issues that, despite our unity as Orthodox, still divide us.

Historical Method and Competing Logics
A Response to Archimandrite Elpidophoros Lambriniadis

Elizabeth H. Prodromou[1]

Introduction and Method

WHEN ASKED BY THE organizers of the conference on *Hellenism and Orthodoxy*[2] to offer a comment on the presentation by Archimandrite Elpidophoros Lambriniadis,[3] several reasons prompted me to enthusiastically accept the invitation. I will return to identify those reasons at the conclusion of this comment, which elaborates on the schematic outline that I presented at the conference whose proceedings now constitute this special issue on "Hellenism and Orthodoxy."

A comment necessarily restricts me to a laconic treatment of a matter that is, in fact, remarkable for its intellectual complexity and existential urgency; the "... perception of the Church of Constantinople with regard to the ecclesiastical situation in the United States and ... [the Ecumenical Patriarchate's] vision for the future of Orthodoxy in this land [i.e., the

---

[1] All views expressed in this article are those of the author alone and in no way reflect the views of or bind the United States Commission on International Religious Freedom, on which the author serves as Vice Chair. The article reflects the author's research in her academic capacity as Asst. Professor of International Relations at Boston University.

[2] St Vladimir's Orthodox Theological Seminary's Annual Summer Symposium: Hellenism and Orthodoxy (Crestwood, NY: 10–12 June 2010).

[3] Archimandrite Elpidophoros Lambriniadis, "Greek Orthodoxy, the Ecumenical Patriarchate, and the Church in the USA." [In the present volume, pp. 273–90.—*Ed.*] Paper presented at the conference in note 2.

United States]."⁴ Therefore, given space constraints, I will concentrate exclusively on one key aspect of Lambriniadis' reflection on the problematic of "Greek Orthodoxy, the Ecumenical Patriarchate, and the Church in the USA." Specifically, Lambriniadis' methodological choice in favor of a historicized narrative of the linkages between Greek Orthodoxy and the Ecumenical Patriarchate deserves attention and deconstruction, for the hints offered regarding the causes and consequences of the divergence between Hellenism and Orthodox Christianity, as well as for the application of those insights to the current renegotiation of the relationship between the Ecumenical Patriarchate and Orthodox Christians in the United States.

My reading of Lambrinidis' text and the rationale for concentrating my comment on the implications of his methodological approach is the product of my location at the interstices of political science and public policy. As a political scientist working on the linkages between religion, security, and democracy, especially within the regional space of Southeastern Europe and the Near East, I am continually struck by the persistence and repetition of certain conventions and stereotypical assumptions which are commonly applied to Orthodox Christianity. Whether in research on European integration and enlargement, democratization in the Greater Middle East, or the interpretation and encounter of Orthodox theology with modernity, the standard claims of social science research around such issues posit either the incompatibility or the defensiveness of Orthodoxy, *writ large*, with the ideas, institutions, and processes identified as modern.⁵ I have seen firsthand how this trope⁶ has seeped into public policy

---

⁴Lambriniadis, "Greek Orthodoxy, the Ecumenical Patriarchate, and the Church in the USA," 421 [above, 273].

⁵Representative works in this genre include Nikiforos Diamandouros, "Cultural Dualism and Political Change in Greece, "Juan March Institute Working Paper 1994/50," http://www.march.es/ceacs/ingles/publicaciones/working/archivos/1994_50.pdf; Samuel P. Huntington, *The Clash of Civilizations and the Remaking of World Order* (New York: Simon & Schuster, 1998); Keith R. Legg and John M. Roberts, *Modern Greece: A Civilization on the Periphery* (Boulder, CO: Westview Press, 1996). Representative of journalistic accounts that reproduce this conventional wisdom for broader reading audiences is Victoria Clark, *Why Angels Fall: A Journey through Orthodox Europe from Byzantium to Kosovo* (London: Picador, 2001).

⁶Maria Todorova offers a masterful critique of the origins, reiteration, and consolidation

debates which assume, even in cases where there is empirical evidence to the contrary, that Orthodox churches and peoples axiomatically support chauvinistic nationalism and authoritarian politics, including the use of force by states against their own citizens.[7]

What unifies the above corpus of scholar-practitioner literature—which deals, as a whole, with Orthodox Christianity and international relations—is the absence of rigorous, nuanced, empirically-grounded, historical analysis. My research and policy experiences have convinced me that the most promising remedy for deficits in the scholarship on Orthodoxy and world affairs is to begin by thinking about *how to ask the questions* and, then, to take great care in deciding *what methodology we use to answer the questions*.

This conviction brings me to the focus of my comment on the Lambriniadis text. He has already identified the question, but at the core of his introspective on the connections between Orthodoxy and Hellenism, which he treats in the form of a rumination on the vision of the Ecumenical Patriarchate for Greek Orthodoxy in America, is a single question: namely, how has Orthodox Christianity spread, diffused, expanded, beyond its original geographic and cultural origins? To ask Lambriniadis' question in another way, would be to phrase it as follows. How we can make sense of the globalization of Orthodoxy, and how is the general experience of the globalization of Orthodoxy relevant for problematizing the relationship between the Phanar and the Orthodox jurisdictions/churches in the United States?

---

of these assumptions within the context of what she defines as the specific discourse of Balkanism. See *Imagining the Balkans*, updated edition (Oxford: Oxford University Press, 2009). The centrality of Orthodox Christianity to the discourse and broader intellectual and applied rubric of Balkanism is explored in Elizabeth H. Prodromou, "Paradigms, Power, and Identity: Rediscovering Orthodoxy and Regionalizing Europe," in John Madeley, ed. *Religion and Politics*, series of International Library of Politics and Comparative Government (Farnham, UK: Ashgate Publishing Limited, 2003). Also, see the special issue of *Balkanologie*, on "Europe du Sud-Est: histoire, concepts, frontières," 3.2 (December 1999).

[7] See, for example, *The Other Balkan Wars: A 1913 Carnegie Endowment Inquiry in Retrospect with a New Introduction and Reflections on the Present Conflict by George F. Kennan* (Washington, DC: Carnegie Endowment for International Peace, 1993).

Lambriniadis' questions, and especially, his methodology, converge neatly with the approach of the historical institutionalist school in political science,[8] which emphasizes the importance of ideas and institutions as primary causes of and explanations for patterns of historical change. Indeed, a focus on how Orthodox ideas (dogma/doctrine) and institutions (the Church *qua* eucharistic community comprised of hierarchical, priestly, and lay strata) interact to produce a conception of and engagement with the world, time, and history, offers great promise for analyzing the spread of Orthodoxy in global context.

What insights can we garner from Lambriniadis' historicized treatment of Orthodoxy's spread into global context, keeping in mind the broader problematic of this conference, which are the nature of the linkages between Orthodoxy and Hellenism?

Orthodoxy in Global Context, and Relations between the Ecumenical Patriarchate and Orthodoxy in America

First and most broadly, Lambriniadis' exploration of Orthodoxy and Hellenism turns on his treatment of the content and evolution "... of the phrase 'Greek Orthodoxy,' in terms of its relationship to the Ecumenical Patriarchate,"[9] by which he requires us to recognize the existence of two distinct worldviews—Hellenism and Orthodox Christianity—whose integral origins, as well as synergies and tensions, lie in the specific "... political, administrative, and cultural context of the Roman Empire."[10] In a word, history matters, but what may seem a self-evident observation about the historical particularity of the founding conditions of the early Roman Empire is far from simple. Instead, history reminds us that Christianity and Hellenism in the Roman Empire were foundationally correlated as *ecumenical* and *universal* worldviews, respectively. Furthermore, Lambriniadis'

---

[8]For a classic summary of the historical institutionalist methodology, see Paul Pierson and Theda Sckocpol, "Historical Institutionalism in Contemporary Political Science," in Ira Katznelson and Helen V. Milnder, eds., *Political Science: The state of the Discipline* (New York: W.W. Norton & Co., 2002).

[9]Lambriniadis, 421 [above, 273].

[10]Ibid.

narrative forces us to problematize on the nuanced, subtle, yet critically important, distinctions that emerged between two concepts—*ecumenical* and *universal*—that are usually deployed as absolute synonyms.

When informed into the institutional (i.e., administrative and organizational) structure of the early Church, the correlation, compatibility, and synergy between ecumenical and universal worldviews implied that the "Greek" prefix to Orthodoxy was understood as the equivalent of "Hellenism" as prefix to Orthodoxy; while cumbersome, "Hellenism Orthodoxy" clarifies the fact that the Greek prefix was a universal, linguistic and cultural marker that reinforced, rather than contradicted or stood in tension to, the ecumenical nature of Orthodoxy. Lambriniadis amplifies the above point in observations about the "syncretism, multiethnicism [sic] and multiculturalism"[11] of the Roman Empire, as well as in references to Hellenism (i.e., the Greek language and thought) as intellectually and linguistically intrinsic to the ideas and institutions that grew out of the codification of "apostolic teaching, the church experience and the patristic tradition."[12]

However, correlation should not be mistaken for unity and sameness, and indeed, the tensions between the universality of Hellenism and the ecumenicity of Orthodox Christianity begin to emerge quickly with the expansion of the Church in the East beyond the incubatory geographic space of the Eastern patriarchates and into the geographic regions of Southeastern Europe and, gradually, to Russia.

While Lambriniadis presents an excessively stylized depiction of the spread of Hellenism with the embrace of Christianity by the Slavic populations in Southeastern Europe and Russia,[13] his account leads to the second crucial point about Orthodoxy in global context. Specifically, tensions and differences between Hellenism as universal philosophy and Orthodoxy as ecumenical worldview began to be revealed—arguably, as early as the medieval period, but most incontrovertibly, during the Ottoman period—in the reactions of Slavs and Romanians against what they perceived as the

[11]Ibid., 422 [above, 274].
[12]Ibid., 423 [above, 275].
[13]Although he concentrates on the transmission of Orthodoxy to Slavic populations, Lambriniadis' arguments are just as easily applied to the Romanian and Illyrian (Albanian) populations of the Balkans.

disproportionate Greek influence over both doctrinal interpretation and ecclesiastical control in the Church.[14]

What bears emphasis, however, is the *mechanism by which* those tensions were catalyzed, and the implications of those mechanisms. The history of the spread of Orthodoxy belies a break with a geographic model, and a shift to a territorial model, of ecclesiastical organization. This shift implied a change in the very ideas and institutions by which the Church conceived of and engaged in its transformative mission as it spread the gospel message. Lambriniadis' brief discussion of the consolidation of the administrative and organizational structure of the Church in Byzantine times along *geographic* lines is instructive. Regardless of ethnicity, language, or race, the "Roman Christian would be a faithful [sic] under the *one* bishop of a particular city that served as either temporary or permanent residence."[15] In short, "the basis and criterion of organization was always geographical, with one bishop elected for every city, to whom all inhabitants of the region were submitted without any discrimination (linguistic or other),"[16] according to the Pauline injunction.[17]

If the geographic model of the Church reinforced the synergies between the universality of Hellenism and the ecumenicity of Orthodoxy, the shift to a territorial model accentuated the tensions between Hellenism and Orthodoxy. What accounts for the shift? Lambriniadis highlights several well-known developments, and there is an extensive, inter-disciplinary literature that analyzes and, increasingly, contests the interpretation of the causes for the disconnections between Hellenism and Orthodoxy.[18]

---

[14]For varying treatments of this point, see Dennis P. Hupchick, *The Balkans: From Constantinople to Communism* (New York: Palgrave Macmillan, 2002); and Barbara Jelavich, *History of the Balkans*, vols. 1 & 2 (New York: Cambridge University Press, 1983).

[15]Lambriniadis, 422 [above, 274].

[16]Ibid.

[17]Gal 3.28.

[18]Amongst the large and contested literature, especially useful treatments include Dusan I. Bjelic and Obrad Savic, eds., *Balkan As Metaphor: Between Globalization and Fragmentation* (Cambridge, MA: MIT Press, 2002); Paschalis Kitromilides, *Enlightenment, Nationalism, Orthodoxy: Studies in the Culture and Political Thought of Southeastern Europe* (Surrey, England: Variorum, 1994); and J. Sutton and W. van den Bercken, *Orthodox Christianity and Contemporary Europe* (Louvain, Belgium: Peeters Publishers, 2003).

Therefore, attention deserves to be focused, instead, on the *conceptual distinction* and consequent *operational differentiation* between geography and territory, because the Church's reframing of how to think about space and boundaries had direct consequences for the implementation of an institutional strategy for dealing with the global spread of Orthodoxy—with crucial implications for the contemporary issue of relations between the Ecumenical Patriarchate and Orthodox Churches in America.

The erosion of the geographic model and its replacement by a territorial model had begun with the fragmentation of European Christendom, with the divergence between the Greek East and Latin West[19]—in other words, with the proto-footprint of the Great Schism. The geographical model was initially compromised when the barbarian invasions produced an administrative restructuring in the Western Roman Empire, based on an operational logic of power, as well as identity markers of tribe, ethnicity, and language. A similar weakening in the capacity to sustain the geographic model in the Orthodox Church occurred in the Eastern Roman (Byzantine) Empire, albeit for very different reasons. Signal experiences, however, were the event of the Fourth Crusade, which began the reconstruction of Orthodoxy as suffix to a version of Hellenism reduced to ethno-linguistic, Greek identity; as well as the *longue durée* of Ottoman rule over Orthodoxy, given that the *millet* system formally compromised the Church's geographic model by restructuring the Ecumenical Patriarchate as an ethnarchy whose political and religious prerogatives were explicitly territorialized.

Historical analysis reminds us, then, that the Ecumenical Patriarchate had been "... organically shaped in the historical context of a non-ethnic, ecumenical Empire ... recorded and codified in the decisions of the ecumenical councils ... [with] ... the organization of church life purely on the basis of geographical criteria and not any linguistic or ethnic origin."[20]

---

[19]See Deno J. Geanakoplos, *Byzantine East and Latin West: Two Worlds of Christendom in Middle Ages and Renaissance* (Oxford, England: Basil Blackwell, Ltd., 1966); Andrew Louth, *Greek East and Latin West: the Church AD 681–1071* (Crestwood, NY: St Vladimir's Seminary Press, 2007); and, Phillip Sherrard, *The Greek East and the Latin West: A Study in the Christian Tradition*, second edition (Athens, Greece: Harvey & Co., 1995).

[20]Lambriniadis, 427 [above, 278].

At the same time, the expansion of Orthodox Christianity, as well as profound changes in the original historical context in which the Ecumenical Patriarchate was shaped, help to explain the unmistakable shift towards a territorial model and the fissure between Orthodoxy and Hellenism, both of which constitute the confining conditions in which the renegotiation of relations between the Phanar and Orthodox Churches in America is taking place.

This is the third and final point deriving from historical institutional reading of Lambriniadis' text. In short, the spread of Orthodoxy in global context has been definitively shaped by the formation of a world order according to the hegemonic power of the state and the dominant ideology of nationalism. Indeed, embedded in Lambriniadis' theological exposition is a political science subtext whose salience deserves mining and critical analysis. Specifically, Lambriniadis' narrative strikingly exposes what I would identify as the logic of Westphalianism as the source of an unrivalled, continuing pressure on the Church's conceptualization of and interaction in contemporary global context. Indeed, it is the logic of Westphalianism that informs the ideation and institutional parameters which, until recently, have largely driven the course of relations between the Ecumenical Patriarchate and the various Orthodox jurisdictions/churches in the United States.

What do I mean by the logic of Westphalianism? I refer to the Peace of Westphalia in 1648, which marked the formal origins of the state as the unit for world order; the entity of the state, coupled with the ideology of nationalism had, by the early 20th century, remapped all of Europe and, indeed, via European imperialism, the globe. The consolidation of a global order built on the nation-state has imposed a global map based on state, territory, and non-religious community, on the *oikoumenē* of the Ecumenical Patriarchate; indeed, the origins of the state and nationalism intrinsically involved a renegotiation and subordination of religious authority and operations to the nation-state.[21]

---

[21] Excellent discussions of my claims about the logic of Westphalianism can be found in Richard A. Falk, *The Declining World Order: America's Imperial Geopolitics* (New York: Routledge,

There is ample evidence suggesting that the Ecumenical Patriarchate recognized the implications of the logic of Westphalianism, even if the Church has never labeled the phenomenon as such. After all, Lambriniadis references the widely-cited examples of the Phanar's condemnation of ethnophyletism, and the Helladification (exclusivist territorialization) of Hellenism ruptured the correlation between Hellenism and Orthodoxy. Moreover, the collapse of empires in late-19th and early-20th-century Europe, as well as the globalization of the nation-state with imperialism, marked the disintegration of ecclesial unity that had been organized geographically and transnationally.

The logic of Westphalianism is at the core of the complexities of relations between the Ecumenical Patriarchate and Orthodox jurisdictions/churches in the United States, and lest it be overlooked, is at the crux of the challenges to the project of Orthodox unity in America. How so? Given impositions of space, I turn to concluding remarks by way of sketching some responses to that question.

Conclusion

Prior to the era of the nation-state, the globalization of Orthodoxy occurred via a clear methodology. When Orthodoxy spread to regions beyond the boundaries of the Roman Empire, pastoral responsibility for these regions was assigned to the Ecumenical Patriarchate, and the geographic model entailed the creation of "jurisdictions of the churches and patriarchates . . . [codified and validated by the previous decisions of] . . . the ecumenical councils [thereby] . . . assuring and expressing the pan-Orthodox [ecumenical] conscience and consent."[22]

The relatively protracted lack of consensus on the pastoral prerogatives of the Ecumenical Patriarchate over all Orthodox Christians in the United States, which presumes the eventuality of an Orthodox Church unifying all current jurisdictions, underscores the potency of Westphalian logic on

---

2004) and, especially as related to the state and religion, Daniel Philpott, "The Religious Roots of Modern International Relations," in *World Politics* 52 (January 2000).

[22]Lambriniadis, 427 [above, 278].

the ideas and institutions of the Church *writ large*. Lambriniadis illustrates the point, when he states that

> The canonical question that arises is the following: Does the territorial expansion of a state comprise a self-evident extension of the jurisdiction of that Church in that particular region? And by analogy: Does the development of missionary activity in a geographical region outside a particular jurisdiction at the same time imply a claim by that jurisdiction?[23]

The response to this question was historically resolved by the application of Canon 28 of the Fourth Ecumenical Council. However, the sharp disagreements over the relevance and interpretation of that canon as applied to the primacy and authority of the Ecumenical Patriarchate vis-à-vis Orthodox Christianity in the United States can only be understood within the logic of the statism of Westphalia.[24] The associated, equally intense debates about jurisdictional unity, which turn on matters of institutional power and language of administration and worship, also indicated that the universality of Hellenism has been significantly captured by the Westphalian ideology of ethno-nationalism.

Indeed, I mentioned at the outset that there were several reasons why I eagerly accepted the conference organizers' and editors' invitation to write a comment on the Lambriniadis text. Most importantly, the text required that I reflect on my nagging unease about the scholarly treatment of the engagement of "... the Church of Constantinople with regard to the ecclesiastical situation in the United States and ... [associated] vision for the future of Orthodoxy in ... [America]."[25] Lambriniadis' text, by virtue of his methodological decision to historicize the topic, was an enlivening call for an inter-disciplinary inquiry into what has been far too frequently conceived as an exclusively theological issue. I have attempted to respond

---

[23] Ibid.

[24] A fascinating analysis of the interpretive differences utilized to justify application of Canon 28 of the Fourth Ecumenical Council within the context of contemporary geopolitics—i.e., using the logic of Westphalia—is provided by Alicja Cyranović, "The Attitude of the Moscow Patriarchate Towards Other Orthodox Churches," *Religion, State & Society*, 35.4 (Dec. 2007).

[25] Lambriniadis, 421 [above, 273].

to that call by demonstrating how social science analysis provides useful tools for understanding the stalemate over relations between the Old World Patriarchates and New World churches, distilled in the challenges to the Ecumenical Patriarchate's primacy based on Canon 28 of the Fourth Ecumenical Council, and woefully expressed in the institutional fragmentation and cleavage of Orthodoxy's jurisdictional multiplicity in America.

Also crucial to my affirmative response to participate in the conference was a sense of responsibility to appreciate the openings of the recent events of the Pre-Conciliar Pan-Orthodox Conferences in Cyprus and Switzerland, as preparation for a Great and Holy Council to be convened by the Ecumenical Patriarchate, as well as the establishment of the Episcopal Assembly of North and South America. As a social scientist, I view the simultaneity of these efforts as suggestive of the ways in which the ideational and institutional resources of Orthodoxy are being retrieved, mined, and redeployed, with fascinating and hopeful possibilities for creating a global Orthodox *ekklēsia*. The goal of my comment, then, has been to foreground a core theme developed in the Lambriniadis text and embedded in the conference: namely, to illustrate the analytical relevance of the logic of Westphalianism to both reveal, and encourage a move beyond, its operational and existential dominance in the Orthodox Church in global context.

Fr John Meyendorff and the Autocephaly of the Orthodox Church in America[1]

Paul Meyendorff

St Vladimir's Theological Quarterly 56.3 (2012): 335–352

FR JOHN ARRIVED IN AMERICA with his family in October of 1959 to assume a teaching position at St Vladimir's Orthodox Theological Seminary, at a time when Orthodoxy in America was emerging from its ethnic cocoon.

In 1960, just months after his arrival, The Standing Conference of the Orthodox Christian Bishops in America (SCOBA) was founded. The three largest Orthodox jurisdictions in America were at this time led by three visionary leaders: Archbishop Iakovos of the Greek Orthodox Archdiocese, who became the first chairman of SCOBA; Metropolitan Leonty of the Metropolia; and Metropolitan Anthony Bashir of the Antiochian Orthodox Christian Archdiocese. High on the agenda of SCOBA was the express desire for canonical unity in North America, and all three of these hierarchs repeatedly spoke on this subject. Indeed, Archbishop Iakovos, in his opening remarks at a January 1965 meeting of SCOBA, praised Metropolitans Leonty and Anthony for their vision and emphasized that the Standing Conference must acquire a regular canonical status, as the provincial synod of the American Church, according to the canons and with the blessing of the mother churches.[2]

In 1965, Fr John was appointed editor of the new Metropolia newspaper, *The Orthodox Church*, a position he held until his retirement in 1992. As editor of this monthly publication he wrote numerous editorials calling for Orthodox unity, and later defending the autocephaly of the Orthodox

---

[1] This paper was presented originally at a symposium honoring Fr Meyendorff on the twentieth year of his death, held at St Sergius Institute in Paris on February 8–11, 2012.

[2] As reported in *The Orthodox Church*, February 1965.

Church in America (OCA) after this was granted in 1970. His very first editorial, published in February 1965, concludes with the following words:

> It seems, however, that we are approaching a new period in the history of our church. Practically everyone understands that the present situation cannot last. The Standing Conference of Orthodox Bishops is watched by millions of laymen with great expectation. Nothing, however, will be done unless all realize exactly *why* Orthodox unity is necessary.
>
> The reasons are spiritual, canonical, and practical.
>
> Spiritually, it is obvious that when we confess our belief in "one, holy, catholic and apostolic Church," this belief is meant to be the guiding principle of our lives: God is one, the Lord Jesus Christ is one, and the Church must be one also. "National" churches can exist only inasmuch as they accept to submit their particular interests to that of the whole Body of Christ.
>
> Canonically, the rules and canons of *all* churches strictly forbid the existence of parallel ecclesiastical organizations on the same territory.
>
> Practically, the Orthodox witness in this country will be immensely strengthened if the three million Orthodox pray and work together; if others are able really to see in us the one true Church, and not a conglomeration of mutually exclusive factions; if we can all join our forces in the education of our youth.[3]

A year and a half later, at a time when the autocephaly of the Metropolia was still a distant dream, his call for a resolution to the canonical issues grew louder. I cite extensively from an editorial entitled "'Mothers' and 'Daughters,'" published in the August-September 1966 of *The Orthodox Church*:

> The fate of the Church in the Western world is in our hands or rather *should be* [emphases in original] in our hands. The canonical conditions of normal church life are clearly spelled out by the tradition of

---

[3] *The Orthodox Church*, February 1965; reprinted in John Meyendorff, *Vision of Unity* (Crestwood, NY: St Vladimir's Seminary Press, 1987), 15–16.

the Church: everywhere, Orthodox Christians must constitute *one* Church, led by its own bishop and priests. Through its bishop, each church must be in communion with the Church universal. All the institutions of the Church—patriarchates, metropolitan districts, autocephalies, archdioceses—exist in order to secure this essential order of the Church.

The tragedy of our times—and the origin of the disorder in which we live—is that these institutions are being used for non-ecclesiastical purposes: patriarchates, while considered by some as infallible criteria of canonicity, are being used by the governments of the countries in which they are situated *as political tools*; archbishops and metropolitans consider themselves as national, and not ecclesiastical leaders. Meanwhile, Orthodox canon law does have provisions against those abuses: *it clearly requires that all ecclesiastical questions are to be solved in the area where they arise.* African bishops in the fifth century even excommunicated those who appealed "beyond the seas" to solve their problems. They would certainly consider as highly uncanonical that the Antiochian American Archdiocese, for example, should have its fate resolved by a synod meeting in a foreign country thousands of miles away.

Our conclusion today is that our internal disunity and disorder in America will last until the time when the patriarchates—the "mother churches"—as well as their representatives here and all the other ecclesiastical institutions will at last realize their proper function and will prove themselves able to perform it. For the time being, by simply demanding that we submit to them, they continue to divide the Church and, in fact, want only that we serve their interests—which *are not* the interests of the Church in America. *Their proper and obvious ecclesiastical duty is to urge and help American Orthodox to realize their unity* while at the same time preserving all the national traditions, languages, and customs which need to be kept.[4]

---

[4]Reprinted in *Vision of Unity*, 18–19. Italics in original.

These two examples—and there are many more—clearly indicate Fr John's public role in the search for Orthodox unity in America and for the eventual granting of autocephaly. Behind the scenes, much was going on as well, and here too he played a central role.

It was at the 1961 World Council of Churches Assembly in New Delhi, India, that the Russian Orthodox Church joined the ecumenical movement, and this allowed contact between the Metropolia and the Russian Orthodox Church to resume after a hiatus of nearly forty years. Here Fr John was able to meet and to speak informally especially with Metropolitan Nikodim of Leningrad, chairman of the External Affairs Department of the Russian Church. This informal meeting led to further encounters in 1963, this time in the United States, and then again in November 1967, at which time Metropolitan Nikodim asked for a "sign" from the Metropolia that it desired to enter into negotiations. Throughout the 1960s, Fr John maintained informal contacts with Metropolitan Nikodim, as well as Metropolitan Anthony Bloom, who encouraged the Metropolia to develop and maintain contact with the Moscow Patriarchate.[5] Then in August 1968, this time at the WCC Assembly in Uppsala, Sweden, Nikodim informed the Metropolia's delegation that the Patriarchal Synod was ready to enter into negotiations. At each of these encounters, Fr John was present and took a leading role.

Fr Meyendorff reported on this conversation to Metropolitan Ireney, primate of the Metropolia, who indicated his willingness to continue the dialogue. On September 22, 1968, Fr John sent a personal letter to Metropolitan Nikodim informing him that the Metropolia was ready to hold a secret and informal meeting between representatives of the two churches.[6] The letter further proposed that the meeting take place either in Belgrade or Geneva. An affirmative response from Moscow, signed by Metropolitan Nikodim, was sent on December 20, 1968.[7]

---

[5]The OCA archives contain a number of letters exchanged between Fr Meyendorff and the two metropolitans.

[6]A copy of this letter, found in the Archives of the Orthodox Church in America, was made available to me by Mr Alexis Liberovsky, Archivist of the OCA. The letter, on stationary of the Department of External Affairs, was cosigned by Fr John and Prof. Sergius Verhovskoy.

[7]Letter found in OCA Archives.

The immediate result was a series of "unofficial" meetings in New York, the first on January 21, 1969, at the New Yorker Hotel, the second on February 3, 1969, in Syosset, NY, at the residence of Metropolitan Ireney. The Moscow delegation was at both meetings headed by Metropolitan Nikodim. The Metropolia delegation consisted of a special commission for this purpose appointed by Metropolitan Ireney and headed by Bishop Kiprian of Pennsylvania, and including Fr Joseph Pishtey, Chancellor of the Metropolia, Frs Alexander Schmemann, John Skvir, John Meyendorff, Kirill Fotiev, as well as Professor Sergius Verhovskoy.

At the January 21 meeting,[8] it was agreed that this meeting would be considered unofficial, but that the subsequent meeting in February would be official and would draft a formal agreement for presentation to the Holy Synods of the Moscow Patriarchate and the Metropolia. Metropolitan Nikodim began by pointing out that the situation in America was fundamentally different from that in Western Europe, where there had never been a diocese of the Russian Church, while a Russian diocese existed in America until 1922. He further stated that it would be pointless to speak of the reasons that led to the break between the mother church and the Metropolia; rather, the focus should be on the future. At this point, Fr Meyendorff summarized the points discussed back in 1963: 1) the granting of autocephaly in accordance with canon law, and its recognition by the other local churches; 2) the recognition by Moscow of the new autocephaly as the complete successor of the mission and exarchates of the Russian Church; and 3) the suppression of the Exarchate, with the exception of a representation church. Metropolitan Nikodim expressed his agreement, but stated that the St Nicholas Cathedral in New York must be kept by the (Moscow) Patriarchate. In the ensuing discussions, Fr Schmemann asked Metropolitan Nikodim how the local churches, particularly Constantinople, would receive the granting of autocephaly. Nikodim replied that Constantinople would not be happy, but that this would not be a problem. Did Constantinople ask anyone when it established its new diocese in America in 1922? He then expressed his certainty that other groups would

---

[8] A confidential report of this meeting, prepared by Fr Kirill Fotiev, one of the participants, was provided to me by the OCA archivist.

eventually join the autocephaly. Further, the non-recognition of the autocephaly might well lead to an inter-Orthodox meeting: by what right can the Greek churches not recognize the right of the Russian Church to grant [autocephaly] to its former diocese, the first on this [American] continent, whose jurisdiction over America no one considered challenging before 1922? After discussion of the church in Japan and several minor issues, the meeting concluded with an agreement to meet on February 3.

Though still officially an "informal" meeting, this gathering discussed the formal details of the granting of autocephaly and agreed upon a formula to be presented as a formal request to the Holy Synod of the Russian Orthodox Church from the Holy Synod of the Metropolia. The proposal was set on paper and signed by Metropolitan Nikodim and Bishop Kiprian.

The agreement listed the following points:

1) the Russian Patriarchate would terminate its jurisdiction in America;

2) the Patriarchate would grant autocephaly to the Metropolia;

3) all property and rights belonging to the Patriarchate would be transferred to the autocephalous church, with the exception of St Nicholas Cathedral, which would have the status of "podvorie" (representation church);

4) the securing by the Patriarchate of the recognition of the autocephaly by all local Orthodox churches.

After the agreement reached in Syosset was approved by the Holy Synods of both churches, an official meeting was held in Geneva, Switzerland, on August 24–25, 1969, to prepare the final steps for the formal declaration of autocephaly and the issuing of the Tomos. One of the Russian representatives at this meeting was Hieromonk Kirill (Gundiaev), a close associate of Metropolitan Nikodim and the current Patriarch of Moscow. Among the details resolved at this meeting was the continued presence in America of a small number of parishes under Moscow, as well as an agreement to hold a meeting in Tokyo of representatives of the Moscow Patriarchate, the Metropolia, and the Japanese Orthodox Church to resolve the canonical situation in Japan, and to resolve some final questions about the autocephaly of the Metropolia.[9]

It was following this meeting that the negotiations and final agreement became public, and the External Affairs Department was charged with informing the dioceses about these developments. Bishop Kiprian and Frs Pishtey and Schmemann personally presented reports to the various diocesan assemblies that fall, and the Metropolitan Council (the administrative body of the Metropolia in the intervals between all-church councils) was briefed. Fr Meyendorff, in his role as editor of the church newspaper, *The Orthodox Church*, wrote a series of editorials that appeared in each issue, all addressing the issue of autocephaly and answering the objections of doubters.[10] I cite from his December 1969 editorial:

> The establishment of an autocephalous "Orthodox Church of America" by the patriarchate which first brought and organized Orthodoxy in America will solve the painful conflict between the Metropolia and its mother church. But it also will provide American Orthodoxy as a whole with a new and unquestionable opportunity. The existence in the same country of several parallel Orthodox jurisdictions—the Greek, the Russian, the Syrian, the Romanian, the Albanian, etc.—is a canonical abnormality which hampers the spiritual and social witness of Orthodoxy. In the eyes of an outsider, we appear as a congregation of ethnic tribes. All must find their place in the one Orthodox Church of America.
>
> Obviously, there can be no question of making this unity "under the Russians." Autocephaly implies the end of ecclesiastical colonialism: Church life in America must have no other goals than the progress of

---

[9] The full report of the Geneva meeting, signed by Metropolitan Nikodim and Bishop Kiprian, is available in the OCA Archives, as is the agreement finalized in Tokyo at the November 26–28 meeting.

[10] "Towards Autocephaly," December 1969; "An 'American' Church," January 1970; "What Is Autocephaly?" February 1970; "Towards Unity," March 1970; "A New Beginning," April 1970; "Responsibility," May 1970; "Coming of Age," November 1970. All are reprinted in *Vision of Unity*.

Orthodoxy in this country and the contribution to the progress of the faith everywhere. It cannot serve particular interests. But it can and must preserve and guarantee all national traditions.[11]

The rest of the story is well-known. On April 10, 1970, the Tomos of Autocephaly was signed, and on May 18 of the same a year, a delegation from the Orthodox Church in America, led by its youngest hierarch, Bishop Theodosius of Sitka and Alaska, traveled to Moscow for the official ceremony. It is interesting to note that neither Fr Meyendorff nor Fr Schmemann made the journey for this event, and it was not until years later that Fr John first traveled to Russia.

The autocephaly of the Orthodox Church created what Fr Schmemann called "a meaningful storm."[12] Although the leading hierarchs in America, particularly Archbishop Iakovos of the Greek Archdiocese and Metropolitan Philip of the Antiochian Archdiocese were kept fully informed during the negotiations that led to autocephaly and had expressed their public support for Orthodox unity in America, a strong negative reaction followed, particularly from the Greek side. Archbishop Iakovos even broke communion with the OCA for a brief time. And in the years immediately following the issuing of the Tomos, a lively debate ensued, in which Fr John took an active part. He did so on several fronts.

First was a series of editorials in *The Orthodox Church* defending the position of the OCA.[13] Perhaps the strongest language he used was in an editorial published in December 1970 and entitled "Against Myths": He first rejects the misconception that SCOBA (the "Standing Conference of Bishops in America") had itself been planning for American autocephaly,

---

[11]"Towards Autocephaly," *The Orthodox Church*, December 1969 (*Vision of Unity*, 31–32).

[12]Alexander Schmemann, "A Meaningful Storm: Some reflections on Autocephaly, tradition and Ecclesiology," in *Autocephaly: The Orthodox Church in America* (Crestwood, NY: St Vladimir's Seminary Press, 1971), 3–27. This volume is a reprint of *St Vladimir's Theological Quarterly* 15.1–2 (1971), of which Fr Meyendorff was editor. [In the present volume, 149–178.—*Ed.*]

[13]"A New Beginning," April 1970; "Responsibility," May 1970; "Coming of Age," November 1970; "Against Myths," December 1970; "The Real Issue at Last," June-July 1971; "The Forgotten Principle," January 1972; "Where Do We Stand? Hope from Constantinople," December 1972; "The Standing Conference: Past and Future," June-July 1973; "The Church and Ethnicity," January 1974; "Orthodox Unity: Where Do we Stand?," January, 1975; "Ethnicity, Americanization, and Orthodox Unity," June 1976; etc. All are reprinted in *The Vision of Unity*.

a project that was then derailed by the unilateral actions of the Metropolia and the Russian Church. Fr John then reports that an appeal was made to the Pan-Orthodox Conference in Chambésy, Switzerland, "but THE ECUMENICAL PATRIARCHATE REFUSED TO PLACE THE ISSUE ON THE AGENDA" (capitalization in the original text). He reports further that, back in 1967, Metropolitan Ireney of the Metropolia had written a letter to all Orthodox patriarchs of the necessity of unity, and that he later requested an audience with the ecumenical patriarch (a request supported by Archbishop Iakovos), but that this request was turned down in a telegram. Through unofficial channels, Constantinople stated that the Metropolia would first have to solve its problems with Moscow. He continues:

> During the negotiations with Moscow, the Chairman and the Vice-Chairman of the Standing Conference [Archbishop Iakovos and Metropolitan Philip] were receiving detailed briefings; and nothing, at any time was done secretly.
>
> The myth of the autocephaly undermining the efforts of the Standing Conference must therefore be fully dispelled. The Standing Conference was facing a stalemate mainly because neither Istanbul nor the other "mother churches" were desiring Orthodox unity in America. Now the situation is drastically changed, the issue CANNOT be avoided any more.
>
> The main argument of Constantinople is that autocephalous churches are to be established by ecumenical councils. The argument is rather astonishing for anyone who knows the history of the Orthodox Church, since the last ecumenical council was in 787. But there it is—proposed by the first see of Orthodoxy.

He then concludes the editorial with two strong paragraphs:

> So, let us abandon myths and come down to reality. The autocephalous Orthodox Church in America is here to stay. It will eventually unite all those Orthodox Christians who want to be simply Orthodox in America, with absolute freedom for all of them to preserve their

languages, ethnic customs, practices, etc. There will also be for a time a number of ethnic jurisdictions which will prefer to identify themselves with their foreign connections. No one has the power to forbid them, and the autocephalous American Church has repeatedly pledged to respect their desires and the rights of their mother churches. All of them, however, can and must continue to cooperate through the Standing Conference.

Before the autocephaly the situation of all churches was uncanonical, because the canons formally exclude the existence of several jurisdictions on the same territory. Today, the door is open for the restoration of canonicity. If the ecumenical patriarch wants to assume the role which should be his— to be the convener, the arbiter, the center of conciliarity, let him exercise this role instead of appealing to non-existing rights! The autocephalous Orthodox Church [in America] will be the first to cooperate in any pan-Orthodox consultation on the future of Orthodoxy in America.[14]

In the ensuing years, Fr John remained thoroughly engaged in the ongoing discussion, not simply in defending autocephaly to the broader Orthodox public in his newspaper editorials and public presentations, but also in personal correspondence with Orthodox leaders worldwide and in the preparation of a study paper for the Pre-Conciliar Commission of the Holy and Great Council, entitled "Remarks on the Contribution of the Ecumenical Patriarchate to the Discussion of the Topics: 'Autocephaly and Autonomy in the Orthodox Church and the Manner of Their Proclamation' and 'The Orthodox Diaspora.'"[15] Allow me to cite two examples. The first is a personal letter to Archbishop Hieronymos of Athens, dated April 5, 1971. After opening greetings, in which Fr John thanks the archbishop for his longtime support of Syndesmos (of which Fr Meyendorff was a co-founder) and other pan-Orthodox initiatives, he continues:

---

[14] "Against Myths," *The Orthodox Church*, December 1970. Reprinted in *The Vision of Unity*, 51–53.

[15] A typewritten draft of this undated and, to my knowledge, unpublished paper is located in the OCA Archives and was provided to me by Alexis Liberovsky, OCA Archivist.

It appears to me, Your Beatitude, that no one other than yourself, as the head of the only large Orthodox Church in the non-Communist world, could help in this matter, before irreparable steps are taken and the mission of Orthodoxy in the world is seriously prejudiced.

The problem which concerns me particularly is the attitude adopted by the Ecumenical Patriarchate towards the autocephaly granted by the Moscow Patriarchate to the "Orthodox Church in America." This concern comes not so much from the negative reaction itself, but from the fact that it is *only* negative. The only positive suggestion made by the Patriarchate is that we should wait until the meeting of an ecumenical council. But Your Beatitude knows that the hope for a "Great" Council of Orthodoxy is only a distant hope . . .

Fr John then briefly describes the composition of the former Metropolia, noting that it was made up almost entirely of "American citizens, speaking and worshipping in English, with the vast majority of its members having no human connection with Russia whatsoever." For the past fifty years, this body was de facto autocephalous, but with no formal canonical status, and with its bishops suspended by the Moscow Patriarchate.

Repeatedly, in the last years, this church has tried to contact the Ecumenical Patriarchate, but was always formally told by the Phanar that it must submit to Moscow jurisdiction! Metropolitan Ireney was denied an audience with the ecumenical patriarch and was refused the right to celebrate Divine Liturgy at the Holy Sepulchre by the Patriarch of Jerusalem. These facts clearly show that negotiations with Moscow were inevitable and, since administrative submission to the Russian Patriarchate were [sic] impossible, what other solution than autocephaly could be envisaged?

The fact that it was granted so easily was a surprise, but also a proof for many of us, that Moscow was still capable to accomplish positive ecclesiastical acts.

In all the criticism of the autocephaly, we have heard so far no *positive* alternative, only references to a future council, which, as I wrote earlier, is unlikely to meet soon. Your Beatitude, such an attitude is pastorally irresponsible: one cannot condemn, without offering an alternate way. . . .

I am sure that You Beatitude understands that Orthodox unity is needed today, as never before. . . .

Your Beatitude also knows very well that the Orthodox churches do not agree upon a uniform procedure on establishing autocephalies. The Church of Greece has, so far, adopted a wise and non-committal attitude on the subject. For example, Your Beatitude and the Holy Synod have recently welcomed the Metropolitan of Prague and all Czechoslovakia—the head of an autocephalous church which is also deprived of official recognition by the Ecumenical patriarchate. What I wish to suggest is that a similar attitude of brotherhood and *constructive* fellowship be applied to the American situation . . .

Here, Fr Meyendorff shows himself to be a pragmatist. Well aware that Constantinople and the Greek-speaking churches are not ready to accept the autocephaly of the OCA, he proposes a *modus vivendi* until such a time that the canonical situation can be resolved in a pan-Orthodox context. Given recent developments, it seems that this *modus vivendi* will need to last a bit longer.

Of significant interest is the second document, a so-far unpublished response to Constantinople's (also unpublished) position paper on issues of autocephaly, autonomy, and the diaspora prepared for the Pre-Conciliar Commission of the Great and Holy Council. Fr John prepared this response at the request of the Ecumenical Patriarchate, as indicated in a personal letter to him from the Phanar, dated January 28, 1984, and signed by Metropolitans Chrysostomos of Myra and Bartholomaios of Philadelpheias (the current ecumenical patriarch).[16] I take here the liberty of quoting extensively from this paper, as it reflects Fr John's thoughts some 15 years after the autocephaly, and only a few years before his untimely death. Following an introduction in which he thanks the patriarchate for the serious attention it has paid to the subject at hand, he divides his response

---

[16]Letter in OCA Archives, provided to me by Alexis Liberovsky.

into four sections: ecclesiological, historical, pastoral, followed by a general conclusion.

Ecclesiological

The ecclesiological basis defined at the outset ("Autocephaly and Autonomy" 1–14) must be accepted by all the Orthodox churches today as the only Orthodox approach to the issues under discussion: one bishop, presiding over one church in each place. Unless one accepts this principle as an absolute norm, there will never be any real hope to solve our other problems in an Orthodox way. The Ecumenical Patriarchate, in affirming this principle in such an unambiguous way, has the truth itself on its side. The most tragic aspect of contemporary Orthodoxy is that it has *de facto* ceased to *act* as the one Church, and, instead, has adopted a system where local—predominantly national or ethnic—churches live a totally independent life, establishing communities everywhere, and preserving only "intercommunion" with each other, as if sacramental communion did not imply unity in ecclesial structures and administration. This phyletism *de facto* is precisely what was so fortunately condemned by the Council of Constantinople in 1872.

Implicit in this brief statement is a strong critique of the contemporary understanding of autocephaly as complete independence, along the lines of the 19th-century European nation-state. It was precisely during the 19th century, following the collapse of the Ottoman Empire, that many of the modern autocephalous churches were proclaimed. Fr John continues:

The ecclesiological basis defined in the documents is also entirely correct when it describes the relationships between the "local" church, each headed by its bishop, with other churches: a local church cannot live in isolation, but is always associated with other churches within a "province," headed originally by a "metropolitan," the ordination of new bishops being the primary function of the provincial synod, headed by its *protos*. The text is also right in pointing out that apostolicity or antiquity were not the only criteria which motivated the establishment of the *proteia* of metropolitans and, later, patriarchs. The system was rather one of practicality and pragmatism ("major cities"), but it assured the unity of local churches throughout the world.

Historical

The documents [prepared by the Ecumenical Patriarchate] seem to attribute an exaggerated importance to the concept of "autocephaly," and, thus, inadvertently surrender to the modern exaltation of that concept by ecclesiastical nationalists. While, on the one hand, recognizing that "autocephaly" is nothing but an "instrument of church unity" ("Autocephaly and Autonomy," 20–21), and, therefore, a pragmatic administrative arrangement for allowing bishops of an area to elect and ordain their primate, the documents, on the other hand, seem to consider it as a major institution, to be dealt with by ecumenical councils only (and only temporarily by the Ecumenical Patriarchate). In fact, local *de facto* independent primacies (which we today call "autocephalies") represented the norm of church organization before the establishment of the great patriarchates. In later centuries, they were often established, only to be re-structured or suppressed later. It seems to me quite inevitable, therefore, that in order to meet the requirements of our present complicated and rapidly changing world, that there must be more flexibility in form and procedures *with the absolute condition that ecclesiological principles defined above be respected*, and accepted as the norm towards which all temporary arrangements must tend.

In a second part of the historical section, Fr Meyendorff discusses the process of granting autocephaly, quoting Theodore Balsamon's affirmation that the privilege of establishing autocephalies belongs to an ecumenical council, to the emperor, and to individual patriarchates.[17]

The documents are right, however (cf. particularly "Autocephaly and Autonomy," 43), in affirming that the establishment of autocephaly fundamentally belongs to the entire episcopate of the Church (this can be said of *any* important ecclesiastical act) and that the ecumenical patriarch as "first bishop" possesses the responsibility of assuring that the

[17]Here, Fr Meyendorff cites from J.-P. Migne, PG 137:317–20.

opinion of all the bishops of the world be properly expressed in each case. He also has the right to express *his* opinion, and exercise leadership in achieving a consensus. This ministry of leadership, however, is different from claiming formal "rights" which cannot be substantiated by texts, or precedents.

The third historical section deals with Canon 28 of Chalcedon. This canon, Fr John, argues, gives Constantinople jurisdiction over "barbarian" (i.e., non-Greek) lands in the diocese of Thrace, Pontus, and Asia, but certainly not over all barbarian lands. Russia, he points out, was considered in Byzantium as part of Thrace,[18] but Constantinople never claimed any jurisdiction over Georgia (known as Iberia), and considered it natural that it was granted autocephaly by the patriarch of Antioch.[19]

In the pastoral section, Fr John reflects on the use of the term "diaspora":

Although the documents are, in general, written on a theoretical level, they also fortunately show sensibility for the extremely complex and diversified situations existing in the various parts of the world. For instance, a clear difference is recognized between the Orthodox "diaspora" in Europe and Australia, and the situation in America ("Orthodox diaspora," 29). This pastoral sense could, in my opinion, be extended even further and lead to the conclusion that the very concept of "diaspora" reflects more a psychological and cultural reality than a canonical one. Indeed, the ancient apostolic patriarchates of Alexandria and Jerusalem today represent "psychologically" a form of Greek "diaspora," whereas a third-generation Geek-American hardly considers himself as living "in dispersion." It is, therefore, much more helpful—in our attempts to solve contemporary issues— to return to the ecclesiological principles of "territoriality," and work towards the establishment of canonically-organized local churches, which would, of course, allow κατ' οἰκονομίαν [*kat' oikonomian*] for temporary pluralism in their organization, reflecting the ethnic and cultural diversity

---
[18]Fr John refers here to Rhalles-Potles, *Syntagma* 2:283, 285.
[19]Again, Fr John quotes Balsamon, PG 137:317–20.

of their membership. In any case, it is a fact that a large percentage of Orthodox Christians in America (and also in Europe, particularly in France) psychologically resent being identified with foreign jurisdictions which classify them as "diaspora." ...

In his conclusion, certainly respectful and sympathetic to the positions taken by Constantinople, he offers his own suggestion:

> The Orthodox Church always recognized a "first bishop," whose ministry is to lead, to coordinate, and to gather around himself the local churches of the world. Following the schism between East and West, that ministry belongs to the bishop of Constantinople. It is very unfortunate indeed that the various historical developments [over] the last two centuries have led national, ethnic Orthodox churches to act as if this universal leadership did not exist. Nevertheless, they all recognize Constantinople's privileges *formally*, although, very often, they fail to acknowledge, or understand the real content of such privilege.
>
> In my opinion, the future witness of Orthodoxy in the world depends on a revival of ecclesiological consciousness which would necessarily involve new awareness of the role of the "first bishop." It is essential, therefore, that this role be defined in terms which would be ecclesiologically uncontroversial and pastorally realistic.
>
> ... It seems to me, however, that to define the role of the Ecumenical Patriarchate as possessing the *formal* exclusive right to grant autocephaly or autonomy (before a still problematic ecumenical council meets to confirm them), and the *formal* right of jurisdiction everywhere (outside the established autocephalous churches) is unrealistic and, therefore, harmful to the eventual revival of ecclesiological consciousness. As formal *rights*, these privileges are today clearly denied not only by the Slavic and Romanian churches, but also practically by the Patriarchate of Alexandria[20] and (certainly) Antioch. Actually, the Ecumenical Patriarchate itself has been rather inconsistent in asserting such rights (cf. the action of Patriarch Joachim III entrusting Greek communities in America to the Church of Greece; or the action of

---

[20] At the time this response was composed.

Patriarch Athenagoras dissolving his Russian Exarchate in Western Europe and calling its members to return to the Patriarchate of Moscow).

Much more practical and more unquestionably canonical would be for the Patriarchate to initiate a sustained, consistent, and charitable series of initiatives, aiming at establishing a normal, canonical, territorial order in Western Europe, in Australia and, indeed, in America. Whether the ultimate result will be new autocephalous churches, or churches under the jurisdiction of the Ecumenical Patriarchate, is ecclesiologically indifferent: it is unity, not jurisdiction which is—and should be—the only real goal. Episcopal committees for coordination and collaboration (cf. "Orthodox Diaspora," 32) could be a useful tool, but only if their ultimate goal is clear, and if they are not used in fact (as is the case of SCOBA in America) to perpetuate an uncanonical *status quo*.

... Some issues of our beloved Orthodoxy wait centuries for a solution. I do not think that the issues debated in the documents can wait as long.

What is perhaps most significant in these words is Fr John's relativizing of the significance of autocephaly. He clearly rejects the modern tendency to view it as absolute independence, along the model of the nation-state. Even autocephalous churches cannot exist in isolation, but are to remain mutually accountable. Even more, it is unity in each place, rather than autocephaly, which is the real goal. Though he did not state this explicitly in this response, he regularly stated that even the autocephaly of the Orthodox Church in America is only a step toward unity in America, and not an end in itself. The Tomos of Autocephaly itself implies this in requiring the OCA to continue working with all the other jurisdictions and local churches toward the goal of unity. But the above words, written over a quarter of a century ago, still ring true.

Ethnophyletism, Autocephaly, and National Churches
A Theological Approach and Ecclesiological Implications

Paul Meyendorff

St Vladimir's Theological Quarterly 57.3–4 (2013): 381–394

I WOULD LIKE TO BEGIN by thanking the organizers of this conference for the timeliness of the topic. Ecclesial developments over the last two centuries have led to a complex and problematic situation for world Orthodoxy. First came the collapse of the Ottoman Empire and the subsequent development of independent nation-states in Eastern Europe—followed soon after by the creation of autocephalous, national Orthodox churches in those states during the 19th century. The 20th century brought two World Wars, one crisis after another in the Middle East, the spread and then the collapse of Communism, with the resulting church persecutions, as well as the migration of many Orthodox to the West—to Western Europe, North and South America, and Australia – upheavals that led to anomalous church structures in these areas, with parallel jurisdictions and competing ecclesiological visions. Now we in the 21st century are left to untangle this mess and to restore proper canonical order, consistent with the Orthodox ecclesiological tradition.

As recent decades have shown, this is no easy task. Nationalism has only grown in both the political and religious spheres. We are today witnessing the difficulties in maintaining unity within the European Union, as well as conflicts and power struggles among the various national churches. And in the West, whether in Western Europe, Australia, or the Americas, canonical order has totally broken down with the existence of multiple jurisdictions and multiple bishops in the same place. Worse yet are the attempts to justify this situation with claims that this situation poses no problem, because "we are all in communion," or, more recently, that the national churches have the responsibility to minister to their "diasporas" outside their canonical boundaries. In this sense, we have moved backward in the last fifty years. In the 1960s, everyone acknowledged that the "diaspora" situation was scandalous. Today, the tendency has been rather to rationalize and justify the status quo.

Ethnophyletism and Nationalism

The relationship between church and state is hardly a new problem, though it has been accentuated in recent centuries with the creation of national churches. On the one hand, primitive Christianity existed within the Roman Empire, and Christians were taught to render unto Caesar what is Caesar's (Mt 22.21) and to pray for the ruling authorities, even long before these were Christian (1 Tim 2.1–2). On the other hand, these Christians clearly understood that, while they were in the world, they were not of the world (Jn 15.19). Thus St Paul, in addressing the various churches, uses expressions such as "To the Church of God which is at Corinth" (τῇ ἐκκλησία τοῦ θεοῦ τῇ οὔσῃ ἐν Κορίνθῳ [tē ekklēsia tou theou tē ousē en Korinthō]) (1 Cor 1.2, etc.). He did not use terms such as the "Corinthian Church," or the "Church of Corinth." These Christians had a strong sense that their home was not in this world, because "here we have no lasting city" (Heb 13.14). Indeed, the very word that we use today for the local eucharistic community, "parish" (Gk: παροικία [paroikia]), implies precisely this idea of a temporary sojourning. And this term was originally used not simply for the local parish, but for any community of Christians organized as a geographical unit, including a diocese or an ecclesiastical province.[1]

"In the world, but not of the world"—this is the ambiguity that has challenged Christians throughout history. And the answers to this challenge have varied throughout history. Following the Peace of Constantine

---

[1]For the various meanings and uses of the term παροικία [paroikia], see G. W. H. Lampe, *A Patristic Greek Lexikon* (Oxford: Clarendon Press, 1961), 1042.

and the eventual establishment of Christianity as the official religion of the Roman Empire, the Church grew closer to the state. Bishops achieved a high rank in the empire and in society, and the organization of the Church followed imperial structures. Constantine and his successors launched a massive program of building churches, and imperial court ceremonial influenced the development of what we know today as "cathedral worship." The rapid spread of monasticism in the fourth century was at least in part motivated by a sense that the leadership of the Church was compromised by this close connection between Church and state; and for many centuries since, the monks served as a check against church authorities that were often controlled or dominated by civil authorities. Of course, monks were themselves not above involving themselves in political affairs of Church and state, for example during the "hesychast" period in the 14–15th centuries, when a number of hesychast monks, including Philotheos Kokkinos, assumed the patriarchal throne in Constantinople and struggled to enhance the power and prestige of the imperial city and church.[2] This history is well-known and need not be repeated here.

A major characteristic of this entire period, however, was its non-nationalistic character. The Roman, as well as the Byzantine, Empire was multi-ethnic and multi-national—as, indeed, was the Russian Empire in later centuries. In these contexts, the Church was similarly not organized according to nationality. Any idea of organizing church life according to ethnic criteria was rejected, as exemplified by the famous Canon 28 of Chalcedon, whose intent was precisely to include the barbarians (i.e., non-Greek speakers) within the local structures in the territories of Pontus, Asia, and Thrace, areas already under the jurisdiction of Constantinople. The principle that "there is neither Jew nor Greek" (Gal 3.28) was taken

---

[2]See, for example the recent work on Metropolitan Cyprian (Tsamblak) of Kiev, a disciple of Philotheos, by Job Getcha, *La réforme liturgique du métropolite Cyprien de Kiev* (Paris: Cerf, 2010). Cyprian was sent to Kiev by Patriarch Philotheos to mediate a difficult political and religious situation involving Moscow, Kiev, and Lithuania. In 1375, Cyprian was consecrated as "Metropolitan of Kiev [Little] Russia, and the Lithuanians," with the expectation that, following the death of Alexis, the then Metropolitan of Moscow, Cyprian would become the head of a single, united Church of all Russia.

seriously in the canonical tradition of the Church, as was the territorial principle.

In recent centuries, the situation has changed dramatically. The old imperial structures have collapsed, including the Byzantine, then the Ottoman, and finally the Russian (twice, in 1917 and 1991). As a result, new nations arose in the old Orthodox world, in Eastern Europe and the Middle East. Repeated wars and other cataclysms in these regions also led to large migrations of people, not just within these traditionally Orthodox areas, but also beyond, to Western Europe, the Americas, and Australia. Obviously, each area has its own history, its own particular characteristics, but there are common trends that pose serious challenges to Orthodox ecclesiology.

The first consequence of the collapse of empires was the redrawing of the map of Europe and the creation of numerous nation states, frequently on the basis of ethnicity. Following upon the creation of these states came the creation of autocephalous Orthodox churches in each state. In one sense, this was certainly in conformity with Orthodox canonical tradition, since from ancient times autocephalous churches were established in accordance with existing political structures. The difference here was the ethnic factor, which risked becoming more significant than the territorial factor. We can trace the roots of this ethnic factor back into the period of the Ottoman Empire, when the patriarchs of Constantinople functioned as the head of the Orthodox Christian population, which resulted as well in the subordination of the ancient churches of Antioch, Alexandria, and Jerusalem to Constantinople, with the resulting Greek hegemony in these struggling churches. Despite the condemnation of ethnophyletism at the 1872 council in Constantinople, ethnic identity became an important factor, alongside the territorial principle, in the self-identity of the newly-established, autocephalous churches. Thus, it has become customary today to refer to Orthodox churches with an ethnic tag: the "Russian Orthodox Church," or the "Greek, Romanian, Bulgarian, Polish," etc. Lost is the original Pauline understanding of "the Church which dwells in Greece, or in Russia . . ."

The situation grew more complicated, and more problematic, with the migration of many Orthodox Christians from their traditional homelands into areas without organized Orthodox dioceses. The size and ethnic composition of these migrations varied from place to place, and I have chosen to focus my attention on North America—because it is the situation with which I am most familiar, and because it raises the significant issues in the most poignant way.

Orthodoxy in North America began with the Russian mission in Alaska that began in 1794 and was in fact part of the missionary outreach of the Church of Russia to Siberia and the Far East that began in the 17th century and continued through the 19th.[3] At that time, Alaska was a Russian territory, and the mission was directed at the many native tribes in this northern region. In 1840, Alaska became a missionary diocese, and Fr John Veniaminov (the future St Innocent) was ordained as its first bishop. Following the sale of Alaska to the United States (1867), the missionary diocese moved its headquarters from Sitka first to San Francisco (1870), and then in 1905 to New York, when St Tikhon, the future Patriarch of Moscow, was bishop in America (1898–1907). During the 19th century came the first waves of immigration and the establishment of the first Orthodox parishes in the "lower 48." Some of these new parishes received support from the missionary diocese, while others were independent of episcopal authority and were controlled by lay boards of trustees. During the latter part of the 19th century, with increasing immigration and the mass conversion of several hundred thousand former Uniates, the missionary diocese expanded rapidly.

Thus, in 1905, Archbishop Tikhon submitted a proposal to the Holy Synod in Moscow to reorganize the mission diocese into an independent, multi-ethnic, American diocese with auxiliary dioceses for each ethnic group—he mentioned specifically the "Arabs," the Serbs, and the Greeks. He already expressed his hope that the mission in America would evolve into a local, territorial, autocephalous church. Already in 1904, Tikhon

---

[3]For a good introduction to this history, see Mark Stokoe and Leonid Kishkovsky, *Orthodox Christians in North America, 1794–1994* (New York: Orthodox Christian Publications Center, 1995).

consecrated (now St) Raphael Hawaweeny as auxiliary bishop, with responsibility for the Arab Christian community. In 1907, Tikhon convened the first "All-American Council" in Mayfield, Pennsylvania, assembling hundreds of clergy and lay delegates. Throughout this period, it is evident that the Church of Russia understood itself to be following the well-established Orthodox principle that the creation of new churches was the responsibility of the church that initiated missionary activity in a particular area. We should note as well that no other church at this time challenged this in any way. We should be careful, however, not to paint an idealized picture of the situation, as there were parishes functioning with no episcopal oversight, and there was some resistance to what was perceived as Russian control, particularly among communities of Greek background.

Though the ecclesial situation was not entirely clear in the early 20th century, it was thrown into total chaos following the 1917 Communist revolution in Russia. Support from Russia disappeared, and soon the church in America was racked by divisions, both ethnic and political. As a result, during the 1920s the various ethnic jurisdictions were created by the Old World churches, and several jurisdictions subsequently split again, typically for political reasons. In particular, several of the Slavic jurisdictions, as well as the Antiochian, each underwent further splits as a result of political disputes, ecclesiological disagreements, and external pressures. The result was the scandalous situation of multiple jurisdictions, divisions along ethnic and/or political lines, and multiple bishops in the same city. And Orthodox Christians in America came to refer to themselves not simply as "Orthodox Christian," but as "Greek-Orthodox," "Serbian-Orthodox," nearly always with an ethnic designator.

This has led to a caricature of Orthodoxy in America, exemplified in the popular film, "My Big Fat Greek Wedding," in which the fiancé of a Greek woman, after being baptized, is told: "Now you are Greek." Unfortunately, this perception appears not simply in the broader American culture, but comes from within the heart of the Orthodox community itself. I vividly remember a priest and professor from Holy Cross Greek Orthodox School of Theology commenting, after hearing his audience at St Vladimir's Seminary sing "O Heavenly King": "Oh, you Russians sing so well!" Ironically, there was not a single Russian in the room, and most of the audience consisted of American converts to Orthodoxy, with a few "cradle Orthodox," of various ethnic backgrounds, thrown in.

One jurisdiction, the direct descendant of the old Russian mission and known before 1970 as the "Metropolia," refused to submit to Soviet control and, as a result, was in 1933 excommunicated and declared schismatic by the Communist-controlled Church of Russia. It was this group, later joined by several other ethnic jurisdictions (Romanian, Albanian, and Bulgarian), that was eventually to become the Orthodox Church in America. This jurisdiction, alone in this constellation of ethnic churches, understood itself as multi-ethnic and, despite its at times desperate material situation, always sought to maintain Archbishop Tikhon's vision of a united territorial church in North America. The Metropolia opened two seminaries in 1938, translated service books into English, and participated diligently in inter-Orthodox and ecumenical activities. St Vladimir's Seminary, its leading theological school, gained a worldwide reputation as a center of Orthodox theological thought, chiefly in the persons of three of its deans, Frs Georges Florovsky, Alexander Schmemann, and John Meyendorff.[4] Most significantly, this jurisdiction did not see itself as being "in diaspora," but understood itself as being placed providentially in America to witness to the truth of Orthodoxy in a new, missionary context.

It is this last fact which, I believe, highlights precisely the theological problem with any sort of ethnophyletism, nationalism, and jurisdictional pluralism. While it is clear that Orthodoxy is an incarnational religion, and therefore one that is able to insert itself into and transform any culture, it is equally clear that Orthodoxy cannot be bound by any particular nationality or culture. This issue is as old as the Church itself and was faced by Peter and Paul, by the apologists in the 2–3rd centuries, and in every period since. The challenges of each age have differed, and so too the Church's responses. Whatever challenges the Church faces, however, the principle remains the same: in the Church, there can be no division

---

[4]It should be noted here that Schmemann and Meyendorff grew up in the midst of the Russian emigration in Paris, studied and then taught at the St Sergius Institute in Paris, and moved to America in the 1950s to assume academic positions at St Vladimir's Seminary.

between Jew and Greek, no division based on nationality, race, or gender. The warning that St Paul addressed to the Corinthians who are split into factions, "It is not the Lord's Supper that you eat" (1 Cor 11.20), remains applicable to us today. Similarly, the paradoxical tension between being "in the world but not of the world" must never be lost—a clear danger when the Church becomes too closely allied with the state, with any single political faction within the state, or with any particular political ideology. In fact, the Church is at times most effective when it stands against the civil authorities, as when the Russian missionaries in Alaska defended the natives from abuse and exploitation by the very Russian-American Trading Company that brought the Church to Alaska. St Herman of Alaska, for example, left Kodiak for Spruce Island precisely to avoid persecution and possible death at the hand not of natives, but of representatives of the Russian company![5]

Ultimately, then, ethnophyletism and the divisions in church life that it creates hinder the Church's missionary efforts, both inside traditionally Orthodox lands and in the West. Our increasingly secularized world needs the answers that Orthodoxy can provide; but our excessive identification of the Church with particular cultures or ideologies, be they Greek, Russian, or any other, as well as our many divisions in the West, greatly reduce Orthodox credibility in a world that has become ever more secular and cynical.

Autocephaly

No topic has been more controversial within world Orthodoxy in recent years than autocephaly, and particularly how it is attained. It is precisely this issue that has slowed the convening of a pan-Orthodox council and may derail it altogether. The controversy includes different interpretations of Canon 28 of Chalcedon, as well as claims by Constantinople that it alone, in the absence of an ecumenical council, can grant autocephaly. The details of this debate are well-known and, in my opinion, avoid, and indeed mask, some more fundamental issues.

---

[5]Cf. M. Stokoe and L. Kishkovsky, *Orthodox Christians in North America*, 5–17.

The first concerns the very nature of autocephaly. For modern debates on autocephaly, in the words of John Meyendorff, "attribute an exaggerated importance to the concept of 'autocephaly,' and, thus, inadvertently surrender to the modern exaltation of that concept by ecclesiastical nationalists."[6] I would like here to summarize some of his conclusions, which seem worthy of our consideration at this symposium. He criticizes the Ecumenical Patriarchate for considering autocephaly as a major institution, therefore "to be dealt with by ecumenical councils only (and only temporarily by the Ecumenical Patriarchate)."

> In fact, local *de facto* independent primacies (which we today call "autocephalies") represented the norm of church organization before the establishment of the major patriarchates. In later centuries, they were often established, only to be re-structured or suppressed later. It seems to me quite inevitable, therefore, that in order to meet the requirements of our present complicated and rapidly changing world, there must be much in forms and procedures *with the absolute condition that the ecclesiological principles defined above be respected*, and accepted as the norm towards which all temporary arrangements must tend.[7]

The ecclesiological principles which he enumerates at the beginning of his response represent full agreement with the position of Constantinople: "One bishop, presiding over one church in each place." But then Meyendorff goes on to critique the current situation:

> The most tragic aspect of contemporary Orthodoxy is that it has de *facto* ceased to *act* as the one Church, and, instead, had adopted a system where local—and predominantly national or ethnic—churches live

---

[6]Quoted from an unpublished response by Fr John Meyendorff to two study papers prepared by the Ecumenical Patriarchate for the Pre-Conciliar Commission of the Great and Holy Council: "Autocephaly and Autonomy in the Orthodox Church and the Manner of Their Proclamation," and "The Orthodox Diaspora." The response came following a personal invitation to Meyendorff, signed by Metropolitans Chrysostomos of Myra and Bartholomaios of Philadelpheias, dated January 28, 1984. The text of the response was provided to me by Alexis Liberovsky, Archivist of the Orthodox Church in America. Citation on p. 3.

[7]Ibid. Emphasis in original.

a totally independent life, establishing communities everywhere, and preserving only "intercommunion" with each other, as if sacramental communion did not imply unity in ecclesial structures and administration. This phyletism *de facto* is precisely what was so fortunately condemned by the Council of Constantinople in 1872.[8]

In short, autocephaly has gradually changed from its original function, in which it was a practical mechanism by which the church in a particular region could form its own synod, elect its own primate, and settle its local affairs, while at the same time assuring "the unity of local churches throughout the world."[9] During the modern era, the model for autocephaly has become the nation state, with its focus on promoting self-interest and absolute independence. And this is a model that leaves little room for any form of primacy at the universal level.

So it is that today we see national churches not just competing for power and territory, but establishing ethnic churches across the whole world to minister to their "diasporas." In some cases, this is even enshrined in contemporary church statutes: I cite but two examples:

> The membership of the Orthodox Church of Cyprus includes: 1) all Christian Orthodox Cypriots who entered into the womb of their church through baptism and who reside permanently in Cyprus, as well as 2) all those who are of Cypriot origin and who today live abroad.[10]

> The jurisdiction of the Russian Orthodox Church extends to: 1) persons of Orthodox faith residing in the USSR, residing on the canonical territory of the Russian Orthodox Church, as well as to 2) persons [of Russian origin] residing abroad and voluntarily accepting its jurisdiction.[11]

---

[8]Ibid., 2.

[9]Ibid.

[10]1980 Statute of the Church of Cyprus, article 2, as quoted in Jean-Claude Larchet, *L'Église, corps du Christ*, Vol II, *Les relations entre les Églises* (Paris: Cerf, 2012), 133. My English translation. The Church of Cyprus has recently revised its statute and removed the reference to Cypriots living abroad.

[11]1988 and 2000 Statute of the Church of Russia, article I, § 3, as quoted in Larchet, ibid. My English translation.

In this way, nationalism and ethnic identity are placed above the territorial principle, and local unity is destroyed. The result is a kind of colonialism which in fact creates local divisions and prevents bishops in America, for example, from effectively resolving local problems, as all issues need to be referred to synods in the "home churches." It remains to be seen whether the recently-established "episcopal assemblies" in America and elsewhere will boldly take a leadership role in the creation of normal, canonical ecclesial structures, or whether they will abdicate their responsibilities and wait for others to decide their fate.

As already noted above, not only has the idea of autocephaly been overemphasized, but so also the process by which it is granted. Fr Meyendorff repeatedly points to Theodore Balsamon, an authoritative interpreter of the canons, who states that the privilege of establishing autocephalies belongs to ecumenical councils, to the emperor, and to individual patriarchates—and he considers it quite normal, for example, that it is for the Patriarch of Antioch to affirm the autocephaly of the Church of Georgia (known as Iberia in the ancient texts), because it was under its jurisdiction.[12] In the case of Russia, which was connected with the diocese of Thrace, it fell within the jurisdiction of Constantinople, and thus received its autocephaly from Constantinople.

We should note as well that, in most cases, autocephaly in each place was a de facto reality before any official proclamation or recognition. The Church of Russia, for example, became ecclesiastically independent (i.e., began selecting its own primate) some 150 years before this was formally recognized by the Patriarch of Constantinople in 1589—a recognition in fact granted only under duress—and then later affirmed by councils in Constantinople in 1590 and 1593. In the last two centuries, as new national churches were created in Central and Eastern Europe as the Ottoman Empire retreated, recognition typically came decades after the fact: On the basis of these facts, one could conclude that autocephaly typically begins as

---

[12]PG 137:317–320, cited in the Meyendorff response, pp. 3–4. For an excellent overview of the process of establishing autocephalous churches, see Alexander Bogolepov, *Towards an American Orthodox Church*, revised ed. (Crestwood, NY: St Vladimir's Seminary Press, 2001).

a reality on the ground and as a result of local initiative, with recognition granted often only grudgingly, and typically after the fact.

The process then, is rather messy, and the canons provide no clear guidelines. The situation of the so-called "diaspora," the Orthodox churches in Western Europe, America, and Australia, is particularly complex. Is autocephaly the answer? Is some form of autonomy? Certainly, the present situation, with multiple ethnic jurisdictions, with multiple bishops in the same city, is intolerable and violates proper church order. The key issue, however, is not autocephaly, but unity. No canons absolutely require autocephaly, but Orthodox tradition and the canons do require unity in each place. And this unity can be achieved only when the bishops in these areas themselves bring it about through local, conciliar action, unrestrained by external control. Do they have the desire for this unity? And, equally important, are the "mother churches" ready and willing to allow this territorial unity to happen? That remains to be seen.

Conclusion

Absolutely central is the need to restore a proper ecclesiological vision, a vision that has been severely hampered by historical developments in recent centuries. Yes, historical circumstances have created what can only be considered as an anomalous situation. It was pastoral need that led to the creation of parallel, ethnic jurisdictions in the West. The tragedy lies not so much in these historical realities, but in their acceptance as normal! How often we hear the refrain that, though divided, we share the same faith and are all in communion. Similarly, the problem lies not so much in the existence of autocephalous churches coterminous with national boundaries, but in the often overly close relation between church and state, in the identity of church with ethnicity, and especially in a new understanding of autocephaly as absolute independence, with no accountability to sister churches, and sometimes even jurisdiction extending beyond canonical boundaries to one's ethnic group.

How are these challenges, both practical, but essentially theological, to be addressed? One desirable step, which touches peripherally on the topic of the present conference, but which also raises profound theological issues, is a rediscovery of the proper function of primacy as bearing the responsibility for maintaining unity, not simply at the local, but also at the international, level. Permit me to conclude with an extensive citation from Fr John Meyendorff, again from his 1984 response to the Ecumenical Patriarchate's position papers on questions of autocephaly and the diaspora:

> The Orthodox Church always recognized a "first bishop," whose ministry is to lead, to coordinate, and to gather around himself the local churches of the world. Following the schism between East and West, that ministry belongs to the bishop of Constantinople. It is very unfortunate indeed that the various historical developments [over] the last two centuries have led national, ethnic Orthodox churches to act as if this universal leadership did not exist. Nevertheless, they all recognize Constantinople's privileges *formally*, although, very often, they fail to acknowledge, or understand the real content of such privilege.
>
> In my opinion, the future witness of Orthodoxy in the world depends on a revival of ecclesiological consciousness which would necessarily involve new awareness of the role of the "first bishop." It is essential, therefore, that this role be defined in terms which would be ecclesiologically uncontroversial and pastorally realistic.
>
> ... It seems to me, however, that to define the role of the Ecumenical Patriarchate as possessing the *formal* exclusive right to grant autocephaly or autonomy (before a still problematic ecumenical council meets to confirm them), and the *formal* right of jurisdiction everywhere (outside the established autocephalous churches) is unrealistic and, therefore, harmful to the eventual revival of ecclesiological consciousness. As formal *rights*, these privileges are today clearly denied not only by the Slavic and Romanian churches, but also practically by the Patriarchate of Alexandria[13] and (certainly) Antioch. Actually, the Ecumenical Patriarchate itself has been rather inconsistent in asserting such rights (cf. the action of Patriarch Joachim III entrusting Greek communities in America to the Church of Greece; or the action of

---

[13] At the time this response was composed.

Patriarch Athenagoras dissolving his Russian Exarchate in Western Europe and calling its members to return to the Patriarchate of Moscow).

Much more practical and more unquestionably canonical would be for the Patriarchate to initiate a sustained, consistent, and charitable series of initiatives, aiming at establishing a normal, canonical, territorial order in Western Europe, in Australia and, indeed, in America. Whether the ultimate result will be new autocephalous churches, or churches under the jurisdiction of the Ecumenical Patriarchate, is ecclesiologically indifferent: it is unity, not jurisdiction which is—and should be—the only real goal. Episcopal committees for coordination and collaboration (cf. "Orthodox diaspora," 32) could be a useful tool, but only if their ultimate goal is clear, and if they are not used in fact (as is the case of SCOBA in America) to perpetuate an uncanonical *status quo*.

. . . Some issues of our beloved Orthodoxy wait centuries for a solution. I do not think that the issues debated in the documents can wait as long.[14]

These words, written over a quarter of a century ago, still ring true today.

---

[14] See note 6 above. Citation on pp. 6–7. Emphases in original.

Autocephaly and Autonomy[1]

John H. Erickson

St Vladimir's Theological Quarterly 60.1–2 (2016): 91–110

OVER THE LAST CENTURY few subjects provoked as much controversy in the Orthodox world as autocephaly and, closely related to this, autonomy. One need only mention disputes between the Russian Orthodox Church and the Patriarchate of Constantinople concerning the autocephalous status of the Polish Orthodox Church, the Orthodox Church in the Czech Republic and Slovakia, and the Orthodox Church in America (OCA). The Russian Orthodox Church recognizes all three as autocephalous, on the basis of tomes of autocephaly issued by it as their "mother church" in 1951 (for Poland and Czechoslovakia) and 1970 (for America). Constantinople, on the other hand, recognizes only the first two as autocephalous, on the basis of its own tomes of autocephaly issued in 1924 (for Poland) and 1998 (for the Czech Republic and Slovakia), and it has denied the autocephalous status of the third. Less often considered, but no less controversial, have been the unilateral claims to autocephaly put forward by "the Ukrainian Orthodox Church–Kiev Patriarchate," "the Ukrainian Autocephalous Orthodox Church," and "the Macedonian Orthodox Church."

Autonomy also has been a source of controversy. Part of the Russian Orthodox Church in tsarist times, the Finnish Orthodox Church, autonomous under Constantinople since 1923, was recognized as such by the Russian Orthodox Church only in 1957. More dramatic was the much-publicized dispute between Constantinople and the Russian

[1] [This article was originally presented at the conference titled "Comprendre les enjeux du prochain Concile de l'Église orthodoxe," organized by *Institut de théologie orthodoxe Saint-Serge* and *Centre oecuménique de l'Université catholique de Leuven* (Paris, October 2012). It was published first in French translation (in *Contacts—Revue française de l'Orthodoxie* 65 (2013): 391–412).—*Ed.*]

Orthodox Church over Estonia, which in 1996 led briefly to a break in communion. In the wake of this clash, two Orthodox jurisdictions now divide the Orthodox population of Estonia: the Estonian apostolic Orthodox Church, an autonomous church under Constantinople, with about 20,000 faithful, mostly Estonian speaking; and the Estonian Orthodox Church of the Moscow Patriarchate, a semi-autonomous diocese of the Russian Orthodox Church, with about 150,000 faithful, mostly Russian speaking. The Japanese Orthodox Church, autonomous under the Russian Orthodox Church since 1970, has not been recognized as such by Constantinople. The same holds true for a number of now-autonomous churches that were integral parts of the Russian Orthodox Church before the break-up of the Soviet Union, most notably the Ukrainian Orthodox Church (as distinct from both "the Ukrainian Orthodox Church–Kiev Patriarchate" and "the Ukrainian Autocephalous Orthodox Church") and the Moldovan Orthodox Church (whose role in independent Moldavia is contested by the Romanian Orthodox Church's revived Metropolis of Bessarabia). The list of controversies and conflicting claims could go on and on.

Most often disagreement concerning autocephaly has centered on accession to autocephaly, i.e., the way in which autocephalous status is attained. But while debate on this subject has proceeded with great acrimony, the nature and content of autocephaly itself has been left relatively undefined. The word is assumed to have a simple, univocal meaning. In fact those who use the term tacitly make certain assumptions that others may not share, but which nonetheless color their outlook and arouse their emotions. Much the same can be said for disagreement concerning autonomy. Clearly no term can be properly understood without considering the wider historical context in which it is used. Clearly, neither autocephaly nor autonomy can be properly understood without careful attention to the wider historical context in which the terms are being used.

In present-day usage, a church is termed *autocephalous* if it possesses (1) the right to resolve all internal problems on its own authority, independently of all other churches, and (2) the right to appoint its own bishops, among them the primate or head of the church, without obligatory expression of dependence on another church.² An *autonomous* church, on the other hand, is one whose primate must be appointed or approved in some way by the "mother church" that granted it autonomy. Similarity between the two aspects of autocephaly just noted and the internal and external sovereignty of the modern state, as presented in textbooks on political science, is hardly coincidental. From the nineteenth century onward, autocephaly typically has been understood as radical independence analogous to that which the modern sovereign state enjoys in the secular sphere. The autocephalous church, often referred to as the "local church,"³ is regarded as the fundamental ecclesiastical organism, of which all lesser bodies are but parts, administrative subdivisions, or dependencies. This tendency is reflected in many governing statutes and in older canon law textbooks, which are preoccupied with identifying and defining the competence of the highest authority within the church (holy synod, patriarch, council . . .). While detailed regulations may also be drawn up for the erection or suppression of "lesser bodies" (dioceses, exarchates, monasteries, and other institutions) and for their operation, the ecclesiological significance of these bodies is seldom explored.

The weaknesses of this understanding of the autocephalous church have become ever more conspicuous over the past century. Like the international system of sovereign states, on which in so many respects it was patterned, the modern system of autocephalous churches has failed to meet demands placed on it in a rapidly changing world. Possession of internal sovereignty has by no means assured spiritual health within an autocephalous church. Insistence on external sovereignty, according to which "every autocephalous church is a full and equal subject of international law,"⁴ has inhibited the creation of effective structures for maintaining communion

---

²Alexander Bogolepov, *Toward an American Orthodox Church*, rev. ed. (Crestwood NY: SVS Press, 2001), 8. Much the same definition is given in typical popular presentations, such as Ronald G. Roberson, *The Eastern Churches: A Brief Survey* (Rome: PIO, 1995), 40.

³*Pomestvennaia tserkov'/topikē ekklēsia*, "local church," "church of the place," in the standard Russian and Greek canon law text books, but "Partikularkirche" in Nikodim Milash, *Das Kirchenrecht der morgenländischen Kirche* (Czernowitz: 1897), 200–09.

⁴S. V. Troitskii, "O tserkovnoi avtokefalii" [About the autocephaly of the Church], *Zhurnal Moskovskoi Patriarkhii* 7 (1948): 48.

(or even communication) between autocephalous churches. The result too often has been indifference, absence of common activity, and periodic confrontations on such matters as the recognition of new autocephalous and autonomous entities.

The approach to ecclesiology lying behind this modern understanding of autocephaly now is generally discredited in Orthodox theological circles, though its continuing influence can still be felt in the practice and official utterances of the autocephalous churches. Its reliance on the language and thought-patterns of law and diplomacy has given way to a more "churchly" approach, with emphasis on Scripture, the liturgy, and the church fathers.

The point of departure for this more recent approach to ecclesiology has been the Eucharist—or more specifically the Eucharist as it is revealed in the letters of St Ignatius of Antioch and other early Christian texts. The Eucharist is seen now, not just as one of several means of grace at the disposal of the Church conceived as a divinely instituted body politic, but as the very basis for the Church's life. It is when all the clergy and faithful, with all their diverse gifts, are gathered under the presidency of the one bishop in eucharistic celebration that the Church becomes truly herself, the very icon of the Kingdom which is to come. But even as the Eucharist proclaims, anticipates, and participates in the banquet of the Kingdom, gathering up the faithful of all times and all places and indeed the whole creation in its prayer, it is celebrated in the time and space of this world. Until the coming again of the Lord, the Eucharist is necessarily a local event, "placed" in a specific context.

The insights of "eucharistic ecclesiology" help explain the evolution of church structures in antiquity. The fundamental ecclesiastical organism was understood to be the local church—"local" in this case meaning the church of a relatively compact face-to-face community, considerably more limited in its geographic extension than the modern autocephalous "local" church. Though modest in scale, each local church was "the sacramental manifestation of ecclesial plenitude," as the late Archbishop Pierre L'Huillier put it.[5] They related to each other "not as parts of a whole, but

---

[5] P. L'Huillier, "Problems Concerning Autocephaly," *Greek Orthodox Theological Review* 24 (1979): 165–91, at 168.

on the principle of *mutual identity*."[6] Each in its place was the concrete realization of the Church of God.[7] This, however, did not negate the need for communion with the other local churches but rather implied it.

The mutual identity of the local churches—the profound communion uniting them with Christ and with each other—was expressed most tangibly in and through the collegiality of their bishops, especially as these met together in council. Long before the establishment of Christianity as the favored religion of the state, before structures for coordination of church life were defined in the form of conciliar canons, ecclesiastical organization in the Roman Empire tended to follow the lines of civil administration. By the fourth century, synods of bishops were meeting with some regularity in most provinces of the Roman Empire, typically under the presidency of the bishop of the metropolis, i.e., the chief city of the province, to address matters of common concern, to resolve disputes, and to elect and ordain their comprovincial colleagues, including their primate, the bishop of the metropolis. Roughly speaking, and with several important exceptions, the churches of each province constituted an autocephalous entity. They did not *become* autocephalous, they *were* autocephalous. To be sure, the word *autokephalos*—coined several centuries later—was not applied to them at the time. But Byzantine canonists and other later writers will have recourse to that word because it aptly expressed an existing reality. As Peter L'Huillier concludes after extensive study of the relevant sources, Byzantine canonists clearly identified the fundamental meaning of autocephaly:

> It consists precisely and uniquely in the fact that all the bishops of a territory are elected and consecrated by the episcopal college of that territory and that the primate . . . does not need to receive his investiture from any other primate.[8]

---

[6] Kallistos Ware, "Communion and Intercommunion," *Sobornost* 7.7 (1978): 554.

[7] Cf. the beautiful address of the *Martyrdom of Polycarp*: "The Church of God which sojourns at Smyrna, to the Church of God which sojourns at Philomelion, and to all the communities in each place of the Holy and Catholic Church. . . ."

[8] P. L'Huillier, "Problems Concerning Autocephaly," 168. For the historical overview that follows, see also his later and more complete "Accession to Autocephaly," *St Vladimir's Theological Quarterly* 37 (1993): 267–304, and John H. Erickson, "Autocephaly in Orthodox Canonical Literature to the Thirteenth Century," *St Vladimir's Theological Quarterly* 15 (1971): 28–41,

It is not necessary here to trace the complex process of consolidation and centralization that transformed ecclesiastical structures in the Roman Empire in the course of the fourth and fifth centuries. Out of a constellation of autocephalous ecclesiastical provinces, five major ecclesiastical divisions emerged, a *pentarchy* of patriarchates whose preeminence in the universal Church would be assured by imperial legislation and theological reflection even after the rise of Islam in the East and barbarian invasions in the West limited their practical significance. But notwithstanding the ascendency of pentarchic theory from the fifth through the twelfth centuries, in practice there were several exceptions—churches besides the five patriarchates with the right to appoint all their own bishops, including their primate. The status of the Church of Cyprus, a surviving example of the autocephalous ecclesiastical province, was confirmed at the Council of Ephesus (AD 431) against encroachment by Antioch and subsequently bolstered by the discovery of the relics of St Barnabas and by imperial edict. The Georgian Church, originally dependent on Antioch, gradually progressed from a state of autonomy (its catholicos was responsible for the election of diocesan bishops, but his own election had to be confirmed by Antioch) to full autocephaly. The church of Justiniana Prima was established as a fully autocephalous archbishopric, with jurisdiction over much of the Balkan peninsula, by a novella of Emperor Justinian. It is noteworthy that in none of these cases did the patriarch of Constantinople or, for that matter, an ecumenical council, play a determinative role.

These ancient autocephalous churches—whether patriarchates or the odd metropolitanate or archbishopric—share certain characteristics that distinguish them from the modern autocephalous church. First of all, they arose and functioned within a single *politeuma*, a single *commonwealth*, multi-ethnic, multi-lingual, in which the coincidence of Church and empire was taken for granted as part of God's plan for the world. As Christian apologists had recognized long before, the Church's universal vocation ("go into all nations . . .") and the Roman Empire's aspirations to universality neatly complemented each other. The geographic boundaries

revised and expanded in *The Challenge of Our Past* (Crestwood NY: St Vladimir's Seminary Press, 1991), 91–113.

of the autocephalous churches might coincide with those of civil administration, but neither civil nor ecclesiastical boundaries were directly related to political independence or to nationality. And while the bishops of the autocephalous entity were expected to manage their own internal affairs, they were obliged to do so in accordance with the norms set forth in the canons. The universal canons, not the particular law of the autocephalous entity, set forth basic principles of church order: the number of bishops required for episcopal elections and ordinations, the relationship between diocesan bishops and their primate, the competence of the synod of bishops, etc. The universal canons also provided mechanisms for the resolution of serious disputes: appeals could be carried to a higher court, contentious issues could be considered by an "enlarged" synod (*meizōn synodos*), etc. Autocephalous entities developed in order to strengthen the bonds of communion uniting the local churches of a given region with each other and with all the churches of the *oikoumenē*. They were intended to unite, not divide. They provided a practical administrative arrangement for self-rule at the regional level without claiming self-sufficiency.

For many centuries, despite adverse changes in circumstances, Roman-Byzantine imperial ideology remained largely intact, and with it the sense of belonging to a single Christian commonwealth. But this began to change in the wake of the 1204 Latin conquest of Constantinople. The thirteenth century saw the establishment of two new autocephalous churches in the Balkans, the Serbian archbishopric of Peć and the Bulgarian Patriarchate of Trnovo. Both came into existence through bilateral treaties between the emerging Serbian and Bulgarian kingdoms and the Greek rump empire of Nicaea. Autocephaly was on its way to becoming an expression of national and political independence, "the status symbol of a new 'Christian nation.'"[9] Whereas autocephaly formerly had meant independence on a purely ecclesiastical level, it now was related to political independence.

Evident also in this period are signs of incipient nationalism. This is most conspicuous among the Balkan Slavs. For example, the bishops

---

[9] Alexander Schmemann, "A Meaningful Storm," in *Church, World, Mission* (Crestwood NY: SVS Press, 1979), 98. This essay was originally published in *St Vladimir's Theological Quarterly* 15 (1971): 3–27. [In the present volume, pp. 149–178.—*Ed.*]

consecrated by St Sava for his newly autocephalous church were Serbs as distinct from Greeks, and in places where there was a Greek incumbent, he was ousted. A similar sense of national identity can be seen in some Greek circles. Intellectuals in the court of Nicaea praised classical letters and art and even began to use the word Hellene—Greek—in a positive sense. (Hitherto it had meant *pagan* as distinct from Christian.) At the same time, a new sense of (Orthodox) universalism can be detected. Old symbols of unity and order—the emperor and his once-universal empire, the pentarchy of patriarchs—were fading in significance. Taking their place on the institutional level was the patriarch of Constantinople, who effectively replaced the emperor as the symbol of the unity of the Orthodox Christian world. Taking their place on the spiritual and ideological level was what some modern scholars have referred to as "political hesychasm" or the "hesychast international," so called because many exponents of hesychast spirituality also advanced a social, cultural, and political program that profoundly affected the entire Orthodox world.[10] These agents of institutional and cultural continuity would provide a measure of leadership, stability, and unity for the Orthodox *millet-i-rum* during the long centuries of the Turkocratia. In this *Byzance après Byzance*, shared religion, now reinforced by shared marginalization, would continue to unite Orthodox Christians as one people, one Roman nation, trumping whatever power ethnicity, language, and similar factors might have had to divide them.

Nationalism—replete with romantic myths about national origins, language, character, genius, etc.—would reemerge as a significant factor in Orthodox church life only in the late eighteenth and nineteenth centuries—and with nationalism, the modern autocephalous church. The first stirrings of this modern nationalism in the Balkans can be felt among educators and other intelligentsia (e.g., Voulgaris among the Greeks, Dosithei Obradović among the Serbs, Sophrony of Vratsa among the Bulgarians),

---

[10]The terms are used by Fr John Meyendorff, among others. See now Daniel Paul Payne, *The Revival of Political Hesychasm in Contemporary Orthodox Thought: The Political Hesychasm of John Romanides and Christos Yannaras* (Lanham MD: Lexington Books, 2011), and Christopher D. L. Johnson, *The Globalization of Hesychasm: Contesting Contemplation* (New York and London: Continuum, 2010).

who promoted the study of national language, history, and culture. But as Paschalis Kitromilides observes:

> Nationalism became a real, as opposed to a theoretical problem for Orthodoxy once the peoples of the Balkans rose up in arms against Ottoman rule in the early nineteenth century. The protracted revolts in the Balkans [. . .] provided the crucible for the transformation of the Orthodox religious communities of the Balkans into modern nations. Part of the transformation involved the radical reshaping of local ecclesiastical communities from branches of ecumenical Orthodoxy into components of new nations.[11]

Throughout the Balkans, the revolt of subject Orthodox minorities against Ottoman rule involved, on the ecclesiastical level, independence from the *millet-bashi* (the religious and political leader responsible for Christians in the East), that is the patriarch of Constantinople. Because of this coincidence, scholars sometimes explain autocephaly simply as a function of nationalism—as one aspect of national consolidation, a process marked by the nationalization of religion and the sacralization of the nation. Pedro Ramet, writing in the late 1980s as nationalist resurgence in Eastern Europe was again becoming a matter of analytical concern, offers an example of this approach:

> The equation of religious unity with political unity and later with national identity became the *raison d'être* for autocephaly in the Orthodox world. Especially with the growth of nationalism in the nineteenth century, to be a nation meant to have a church of one's own, and to be entitled to one's own state. By contrast, subject peoples, such as Macedonians, Belorussians, and Ukrainians, were described as "lacking a true history"; they were said to speak the "dialects" of other "historical" nations and were denied the right to have their own autocephalous churches.[12]

---

[11] "The Legacy of the French Revolution: Orthodoxy and Nationalism," in *The Cambridge History of Christianity* 5: *Eastern Christianity* (Cambridge and New York: Cambridge University Press, 2006), 229.
[12] Pedro Ramet, "Autocephaly and National Identity in Church-State Relations in Eastern Christianity: An Introduction," in *Eastern Christianity and Politics in the Twentieth Century* (Durham, NC: Duke University Press, 1988), 4–5.

The story, of course, is more complex. As the quotation from Ramet itself suggests, a sense of national identity in the absence of other factors seldom, if ever, has been sufficient for the establishment of an autocephalous church—at least for the establishment of an autocephalous church recognized as such by all its "sister" churches. What has made a decisive difference is state involvement and—closely related to this—changes in "political geography," most often as the result of wars and revolutions. Indeed, examining the case of Greece, Victor Roudemetof has argued that in the Balkans national identity itself has been largely a creation of the state.[13]

Over the last two centuries, state involvement in the establishment of autocephalous churches has taken a variety of forms. Comparatively well-known are circumstances leading to the establishment of the Church of Greece, the Serbian Orthodox Church, and the Romanian Orthodox Church. Attainment of political independence from Ottoman rule was quickly followed by requests—or demands—by the civil authorities of the new states for Constantinopolitan recognition of ecclesiastical autocephaly. Less well-known are some other examples of state involvement in Orthodox ecclesiastical life in this period.

In the nineteenth century, the Austro-Hungarian Empire attempted to manage its multiple Orthodox minorities (Serbs, Romanians, Bukhovinians, etc.) by establishing two autocephalous churches: the Patriarchate of Sremski-Karlovci (Karlowitz), with jurisdiction over all the Orthodox in the vast kingdom of Hungary, and the Metropolitanate of Czernowitz (now Chernovtsy), which exercised comparable jurisdiction over all the Orthodox in the rambling Austrian portion of the empire, from Bukhovina to Dalmatia. This arrangement neatly balanced Hungarian and Austrian interests, but at the expense of the interests of the Orthodox minorities. The

---

[13]See especially V. Roudemetof, "From *Rum Millet* to Greek Nation: Enlightenment, Secularization, and National Identity in Ottoman Balkan Society, 1453–1821," *Journal of Modern Greek Studies* 16 (1998): 11–48. On the subject see also Paschalis M. Kitromilides, "'Imagined Communities' and the Origins of the National Question in the Balkans," *Eastern European Quarterly* 19 (1989): 149–94. For a stimulating discussion of Orthodox and national identity—in this case Greek—today, see Roudometof's article, "Greek Orthodoxy, Territoriality, and Globality: Religious Responses and Institutional Disputes," *Sociology of Religion* 69 (2008): 67–91.

churches in question enjoyed only tacit recognition by the other Orthodox churches of the Balkans, and—when political boundaries changed following World War I—their populations were eagerly gobbled up by the churches of the neighboring Orthodox nation-states, ecclesiastical irredentism going hand in hand with national irredentism.

Equally self-interested was the Sublime Porte's attempt to accommodate Bulgarian national aspirations by the establishment of a Bulgarian Exarchate within the Ottoman Empire in 1870. As is well-known, this prompted the convocation of an ostensibly Pan-Orthodox Council in Constantinople in 1872, which condemned Bulgarian "phyletism" as heresy. (Notably absent from the gathering were representatives of the Patriarchate of Jerusalem and the Russian Orthodox Church, which continued to supply the Bulgarian Church with chrism as well as other forms of support until its eventual recognition by Constantinople.)

As these examples suggest, state involvement in the establishment (or, one might add, suppression) of autocephalous churches has been motivated by state interests, and only secondarily by religious considerations. Many examples could prove it. Whether in the case of the predominantly Orthodox nation-states of the Balkans or in the declining Ottoman and Austro-Hungarian empires, autocephaly assured that the ecclesiastical entity in question would serve state interests, or at least not undermine them. The episcopate of the church in question might have the right to manage its internal affairs and to elect all its bishops, including the primate—of course under close state supervision. But communication with other Orthodox churches was strictly limited. Typically, external church contacts had to go through the state's foreign office.

With new changes in political geography in the wake of World War I, the issue of accession to autocephaly took on new urgency. After the collapse of the Ottoman Empire and the 1923 exchange of Greek and Turkish populations, the patriarch of Constantinople was left with only a tiny flock in the new Turkish republic. Perhaps as a consequence, the Patriarchate of Constantinople became more inclined than before to emphasize its wider primatial authority within the Orthodox world. Meanwhile, relentless Communist persecution of the Russian Orthodox Church brought an end to its once-enormous influence for several decades. This set the stage for a long series of confrontations and controversies concerning autocephaly, autonomy, and related issues during the remainder of the twentieth century.

When political boundaries were redrawn in the wake of World War I, nearly four million Orthodox Christians who hitherto had been under the jurisdiction of the Russian Orthodox Church found themselves within the new Polish republic. Under heavy pressure from the Polish government, a reluctant hierarchy petitioned the Patriarchate of Constantinople for autocephaly, which was quickly granted. Needless to say, the Russian Orthodox Church regarded this as unwarranted interference in its own internal affairs. Similar disagreements arose when Constantinople, acting in response to requests from the newly independent Finnish and Baltic states, granted the status of autonomy to the Orthodox churches in those lands, even though they had been part of the Russian Orthodox Church throughout their history.

In all these dealings, the actual sentiments of the Orthodox populations and hierarchies in question were hardly taken into consideration. In the newly autocephalous Polish Orthodox Church, for example, official documents and even sermons had to be in Polish, even if very few of the Orthodox faithful could understand that language. Similar efforts at re-fashioning national identity took place in Finland. Ecclesiastical autocephaly or autonomy served the interests of the new Polish and Finnish nation-states (e.g., by facilitating Polonization or Finnification). It did not necessarily serve the religious needs of the Orthodox faithful within those nation-states.

Disagreement over the status of these churches—and more recently over the status of the OCA—led the Russian Orthodox Church and the Patriarchate of Constantinople to formulate contradictory positions regarding accession to autocephaly. The resulting polemical literature was uneven in quality. Both parties appealed to historical precedents and the ancient canons, but they showed little sensitivity to their historical context. However, as both parties appear to have recognized, reference simply to the past will not overcome this impasse in inter-Orthodox relations.

Historical evidence does not offer a clear and compelling procedural pattern, particularly if one takes into consideration the ways in which the notion of autocephaly itself has changed under the impact of nationalism, statism, and other extra-ecclesial forces. And as for the canons, it would be difficult not to concur with a statement made by ecumenical patriarch Benjamin (1936–46) in 1937: "It is known [. . .] that concerning the manner of establishing the autocephaly of any part of the Church, none of the sacred canons provides direction or inkling."[14]

Inter-Orthodox cooperation in the early 1990s began to suggest a way forward. As is well-known, the agenda initially developed for a Great and Holy Council of the Orthodox Church back in the 1960s was limited to "easy" topics (e.g., Scripture and tradition, fasting regulations, marriage impediments). In the wake of the "meaningful storm" stirred up by the autocephaly of the OCA in 1970, the list of agenda topics was amended in 1976 to include the "diaspora," autocephaly, autonomy, and the diptychs. Thereafter the Inter-Orthodox Preparatory Commission for the Great and Holy Council worked away, first on the "easy" topics, then on the more challenging ones.

In 1990 and 1993, meetings of the Inter-Orthodox Preparatory Commission addressed two closely intertwined topics, the "diaspora" and "autocephaly and how it is to be proclaimed," and it also touched on "autonomy and how it is to be proclaimed." The commission's point of departure was background reports from the churches—texts that by this point were over ten years old. In them three main lines of thinking can be discerned:

1. The report of the Romanian Orthodox Church argued that each autocephalous national mother church has the right to govern its own national "diaspora." It also acknowledged that churches formed as a result of missionary activity constitute a special case, "since they belong to a different nationality than the members of the missionizing church." In such cases, autocephaly may be envisioned.

---

[14]"Letter to Patriarch Nicholas of Alexandria, December 7, 1937," in Apostolos Glavinas, *Orthodoxē Autokephalē Ekklesia tēs Albanias* [The autocephalous Orthodox Church of Albania] (Thessalonica: 1985): 63, cited by P. L'Huillier, "Accession to Autocephaly," 298.

2. Reports of the churches of Greek heritage (Alexandria, Constantinople, Greece) appealed to I Constantinople canon 3 ("As for the bishop of Constantinople, let him have the *presbeia tēs timēs*—the prerogatives or primacy of honor—after the bishop of Rome, since this city is the New Rome") and above all to Chalcedon canon 28. Because of its *presbeia tēs timēs*, Constantinople and only Constantinople has the right to exercise jurisdiction outside its own territorial limits, in all geographical areas that lie outside the boundaries of the duly established and recognized autocephalous churches. According to this interpretation of Chalcedon, Canon 28, Constantinople has jurisdiction not only over Pontus, Asia, and Thrace, but also the right to consecrate bishops "among the barbarians"—i.e., in the "diaspora"—thus modifying earlier provisions such as I Constantinople, Canon 2, which stated that "the churches of God in heathen nations must be governed according to the custom which has prevailed from the time of the fathers." As for autocephaly, only a council of ecumenical standing (such as a Great and Holy Council) can definitively establish an autocephalous church, and any interim arrangements depend upon approbation by Constantinople acting in its capacity as ultimate "mother church" and "first among equals."

3. The report of the Russian Orthodox Church (and also the much shorter report of Antioch) takes a more pragmatic approach. Like the Romanian report, the Russian report (and also the Antiochian report) rejects the Greek interpretation of Chalcedon canon 28. According to the Russian position, the phrase "among the barbarians" in Canon 28 historically referred to regions adjacent to Pontus, Asia, and Thrace. It did not refer, e.g., to regions adjacent to Orient (Antioch) or Egypt (Alexandria), and in no way did it override I Constantinople, Canon 2 concerning the governance of churches in "heathen" regions. Modern situations are quite different, the report continues. Each should be considered on its own terms—whether arising from mission or from multiple immigrations. But whether born of mission or of immigration, churches of the so-called diaspora "must gradually receive the opportunity to grow into new local churches and to receive autocephaly (or initially autonomy) from their

own mother churches." In America, the multiplicity of jurisdictions is the result in part of mission, in part of immigration. Several possible solutions are conceivable. The best possible solution, the report concludes, would be for Constantinople to grant autocephaly to its Greek Orthodox Archdiocese of America just as Moscow did in the case of the Orthodox Church in America (OCA), so also for the other churches to grant autocephaly in the case of their own "jurisdictions," and for these then to form a single autocephalous church. As for autocephaly and how it is to be proclaimed, any autocephalous Orthodox church has the right to grant autocephaly—the right of self-rule, including election of its head—or autonomy to a dependency, provided that conditions necessary for independent church life are present (e.g., an adequate number of bishops).

How can the positions represented in these highly divergent reports be reconciled? That was the question facing the Inter-Orthodox Preparatory Commission in 1990 and again in 1993. The commission, in effect, chose not to attempt to reconcile the divergent interpretations of the historical record evident in the background reports and chose instead to develop specific proposals for the future. One result was a draft text on the "diaspora," which—after a long hiatus—finally was reviewed, modified at several points, and approved for implementation by the Fourth Pan-Orthodox Pre-Conciliar Conference, which met in Chambésy in June 2009.[15]

The 1993 draft text on autocephaly has fared somewhat less well. As set forth in the draft text, requirements for accession to autocephaly include: (1) consent and action of the mother church, (2) the obtaining of a Pan-Orthodox consensus, in a process overseen by the Ecumenical Patriarchate, and (3) the issuance of a tomos proclaiming the autocephaly of the applying church. At the time, the Preparatory Commission did not reach agreement concerning who is to issue and sign the tomos of autocephaly, and it referred the matter to a future meeting of the Preparatory Commission.[16]

---

[15]The approved text of this "Decision on the Diaspora" and its supplementary "Rules of Operation of Episcopal Assemblies in the Orthodox Diaspora" are widely available online at this point. In an English translation they can be found at http://www.scoba.us/resources/chambesy_documents.html, accessed August 8, 2012.

[16]Draft texts for eventual submission to a Great and Holy Council are prepared by the

After a hiatus of over fifteen years, the draft text was taken up again at a December 2009 meeting of the Inter-Orthodox Preparatory Commission. One may infer from press releases and follow-up interviews that this was a difficult meeting. According to Metropolitan Hilarion Alfeyev, head of the Russian Orthodox delegation,

> This procedure should conform to the principle of *sobornost*, traditional for the Orthodox Church in making decisions on important common church matters. In this understanding, a tomos on autocephaly should be signed by the heads of all the local churches.... At the same time, the delegations of some churches insisted that the signature of the ecumenical patriarch alone was sufficient for granting autocephaly. As a result of a prolonged discussion the commission adopted a wording that presupposes signatures of the primates of all the autocephalous churches. It was also agreed that the actual contents and procedure for signing a tomos would be specified by the next meeting of the Preparatory Commission.[17]

The Final Statement issued at the conclusion of the December 2009 meeting offers the official final wording of the controversial paragraph:

> With the agreement of the mother church and the obtaining of pan-Orthodox consent, the ecumenical patriarch will officially proclaim

---

Inter-Orthodox Preparatory Committee, but in principle these drafts are not to be published before being reviewed, possibly revised, and then approved for publication by a Pre-Conciliar Pan-Orthodox Conference. The 1993 draft text on autocephaly in fact has been published at least twice, in French in Vlassios I. Phidas, *Droit Canon: Une Perspective Orthodoxe* (Chambésy: Centre Orthodoxe du Patriarcat Oecuménique, 1998), 136–38, and in English in John H. Erickson, Foreword to Bogolepov, *Toward an American Orthodox Church*, xvi-xix. Pre-Conciliar Conferences prior to the fourth met in 1976, 1982, and 1986. A Fifth Pre-Conciliar Conference is expected to consider draft texts on autocephaly, autonomy, and the diptychs, thus completing work on topics in the announced agenda for the Holy and Great Council. It would be hard to predict when this Conference actually will meet. [The theme of autocephaly was not discussed at the Fifth Pre-Conciliar Pan-Orthodox Conference (Chambésy, October 2015) and, consequently, was withdrawn from the agenda of the Holy and Great Synod of the Orthodox Church (June 2016).—*Ed.*]

[17]"We have reached consensus on the autocephaly procedure'—DECR chairman's interview with the *Journal of the Moscow Patriarchate*," accessed July 28, 2012, http://www.mospat.ru/en/2010/05/04/news17608/.

the autocephaly of a Church which requests it, by issuing the tomos of autocephaly. This tomos will be signed by the ecumenical patriarch, witnessed by the signatures of Their Beatitudes the heads of the most holy Orthodox churches invited to do so by him.[18]

This wording, however, does not appear to have been met with universal satisfaction. Meeting again in February 2011, the Inter-Orthodox Preparatory Commission failed yet again to reach agreement on outstanding issues relating to autocephaly. According to a press release from the Russian Orthodox Church, "As a long discussion has not led to a unanimous decision, the necessity of further studying the issue of autocephaly was recognized."[19]

While the Inter-Orthodox Preparatory Commission still has not reached full agreement on the subject of autocephaly, it has reached agreement on autonomy. In accordance with accepted practice, the agreed upon text has not been officially published, but a fairly detailed summary has appeared in at least one press release:

> It was agreed that the initiation and completion of the procedure for granting autonomy to a certain part of its canonical jurisdiction is exclusively under the competence of the respective autocephalous Church. It is noted that in church practice there are different degrees in which an autonomous Church depends on the autocephalous Church that has granted autonomy to it. A petition for autonomy is considered by the autocephalous Church which, having assessed the prerequisites and reasons for this petition and taken a favorable decision, issues an appropriate tomos defining the territorial boundaries of the autonomous Church and its relationships with the autocephalous Church to which it belongs in accordance with the established criteria of church Tradition. Then the primate of the autocephalous church notifies the

---

[18] "The Inter-Orthodox Preparatory Committee for the Holy and Great Council meets at Chambésy," accessed July 28, 2012, http://www.antiocheurope.org/en/news/details/105/.

[19] "Inter-Orthodox Preparatory Commission completes its work," accessed July 28, 2012, http://www.mospat.ru/en/2011/02/26/news36896/.

Ecumenical Patriarchate and other autocephalous Orthodox churches on the declaration of an autonomous church.

The draft document also provides for measures to find a canonical settlement of an issue in case of differences arising from two autocephalous churches granting the autonomous status to church communities in the same geographical church region.[20]

How are we to evaluate these texts on autocephaly and autonomy in light of the historical considerations raised earlier in this paper? A few observations may be in order.

Many decades ago, when the topics of autocephaly and autonomy and the closely related topic of the "diaspora" were added to the agenda for a Great and Holy Council, two sharply divergent positions were evident. According to the Russian Orthodox Church and its allies, any autocephalous church has the right to grant autocephaly or autonomy to one of its parts. According to Constantinople and its allies, on the other hand, only an ecumenical council or its equivalent can definitively establish an autocephalous church, and any interim arrangements relating whether to autocephaly or to autonomy depend upon approbation by Constantinople.

Notwithstanding their obvious differences, both of these positions envisioned accession to autocephaly and accession to autonomy as being very similar processes. The draft documents on autocephaly and autonomy, on the other hand, envision these processes as dissimilar. The process for accession to autonomy prescribed in the draft text is consonant with what the Russian Orthodox Church envisioned for both accession to autonomy and accession to autocephaly in its original background reports. The process seems straightforward, realistic, appropriately flexible, and pragmatic. It is harder, however, to characterize the draft text on accession to autocephaly. It could be described as "balanced," inasmuch as it tries to take into consideration multiple factors, including the role of the mother church, the role of Constantinople, and the importance of pan-Orthodox consensus. But is it realistic, even if agreement can finally be reached on how the tomos of autocephaly is to be signed? The draft text

[20]"Second Chambésy meeting discusses autocephaly, autonomy," accessed August 8, 2012, http://www.mospat.ru/en/2009/12/17/news10309/.

envisions a "best-case" scenario. Few, if any, historical accessions to autocephaly have gone so smoothly. Let us consider just one possible sticking point. According to the draft text, "Pan-Orthodox consensus is expressed by the unanimous decision of the synods of the autocephalous churches" (para. 3.b). It would appear that failure of just one Orthodox church, for whatever reason, to approve a proposal for accession to autocephaly would effectively kill that proposal.

If the draft text on accession to autocephaly is unrealistic, this may be because it fails to consider the nature and content of autocephaly itself. The draft text affirms that

> the institution of autocephaly expresses in an authentic way one of the fundamental aspects of the Orthodox ecclesiological tradition concerning relations between the local church and the universal Church of God (para. 1),

but it does very little to elucidate and demonstrate the truth of this proposition. What is meant here by "local church"? Is it "the sacramental manifestation of ecclesial plenitude" epitomized in the gathering of all the clergy and faithful of a given place, under the presidency of the one bishop, in the Eucharist? That would be the point of departure favored by many modern Orthodox theologians and historians. Or is it the autocephalous church as we now know it? The draft text on accession to autocephaly fails to address basic ecclesiological questions of this sort.

Like so many of the texts developed in the course of the Great and Holy Council process, the draft text on accession to autocephaly ducks the hard issues. It avoids any reference to the many extra-ecclesial factors that have affected and, in many ways, transformed our understanding of autocephaly, most notably nationalism and statism. This makes it difficult to imagine any real progress in inter-Orthodox relations, even if a Great and Holy Council does eventually meet to approve the texts now under discussion. What is needed is constructive engagement with our past—something that may be painful, yet also invigorating. If we know where we have been, it will be easier to know the way forward to fuller communion with God and with each other.

Church Autocephaly as Sovereignty
A Schmittian Approach

Andrey Shishkov[1]

St Vladimir's Theological Quarterly 60.3 (2016): 369–395

Autocephaly and Sovereignty: Definition of the Problem

THE SYNAXIS OF HEADS of local Orthodox churches held in March 2014 in Istanbul decided to convene a pan-Orthodox council in two years' time. The history of attempts to convene a council is over 90 years old.[2] Since 1923 and officially since 1961 the pre-conciliar pan-Orthodox process has become one of the primary aspects in inter-church relations.[3]

The first attempt to organize a pan-Orthodox forum for dealing with pressing problems facing the world Orthodoxy was made in 1923, when the patriarch of Constantinople initiated the convening of a pan-Orthodox congress in Istanbul. However, that attempt failed since some autocephalous churches, including the Russian Orthodox Church, refused to recognize the church-wide status of the congress and its decisions. Further initiatives, such as the 1930 inter-Orthodox conference on Mouth Athos

---

[1] An earlier version of this paper was published in Russian in the leading Russian academic journal on Religion studies, *State, Religion, Church in Russia and Worldwide*. This version includes some new facts and sources.

[2] On the history of the pre-conciliar pan-Orthodox process, including the decisions of the official pre-conciliar conferences, see: Viorel Ioniță, *Towards the Holy and Great Synod of the Orthodox Church* (Fribourg: Institute for Ecumenical Studies, University of Fribourg, 2014). For a brief survey of the history of the pre-conciliar process, see the report of the chairman of the Moscow Patriarchate Department for External Church Relations, Hilarion Alfeyev, "Inter-Orthodox Cooperation on the Preparations for a Holy and Great Council of the Orthodox Church," Department for External Relations of the Moscow Patriarchate, accessed June 04, 2014, https://mospat.ru/en/2011/11/03/news50923.

[3] The term 'inter-church relations' is understood as the sphere of relations between autocephalous local Orthodox churches.

and the 1948 conference of heads and representatives of local Orthodox churches in Moscow, called by the Patriarchates of Constantinople and Moscow respectively, failed to gain church-wide recognition as well. It was only in 1961 that the Pan-Orthodox Conference on Rhodes, attended by representatives of all the autocephalous local churches, decided to begin the work to prepare a pan-Orthodox council. It also drafted a list of over one hundred themes to be discussed jointly.[4] Later, in 1976, this list was reduced to ten themes: (1) The Orthodox Diaspora; (2) Autocephaly and its manner of proclamation; (3) Autonomy and its manner of proclamation; (4) The diptychs; (5) The problem of the new calendar; (6) Impediments to marriage; (7) Adapting the church rules concerning fasting; (8) Relations of the Orthodox Church with the rest of Christian world; (9) Orthodoxy and the Ecumenical Movement; and (10) The contribution of the local Orthodox churches to the realizations of the ideals of peace, freedom, brotherhood, and love among peoples and the removal of racial discriminations.[5]

A proposal was to be drafted on each of these themes so that it could be approved by all the autocephalous churches. Then the drafts and agreed decisions were to be considered and approved by the council. To achieve this goal a standing body was set up, a pre-conciliar pan-Orthodox conference, which was and is engaged in developing and coordinating decisions.

By the mid-1980s, six themes (Nos. 5–10) had been successfully developed and agreed upon,[6] but three themes (Nos. 1–2, 4) concerning inter-Orthodox relations ("Orthodox Diaspora,"[7] "autocephaly and the

---

[4]See the whole list in Ioniță, *Towards the Holy and Great Synod of the Orthodox Church*, 125–30.

[5]Ibid., 147. This list was corrected by the 5th Pre-Conciliar Pan-Orthodox Conference in October 2015: (9) was included into (8), and (10) was renamed as "Mission of the Orthodox Church in the modern world".

[6]During the 2014–15 agreed documents were revised and the 5th Pre-Conciliar Pan-Orthodox Conference fixed consensus only on (3), (7), (8–9), see decision 71, "Decisions of the Holy Synod of the Russian Orthodox Church (Oct. 22, 2015)," Moscow Patriarchate official site, accessed October 27, 2015, http://www.patriarchia.ru/db/text/4250904.html.

[7]The decision on the Orthodox Diaspora adopted by the 4th Pre-Conciliar Pan-Orthodox Conference is an interim one. The official document "The Orthodox Diaspora," par. 1a, states, "The problem of the Orthodox Diaspora needs to be sorted out as soon as possible" (Ioniță, *Towards the Holy and Great Synod of the Orthodox Church*, 188).

procedure of its proclamation," and "diptychs"[8]) have remained undecided to this day. These are themes concerning church governance and church authority; to be more precise, the question of who exercises the supreme power in the Orthodox Church. In other words, the question is: Does the Orthodox Church have a center of power that governs the whole Orthodox diaspora, makes decisions on granting autocephaly, and exercises additional powers, by virtue of its first place in the church diptychs? Alternatively, is the authority in the Church basically decentralized and limited to the boundaries of equal autocephalous local churches?

The whole set of problems in the area of inter-church relations on the agenda of a pan-Orthodox council can be united around the notion of "autocephaly," which expresses the main principle of church order in world Orthodoxy today.[9] It consists in that an autocephalous church has the source of its power in itself: it elects its head on its own and makes decisions concerning church life—that is, it is not subordinate to any other

---

[8]The sacred diptychs represent a list of autocephalous local Orthodox churches "in order of honour." Atop the diptychs are autocephalous churches that have the status of patriarchate, and then follow those that have the status of archdiocese or metropolitanate. The first four listings in the diptychs are occupied by the so-called Ancient Eastern patriarchates, whose place in the diptychs is defined by the canons of Ecumenical Councils. The rest of the autocephalous churches are placed in the diptychs according to the date of the recognition of their autocephaly (separately for patriarchates and then for archdioceses and metropolitanates). The primacy in honor in the Orthodox Church belongs to the Patriarchate of Constantinople. The Russian Orthodox Church occupies the fifth place and appears in the diptychs immediately after the Ancient Eastern patriarchates. The diptychs are used at liturgical commemorations when the primate of each autocephalous church mentions the names of primates of other local churches. This order of diptychs is also used in church diplomatic protocol. In the 20th century, through the efforts of the Patriarchate of Constantinople, the diptychs began to acquire an increasing importance in inter-church relations and church governance. According to the Church of Constantinople, its primacy of honor in the diptychs gives it additional privileges and power at the pan-Orthodox level (in the sphere of court of justice and in some matters of church governance).

[9]The use of the notion of autocephaly can go far beyond the actual mechanisms of church governance to turn into a myth, as for instance Archimandrite Cyril Hovorun points out in his work: Cyril Hovorun, "Avtokefaliia: ot kanona k mifu" [Autocephaly: from canon to myth], *Religiia v Ukraini* 1 (2009): 31–36. The author understands by myth "a set of ideas which go far beyond the original conceptual meaning," adding, "Nowadays the category of autocephaly includes a lot of aspects which have nothing to do with canon law or even ecclesiology. They turn autocephaly into a myth" (ibid., 32). However, becoming a myth, autocephaly does not lose its importance for church governance and church authority but perhaps even strengthens it.

autocephalous church, thus being independent of other churches in everything except doctrinal matters.

Today, the theme of autocephaly is not limited to the problems involved in granting/obtaining (and abolishing) autocephaly, but it also includes such issues as the possibility for interference in the internal affairs of an autocephalous local church, governance over the parishes located outside the canonical territories[10] of autocephalous churches (i.e., in the Orthodox Diaspora), the functioning of pan-Orthodox (supra-autocephalous) institutions and the need for them in inter-church relations. In this article, we will consider the problems of autocephaly precisely in this broad vein.

The question of autocephaly is one of supreme power, and therefore sovereignty. If it is declared that an autocephalous church has the source of power in itself and is independent of other churches, then there can be

---

[10] The territorial dimension of modern autocephalous Orthodox churches includes two elements: so called canonical territory and diaspora. Canonical territory is an ecclesial-geographical term denoting the historically shaped territory of an autocephalous church whose boundaries no other autocephalous church has the right to violate. The canonical territory of an autocephalous church consists of church administrative entities, such as dioceses, metropolises, exarchates, etc., subordinate to this church. The establishment of other church's dioceses and parishes in this territory (that is, the creation of a parallel jurisdiction) is a violation of the principle of autocephaly. This ban on the existence of parallel jurisdictions goes back to the ancient principle of church order: "one city, one bishop." Church territory in diaspora is ordered in a different way, as the principle of a single jurisdiction is not applied to it today, so that dioceses and parishes of different autocephalous churches can coexist in the same diaspora territory. This situation is due to the fact that immigrants from various Orthodox countries who belong to different autocephalous churches wish to preserve contacts with their mother church. The existence of parallel jurisdictions in diaspora is believed to be "not quite consistent with church canons" (see, Alfeyev, "Inter-Orthodox Cooperation"). Among possible resolutions of this "non-canonical" situation in the diaspora is to place it under the authority of the Patriarchate of Constantinople, but this initiative of the Church of Constantinople is not appreciated by most autocephalous churches, which preserve their dioceses and parishes in the diaspora. The term "canonical territory" became current in the Church in the early 90s of the 20th century, but, as Metropolitan Hilarion Alfeyev writes, "the ecclesiological model standing behind it goes back to apostolic times" (Hilarion Alfeyev, "Printsip 'kanonicheskoi territorii' v pravoslavnoi traditsii" [Principle of "canonical territory" in Orthodox tradition], Official web-site of Metropolitan Hilarion Alfeyev, accessed on Aug. 26, 2014, http://hilarion.ru/2010/02/25/1048. On the history of the development of canonical territories of autocephalous churches, see also Cyril Hovorun, "Kanonicheskaia territoriia: vektory razvitiia tserkovno-kanonicheskoi kategorii" [Canonical territory: the vectors of development of the church-canonical category], *Trudy Kievskoj duhovnoj akademii* 20 (2014): 349–58.

no power above it and it is sovereign. Therefore, what is called autocephaly in the Church corresponds to what is understood as sovereignty in the political, inter-state relations sphere.

Below we will consider the theme of autocephaly through the lens of the theory of sovereignty proposed by German lawyer and political philosopher Carl Schmitt in his work *Political Theology*,[11] and developed by Yale theoretician of law Paul Kahn in his book of the same title.[12] In the first place we will be interested in the aspect that relates the notion of sovereignty to a state of emergency, i.e., sovereignty-as-exception.

The Schmittian theory of sovereignty[13] is only one of many today. In our view, however, its instruments can be successfully applied to church autocephaly, since the very notion proves to be closely linked with basic elements of the concept of a state of emergency and its wilful introduction. Such important matters concerning sovereignty as proclamation/abolishment of autocephaly and the extension of a territory, both canonical and in the diaspora, are resolved through the introduction of a state of emergency, as we will see below.

It should be noted that the problems of church authority will be limited in this article to the area of interaction between church hierarchical institutions, primarily autocephalous local churches, which comprise together the universal Orthodox Church. We will not consider the problem of sovereignty in church-state relations, since this area is beyond the scope of this analysis.[14]

---

[11] Carl Schmitt, *Political Theology: Four Chapters on the Concept of Sovereignty* (Chicago and London: Chicago University Press, 2015).

[12] Paul W. Kahn, *Political Theology: Four New Chapters in the Concept of Sovereignty* (New York: Columbia University Press, 2011).

[13] In Russia there is continuing interest in the works of Carl Schmitt, including his theory of sovereignty. There are many studies on various aspects of this political philosophy. Prominent among them are works by Prof. A. F. Filippov of the Higher School of Economics National Research Institute. *Logos* journal Issue 5, which came out in 2012, was fully devoted to C. Schmitt. Some researchers point to a growing interest in the Schmittian tradition in the West as well (see, for example, Chantal Mouffe, ed., *The Challenge of Carl Schmitt* [New York: Verso, 1999]).

[14] Since this article considers the basic principles of the order of the Orthodox Church and inter-church relations, it should be pointed out right away that the inter-church relations in the 20th–early 21st century do not presuppose the involvement of secular authorities.

Schmitt's Approach to Sovereignty

In the first chapter of his *Political Theology*, Carl Schmitt gives this definition to the sovereign: "Sovereign is he who decides on the exception."[15] This definition includes three notions: "sovereign," "decision," and "state of emergency'" (or "exception"). Each of these terms, as Paul Kahn rightly observes, "can be defined only in terms of the others," but "together, they point to a single political phenomenon."[16] Schmitt says that his definition "can do justice to a borderline concept."[17] Only an ultimate situation becomes possible for the authority to prove itself as supreme power, the sovereign. This ultimate situation is that political phenomenon which is referred to by Kahn and which is described through the notions of "sovereign," "decisions," and "exceptions."

"[The Sovereign] stands beyond the normally valid legal system, he nevertheless belongs to it."[18] A state of emergency sets up the parameters of an ultimate situation; it implies going beyond the limits of the existing order of things and rules which regulate this order. Certainly, it does not mean that sovereign power exists only in situations of exception, but it is in a situation of emergency that its supremacy becomes "visible."

As Paul Kahn writes, "sovereignty is not the alternative to law, but the point at which law and exception intersect";[19] "sovereign power operates beyond law to create and protect law."[20] Kahn believes that "there can be no exception without reference to a norm,"[21] otherwise a situation of emergency will become mere anarchy and lawlessness. In other words, a situation of emergency represents the point at which the supreme power "rebuilds" the order. The sovereign himself establishes the order and to this end he goes beyond the existing order to the point of extreme exception. It is important here that an exception generates a certain order. This is

---

[15] Schmitt, *Political Theology*, 5.
[16] Kahn, *Political Theology*, 31.
[17] Schmitt, *Political Theology*, 5.
[18] Ibid., 7
[19] Kahn, *Political Theology*, 34.
[20] Ibid., 52.
[21] Ibid., 34.

how Giorgio Agamben describes this "paradox" of sovereign power: "The sovereign is, at the same time, outside and inside the juridical order."[22]

However, the situation of exception alone is not sufficient for defining supreme power. Sovereignty is impossible without decision-making. To be supreme the authority cannot but manifest itself, and it can do it only by making decisions. A decision on the state of exception is a manifestation of the supreme power in the political space. At the same time, as Kahn observes, "the sovereign power is not that of recognizing or identifying the exception; it is the power to decide on the exception."[23] In his opinion, such a power cannot exist only as potential, for it necessarily should be expressed in an act of decision-making. Kahn believes that "a decision with no effect is not a decision."[24] He associates this kind of decision with a loss of power.

Kahn sets rather a tough framework linking sovereignty with decision as a concrete act of will. He suggests that sovereign power does not accept any potentiality of decision. However, the declaration of the intent to create an exception can have the same effect of "decision" as the decision itself. In the matter under consideration here, the demonstration of the ability to make a decision on the exception is no less important than the decision itself. For instance, attempts to manipulate the possibility for making a decision to isolate any of the autocephalous churches in inter-church relations, or a threat to deprive a particular local church of autocephaly, can be regarded as a claim to supreme power.

Another question to be considered is who is sovereign—a person or a political body? Kahn writes this about this: "The location of sovereign power is not an issue of definition but of the functioning of an actual political organization."[25] The sovereign is he who makes a decision on the exception, be it a person, a group of people, a political body, or a nation.

---

[22] Giorgio Agamben, *Homo sacer: Sovereign Power and Bare Life* (Stanford, CA: Stanford University Press, 1998), 17.
[23] Kahn, *Political Theology*, 40.
[24] Ibid., 40.
[25] Ibid., 39.

Proclamation of Russian Autocephaly as Sovereign Decision

If the problem of church autocephaly represents a problem of supreme power (sovereignty) in the Church, then in church history we would inevitably encounter examples of sovereign decisions that create exceptions to generate a new (canonical) order. Among them are the proclamation of autocephaly, the extension of a canonical territory by annexing it from another autocephalous church, or the establishment of a parallel jurisdiction,[26] etc.

Let us consider the situation of the proclamation of autocephaly, using as an example the Russian Church. The sovereignty of the Russian Church was born in the situation of weakness of Constantinople's church and state power. The separation from the Patriarchate of Constantinople was preconditioned by the conclusion of *unia* between the patriarch, the emperor of Constantinople and the see of Rome at the 1439 Council of Ferarra-Florence.[27] Among the participants and active proponents of the *unia* was Metropolitan Isidore of Moscow, who was installed in the see of Moscow in 1436 instead of Bishop Jonah of Ryazan, who had been nominated by the Russian bishops.

Upon his return to Moscow from Florence in 1441, the Uniate Metropolitan Isidore made public the council's act on *unia*, for which he was arrested and condemned by the council of the Russian clergy convened by the prince of Moscow. The Russian Church found itself in a difficult situation, as the metropolitan of Moscow was deposed in punishment for the *unia*; the patriarch and the emperor were also Uniate while the see of Moscow remained vacant and in need of filling the vacancy. It took several

---

[26] On parallel jurisdiction see note 10 above.

[27] The Council of Ferrara-Florence, a council of Christian churches convoked by the Pope of Rome, Eugene IV. It began in Ferrara 1438–39, continued in Florence in 1439–42, and concluded in Rome in 1443–45. The *unia* conditions presupposed acceptance of the doctrinal teachings of the Catholic Church (including the addition of *filioque* to the creed, the primacy of the pope, and purgatory). The Orthodox Church was represented at the council by Emperor John VIII, Patriarch Joseph II of Constantinople, and a few dozen bishops of the Church of Constantinople (including the Moscow Metropolitanate), with some of them assuming the functions of legates of the patriarchs of Alexandria, Antioch, and Jerusalem. The *unia* was signed by the Byzantine delegation (except for several bishops who were against it), but most of Orthodox churches did not accept it.

years to find a canonical way out of the situation (the developments in those years are of no great importance for our present analysis).

Finally, in 1448, the council of Russian bishops convened by Prince Basil II installed Bishop Jonah as Metropolitan of Moscow. This decision was the first sovereign act of the Russian Church. It created a situation of emergency (exception) in which the existing canonical order was changed as the Russian Metropolitanate removed itself from the control of the Patriarchate of Constantinople.

It is noteworthy that the sovereignty of the Russian Church was not born of the situation of an ecclesial-political revolt generated by the *unia* (there is a temptation to see in it alone the source of the emergency situation). Rather, it was born of the council's decision to install the metropolitan to the see of Moscow. It is confirmed by the fact that at the same time bishops in Western Rus' (with its center in Kiev), despite the *unia*, preserved their relations with the see of Constantinople.[28] It also indicates that the autocephaly of the Russian Church came into effect only seven years after the deposition of Metropolitan Isidore, rather than immediately after it. That is to say, the state of emergency brought about by the proclamation of autocephaly was caused by the will of the sovereign, the bishops' council in this case, rather than by external circumstances, even if they opened up a "corridor of opportunities" for making such a decision. It can be stated that the 1448 Council of Moscow transformed the situation, which arose in the Patriarchate of Constantinople, into a state of emergency (exception) compelling the Russian Church to establish a new order (something which, for instance, bishops of Western Rus', led by the metropolitan in Kiev, failed to do).

Certainly, after the accession of Emperor Constantine XI to the imperial throne in 1451, the Russians had some hesitations about the autocephaly. Indeed, the new emperor claimed to be a supporter of Orthodoxy and expelled the Uniate Patriarch Gregory Mammas. In 1452, Prince Basil II of Moscow even drafted a message to the emperor setting forth the case of Metropolitans Isidore and Jonah, but it was never sent to the

---

[28] Anton Kartashev, *Sobranie sochinenii*, 2 vols, vol. 1: *Ocherki po istorii Russkoi Tserkvi* [Essays on the history of the Russian Church] (Moscow: TERRA, 1992), 359.

addressee.²⁹ That same year, Emperor Constantine XI moved to the *unia*, and a year later Constantinople was captured by the Ottoman Turks and Orthodox Byzantium ceased to exist.

Church historian Anton Kartashev speaks ironically of those hesitations of the Russians, describing them as "modest revolutionaries" who "did not mature enough to seize the occasion [uniatism of the patriarch of Constantinople] to win church autocephaly for themselves once and for all."³⁰ For the record, it should be noted that these hesitations never resulted in a decision, and the Russian Church remained autocephalous from 1448 on. To the contrary, in our view the very fact of the Russians' hesitations rather confirms the urgency of the situation created by the Council of Moscow and points to the radical novelty of the established order.

The birth trauma of Russian autocephaly linked with the "the Greeks' apostasy" gave rise to the Russian Church's fervent attitude regarding her own sovereignty, which can be traced through her further history. By the end of the 15th century, this attitude concerning her own sovereignty led to the emergence of an ecclesial-political myth about Moscow as the Third Rome. In the 20th century, it was sealed in the form of the label of the "absolute autocephaly of Moscow."

Fr George Florovsky connects the events of "the Greeks' apostasy," the fall of Constantinople, and the development of the myth of the Third Rome.³¹ The political myth of the Third Rome was grounded in the idea of the exclusiveness of the Russian Church in the Orthodox world as the only guardian of the true faith and of the Russian sovereign as the last defender of Orthodoxy. The close attention to its own sovereignty, not only administrative but also doctrinal, led to isolation "within the limits of its local national memory" and amounted to "a full exception and denial of the Greek mediation also in the past."³² In no less measure, the distrust towards the Greeks caused a schism in the Russian Church in the 17th century.³³

---

²⁹Ibid., 362.
³⁰Ibid., 361–62.
³¹George Florovsky, *Puti russkogo bogoslovija* [Ways of Russian Theology] (Minsk: Izd-vo Belorusskogo ekzarkhata, 2006), 14.
³²Ibid., 15.
³³Ibid., 66.

The disintegration of the Russian Empire and the abdication of the Russian emperor, the defender of the Church and Orthodox faith, became a real test for the sovereignty of the Russian Church. The new era began with the 1917–18 Moscow Council and continued with the destruction of the church infrastructure and repression, which literally immobilized the church power of Moscow.

From the viewpoint of the theory of sovereignty under consideration, the decisions of the 1917–18 Moscow Council and first of all the restoration of the patriarchal office became a powerful testimony to the sovereignty of the Russian Church. However, the subsequent events weakened (one can say even paralyzed) church authority so much that some member dioceses of the Russian Church fell away, with the territories remaining under it seeing the emergence of parallel schismatic jurisdictions and a considerable part of the Russian diaspora also falling away from the mother church. The ROC managed to preserve her sovereignty,[34] but the situation of power paralysis opened up an opportunity for the Georgian and Polish churches to establish their own sovereignty, which they seized. The weakness of the Russian Church's power was also the reason for the interference in the ROC's internal affairs by other autocephalous churches, primarily the Patriarchate of Constantinople, which certainly became one of the main factors of growing "Moscow autocephalism" on the international arena once the crisis was over.[35]

---

[34]Support by the Soviet power, which replaced direct repression, made it possible for the Russian Orthodox Church to preserve sovereignty in inter-church relations. The same happened to the Church of Constantinople under the Ottoman rule. The subjection of the church to an ideologically atheistic state, in its turn, provoked distrust for the Russian Church rather than for "Greek apostates." For many, this subjection, symbolized by Metropolitan Sergius' (Stragorodskii) declaration of loyalty to the Soviet regime, which was published in 1927, became evidence of "the apostasy of the Russians" and "the heresy of Sergianism." Having become an instrument of Stalin's foreign policy in the second part of the 1940s, the ROC could again advocate her sovereignty in inter-Orthodox relations, which was difficult to do earlier.

[35]The crisis came to an end in 1945 when a local council of the ROC took place under the patronage of the Soviet authorities. It elected Patriarch Alexis I (Simansky) to the see of Moscow. This council, attended also by primates of churches of Alexandria, Antioch, and Georgia and representatives of other autocephalous local churches, showed that the ROC was a legal successor of the All Russia Orthodox Church led by Patriarch Tikhon—which, in its turn, helped to bring back to her some of her bishops and faithful who stayed outside the USSR.

In the characteristic works on the issue of autocephaly written by Moscow canonists and theologians in the period from 1940–50s, we invariably encounter an attitude rigorously advocating the sovereignty of an autocephalous church in inter-church relations. This line is continued in the Russian Orthodox Church's official stand on the issues of autocephaly placed on the agenda of the Pan-Orthodox Council.[36]

Sergius Troitsky as a Theoretician of "Absolute Autocephalism"

The prominent Russian canonist of the 20th century Sergius Troitsky (1878–1972) became the main theoretician of "Moscow's absolute autocephalism." His approach was to make an enormous impact on the official stand of the Russian Orthodox Church on the whole range of issues concerning the problems of autocephaly for decades ahead. The basic text reflecting Troitsky's views on our theme is his article "About the Autocephaly of the Church."[37]

Troitsky defined the term "autocephalous" as applied to secular and ecclesial organizations "which are self-headed, that is, have their own head, their own *supreme or sovereign power* (italics are mine, A.Sh.),"[38] independent of any other. The principle of church autocephaly essentially lies in that "its first bishops and the rest of bishops . . . are elected and installed by bishops on their own, not bishops from any other church."[39]

An autocephalous church, according to Troitsky, enjoys full independence in administrative and judicial areas of church work so that "local councils of bishops have the powers to judge even their own primates."[40] It "enjoys full freedom in producing the holy myrrh for itself, canonizing its own saints, composing new hymns, determining the time of the liturgy,

---

[36]See more about the position of the Russian Orthodox Church in my paper: Andrey Shishkov, "Einige Besonderheiten der Position der Russischen Orthodoxen Kirche im panorthodoxen vorkonziliaren Prozess," *Una Sancta* 70.2 (2015): 119–29.

[37]Sergius Troitsky, "O tserkovnoi avtokefalii" [About the Autocephaly of the Church], *Zhurnal Moskovskoi Patriarkhii* 7 (July, 1948): 33–54.

[38]Ibid., 36.
[39]Ibid., 45.
[40]Ibid., 48.

etc."⁴¹ However, in the area of dogmatic teaching, an autocephalous church has no independence; and in the area of liturgy as well it is bound by "the link between the liturgy and dogmatic teaching and the desire to unify the liturgy."⁴²

Among the important points is the independence of an autocephalous church in the area of inter-church relations, which Troitsky describes as analogous to international relations.⁴³ Accordingly, interference of any autocephalous church into the affairs of another is a violation of the latter's sovereignty. In his articles written at various times, Troitsky criticizes the Patriarchate of Constantinople for continued violation of the sovereignty of autocephalous churches.⁴⁴

Troitsky considered the entire Orthodox episcopate acting as one body with the ecumenical council⁴⁵ as the supreme power in the Orthodox Church. During an ecumenical (or pan-Orthodox) council, the principle of autocephaly ceases to play any role in settling church matters, just as the order of honor of autocephalous churches, also known as the "sacred diptychs"⁴⁶ ceases to play any role. A council is an extraordinary event, and during an inter-council period the supreme power returns to the autocephalous churches.

As regards the proclamation of autocephaly, Troitsky maintained that "since any autocephalous church has supreme sovereign power, it is evident that only the organization or the person who themselves exercise supreme power can establish an autocephalous church."⁴⁷ He singles out the three subjects of supreme power capable of founding an autocephalous church: apostles, all the Orthodox episcopate (through an ecumenical or

[41] Ibid.
[42] Ibid.
[43] Ibid.
[44] See, for instance, Sergius Troitsky, "O granitsakh rasprostraneniia prava vlasti Konstantinopol'skoi Patriarkhii na diasporu" [On the limits of the territorial expansion of the patriarchate of Constantinople over the diaspora], *Zhurnal Moskovskoi Patriarkhii* 11 (1947): 34–45; Sergius Troitsky, "Kanony i vostochnyi papizm" [The canons and eastern papism], *Vestnik Russkogo Zapadno-Evropeiskogo Patriarshego Ekzarkhata* 22 (1955): 124–35.
[45] In Troitsky's terminology, the terms "ecumenical" and "pan-Orthodox" are synonymous with regard to a future council.
[46] Troitsky, "O tserkovnoi avtokefalii," 49.
[47] Ibid., 37.

pan-Orthodox council), and the episcopate of an autocephalous church (through a council of the autocephalous church). As the first two, according to him, belong to the distant past (or indefinite future, such as an ecumenical council), so the actual subject is the last of the three—the episcopate of an autocephalous church. He condemns an arbitrary proclamation of autocephaly by a part of an autocephalous church, except for the case where a "kyriarchal church"[48] falls into a heresy. It enables him to justify the self-proclamation of Russian autocephaly in 1448, and it is the only case where Troitsky justifies the self-proclamation of autocephaly by a local church. In any other case, the self-proclamation of autocephaly is impossible. Only a kyriarchal church can grant autocephaly to a part of itself.

On the whole, Troitsky's method can be considered legalistic, since it is based on the observance of the Orthodox Church's canon law. Troitsky appeals to law and church history (as description of precedents of the application of law) as the primary source of his reasoning. However, the problem is that, in the Orthodox Church, there is no single code of canon law nor instances that monitor church-wide application of law. Each autocephalous church is free to interpret canonical sources as it finds suitable.

However, Troitsky's legalistic approach cannot explain the changes of canonical order related to the self-proclamation of autocephaly. On the one hand, he speaks of autocephaly as supreme sovereign power. On the other hand, the legalistic approach he chooses compels him to assert that autocephaly is possible only as a result of its being granted by the mother church (except for the situation of a heresy upheld by a kyriarchal church). Troitsky, however, does not take into consideration that the very fact of granting represents an act of exercising supreme power by a kyriarchal church towards its part that receives autocephaly. As we will see below, it can lead to a situation where a kyriarchal church could threaten to abolish the autocephaly it had granted—which certainly restricts the sovereignty of a newly-proclaimed autocephalous church. Therefore, Troitsky's method does not allow the possibility of explaining how sovereign power

[48] A kyriarchal church is a local church which is the mother church for a separated part of itself.

appears in proclaiming autocephaly. And the time period from the self-proclamation of autocephaly to its recognition by others becomes a "blind spot" in his approach.

An Alternative: The Patriarch of Constantinople as the Sovereign

Along with the above model of sovereignty in the Orthodox Church, which links this notion with church autocephaly, there is in Orthodox theology an alternative model bestowing on the first hierarch in honor, the patriarch of Constantinople, the prerogatives of sovereign on the universal scale. Though this model does not presuppose the establishment of a single universal jurisdiction after the example of the pope of Rome, it bestows on the patriarch of Constantinople a number of powers, which put his power above the power of primates and councils of other autocephalous local churches. In particular, it includes special judicial powers, as well as the right to proclaim the autocephaly of a particular church.

This model appeared in the beginning of the 20th century, after the disintegration of the Ottoman Empire, and it is necessary at this point to say a few words about the status of the patriarchs of Constantinople in that empire. Among the basic peculiarities of the government system in the Ottoman Empire was a division into religious rather than ethnic communities, the *millets*. The Ottoman political system, built on Islamic law, presupposed the existence of only one head, the *millet-bashi*, in a religious community. The patriarch of Constantinople was the head of the Orthodox community, the largest among the non-Muslim communities of the empire. The sultan extended considerably the powers of the patriarch of Constantinople by turning over to him matters of police supervision, the collection of taxes, and litigation among Christians.[49] At the same time, it should be remembered that these powers were given not to an episcopal see, but personally to the patriarch (or, to be more precise, to the institution of the patriarch). The Ottoman Empire developed a system of

---

[49] Peter F. Sugar, *Southeastern Europe under Ottoman Rule, 1354–1804*, A History of East Central Europe, vol. 5 (Seattle: University of Washington Press, 1977), 46.

church governance in which the powers of the patriarch of Constantinople exceeded those of any primate of an autocephalous church in the territory of the empire (i.e., in the area of inter-church relations, the supreme power belonged to the patriarch of Constantinople, though formally his ecclesial jurisdiction did not extend to the territory of other autocephalous churches in the Ottoman Empire).[50]

The disintegration of the empire led to the patriarchs of Constantinople losing the extraordinary powers granted them by Ottoman rulers, and their territory rapidly decreased to the size of today's Turkey; moreover, a considerable part of the Orthodox population was deported. In this situation, the patriarchs of Constantinople began claiming worldwide sovereignty on the grounds of their primacy in the sacred diptychs of the Orthodox Church.[51] The activities of the Patriarchate of Constantinople throughout the 20s and 30s of the 20th century were essentially innovative for the Orthodox Church. The Church of Constantinople generated an enormous number of sovereign decisions (as compared to other churches), which created situations of exception, thus eventually changing the whole order that existed at that time. These decisions mostly concerned the extension of power jurisdiction of the Patriarchate of Constantinople, especially in the diaspora.[52]

---

[50]Certainly, matters did not always stand in practice as they did in theory. For instance, the special powers did not at all exclude some weaknesses of the patriarch of Constantinople's powers, which allowed other primates to pursue a more or less independent policy. The archbishop of Cyprus in the second half of the 17th century as much as obtained from the sultan the same title of *millet-bashi* as the patriarch of Constantinople and became the political and religious leader of the Christians in Cyprus. However, the status and powers of the patriarch of Constantinople as *millet-bashi* generated the idea of him as head of all the Orthodox Christians in the Ottoman Empire, which was to transform later into the claim to primacy on the pan-Orthodox scale.

[51]See the details of the situation that compelled the patriarchs of Constantinople to choose this line of conduct in Pavel Ermilov, "Proiskhozhdenie teorii o pervenstve Konstantinopol'skogo patriarkha" [The origin of the theory of the Patriarch of Constantinople's Primacy], *Vestnik PSTGU* 51.1 (2014): 36–53.

[52]See concrete examples, for instance in Troitsky, "O granitsakh rasprostraneniia prava vlasti Konstantinopol'skoi Patriarkhii na diasporu," 35; Maximos, Metropolitan of Sardis, *The Oecumenical Patriarchate in the Orthodox Church* (Thessaloniki: Patriarchal Institute for Patristic Studies, 1976), 312–13.

It cannot be stated that all the claims of the Patriarchate of Constantinople were fully realized, but its active, if not aggressive, positioning itself as the universal sovereign enabled the patriarchs of Constantinople to extend their power considerably. It even came to ascribing some "ontological" characteristics to the Church of Constantinople. Thus, in 1950 Patriarch Athenagoras of Constantinople issued an encyclical letter stating in particular that it was through the communion and contact with the see of Constantinople that individual autocephalous Orthodox churches are united in the body of one, holy, catholic, and apostolic Church.[53] A rupture of communion with the patriarch of Constantinople, according to Athenagoras, meant a rupture with the Orthodox Church herself.

In the period from 1950 to the 1970s, Constantinopolitan theologians, historians, and canonists began elaborating a teaching on the special role played by the Patriarchate of Constantinople in the life of the universal Orthodox Church. Its principal ideologist was Metropolitan Maximos of Sardis, who published a book entitled *The Oecumenical Patriarchate in the Orthodox Church*.[54]

Unlike the Moscow patriarchate, Constantinople's official theology did not restrict itself to a historical-canonical approach. Since the mid-1990s, the primacy and special powers of the patriarch of Constantinople have been theologically advocated by Metropolitan John Zizioulas of Pergamon. In January 2014, the official website of the Patriarchate of Constantinople published an article by Metropolitan Elpidophoros Lambriniadis of Bursa who, developing Zizioulas' ideas, proposed that the patriarch of Constantinople should be considered "the first hierarch without equals" (in contrast to his traditional designation as *primus inter pares*, "the first among equals").[55] The article states in particular that the primacy of the

---

[53] Alexander Schmemann, "Vselenskii Patriarkh i Pravoslavnaia Tserkov" [The ecumenical patriarch and the Orthodox Church], in *Sobranie statei, 1947–1983* [Collection of essays, 1947–1983] (Moscow: Russkii put', 2009), 364.

[54] Maximos, Metropolitan of Sardis, *The Oecumenical patriarchate in the Orthodox Church*.

[55] This line of ecclesiological thinking continues in the works of Archimandrite Panteleimon Manoussakis: John Panteleimon Manoussakis, "Primacy and Ecclesiology: The state of the Question" in *Orthodox Constructions of the West*, ed. George E. Demacopoulos and Aristotle

patriarch of Constantinople is expressed in special privileges, such as "the right of appeal and the right to grant or remove autocephaly."[56]

Among the important claims of the Church of Constantinople to sovereignty on the pan-Orthodox scale is the statement of his right to convene a pan-Orthodox council and to preside over it. Today, Constantinople stands only a step away from the realization of this claim. The official communiqué of the conference of the heads of local Orthodox churches, which took place in March 2014 in Istanbul, states, "It [the Pan-Orthodox Council] will be convened and presided by the ecumenical patriarch in Constantinople in 2016."[57]

The patriarch of Constantinople has come far toward the actual acquisition of this right. His initial attempts to convene a pan-Orthodox conference were made in 1923 and 1930. Since 1961, at the initiative of Patriarch Athenagoras of Constantinople, Pre-Conciliar Pan-Orthodox Conferences began to be chaired, according to the procedure, by the head of Constantinople's delegation. In 1986, Constantinople managed to include in the conference procedure a point giving the patriarch of Constantinople the right to convene Pre-Conciliar Pan-Orthodox Conferences "after an agreement with the primates of local Orthodox churches."[58] Concurrently with the pre-conciliar process, the patriarch of Constantinople began convening synaxes of the primates of the autocephalous local Orthodox churches, with the last one ending in the decision to convene a pan-Orthodox council.

Therefore, Constantinople's conception of sovereignty presupposes that on the pan-Orthodox level there is a certain supreme power localized

Papanikolaou (New York: Fordham University Press, 2013), 229–39; John Panteleimon Manoussakis, *For the Unity of All: Contributions to the Theological Dialogue between East and West* (Eugene, OR: Cascade Books, 2015), 21–43.

[56]Elpidophoros Lambriniadis, "First without equals: A response to the text on primacy of the Moscow Patriarchate," official website of the Ecumenical Patriarchate, accessed January 07, 2014, http://www.patriarchate.org/documents/first-without-equals-elpidophoros-lambriniadis.

[57]"Communiqué of the Primates of the Orthodox churches," official website of the Ecumenical Patriarchate, accessed June 04, 2014, http://www.patriarchate.org/documents/synaxis-2014-communique.

[58]Ioniță, *Towards the Holy and Great Synod of the Orthodox Church*, 179.

in the patriarch of Constantinople who, as a consequence, turns out to be the sovereign of the entire Orthodox Church. Within this model, while the patriarch of Constantinople as sovereign does not extend his administrative power to other autocephalous churches, he still can interfere in their internal affairs as supreme arbiter. That is to say, he enjoys the right to consider appeals on the pan-Orthodox scale and to make decisions on them; he has the power to grant or remove autocephaly; he appropriates to himself the right to govern the entire Orthodox diaspora. Accordingly, the patriarch of Constantinople can unilaterally admit into his jurisdiction the dioceses and parishes in the diaspora which "illegally" and "for a certain time" have found themselves under the jurisdiction of other autocephalous churches.

This approach also provides for the patriarch of Constantinople to have the right to convene pan-Orthodox conferences, conferences of the heads and representatives of autocephalous local churches, and finally a pan-Orthodox council— and to preside over all these assemblies, including the council. The system of church autocephalies is preserved, but the patriarch of Constantinople is assigned the right to emergency interference in the affairs of other churches in the above-mentioned matters. Therefore, in this model the sovereignty of autocephalous churches actually becomes *limited*.

At the same time, it is noteworthy that this model of "autocephalies with limited sovereignty" represents rather an action program, that is, it is predetermined rather than given. The claims of the patriarchs of Constantinople are far from all being realized in practice (for instance, church communities in the Orthodox diaspora are not governed from a single center). However, the Patriarchate of Constantinople continues giving numerous examples of sovereign decisions that work for the implementation of the program it has announced.

The Condition of "Sovereign Autocephaly"

Despite Constantinople's clams, what is generally accepted in the Orthodox Church today is the model of "sovereign autocephaly," upheld not only by the Moscow Patriarchate but also by many other autocephalous local churches. Most of today's autocephalous churches have traveled a path towards autocephaly similar to that covered by the Russian Church. Many of them adhere to the same principle in inter-church relations, namely, identification of autocephaly and sovereignty after the pattern of inter-state relations.[59] This principle presupposes the following: non-interference in the internal affairs of an autocephalous church by other autocephalous churches; integrity of canonical territorial borders; and the equal rights of autocephalous churches as subjects of inter-church relations.

From the viewpoint of the theory of sovereignty under consideration, the principal condition of autocephaly is precisely the proclamation of autocephaly, not receiving it from outside.

The sovereignty of an autocephalous church is realized at the moment when it proclaims autocephaly. An autocephalous church acquires supreme power only if it creates a situation of emergency (exception), which gives rise to a new order. First, a newly-proclaimed autocephalous (local) church comes to have its own canonical territory, which other autocephalous churches cannot by definition invade administratively. After being recognized as autocephalous by other local churches, this church becomes the subject of inter-church relations, which is symbolicly sealed by including this local church in the diptychs.

However, if a local church does not proclaim autocephaly on its own but receives it from a kyriarchal church, then the sovereignty of a new autocephalous church is limited. It is the *granting* of autocephaly that manifests supreme power and represents a sovereign decision; and, therefore, it is the kyriarchal church that acts as sovereign with regard to the new autocephalous church. And since the autocephalous church with granted autocephaly has an external sovereign, its autocephaly can be removed by the same kyriarchal church.

Among the examples of autocephaly that is not self-proclaimed but granted is that of the Orthodox Church of the Czech Lands and Slovakia

---

[59]Fr Cyril Hovorun believes that "the modern system of inter-church relations also reflects some later forms of the development of the Westphalian model of sovereignty" (Hovorun, "Kanonicheskaia territoriia," 355).

(OCCLS), which was recognized by world Orthodoxy. At the same time, it is interesting that the granting of autocephaly to this church happened twice: in 1951 it received it from the ROC as a part of it at that time; and in 1998 it received it from Constantinople.[60] In 2012, an exchange between Patriarch Bartholomew of Constantinople and the primate of the OCCLS, Metropolitan Christopher, was published on the internet, in which the former openly stated that this autocephaly could be abolished.[61] Rather characteristic is also the situation with the election of a new primate of the OCCLS in 2013–14, in which representatives of the two sovereign churches, Constantinople and Moscow, took an active part. The Church of Constantinople only recognized the outcome of that election in 2016,[62] because it was won by the candidate supported by the ROC.

Another example is the Orthodox Church in America (OCA), which received autocephaly from the Russian Orthodox Church in 1970. That act was recognized only by some local Orthodox churches, while quite a number of autocephalous churches (the Church of Constantinople in the first place) still consider the OCA a metropolitanate of the ROC. During Pre-Conciliar Pan-Orthodox Conferences, representatives of the OCA came as members of the Russian delegation.

It is quite interesting that supporters of the autocephaly of the Ukrainian Orthodox Church keep discussing the theme of "receiving autocephaly" from Moscow or (more often now) from Constantinople.[63] In doing

---

[60]The Patriarchate of Constantinople did not recognize the OCCLS's autocephaly granted by Moscow, and until 1998 it regarded OCCLS as a part of the ROC.

[61]In his letter, Patriarch Bartholomew was indignant at the fact that the OCCLS celebrated the 60th anniversary of its reception of autocephaly from Moscow: "We firmly announce that in case of recurrence of similar events to celebrate the autocephaly considered as if non-existent and recognized as invalid from the very beginning as it was imposed on the Church of the Czech Lands and Slovakia by an act of the Moscow Patriarchate, the Ecumenical Patriarchate will be regrettably compelled to abolish the canonical autocephaly granted to your church fourteen years ago" (Pis'mo Vselenskogo Patriarkha Varfolomeia mitropolitu Cheshskomu Khristoforu [The Letter of ecumenical patriarch Bartholomew to the Czech Metropolitan Christopher], Portal "Romfea," accessed June 04, 2014, http://www.romfea.gr/romfea-russian/12090–2012–03-30-15-13-01).

[62]See http://basilica.ro/new/en/reconciliation-in-the-orthodox-church-of-the-czech-lands-and-slovakia/.

[63]See the text of such a theoretician of the Ukrainian autocephaly as Prof. Yury

so, they tend to bear in mind that such an appeal to an external sovereign can only led to acquiring "limited sovereignty."

At present, the Pre-Conciliar Pan-Orthodox Conferences are discussing a procedure for proclaiming autocephaly. As is evident from the report by Metropolitan Hilarion Alfeyev, a range of possible solutions of this problem stretches from the right of a kyriarchal church to grant autocephaly to a part of itself to proclamation of autocephaly by the Patriarchate of Constantinople. In other words, the different and conflicting positions are similar in that a local church seeking autocephaly plays a passive role in this process, since it may only ask for autocephaly, while the decision is made by some external sovereign instance (a kyriarchal church, the patriarch of Constantinople, a pan-Orthodox conference or a conference of primates, a pan-Orthodox council). At the same time, Metropolitan Hilarion points out that "most often in the past it happened so that a particular Church would unilaterally declare her own autocephalous status and only years later her autocephaly would be recognized by other churches."[64] It turns out therefore that, except for the latter option—a pan-Orthodox council, all the other solutions lead to the "production" of autocephaly with limited sovereignty.

The Pan-Orthodox Council and the Sovereign Power of Autocephalous Churches

Finally, the last issue concerning the theme of this article—how does the sovereignty of autocephalous churches correlate with such a supra-autocephalous institution as a pan-Orthodox council?

The power of a council as an instance that makes decisions of church-wide importance and scale should exceed (hence, limit) the sovereign

Tchornomorets and Archpriest Andrey Dudchenko: Yury Tchornomorets, "Vselens'kist' pomisnoï tserkvi iak vimoga ekleziologiï ta perspektivi kiïvs'kogo khristijanstva" [Universality of the local church as a requirement for ecclesiology and perspectives of Kyivan Christianity], Theology in Ukraine, accessed June 04, 2014, http://theology.in.ua/ua /bp/theologia/ukrainian/56 376/; Andriy Dudchenko, "Ukraï'ns'ka Pravoslavna Cerkva v poshukah ukraï'ns'koï' identychnosti" [Ukrainian Orthodox Church looking for Ukrainian identity], Theology in Ukraine, accessed June 04, 2014, http://theology.in.ua/ua/bp/theologia/ukrainian/56 377/.

[64] Alfeyev, "Inter-Orthodox Cooperation."

power of autocephalous churches. In the period when a pan-Orthodox council is held, it is this council that becomes the church sovereign which can establish a new order by making a decision obligatory for all the autocephalous churches. Below we will consider how the sovereign power of a council is manifested, and what happens to the sovereignty of autocephalous churches from the viewpoint of theory proposed by Carl Schmitt.

According to the Schmittian approach, sovereignty is described through interaction between its three basic elements: "sovereign," "situation of emergency (exception)," and "decision" (and its implementation). Let us consider each of these elements in detail.

In the case of a pan-Orthodox council, the very event, i.e., its conduct, is an emergency (exception) for the Orthodox Church today. Accordingly, the very proclamation of a council as pan-Orthodox constitutes the decision to introduce "a state of emergency," which is made by a new sovereign—the assembly representing all world Orthodoxy.

The holding of a pan-Orthodox council represents an emergency event since it goes beyond the existing order of governance in the Orthodox Church (to be more precise, in the various Orthodox churches). In "normal situations," the supreme power in the Orthodox Church is concentrated on the level of autocephalous churches. In case of the holding of a council, however, understood as the supreme power instance on a church-wide scale, the sovereignty of autocephalous churches becomes limited. The emergency nature of a council enables it, as the sovereign exercising supreme power, to change the order existing throughout the Church and to introduce a new order, so that after the council none of the autocephalous churches will be able to revoke this order since the supreme power of autocephalous churches applies only to autocephalous churches themselves. Precisely for this reason, a new autocephaly proclaimed by a council will be fully sovereign and cannot therefore be abolished by any of the already existing autocephalous churches.

It should be stressed that a state of emergency in the Orthodox Church is introduced precisely through the proclamation of the assembly that represents the entire Orthodox Church as a pan-Orthodox council, not at all through a decision to convene it sometime in the future (even in the nearest future, as was the case at the Pan-Orthodox Summit in March 2014). Only if an already convened council declares itself pan-Orthodox (i.e., church-wide) does it become the church-wide sovereign. The decision to hold such a council (even made by a church-wide assembly) only points to a possibility for the emergence of a church-wide power instance, since there is always the possibility that the council will not take place for whatever reason.

According to P. Kahn, sovereign power does not presuppose any "potential decisions." Precisely for this reason the claim of the patriarch of Constantinople to the right to convene a pan-Orthodox council is not a manifestation of sovereign power over the whole Orthodox Church (from the point of view of the Schmittian sovereignty concept). The instance that convenes a council does not become the sovereign, as it is only a pan-Orthodox council itself, which has proclaimed itself as such, that can become the sovereign.

The decision to proclaim a council as church-wide also has another aspect. It is a decision to limit the sovereignty of the existing autocephalies. By proclaiming a council as pan-Orthodox, its participants themselves, i.e., the autocephalous churches, voluntarily limit their sovereignty.

However, it raises another question, namely, the *representation* of the sovereign autocephalous churches at a pan-Orthodox council. The emergence of a new "conciliar" sovereign involves, so to say, the collective transfer of sovereignty from local churches to a church-wide assembly. How can this transfer take place? What format of a pan-Orthodox assembly/council can make it really church-wide?

The March 2014 synaxis of the primates of churches in Istanbul considered two formats for conducting the Pan-Orthodox Council planned for 2016. The first presupposes that the council will be attended by *delegations* of autocephalous Orthodox churches, which alone will have the right to vote. According to the second format, the council should be attended by *all Orthodox bishops*, with each having the right to vote.

The synaxis agreed that the Pan-Orthodox Council will be attended by delegations of universally recognized local Orthodox churches. Each delegation should consist of the primate of an autocephalous church and no more than 24 bishops. At the same time, "the churches which do not have that many bishops will be represented by the full membership of their hierarchy led by the primate."⁶⁵ Therefore, it is *delegations*, not individual bishops, who will exercise the right to vote at the Council.

In other words, the point is that the new supreme sovereignty in the universal Orthodox Church (i.e., the sovereignty of the Pan-Orthodox Council) should emerge through a joint "symphonic" will of all the church autocephalies represented at a council by full-fledged and empowered church delegations of the church sovereigns existing today. Therefore, in this case it is immaterial who comprises these delegations—a group of representatives authorized by an autocephalous church (led by the primate) or all the bishops of each autocephalous church.

Accordingly, at present the decision to convene a pan-Orthodox council opens up an opportunity for the emergence of a sovereign in world Orthodoxy *different* from the sovereignty of church autocephalies. Paradoxically, this new church sovereign will at the same time be the result of the common decision of today's sovereigns and an (emergency) decision that undermines the "individual" sovereignties of the participants who together make this decision.

In this case, already contrary to Schmitt, sovereign power is based not only on a state of emergency, such as the holding of a pan-Orthodox council, but also on the power and authority of indisputable sovereigns-autocephalies. This introduces a certain continuity in the question of the emergence of sovereignty, whereas the Schmittian approach actually presupposes the creation of sovereign power "from nothing." Therefore, this paradox, if realized, already takes us out of the Schmittian pattern into a new conceptual space presupposing our address to other than Schmittian approaches existing in the discourse about *political* sovereignty as well as our consideration of the specific nature of precisely church power.

---

[65] "'Gotovilis' s 1961 goda'. Pavel Korobov beseduet s mitropolitom Volokolamskim Ilarionom" ['We have been preparing since 1961'. Pavel Korobov talks with Metropolitan Hilarion of Volokolamsk], Ogonyok, accessed June 04, 2014, http://www.kommersant.ru /doc/2416164.

APPENDIX 1
Some Quotations

St Vladimir's Seminary Quarterly 5.1–2 (1961): 114–117

Meletios IV (Metaxakis), Ecumenical Patriarch, former Greek Archbishop in America

We desire to mention also the question of one administration of the Orthodox Church in the diaspora.... I saw with my own eyes the biggest and the most numerous parts of the Orthodox Church in diaspora and I understood the measure in which the name of Orthodoxy would be exalted, especially in the great country of the United States of America, if the two millions of Orthodox Christian were organized there into one united ecclesiastical organization, as an "American Orthodox Church."[1]

St Tikhon (Bellavin), Archbishop of the Aleutian Islands and North America (later Patriarch of Moscow)

The diocese of North America[2] must be reorganized into an exarchate of the Russian Church in North America. The diocese is not only multinational; it is composed of several Orthodox Churches, which keep the unity of faith, but preserve their particularities in canonical structure, in liturgical rules, in parish life. These particularities are dear to them and can perfectly be tolerated on the pan-Orthodox scene. We do not consider that we have the right to suffer the national character of the churches here; on the contrary, we try to preserve this character and we confer them the latitude to be guided by leaders of their own nationality. Thus, the Syrian Church here received a bishop of its own (the Most Rev. Raphael of Brooklyn),

---

[1]Declaration of Enthronement as Ecumenical Patriarch, Constantinople (January 24, 1922). Quoted in B. Zoustis, *Hellenism in America and its Activities* [in Modern Greek] (New York, 1954), 147.

[2]In 1905, when this statement was made, all Orthodox national groups in America were united in the jurisdiction of Archbishop Tikhon.

who is the second auxiliary to the diocesan bishop of the Aleutian Islands, but is almost independent in his own sphere (the bishop of Alaska having the same position). The Serbian parishes are now organized under one immediate head, who for the time being is an archimandrite, but who can be elevated to the episcopacy in the nearest future. The Greeks also desire to have their own bishop and are trying to settle the matter with the Synod of Athens. In other words, in North America a whole Exarchate can easily be established, uniting all Orthodox national churches, which would have their own bishops under one exarch, the Russian archbishop. Each one of them is independent in its own sphere, but the common affairs of the American church are decided in a synod, presided by the Russian archbishop. Through him a link is preserved between the American Church and the Church of Russia and a certain dependence of the former to the latter. It should be remembered however that life in the New World is different from that of the Old; our Church must take this into consideration; a greater autonomy (and possibly autocephaly) should therefore be granted to the Church of America, as compared with the other Metropolitan sees of the Russian Church. The North American Exarchate would comprise: (1) the archdiocese of New York, with jurisdiction over all Russian churches in the United States and in Canada; (2) the diocese of Alaska, for the orthodox inhabitants of Alaska (Russians, Aleutians, Indians, Eskimos); (3) the diocese of Brooklyn (Syrian); (4) the diocese of Chicago (Serbian); (5) a Greek diocese.[3]

Professor H. Alivizatos, Member of the Greek Academy, Professor of Canon Law at the University of Athens[4]

The language of Americans of Greek descent is the English language and, according to the views of the Orthodox Church, it can be used in the

---

[3]Opinions (Otzyvy) of Diocesan bishops concerning Church Reforms, submitted to the Pre-Conciliar Commission of the Holy Synod, St Petersburg, 1906, Part I, 531.

[4]Lectures on the Orthodox Church given in April 1953 and July 1954 at the University and the Ecumenical Institute of Chicago, IL, published in the "Scientific Journal of the Theological School of the University of Athens," and in a book, *The Greek Orthodox Church* (Athens, 1955), 6–9.

liturgy.... This is the only means by which their interest towards Orthodoxy will be maintained.... The Greek[5] Orthodox Church, in its Hellenic part, together with the other national branches, will become English speaking in thirty or forty years at the maximum, since no effort is able to maintain the national languages. As an immediate consequence, the present canonical chaos in the administration of the Church in America will be replaced, in the nearest future, by a big united American Greek Orthodox Church, governed by a synod of American bishops. This Church, in due time, will evolve, according to the established pattern, into an independent autocephalous Church. It is evident that the first immigrants of Orthodox descent became the creators of a new branch of Orthodoxy, the American Orthodox Church. The future of this Church, if the above conditions are fulfilled, will be truly great and glorious.

Anthony (Bashir), Metropolitan of the Antiochian Orthodox Archdiocese of America

While we must still minister to many who remember the way and customs of another land it is our policy to make our church in the United States an American Church. In my own archdiocese, under my administration we have pioneered in the introduction of English in our services and our sermons. From the beginning of my ministry I began the printing of English service books, and the training of English-speaking priests. We are tied to no sacred language; we recognize all tongues as the creation of God, and employ them in this worship. We have no desire to perpetuate anything but the Gospel of Christ, and that we can do as effectively in English as in any other tongue.[6]

John (Shahovskoy), Archbishop of San Francisco

The time has come for all Orthodox of America, whatever their extraction may be, to understand that the United States of America cannot be

---

[5]The word "Greek" is used here not in its national sense, but in the sense which embraces the whole Orthodox Church (note of H. Alivizatos).
[6]"The Antiochian Church and Christian Unity," *The Word* 1.6 (June, 1957): 145.

considered a colony any more either in political or in ecclesiastical sense. The past is gone. This country has ceased to be an ecclesiastical colony of the English, the Dutch, the Swedes; it cannot remain a spiritual colony of the Greeks, the Serbs, the Romanians, the Russians, whether those of the USSR or those "in exile." Americans have indeed won the right (no less than the Cypriots, the Albanians or the Czechoslovaks) to have their own Orthodox local church, in conformity with the ecclesiastical canons.[7]

The Very Rev. Prof. Georges Florovsky, St Vladimir's Orthodox Theological Seminary, Harvard University, Princeton University

The Universality of the Orthodox faith is obscured by human divisions, and it is often forgotten that Orthodoxy is the Church, and therefore is not, and cannot be confined to any territorial or historical boundaries. There should be no limits to the Orthodox expansion, and in new conditions, the Church may speak a new tongue.

It was the glory of the Orthodox Church that, from the very beginning, and throughout the ages, she did address diverse nations in their own idioms, and the holy liturgy was celebrated in many tongues. It was the glory of the Orthodox Church that she addressed the Slavs in their vernacular and encouraged them to worship God in their own language. That glorious example of Sts Cyril and Methodius, the "Slavic Apostles," has been closely followed by the missionaries of the Russian Church, from the days of when St Stephen of Perm endeavored to evangelize the Finnish tribes in their own language and adapted the liturgy to their vernacular, to the days of the great Orthodox "Apostle of Japan," Archbishop [St] Nikolai of Japan, who laid foundations of a Japanese Orthodoxy. The languages are many, and any one should be used for the propagation of the true faith and for a spontaneous offering of praise and thanksgiving to God, who is God of all nations.[8]

---

[7] *The Russian American Orthodox Messenger* 56.10 (October, 1960): 166.
[8] St *Vladimir's Seminary Quarterly* 2.4 (1954): 3.

Archimandrite Hieronymos Kotsonis, Chaplain of the Royal Palace of His Majesty the King of the Hellenes, Professor of Canon Law, Theological Faculty, University of Thessalonica

The problem of the survival of Hellenism in America is essentially a problem of preserving its Orthodoxy.... The liturgical and sacramental wealth of our Church must become accessible through the performing of the divine liturgy and the other holy sacraments and services in the English language (alongside of the Greek). Since the Roman Church, with its clergy and monastic orders being much better organized than the Orthodox, is obliged today to admit in America as elsewhere the use of the local languages in its liturgy, it is obvious that this is even more necessary for us Orthodox: we do not have the same presuppositions as the Catholic Church, and the use of local language in both liturgy and preaching belongs to the Tradition of our Church....

The unity of all Orthodox Christians in America would very much contribute to the spread of the Orthodox Church in America and would help its prestige, and thus it will better attract the Orthodox youth. Its present influence on the public life of the country is negligible if not non-existant. This situation is due, among other reasons, to our present division into several ethnic groups (Greek, Russian, Romanian, Bulgarian, etc.) ... Every effort should be made to unify the Orthodox Church in the USA This would not mean that the various groups would lose their ethnic character or their inner administrative autonomy.[9]

---

[9]*Anaplasis* (November, 1955): 507–09.

APPENDIX 2

Documents: The Autocephaly of the Orthodox Church in America

St Vladimir's Theological Quarterly 15.1–2 (1971): 42–80

Editorial comment

Published below are the basic documents concerning the establishment of the Autocephalous Orthodox Church in America, and the correspondence which took place between the Patriarchates of Constantinople and Moscow in relation with this event.

Paragraph numbering and sub-titles have been added by the editor for the convenience of the reader.

As is well known, the correspondence between Istanbul and Moscow started in January 1970, when the negotiations were in progress. His Holiness, the late Patriarch Alexis, signed the Tomos of Autocephaly on April 10, 1970, thus providentially sealing this historical act six days before his death. The correspondence was continued by the Patriarchal Locum-Tenens, Metropolitan Pimen.

While the position of the Orthodox Church in America is clearly stated by His Beatitude, Metropolitan Ireney in his report to the council (Document 11), the respective attitudes of the Patriarchates of Constantinople and Moscow can be summarized in the following major agreements and disagreements:

Agreements:

1. Constantinople and Moscow agree on the point that the restoration of "normal" canonical relations between Moscow and the Metropolia was desirable (III.2).

2. They also agree on the crucial principle that in every country there can normally exist only one church and that Orthodox canon law requires unity of territorial jurisdiction (Documents IV.5; V.17). This agreement is particularly important, since some ecclesiastical "nationalists" try to maintain the multiplicity of ethnic jurisdictions in America as a normal canonical order.

3. There is also agreement on the point that an Orthodox ecumenical council, when and if it ever meets, can and must authoritatively solve the existing problems.

Disagreements:

1. Constantinople affirms that no Orthodox Church possesses exclusive territorial rights in America (V.15–16), While the Patriarch of Moscow recalls that, before 1921, "strict canonical order was followed on this continent under the hierarchical leadership of the Russian Church" (VI.17). The exchange on this point is aggravated by the—truly strange—remark in Patriarch Athenagoras' second letter (V.16) about the "propagandistic and proselytizing activity" of the Russian Church, directed at Uniates (as if Constantinople itself was not accepting Uniates also).

2. Constantinople promotes the theory according to which autocephalies are established by Ecumenical Councils only (V, 5–6). It also states that those autocephalies which were created otherwise have disappeared and that the now existing autocephalies (unless they were created by ecumenical councils) also needed confirmation (V.7). According to Moscow, any autocephalous church has the right to grant canonical independence to one of its parts.

3. The patriarch of Moscow recognizes that Constantinople has primacy of "rank," or "honor," but not of power (VI.14), while Constantinople speaks of itself as the "mother church" of all Orthodox churches (V.8).

In the letters of the late Patriarch Alexis and of Metropolitan Pimen, there are certainly some points which may be subject to debate. In Constantinople's attitude, however, there is obvious disregard for historical facts and lack of realism for the present. The theory according to which ecumenical councils were alone empowered to grant autocephaly belongs to pure mythology: as John Erickson's article, published in this issue,[1] clearly shows, the very word "autocephaly" has changed meaning frequently, while the reality which it now reflects—administrative independence of an ecclesiastical body—had been in the jurisdiction of the Byzantine emperor, in that of individual patriarchs, but ecumenical councils never dealt with it directly. On the other hand, to refer the solution of the American ecclesiastical problem to the future "Great," or "Ecumenical" Council of Orthodoxy is, in fact, a simple defense of the present status quo. Everyone certainly hopes that such a council will be able to meet in the near future, and no one denies that it would be able to provide a canonical solution, but, realistically speaking, its convocation is unlikely in the present generation.

A "great" or "ecumenical" council would be a council of all Orthodox bishops of the world. Can one imagine the holding of such a council in one of the Communist dominated countries? Can one imagine the Soviet, or Romanian, or Bulgarian governments to allow all the Orthodox episcopate of these countries to travel simultaneously abroad? Can one imagine the Turkish government to allow the ecumenical patriarch to preside over such a council?

The answers to these questions are so obvious, and are so well known to everyone, that any expectation that such a council would be the appropriate authority to solve the urgent needs of the Church in America is intellectually dishonest. These needs can be solved by the Americans themselves, striving towards order and unity, by the mother churches honestly desiring this order and this unity, and by a consensus of all concerned. The autocephaly granted by the Patriarch of Moscow is the basis for such a consensus, not a substitute for it. It does not close any doors, it widely opens the only realistic possibility for the present and the future, without forcing anyone to follow, but challenging the conscience and responsibility of all the Orthodox churches having branches in this country.—*Ed.*

[1][The editors are referring here to the following article: John H. Erickson, "Autocephaly in Orthodox Canonical Literature to the Thirteenth Century," *St Vladimir's Theological Quarterly* 15.1–2 (1971): 28–41. This article is included in the present volume, pp. 179–195.—*Ed.*]

I
TOMOS
of ALEXIS, by the Mercy of God Patriarch of Moscow and All Russia

For a number of years, the Russian Orthodox Church has observed with maternal love and concern the development of the Orthodox church which she planted on the American continent. In the last few decades she has sorrowfully witnessed the unfortunate appearance there of a pluralism of ecclesiastical jurisdictions, a temporary phenomenon, and by no means a permanent norm of the canonical organization of the Orthodox Church in America, since it is contrary to the nature of Orthodox canonical ecclesiastical unity.

The Holy Russian Orthodox Church, striving for the good of the Church, has directed her efforts toward the normalization of relations among the various ecclesiastical jurisdictions in America, particularly by negotiating with the Russian Orthodox Greek Catholic Church in America, concerning the possibility of granting autocephaly to this church in the hope that this might serve the good of the Orthodox Church in America and the glory of God.

In her striving for the peace of Christ, which has universal significance for the life of man; desiring to build a peaceful and creative church life, and to suppress scandalous ecclesiastical divisions; hoping that this act would be beneficial to the Holy Orthodox Catholic Church of Christ and would make possible the development among the local parts of the one, holy, catholic and apostolic Church of such relations which would be founded on the firm ties of the one Orthodox faith and the love that the Lord Jesus Christ willed; keeping in mind that this act would serve the welfare of universal, mutual cooperation; taking into consideration the petition of the Bishops' Council of the Russian Orthodox Greek Catholic Metropolitanate of North America, which expressed the opinion and desire of all her faithful children; acknowledging as good for Orthodoxy in America the independent and self-sustaining existence of said Metropolitanate, which now represents a mature ecclesiastical organism possessing all that is necessary for successful further growth, Our Humility together with the Sacred Synod and all the venerable hierarchs of the Russian Orthodox Church, who have signified their agreement in writing, having examined the said petition, in sincere love grant autocephaly to the Russian Orthodox Greek Catholic Church in America, that is, the right of a fully independent ordering of church life in accordance with the divine and sacred canons and the ecclesiastical practices and customs of the one, holy, catholic and apostolic Church inherited from the fathers; for which purpose this Patriarchal and Synodal Tomos is directed to His Beatitude, IRENEY, Archbishop of New York, Primate of the Autocephalous Orthodox Church in America, Metropolitan of All-America and Canada, by which we announce:

1. The Russian Orthodox Greek Catholic Church in North America is confirmed and proclaimed an autocephalous church and named, "The Autocephalous Orthodox Church in America";

2. By "autocephaly," which is confirmed in this decision, it is understood that the Autocephalous Orthodox Church in America shall:

a. be independent and self-governing with the right of electing her own primate and all her bishops, without confirmation or the right of veto over such elections on the part of any other church organization or representative of the Eastern Orthodox or any other confession;

b. firmly and inalterably preserve the divine dogmas, being guided in her life by the sacred canons of the holy Orthodox Catholic Church of Christ and governed in accordance with her own Statute as accepted, augmented or amended from time to time by her own highest legislative and executive organ;

c. maintain direct relations with all other churches and confessions, Orthodox and non-Orthodox alike;

d. enjoy all the authority, privileges, and rights usually inherent in the term "autocephaly" in the canonical tradition of the Eastern

Orthodox Church, including the right of preparing and consecrating holy chrism.

3. The following are excluded from autocephaly on the territory of North America:

a. St Nicholas Cathedral and its possessions, located at 15 East 97th Street in New York City and the accompanying residence; and also, the immovable possessions in Pine Bush, New York, together with buildings and edifices which might be constructed in the future on this land;

b. Parishes and clergy in the USA which at present are in the Patriarchal Exarchate and which desire to remain in the canonical and jurisdictional care of the Most Holy Patriarch of Moscow and All Russia—these parishes, desiring to remain in the canonical jurisdiction of the Most Holy Patriarch of Moscow and All Russia and excluded from the Autocephalous Orthodox Church in America, are the following: [a list of parishes and home chapels follows]

c. All parishes and clergy in Canada, which presently constitute the Edmonton, Canada Diocese of the Moscow Patriarchate (they all desired to remain in the jurisdiction of the Most Holy Patriarch).

4. St Nicholas Cathedral and its possessions and residence, and also the property in Pine Bush, NY shall be governed by the Most Holy Patriarch of Moscow and All Russia through a person representing him in the rank of presbyter.

5. Parishes and clergy in the USA which remain in the canonical jurisdiction of the Moscow Patriarchate shall be governed by the Most Holy Patriarch of Moscow and All Russia through one of his vicar bishops, not having a title of the local American Church, especially appointed for this, and until such time as these parishes express their official desire to join the Autocephalous Church in America in the manner described below.

6. Parishes and clergy which at this time constitute the Edmonton, Canada Diocese of the Moscow Patriarchate and remain in the canonical

jurisdiction of the Moscow Patriarchate, shall be governed by the Most Holy Patriarch of Moscow and All Russia through one of his vicar bishops not having a title of the local American Church, especially appointed for this, and until such time as these parishes express their official desire to join the Autocephalous Church in America in the manner described below.

7. The Autocephalous Orthodox Church in America shall have exclusive spiritual and canonical jurisdiction over all bishops, clerics, and laymen of the Eastern Orthodox confession in continental North America, excluding Mexico and including the state of Hawaii, who are presently part of the Metropolitanate, or who shall later enter the Metropolitanate; and over all parishes which now belong or later shall be accepted into the Metropolitanate, excepting the entire clergy, possessions, and parishes enumerated in Paragraph 3, a, b, c.

8. The Moscow Patriarchate shall not lay claim to either spiritual or canonical jurisdiction over bishops, clergy, and laymen of the Eastern Orthodox confession, or over parishes mentioned in Division 1, Paragraph 7, and by the present yields to the Metropolitanate all jurisdiction to which she has laid claim on the above mentioned territory (Paragraph 7), excepting the entire clergy, possessions, and parishes enumerated in Paragraph 3, points a, b, c.

9. The changing of jurisdictions by parishes which are in the canonical care of the Moscow Patriarchate after the proclamation of the Metropolitanate's autocephaly shall occur on the initiative of the parishes themselves and after bilateral agreements in each concrete case between the Moscow Patriarchate and the Autocephalous Church in America.

10. The Moscow Patriarchate shall not receive into its care in North America any clerics without written release or any parishes except parishes from uncanonical ecclesiastical organizations in Canada; and shall not canonically permit clergy and parishes remaining in its care to enter any of the Orthodox jurisdictions but the jurisdiction of the Autocephalous Orthodox Church in America.

11. The Patriarchate assures the parishes remaining in its care of its readiness to defend their status as parishes of the Moscow Patriarchate,

and also defend the enumerated parishes from attempts to change their present status without a free expression of their decision and without the written agreement of the Moscow Patriarchate.

12. The Moscow Patriarchate and the Orthodox Autocephalous Church in America shall maintain sincere fraternal relations, in which they should be guided by the bilateral agreements, signed by His Eminence, Metropolitan IRENEY, and by His Eminence, Metropolitan NIKODIM, Metropolitan of Leningrad and Novgorod, on March 31st, 1970.

13. The Exarchate of North and South America, together with the dioceses in the USA and Canada which comprised it, is abolished.

Confirming the autocephaly of the Russian Orthodox Greek Catholic Church in America, we bless her to call herself, The Holy Autocephalous Orthodox Church in America; we acknowledge and proclaim her our sister church, and we invite all local Orthodox churches and their primates and their faithful children to acknowledge her as such and to include her in the dyptichs in accordance with the canons of the Church, the traditions of the fathers and ecclesiastical practice.

The newly-established local Orthodox Autocephalous Church in America should abide in brotherly relations with all the Orthodox churches and their primates as well as with their bishops, clergy, and pious flock, who are in America and who for the time being preserve their *de facto* existing canonical and jurisdictional dependence on their national churches and their primates.

With profound, sincere joy, we announce this to the fullness of the Church and we do not cease thanking the all-gracious Almighty God, who directs all in the world by his right hand for the good and the salvation of mankind—for the successful and final formation of autocephaly, and we entreat the all-powerful blessing of God upon the younger sister in the family of local autocephalous Orthodox churches, the Autocephalous Orthodox Church in America.

May the consubstantial and life-creating and undivided Trinity—Father, Son, and Holy Spirit—acting in its own wondrous providence, send down on the archpastors, pastors, and faithful children of the holy autocephalous

Orthodox American Church its heavenly, unfailing help, and may it bless with success all her future endeavors for the good of the holy Church.

Signed in the city of Moscow, April 10th, 1970.
ALEXEI, Patriarch of Moscow and All Russia

Members of the Holy Synod:
1. Metropolitan of Krutitsa and Kolomna, PIMEN
2. Metropolitan of Leningrad and Novgorod, NIKODIM
3. Metropolitan of Kiev and Galicia, Exarch of the Ukraine, PHILARET
4. Metropolitan of Orel and Briansk, PALLADY
5. Metropolitan of Alma-Ata and Kazakhstan, IOSIF
6. Metropolitan of Yaroslavl and Rostov, IOANN
7. Archbishop of Irkutsk and Tchita, VENIAMIN
8. Archbishop of Ufa and Sterlitamak, IOV
9. Archbishop of New York and the Aleutians, Exarch of North and South America, IONAFAN
10. Bishop of Kishinev and Moldavia, VARFOLOMEY
11. Bishop of Tula and Belev, IUVENALY
12. Bishop of Chernigov and Nezhinsk, VLADIMIR
13. Bishop of Smolensk and Viazma, GEDEON
14. Chancellor of the Moscow Patriarchate, Metropolitan of Tallin and Estonia, ALEXEI.

II
Report on Autocephaly
By His Beatitude, Metropolitan IRENEY Archbishop of New York, Metropolitan of All America and Canada at the First All-American Council of the Orthodox Church in America. October 20–22, 1970, St Tikhon's Monastery, South Canaan, Pennsylvania

Your Eminences, Your Graces, Dear Fathers and Brethren, Fellow-Laborers in the vineyard of Christ!

1. "I will sing to the Lord who has dealt lovingly with me! I will praise the name of the Lord Most High!" (Ps 12.6)

It befits me to open this report with the words of the Psalmist, at this most significant of all the councils of our Church in America. Indeed, we have never experienced so intensely that the Holy Spirit himself guides and leads the Church, that the Lord Jesus Christ—and not we, unworthy sinners—builds the Church, and that the mercy and grace of God are not lost to her.

I shall begin with the main event which marked the three years since our last council—the proclamation of autocephaly of the Orthodox Church in America. At the All-American Council in 1967 it became evident to all of us that our Church had drawn near to a last stage, and that her further growth required a final clarification of her canonical foundations and our common consciousness of our own churchness. In the wonderful and memorable "straw-vote" on the question of renaming our church, the direction was clearly indicated. Our church—such was the meaning of this vote—truly realized her own maturing into a local, permanent American church, bound for all time with this land and with this people, ready to take on herself the full responsibility of the Church.

Break Healed

2. This fact, which revealed the conciliar maturity of our church, prompted us, the bishops, to seek ways of implementing it in canonical forms, true both to the universal church tradition and to the needs and particularities of our life in America. Everyone is aware of the fact that one massive and contaminating obstruction stood in the way, for almost fifty years: our involuntary, yet necessary, break with our mother Russian Church, a break which for years poisoned church life with animosity, court cases, mutual accusations—and all this served only to hinder Orthodoxy's primary calling—spiritual and missionary—in America. Sad and terrible it is to ponder how much energy, how much money was "used" in these sinful and awful dissensions.

I repeat—this break was necessitated by tragic events, which befell the suffering and martyred Russian Church. But along the unfathomable ways of God, where "the power of Christ is made perfect in weakness" (2 Cor 12.9), this break—despite its tragic character—was possibly beneficial. For it taught us, almost against our will, the hard gift of freedom, of common responsibility for the Church—it taught us "to bear each other's burdens" (Gal 6.2), and having deprived us of material help from the mother church, it taught sacrificial and active participation of all in the life of the Church. When we see to what a degree the other ecclesiastical persuasions in America are bound to far-away centers overseas, we can only thank God for those experiences, by which He enlightened and edified us. And I think that especially on this day, at the very beginning of our Council, we must "with one mouth and one heart" acknowledge the Church's debt in memory and gratitude to those hierarchs, pastors, and laymen, who in the most difficult period of our history guided the ship of the Church unharmed through the turbulent seas. Memory Eternal to them!

Past Forgotten, Future Sought

3. Truly unfathomable are the ways of God! For at the same moment when the sobornal consciousness of our church felt the necessity of a decisive step in the direction of canonical clarification and the freedom of the Church, we encountered understanding on the part of the Russian Church's leaders. For me, as for all of us I'm sure, the main proof that what has been accomplished was the work of the Holy Spirit—is that both sides simultaneously and from the beginning professed their desire to speak not of the past, but of the present and the future, to cover this past with love, to seek not the victory of one side over the other, but to seek instead only the good of the Church, following the words of the Apostle Paul: "Forgetting what lies behind and straining forward to what lies ahead" (Phil 3.13). In the sad reality of church affairs, so poisoned by suspicion and doubt that it seemed that many had already forsaken belief in the all-victorious power of the Holy Spirit and the love of Christ—a sign was given to us that "what is impossible to men, is possible to God" (Lk 18.27).

Talks Successful

4. The talks with the Russian Church in January of 1969 began precisely in the Spirit, and these were crowned with the signing on March 31, 1970 of the agreement you are all aware of. Here there is no need to expound the history—often difficult—of these talks. But, one thing I must say. In view of the fact that there are people ready to spread all sorts of lies and slander in order to sow doubt and dissension, I want to witness with my episcopal and primatial conscience—before God, and before this sacred council of our whole Church—that at no time during these talks, from either side, was an "offer" or "condition" set forth which would in the least limit our freedom and conscience, such being incompatible with our condition and life in America. We turn over to the righteous and just judgement of God those who, imprisoned by human and political passions and blinded by hate, find it possible to mock the work of God. I want also to state, that from the very beginning to the very end, these talks were conducted under the direction and constant and immediate control of the entire Council of

Bishops—upon which lies, according to the doctrine of the Church, the full responsibility for the canonical structure of the Church. That which was accomplished "seemed good to the Holy Spirit and to us" (Acts 15.28). I am happy to express before the entire council our sincere gratitude to all those who, fulfilling our requests, conducted these talks in unshakeable faithfulness to the Church, unspoken obedience to the hierarchy, patience, wisdom, and broadmindedness.

A Miracle of Grace

5. And so, on April 10, 1970, the day on which the entire Orthodox Church sang a joyous song of praise to the Most Holy Theotokos, on the eve of death and the threshold of eternity, preparing to stand before the judgment of God, the primate of the Russian Church, the Most Holy Patriarch Alexis signed the act which, we believe and we confess, shall remain in the memory of the Church as the act which inaugurated a new era in the history of the Church—filled with difficulties and temptations and deceptions, but also with the miracle of God's grace—in her earthly journey towards the day of the Kingdom of God which knows no evening.

New Life

6. For this act is an act of freedom and creativity, an act of faith and trust, a sign that the Church of God "never grows older, but forever younger" and that new channels of life can flow through her ancient arteries. This is an act blessing the young Orthodoxy in America, calling it to grow to the measure of grace bestowed upon it, and to bring its fruit also to the one treasury of universal Orthodoxy. Undoubtedly, years shall pass before the waves of small human passions and misunderstandings raised by it finally subside. But we, witnesses of this act, can even now—with the eyes of faith, hope, and love—foresee the magnitude and the joy of the one holy Orthodox Church in America, inheritors of all the gifts, all the riches, all the traditions of universal Orthodoxy, glorifying God with one mouth and one heart in this great and free country. May this be! May this be!

Prayers of St Herman

7. That work, which was begun 175 years ago in Alaska by a band of monks from Valaam Monastery in Russia, is now fulfilled. And almost as "proof" of this, during the past summer we were blessed with the glorification of the first American saint, our venerable and God-bearing Father Herman of Alaska, Wonderworker of All America. There, at his tomb, during those unforgettable days of his canonization, it was granted us to foretaste that joy, to commune with that light, to experience the power of oneness in the Holy Spirit, to all of which the holy Orthodox Church in America is called. Venerable Father Herman, pray to God for us! Help us in serving and building that church, whose spiritual beauty and joy you are!

Suspicion and Fear

8. We receive the gift of God's mercy with gratitude, which was sent down upon us, we clearly recognize, together with a new responsibility for the fate of Orthodoxy in America. One of the main tasks facing this Council consists precisely in defining this responsibility, and in explaining it to our brethren in the faith.

Let us not delude ourselves: the proclamation of the Orthodox Church in America's autocephaly has brought forth not only joy, but also doubts, questions, and criticisms. Alas, Orthodox Christians are so accustomed to living in their little isolated ethnic worlds, treating each other with suspicion—that the storm raised by the autocephaly was not unexpected. This requires of us patience, love, sincerity, and uprightness. If some of these criticisms are so base and ignoble that it is senseless even to refute them, to certain others we promise to give positive answers.

The Negative Position of Constantinople

9. We are most upset, naturally, by the negative position on the autocephaly taken by the Most Holy Patriarch Athenagoras of Constantinople. Upset, first of all, because with the entire Orthodox Church we honor the ecumenical throne as the center of unity and love, and the most holy patriarch

of Constantinople as the hierarch first in honor among the Orthodox. Upset, secondly, because precisely from him rather than from many others, we were entitled to expect an understanding of the ecclesiastical situation in America, together with a unique concern for its welfare. But, we see instead with sadness that, in his letters on the autocephaly, much is said of the rights and privileges of the churches, and almost nothing of the spiritual plight and ecclesiastical drama of hundreds of thousands of Orthodox Americans.

American Orthodoxy Ignored

10. The Most Holy Patriarch Athenagoras knows, of course, that the jurisdictional and anti-canonical chaos in the New World did not appear yesterday, and was not born because of the autocephaly—but arose rather through the prolonged lack of concern or else simply the inability, on the part of many churches, to admit the FACT of American Orthodoxy, to see in it nothing more than a chaotic mesh of ethnic ecclesiastical "colonies"! Patriarch Athenagoras likewise knows of the numerous and constant attempts on the part of our Church specifically to raise the question of Orthodoxy in America on an international Orthodox scale. In order not to sound inconclusive, I will permit myself to set down certain facts.

Audience Denied

11. First fact: Almost immediately after my election as metropolitan in 1965, I appealed to the heads of all the churches with a long letter in which I entreated them to devote themselves in council to canonical order in America. I also requested a private audience with Patriarch Athenagoras so that we might discuss this problem in a brotherly setting. Patriarch Athenagoras not only did not reply at that time, but even put off my visit on the grounds that we should first normalize our relations with the Moscow Patriarchate.

Synod Rejected

12. Second fact: A number of years ago a special commission of the Standing Conference of Canonical Orthodox Bishops in America suggested that a temporary pan-Orthodox synod be formed in America, under the mantle of the ecumenical throne. This suggestion was not accepted by any of the autocephalous churches having their diocese here, which obviously means that they saw no reasons to replace their own jurisdiction in America with the ecumenical patriarch's, and they recognized no special "Constantinopolitan" rights on American soil. Even then it became quite clear that the choice facing Orthodoxy in America was between full canonical independence, that is, autocephaly—and the preservation of the depressing status quo, that is, a multiplication of national and disjoined "jurisdictions." Why now, when the Russian Church—indisputably the eldest in her jurisdiction in America, and which always included in her American branch Orthodox Christians of different ethnic backgrounds, following in this both the spirit and the letter of church tradition—acknowledges the ecclesiastical maturity of her branch and grants her independence and the possibility of guiding her own life; when the first step has been taken towards dispelling that "phyletism" (i.e., subordination of the Church to nationalism) which was, relatively recently and so solemnly, condemned by the ecumenical throne itself; why is all this condemned and proclaimed as uncanonical?

Chaos Long Tolerated

13. If this action has been condemned as being allegedly "unilateral" then why did the ecumenical throne not condemn the truly "unilateral" creation in America by various Orthodox churches of their dioceses, missions, and metropolitanates? If, as all the acts of the ecumenical throne vis-à-vis the situation in America prove, it recognizes that everybody has the right of acting as he wills on this continent—why is this right denied to the church which planted Orthodoxy here and is indisputably the eldest in her jurisdiction and canonical rights? And, finally, what disrupts the unity of the Church more: A multitude of self-serving ethnic jurisdictions—or the long

overdue application in America of that local principle by which the structure of the Orthodox Church was determined, everywhere and always?

The Autocephaly is Canonical

14. Fully canonical is that which corresponds to the age-old apostolic doctrine of the Church, that which serves her in realizing her eternal and timeless ordination: witnessing to Christ and to the new life in him before the entire world.

The autocephaly of our church is canonical, because it corresponds perfectly to this age-old and universal doctrine of the Church. It confirms and realizes the growth in America of a local Orthodox church—founded not on the earthly, the temporal, the transitory—but on Christ and on unity in him. The autocephaly of our church is canonical, because it was rightly received from the church which planted Orthodoxy in America and which is the mother church in America.

The autocephaly of our church is canonical, because her faith is the faith of the universal Church. Her structure is the structure of the universal Church. Her hierarchical structure is the apostolic structure of the universal Church. Her tradition is the tradition of the universal Church. Canonicity is not determined by recognition or non-recognition, for recognition alone does not make canonicity canonical—but rather its correspondence to the canonical tradition of the Church. Those who do not "recognize" our canonicity are only those, who—not for churchly reasons, but for earthly, temporal, and human ones—do not desire the unity of Orthodoxy in America, who do not believe in it, and who by this attitude break themselves off from the universal Tradition of the Church. We cannot wait patiently for the clarification of churchly consciousness and realization by all in America of the eternal truth of the Church.

No Supremacy of One Group

15. We confess the autocephalous Orthodox Church in America as being the unshakeable foundation of ecclesiastical unity on this continent. We are ready, together with all those who thirst for unity, to seek the best

possible ways of building our common life in love. This life—I repeat again and again—cannot be founded on the supremacy of one group over another. We are ready to review our statutes, so that inside the one church all might feel at home. In our unity there must be room for all that is permanent, eternal, and good in all the traditions of the one Orthodoxy. May our church be the inheritor of all the Orthodox riches accumulated by natives of various lands.

After my report, Archbishop Valerian, the chairman of our Canonical Department, will share with you some practical steps and measures. Autocephaly is not for us alone, but for all. God has given this gift to all, all are called to benefit by it. We call all our brethren in the faith to follow us on this joyous path!

But, of course, the success of our calling depends on each one of us—every parish, every priest, every layman! It is up to us to show not only in words, but also in deeds: our maturity, our love, our understanding. We must broaden our hearts, driving from them every narrowness, provincialism, and patience!

Let us enter with prayer on this fruitful fulfillment of the Church.

III
Letter of Patriarch Athenagoras to Patriarch Alexis

Protocol Number 7

Your Beatitude and Most Holy Alexis, Patriarch of Moscow and All Russia, most beloved and dearest brother, and co-celebrant with my humble self; We respectfully and brotherly embrace Your Beatitude in Jesus Christ and address you with the following:

1. For some time now we have been informed, by the circle of the Russian Metropolia in New York, of negotiations that have long been taking place between Your Beatitude and the Metropolia for the re-establishment of regular relations between this metropolia and the Patriarchate of Moscow.

Contacts with Moscow Welcomed

2. Our Church of Constantinople, being a mother, always pursuing peace within each of the various Orthodox churches, as well as the maintenance among them of the bond of love, has been affectionately following the brotherly efforts that have been taking place on both sides towards the restoration of regular relations, and the preservation of harmony and unity within the compound of our holy Orthodox Church, and always within the framework of the holy canons and the ecclesiastical order and practice that from long ago became law.

Autocephaly Opposed

3. While, then, we were anticipating that, consistent with the deep prudence of Your Beatitude, the negotiations that were taking place would lead towards a blessed and irenic direction, we and our Holy Synod were lately

informed, to our surprise and sorrow, in reports from our Most Reverend Archbishop of North and South America, Iakovos, that the representatives of Your Beatitude are negotiating with the representatives of the said Metropolia for the proclamation of this church as autocephalous.

4. We consider it superfluous and useless to enumerate in detail all the disastrous consequences that such a possible action by the holy Russian Church might result in. For Your Beatitude well knows what an overthrow of our ecclesiastical order, and what a more general upheaval can come about when such proclamations of autocephality are made in violation of jurisdiction, spontaneously and unilaterally, on behalf of a church, by anyone of the autocephalous churches.

Fears Upsetting Relations

5. Turning now to those Orthodox churches in "diaspora" in America, which are subject to various old-country jurisdictions, and which depend on them until there is a pan-Orthodox resolving of the matters involved, it is obvious that the proclamation of the autocephality of any one of these churches, if it is done in the manner now being planned with reference to the Metropolia, constitutes an action which is not only contrary to sacred canons which have been the order of our Orthodox Church for many centuries, but an action which, instead of furthering brotherly efforts for the re-establishment of regular relations, could become a source of problems for Orthodoxy in America. The results of these problems cannot be avoided, nor can the said Metropolia avoid becoming, in a more general sense, the object of upsetting inter-Orthodox relations.

Matter to be Postponed until Great Synod Meets

6. In these days when so many efforts are painstakingly being taken for the promotion of a sacred unity within Orthodoxy, and when lists of subjects referring to the Orthodox Church in general in the diaspora, including autocephality, are being proposed for study and for a definitive resolution by a Holy and Great Synod, we unhesitatingly believe that the plan under

consideration regarding the Metropolia, if put into effect, carries with it great danger, and will undermine the cooperative and harmonious inter-Orthodox efforts for the preparation of the Synod.

7. Your Beatitude knows better than anyone else that our primary duty and concern of late as leaders of our Church, has been to pursue with all our strength, and with every lawful and even ultimate sacrifice if necessary, the task of reconciliation, love, and peace, with all possible condescension, dispensation, and forbearance. These are imposed upon us by the mother church for the promotion and preservation of peace and unity among the autocephalous Orthodox churches.

8. Caring deeply, therefore, for the unity of our Orthodox churches, and for the unity each church displays in taking a firm step towards the Great Synod, and being convinced that Your Beatitude, most beloved as you are, is of the same opinion and intent, we write to you in accordance with the decision of our Holy Synod. And in doing so, we demand of you and of your most holy church, that after weighing the situation and the responsibilities seeming therefrom, you not allow, for the sake of the general interest, this matter to go any further, and that the actions contemplated up to now be cancelled.

Recognition Refused

9. Wishing as we do with all sincere clarity to make known to Your Beatitude in advance what the stance of our holy apostolic and patriarchal ecumenical throne will be in the event that the problem under consideration regarding Orthodoxy should confront us, we accordingly inform you in this brotherly patriarchal letter that:

10. If the holy Church of Russia, so beloved, in spite of our brotherly entreaty and recommendation, and in spite of our every hope, should proceed with the realization of the proposal now being planned to announce the autocephality of the Russian Orthodox Metropolia in America, this throne will neither recognize this action nor enroll this church in the diptychs or in the sacred catalogue of the holy Orthodox autocephalous churches.

Accordingly, we would label this church, which you would choose to proclaim autocephalous, as uncanonical. In this connection also, this throne will take any other action needed to secure canonical order.

Churches Informed

11. Moreover, we consider that we have the duty to make this matter known to our brothers in Christ the patriarchs, archbishops, and presidents of the holy Orthodox autocephalous churches, to each of which we address a copy of this patriarchal letter for their information. A copy also is being sent to the Most Reverend Archbishop Iakovos of North and South America.

12. We have addressed to Your Beatitude this decision of our Holy Synod with the hope that in this instance, any action that would disturb the calm and peace of the Church will be avoided, and we again embrace you with brotherly love and with the greatest esteem in the name of Christ the Savior who made his appearance at the River Jordan.

Your Brother in Christ
Athenagoras of Constantinople

January 8, 1970

IV
Letter of Patriarch Alexis to Patriarch Athenagoras

Your Holiness, beloved in Jesus Christ, Lord and Brother,

1. Saluting Your Holiness, very beloved in Lord, with our whole heart, and sending our brotherly greetings, we notify Your Holiness that, though we have not received your letter, number 7, of 8 January, 1970, which as an official document was sent to the heads of the local Orthodox churches and was distributed among the Orthodox and non-Orthodox Christian communities, and which we received in copies, we, after studying it thoroughly, felt it our duty to notify Your Holiness of our opinion and of that of the Holy Synod of the Russian Orthodox Church concerning the matter of the granting of autocephaly by the Moscow Patriarchate to the Russian Orthodox American Metropolitanate, a matter which is discussed in your letter. Proceeding to an account of the true state of affairs, we consider it necessary to note that Your Holiness' letter, by its form as well as by its content, provokes in us feelings of bewilderment and astonishment.

Which Canons Violated?

2. Your Holiness' letter, concerning the possible elevation of the Russian Greek Catholic Church of America to autocephaly by the Moscow Patriarchate states: "Turning now to those Orthodox churches in 'diaspora' in America, which are subject to various old country jurisdictions, and which depend on them until there is a pan-Orthodox resolving of the matters involved, it is obvious that the proclamation of the autocephaly of any one of these churches, if it is done in the manner now being planned with reference to the Metropolia, constitutes an action which is not only contrary to sacred canons which have been the order of our Orthodox Church for many centuries, but an action which, instead of furthering brotherly efforts

for the re-establishment of regular relations, could become a source of problems for Orthodoxy in America. The results of these problems cannot be avoided, nor can the said Metropolia avoid becoming, in a more general sense, the object of upsetting inter-Orthodox relations." Such an assertion is not only incomprehensible to us, but also seems somewhat strange. Why does Your Holiness consider it "superfluous and useless to enumerate . . . all disastrous consequences?" What are these "disastrous consequences"? What does "violation of jurisdiction" mentioned therein mean? If the intentions of the Russian Orthodox Church are seen by the Patriarchate of Constantinople as an "overthrow of the existing order," then why is there no indication of exactly which canons of the ecumenical or local councils or of the holy fathers would, in such a case, be violated? We would like to consider such and other similar assertions and the absence of concrete explanations as a misunderstanding, and thus we nourish the hope for a solution of the misunderstanding through the grace of God and in the Spirit of love of Christ. In connection with this, our unchangeable love and respect for you impelled us to address our brotherly explanation to Your beloved and revered Holiness.

Territorial Rights of Russian Church

3. It is well known that, during the course of many years, the Russian Orthodox Church, zealous of the glory of God and the welfare of the holy Church, directed her efforts towards the normalizing of the situation of the Orthodox Church in America.

In accord with canonical and ecclesiastical law, legitimate autocephaly may be received only from a legitimate authority. For the Russian Orthodox Greek Catholic Church of America, as the American Russian Metropolitanate is called, as also for the whole of Orthodoxy in America, such authority is the Russian Orthodox Church. No one can challenge the fact that every autocephalous church is fully empowered to give autocephaly to a part of itself.

Historical Precedents

4. Your Holiness, if we turn to history, we will see that the establishment of autocephaly has taken different forms at different times. The basis for the original formation of local churches was, partially, the political importance of cities, which was of central importance for the division of the unified Roman Empire into provinces. In this manner, the churches of Rome, Constantinople, Jerusalem, and Alexandria were constituted as patriarchates. Later, the right to ecclesiastical autocephaly was recognized by the Orthodox Church as belonging to Orthodox peoples, who, by their national development, and by the conditions of their political life, were capable of independent ecclesiastical rule. In this case, autocephaly was granted, not by an ecumenical council, but by a single local church. For instance, through the decisions of the council or synod of the Church of Constantinople, the Bulgarian Church (932, 1234, 1946), the Serbian Church (1218, 1879), the Greek Church (1850), the Romanian Church (1885), and the Albanian Church (1938) were declared autocephalous. The Georgian Church received its autocephaly in ancient times from the Church of Antioch. The churches of Poland (1948) and Czechoslovakia (1951) received their autocephaly from the Russian Church.

Origins of Orthodoxy in America

5. In discussing the question of the possibility of proclaiming the above mentioned autocephaly, we are guided by the viewpoint that the holy Orthodox Church has always considered and considers herself canonically united, based upon the firm principle of hierarchical unity and the unity of local jurisdiction, and that all believers in Christ, wherever they may be, form one Church body, headed by one hierarch, through whom they are united with the universal Church. In North America, from the very beginning, this unity was realized through the Russian Orthodox Church. It is very well known that Orthodoxy on the American continent was established, developed, and organized by the Russian Orthodox Church. The Russian Orthodox Greek Catholic American Metropolitanate is the daughter Church of the Russian Orthodox Church: in 1793—an

ecclesiastical mission; in 1858—21—vicariate in Sitka; in 1870—the diocese of the Aleutian Islands and Alaska; in 1900—the diocese of the Aleutian Islands and North America; and in 1907 "the Russian Orthodox Greek Catholic Church of North America under the jurisdiction of a hierarch of the Church of Russia." From 1794, the year of the arrival of the first missionaries from Russia, until 1921, the year marking the beginning of pluralism in church jurisdiction, the Orthodox Church in North America united all of the Orthodox in America under its hierarchical authority, without regard for their national background. This was recognized by all the local churches, including the holy Church of Constantinople presently headed by Your Holiness. For instance, His Holiness, Patriarch Joachim III, in 1912, led negotiations with the Russian Holy Synod concerning the appointment of a Greek Bishop to America. Such an appointment was supported by the Russian Orthodox Church inasmuch as it followed and met the correct canonical order. The Serbian and Syrian (Arabian) bishops were also appointed with the knowledge and concurrence of the Holy Governing Synod of Russia. However, this order, adequate to church canons and practice, was violated in 1921, when, without the knowledge and canonical approval of the Russian Orthodox Church, a Greek Archdiocese was founded in America.

Need for Autocephaly

6. Aiming at the unity of Orthodoxy, the Moscow Patriarchate is negotiating concerning the granting of autocephaly to the Russian Orthodox Greek Catholic Metropolitanate in America in the hope that this act will help in the unification of Orthodox jurisdictions in America, whose presence contradicts the nature of canonical ecclesiastical unity and can, in no way, serve as the basis of a permanent canonical structure for the Orthodox Church in America. Besides, the growth of Orthodoxy in America and its gradual transformation into the faith of native Americans emphatically demands the creation in America of an autocephalous Orthodox Church. It is the Russian Orthodox Church which must accomplish this act as the mother church, inasmuch as the jurisdiction of her bishops over

the Orthodox in America and the jurisdiction of hierarchical authority of the Russian Orthodox Church over the Orthodox episcopate of America has existed for over a hundred years and possesses the right of historical primacy. Hence, it is obvious that the granting of autocephaly to a part of some other autocephalous church in America would be a violation of the basic canonical principle of the inviolability of the rights of each autocephalous church, and would be condemned by the holy canons as a pretension to an authority not appertaining to that church.

Responsibility of Great Council Recognized

7. In Your Holiness' letter, we found references to the upcoming Great Council of the Orthodox Church as an instance having the power to regularize the canonical situation in America. Undoubtedly, the future Great Council will examine the questions being prepared by the Pan-Orthodox Conferences and will be able to examine the canonical position of all Orthodox churches in the world; but no one of us can, at this moment, say when the preparations will be finished and when the council will meet. Therefore, until that time, the holy local Orthodox churches are obliged to continue the realization of their saving mission on the basis of the Divine and holy canons and of such church practice which conforms to the canons. We consider that the best solution of the above-mentioned matter is the granting of autocephaly to the Russian Orthodox Greek Catholic Metropolitanate, which may be realized only by the mother church, that is, the Russian Orthodox Church; and we believe this will serve only to the good of holy Orthodoxy and the development of church life in the USA.

Striving for Unity

8. Your Holiness knows better than anyone else how many efforts our holy church has undertaken to preserve and strengthen peace and unity between all of the Orthodox churches. With motherly love and sorrow she observes the ecclesiastical schisms in America. Repeatedly, she has called those who have strayed away to return to the bosom of the mother church, and has addressed herself in letters to many heads of local

Orthodox churches, among whom was also Your Holiness, asking to assist her in the elimination of the schism. However, we are forced to note with sorrow that hierarchs of the holy Church of Constantinople repeatedly, willfully or unwilfully, supported the schismatics and the schism. Disregarding all of this, we persistently continued, through our sense of duty, to labor for Orthodox unity and, as a result of contacts with fully empowered representatives of the Russian Orthodox Greek Catholic Metropolitanate of America, have agreed on the manner of resuming communion and canonical relations between the mother, Russian Orthodox Church, and her daughter, the Russian Orthodox Greek Catholic Church of America, and also are considering the matter of granting her autocephaly, which in many ways will assist Orthodox unity in America.

Rights of Other Churches Respected

9. Your Holiness, in intending to grant autocephaly to the Russian Orthodox Greek Catholic Metropolitanate of America, the Moscow Patriarchate is guided by the highest principles of the good of the Church. It is not interfering in the affairs of other sister churches, having their own branches in America. It is not encroaching on their rights, which exist de facto, though uncanonically; and therefore, it is fully determined by all means to defend its rights from everything which may damage the cause of ecclesiastical justice, love, and peace, and the tasks of Orthodoxy.

Decision Taken

10. In candid clarity, informing Your beloved Holiness concerning these matters, we declare that if the Russian Orthodox Church arrives at the conviction that the Orthodox Church in America has matured sufficiently to become autocephalous and that her independence will assist her development and flowering, she will grant her autocephaly in accordance with the church canons and the historical tradition of the holy Church. We hope that the proposed establishment of autocephaly will be met with understanding by the local Orthodox churches, will assist the strengthening of

Orthodox unity on the American continent, and will serve the glory of God and the holy Church.

Other Churches Informed

11. We are addressing copies of our answer to Your Holiness' letter to the heads of the holy local Orthodox churches—for their information. Also, we express our regret that the present correspondence between the heads of two sister churches causes a certain degree of inquietude to Their Holinesses and Beatitudes, the patriarchs, metropolitans, and archbishops. However, since in the copies of Your Letter to us, addressed to them by Your Holiness, some matters of church practice are discussed which touch upon the honor of the holy Russian Church, we considered it necessary to acquaint our beloved brethren, the heads of the local Orthodox churches, with the present letter.

Embracing Your beloved Holiness, we send you our best wishes, and we remain, with constant brotherly love in Christ Jesus, our Lord,

Alexis,
Patriarch of Moscow and All Russia

Moscow, March 17, 1970.

V
Letter of Patriarch Athenagoras to Metropolitan Pimen

Protocol Number 583

Most Reverend Metropolitan Pimen,
Beloved brother in the Holy Spirit, Locum Tenens of the Patriarchal Throne of Moscow, and co-celebrant with my humble self:

May the grace and peace of God be with Your Eminence:

1. We received and read with all required attention in a meeting of our Holy Synod the letter of March 16, 1970 in which His Beatitude Alexis, the Patriarch of Moscow and All Russia, lately deceased and now of blessed memory, sent us in answer to our brotherly letter to him of January 7, 1970 with Protocol Number 7. In his letter, His Beatitude of blessed memory analyzed his reasoning and point of view, as well as that of the Holy Synod of the sister Orthodox Russian Church on what lately happened, though it should not have; that is, the matter of the granting of autocephaly, by the Patriarchate of Moscow, to the Russian Orthodox Metropolia of New York, thereby naming it "The Autocephalous Orthodox Church in America."

Letter Properly Sent

2. We were greatly surprised to be informed by the letter of the late patriarch of blessed memory that our letter to him of January 7, 1970, Protocol Number 7, did not reach his hands, and that he gained knowledge of its contents through a copy that was sent to him by someone else. Our perplexity, which bordered on anxiety, becomes all the more understandable since our letter was sent registered with a receipt of its arrival requested; and indeed, in accordance with the international practice, the mailed receipt was returned to us, bearing the arrival date (in Moscow) of January

16, 1970, as well as the signature of the receiver. In order that you may be exactly informed concerning this, we enclose herewith a photostatic copy of this receipt. We deemed this explanation essential so that your appropriate office can, insofar as it is possible, clarify this situation, which can result in serious misunderstandings. We therefore kindly request Your Eminence to inform us in due course concerning the results of the investigation that will be undertaken to clear up a matter that has also occasioned us reasonable wonder.

Disagreement Stressed

3. Coming now to the answering letter of March 16, 1970, the patriarch of late memory noted that the contents of our letter to him made him experience feelings of surprise and puzzlement. We cannot understand why this should be so; but we must confess that it was precisely his answer to our letter, and the manner in which its contents were phrased, that occasioned us and our Holy Synod the deepest sorrow.

In our letter of January 7, 1970, Protocol Number 7, we had addressed a warm brotherly recommendation that the holy Russian Church refrain from any further activities that might disturb ecclesiastical peace and harmony and bring about a condition that might overturn the established canonical order and cause a more general agitation and confusion at the expense of the unity and accord that came to pass in our holy Orthodox Church through so many efforts and sacrifices.

Though we were hoping to find on your part understanding and a positive response to this brotherly request of ours, we must now conclude, in spite of our every hope and expectation, that the Russian Orthodox Church, unfortunately, persists in her incorrect stand, continuing further with her plans for the realization of this autocephaly—even to the point of proclaiming it.

And though your church calls in support of her activities the need to neutralize the irregularities existing in the relations between the church and her communities, and among the communities themselves, as well as her supposed right to grant the autocephaly in question—yet these explanations and arguments which are brought forth are not at all convincing regarding the canonical regularity of the undertaken venture.

Other Unspecified Action Supported

4. First of all, in reference to the irregularities which you claim exist between the relations of the Russian communities and the Russian Church, and among these communities themselves, there is no reason at all, and no need whatsoever, to have the neutralization of such a situation pursued with another, even greater anomaly, which seriously shakes the governing system of the entire Orthodox Church—especially since there exist other forms of administrative action that the sister holy Russian Church could turn to. As for her alleged right, as well as that of any other autocephalous Orthodox church, to grant the status of autocephaly to another church—such a right does not correspond either to canonical requirements or to existing practices within the Church.

Grant of Autocephaly Reserved to Entire Church

5. Certainly and incontrovertibly, and in accordance with the canonical conception of the Church, the concept behind the granting of autocephaly belongs to the domain of canonical authority. However, what is the legal principle underlying the granting of autocephaly? What are its required conditions and presuppositions?

Specific canons exactly characterizing autocephaly are not to be found in ecclesiastical legislation. However, certain general guidelines and provisions, relative to autocephaly, may be gathered from the basic principles of such legislation. These, moreover, are to be found clearly stamped in the canonical conscience of the Church and in its history, and have been repeatedly expressed, and are distinctly printed in the tomes that were published on the occasions of the founding of the newer local autocephalous churches.

From these basic and valid sources, and also from the very meaning of autocephaly itself as an ecclesiastical act, from which certain changes result relative to ecclesiastical boundaries and to the rise of new jurisdictional and administrative powers that bring about a new order in the Orthodox Church as a whole—it may be concluded that the granting of autocephaly is a right belonging to the Church as a whole, and cannot at all be considered a right of "each autocephalous church," as is stated in the letter of Patriarch Alexis of blessed memory.

Ecumenical Councils Define Independence of Churches

6. Thus the First Ecumenical Council of Nicaea put the stamp of approval on the old custom of considering as churches the regional provinces, thereby validating the existence of the churches of Rome, Alexandria, Antioch and Jerusalem (Canons 6 and 7). The Second Ecumenical Council of Constantinople determined the independence of the exarchs of the dioceses of Asia, Pontus, and Thrace (Canon 2). The Third Ecumenical Council of Ephesus ruled definitively on the differences that existed between the bishops of the Churches of Antioch and of Cyprus, and in so doing made secure the autocephaly of the Church of Cyprus (Canon 8). The Fourth Ecumenical Council of Chalcedon regulated anew the status of the Dioceses of Asia, Pontus, and Thrace, referred to above and made them dependent on the throne of Constantinople (Canon 28): at this Fourth Council also were finally resolved the differences between Antioch and Jerusalem concerning their boundaries. The Fifth-Sixth Ecumenical Council (the Trullo or Dome Council) also occupied itself with boundary jurisdictions, which constitutes another proof that the Ecumenical Councils considered that judgement concerning autocephaly was within their jurisdiction and did not lie outside of their competence.

Unconfirmed Autocephalies Disappeared

7. And the necessity of a common decision concerning autocephaly is supported by history, which reveals that autocephalous churches which did not obtain ecumenical validation and assurance—like the Church of Carthage, the Church of Mediolana (Milan), the Church of Lyons, the Church of Justiniana Prima, the Church of Ochrid, the Church of Trnovo, the Church of Ipek, and the Church of Iberia, as well as some others in this

category—lost their autocephaly with the passage of time. On the other hand, those churches which did have ecumenical recognition of their autocephaly, even though they underwent many trials, and almost came to the point of dissolution, remained as autocephalous churches and obtained a new lease on life, as did the churches of Cyprus, Jerusalem, Antioch, and Alexandria. This same stamp of validity by an ecumenical synod is needed also, for their definitive and continuing autocephalous existence, by the newer autocephalous churches because of the unfavorable circumstances in which they may at times find themselves. These include the churches to which the holy apostolic and patriarchal ecumenical throne gave the stamp of autocephaly with the approval of the other Orthodox churches.

Primacy of Constantinople

8. The Ecumenical Patriarchate could do this because of its attribute as the mother church and its status as the "first among equals" in reference to the other autocephalous Orthodox churches, and because it is at the center of the internal unity of the entire Orthodox Church, helping the other churches in their needs—a duty that derives from its presiding and excelling position within the family of the Orthodox churches.

Rights of Local Churches Limited

9. According to the above, therefore, the final and definitive decisions concerning autocephaly belong to a synod representing more generally the entirety of the local autocephalous Orthodox churches, and especially to an ecumenical synod. Such decisions cannot be made by each local autocephalous church or by a local synod of a church from which a diocese is requesting autocephaly. Such a local synod has the right only to receive the first petitions for autocephaly and to form an opinion as to whether or not the reasons preferred for autocephaly are justified in accordance with the spirit of the 34th Apostolic Canon.

So much for the principles underlying the right to grant autocephaly.

Condition for Autocephaly

10. We come now to the conditions required for the good and proper proclamation of autocephaly. We may surmise from history and from the well imprinted conscience of the Church that the announcement of autocephaly, which aims towards the fulfillment of clearly ecclesiastical needs, basically took into account neither the apostolicity of the see, nor exclusively the prestige of the nation involved, nor the principle that has taken on a quasi-canonical form to the effect that "ecclesiastical affairs should change in accordance with political events." Such contentions, at least in part, were the basis for the proclamation of the autocephaly of the newer Orthodox churches in areas that gained national independence, and were largely inhabited by Orthodox peoples. The expressed opinion of the Christian faithful, of both the clergy and the laity, has always been decisively imposed on ecclesiastical matters. But such expressed opinion has been considered first and foremost as foundational and essential to the factors of autocephaly if it is imprinted in an official synodical act, containing the petition and the stated reasons for the desired independence, concurred in by the entire hierarchy of the local church, without which any move on the part of the laity, or by whoever represents the governing body of the church, would constitute an attempt at usurpation. That is why both the judgement of the mother church, and, finally, the definitive decision of the entire Church, are essential, in accordance with the above, for the canonical establishing of autocephaly, as would be the case with any other ecclesiastical act of the same type and nature.

Churches not to Act Outside of their Limits

11. If, according to the above, it is uncanonical for a local autocephalous church to declare autocephalous a branch church detached from its ecclesiastical realm, not only not comprising a component part of it, but also not having had a canonical relation to it or dependence on it—then how much more uncanonical would be such a declaration of autocephaly in reference to a church completely outside of your boundaries. Such an effort and act would entirely exceed your jurisdiction, as it is clearly ordered in

the divine and sacred canons. That is why the holy apostles and fathers of the Church took great care later to bring about a condition whereby irenic relations would prevail among the various churches. The apostles ordered that "no bishop be permitted to pass over into the province of another" (Apostolic Canons 14 and 34); while the holy fathers assembled at the First Ecumenical Council of Nicaea legislated that "the old customs be kept" and that "each throne rule over the provinces belonging to it" (Canons 6 and 7). Finally, according to Zonaras, the holy fathers who convened at the Second Ecumenical Council of Constantinople ruled that a bishop should not invade the province of another bishop by exceeding his jurisdiction, that is, going beyond the province belonging to him, and entering the territories of churches beyond his own boundaries, which are outside of the defined limits.

Russian Church Oversteps Rights

12. These are the divine and sacred canons on which from the beginning the status of the Church has been based, and by which the ruling system of the Church has been strengthened; and the canonical rights of the churches secured, and scandals dispersed. But the holy Russian Church, not considering these things at all, unfortunately proceeded beyond her jurisdiction with a series of acts and moves that are characteristic of what she was bold enough to do during these last years in Poland and Czechoslovakia, and of what she is now doing in America.

The Case of Poland

13. Having ignored the previous formation of an Autocephalous Orthodox Church in the state of Poland through the Patriarchal and Synodical Tomos of November 13, 1924, issued under the late Ecumenical Patriarch Gregory VII of blessed memory—a decision based on an appropriately supporting tomos—and having ignored also the spirit of love and brotherly communal unity expressed to the entire Church by all other autocephalous Orthodox churches which willingly and unhesitatingly recognized what had been done by the Ecumenical Patriarchate—the Russian Orthodox Church, by

an act of her Holy Synod of June 22, 1948, granted to the Church of Poland a new autocephaly. And this act of the Russian Orthodox Church was done by exceeding her jurisdictional rights, since after the end of World War II, the territories of Ukraine and Byelorussia, which previously belonged to the Church of Poland, were detached from this church; and the areas included in these detached churches reaching Westward as far the Baltic Sea, and being from times past outside the boundaries of the Patriarchate of Moscow, are under the jurisdiction of the ecumenical patriarchal throne.

The Case of Czechoslovakia

14. Unsupportedly and unjustifiably and with transgression of jurisdiction the Russian Orthodox likewise interfered in the ecclesiastical affairs of the Orthodox Church in Czechoslovakia, the territory of which canonically and historically has belonged to the Ecumenical Patriarchate, and was organized by the throne of Constantinople. From the beginning, the Russian Orthodox Church brought pressure to bear on the late Archbishop Sabbatios of Prague and All Czechoslovakia, arbitrarily sending to that archdiocese an exarch, and continuing to the point of finally granting it an autocephaly which was uncanonical and unfounded—and this, again, was done in order to overturn the status of autonomy given to the Czechoslovakian Church by the ecumenical throne from the year 1923, a status recognized as canonical by the local sister Orthodox autocephalous churches.

Russian Usurpation in America

15. Today, the Russian Orthodox Church, proceeding on its uncanonical course, is interfering in American ecclesiastical affairs, and invoking her so-called maternal bond with the Orthodox in America deriving from the mission she once sent to the Aleutian Islands and to Alaska, considers herself as the only legal authority for the "Orthodox Greek Catholic Church of America" as she terms the Russian Metropolia which is under the Most Reverend Metropolitan Ireney. And, indeed, she considers herself as being

the only legal authority "for all Orthodoxy in America," on the basis of which she feels justified in administering American ecclesiastical matters according to her judgment, deeming the analogous activities of every other autocephalous church in America as a trespass against the basic canonical principles. And in so doing she ignores the unshakable rights of each autocephalous church by usurping an authority not belonging to her, which is an act condemned by the holy canons.

No Exclusive Rights on Orthodox Diaspora in America

16. But the fact that the original foreign mission in the Aleutian Islands and in the most westward Alaskan corner of the Western Hemisphere comprised a branch of the Russian Empire at that time and until 1867, when these territories were sold to the United States for a monetary sum; as well as the fact that in later years the Russian Church was engaged in propagandistic and proselytizing activities primarily directed towards the Slavic Uniates who had emigrated to America from Galicia and Hungary—obviously in no way gives to the Russian Orthodox Church the right, which she claims, of having an exclusive jurisdiction in America. From the beginning of the second half of the past 19th century, when the Russian Orthodox began moving southward from the northernmost places towards the industrial centers of the continental United States, and especially from the first decades of the present 20th century, when large masses of Orthodox faithful from all the countries where they lived emigrated to the New World—from then on were formed the now existing Orthodox jurisdictions in America.

Irregularly Overlapping Jurisdiction

17. This constitutes a new phenomenon in the history of the Orthodox Church in America, and a new form of the "diaspora," making for an extraordinary and irregular situation, allowing the co-existence of many hierarchs with the same rank who exercise ecclesiastical jurisdiction over their own people, contrary to explicit canonical orders such as that of the

21st Canon of the Fourth Ecumenical Council of Chalcedon specifying that "two metropolitans not be in the same province."

Waiting for the Great Synod

18. Even though this situation is contrary to the fundamental dogmatic principle of Orthodox ecclesiology, which is the basis of the ecclesiastical organization that underlies the unity of all the faithful who live in the same place in one ecclesiastical organism under the leadership of one bishop, thus manifesting the unity of those new people of God, according to which "there is neither Greek nor Jew ... but Christ is all and in all" (Col 3.2); and even though this situation offends the government and the sacred legislation of the Church—it is nevertheless deemed and confronted by this holy, apostolic, and patriarchal throne as constituting an extraordinary phenomenon, self-peculiar and temporary. We therefore face this situation mindful that it is one brought about by extreme necessity (*oikonomia*); and we face it also with condescension and toleration, in order to serve the securing and the promotion of peace and unity among the sister Orthodox Churches until such a time as this subject [may] be appropriately examined and definitely solved by the future Holy and Great Synod of the Orthodox churches, to which it has already been referred for a pan-Orthodox decision. For this reason, we are at a loss to explain the haste shown by the Russian Orthodox Church in announcing as autocephalous a relatively small section of the Russian Orthodox diaspora in America, and conferring upon this church a title disproportionate with reality, after having only recently recognized her jurisdiction.

Primacy of Constantinople over Russia since 1591

19. Therefore, we think it opportune and essential, for the fulfillment of our debt and responsibility towards the entire Orthodox Church, to urge once again the holy Russian Orthodox Church, in a brotherly way, to refrain from any further action in this matter, reminding her that her boundaries are defined, as is also the scope of her jurisdiction, and cannot be extended beyond what was allotted to her by the Golden Seal Certificate

of ecumenical patriarch Jeremiah II in the year 1591. The Russian Orthodox Church owes her independent existence to this document, as well as to the Newer Tome of February, 1593 issued by this same ecumenical patriarch Jeremiah II. This Newer Tome announces to the Russians the decisions, relative to the recently established Patriarchate of Moscow, that were made at the Great local Synod of Constantinople which was participated in by Patriarch Meletios of Alexandria, who also represented the absent Patriarch Joachim of Antioch, and also by Patriarch Sophronios of Jerusalem and seventy-six other hierarchs. Concerning the patriarch of Moscow, it was ordered that "he be counted among the other patriarchs and his order in the patriarchal ranks and the commemoration of his name in the services come after that of the patriarch of Jerusalem; and that he be obliged to commemorate the name of the ecumenical patriarch, as well as the names of the other patriarchs, but always considering as his head and first in rank, as do the other patriarchs, the apostolic throne of Constantinople." The original of this Newer Tome bears the signature and the waxen imprints of the seals of the patriarchs of Constantinople, Alexandria and Jerusalem, and up to the end of the last century it was kept in the collection of manuscripts of the Moscow Synodical Library.

No Decision Valid before Great Council

20. We sincerely hope that the sister Russian Orthodox Church, retaining the canonical order and having in mind and desiring the peace of the Church, will not only proceed no further in this matter now under judgment, but will also make every effort to dispel the confusion it has caused in reference to canonicity.

If, however, in spite of our hope, the Russian Orthodox Church will want to persist in her views and act in a way that would oppose a pan-Orthodox determination of this question by a future Holy and Great Synod of the Eastern Orthodox Church, we hereby declare that this apostolic and patriarchal ecumenical throne will of necessity find itself obligated, for the good and the interest of the entire Church, to consider any action taken in this matter as not having been done. We so declare since we consider as valid only a pan-Orthodox decision concerning the solution of the entire subject of the Orthodox in the "diaspora."

We thus reply, with fraternal duty, to the letters of March 17, 1970 which we received from the most holy Russian Church, and with humility of heart we entreat the God and Father of peace to direct her desires on this question towards activities worthy of her glorious past and her honorable traditions, for the safeguarding of the canonical order and the sacred legislation of our fathers.

We pray that our Lord may grant peace to his holy Church, and that the years he bestows on Your Eminence be many, healthful, and salutary.

With brotherly and the highest esteem,
Athenagoras of Constantinople

June 24, 1970

VI

Letter of Metropolitan Pimen to Patriarch Athenagoras

August 11, 1970
No. 1505
Moscow

To His Holiness the Most Holy Athenagoras,
Archbishop of Constantinople-New Rome, ecumenical patriarch:

Your Holiness, beloved in our Lord, Most Holy Master:

1. I received Your Holiness' letter of 24 June, 1970, and it was the object of an attentive scrutiny at the meeting of the Holy Synod of our holy church on 30 June, 1970. The Holy Synod, under my chairmanship, expressed its position on the substance of the problem touched upon in Your Holiness' letter, and it is my duty to inform Your Holiness and the Holy Synod of the Constantinopolitan Church of our answer to your above-mentioned Letter.

Delay Explained

2. First, concerning the delay in receiving Your Holiness' letter of 8 January, 1970. As a result of inquiries concerning this matter, it was found that your above-mentioned letter was retained by His Holiness, Patriarch Alexis, together with a multitude of festal greetings.

Explanation Needed

3. Inasmuch as Your Holiness' letter contains the reactions of the holy Constantinopolitan Church to a very important event—the inception of a young autocephalous Orthodox Church in America, and this reaction, to our great sorrow, bears witness to a marked difference in this and several

other incidental questions between members of the one and the same body, which is the holy Catholic Orthodox Church, that, in our aspiration to further the preservation of a unity of spirit in a union of peace, in all humility and love, we consider it necessary to give as detailed as possible an answer to all questions set before us in Your Holiness' letter, and to state our point of view concerning all the problems which, in our opinion, require it.

Christ, Only Head

4. Insofar as our Lord has set us to preserve the dignity of the holy Church of Russia, we consider it necessary, first of all, to state our judgement concerning that section in Your Holiness' letter in which the limits of the jurisdiction of the Moscow Patriarchate are discussed, as in their own time they were delineated by the most revered, most memorable, most holy, and most blessed patriarchs of Constantinople, Alexandria, Antioch, and Jerusalem together with the holy council of the Eastern bishops, at the establishment of a patriarchate in the great imperial city of Moscow. In your letter Your Holiness calls the Church of Russia not to transgress the limits, delineated for her by the Patriarchal Chrysobull of the Most Holy Patriarch of Constantinople, Jeremias II, to whom, as you assert, our holy Russian Church is indebted for her independent status. We believe that, for her existence, our holy Russian Church is indebted to our Great High Priest, our Lord Jesus Christ, who led the greater and lesser peoples inhabiting the land of our fathers to the knowledge of the saving light of Christ's truth by means of the saving mission of a multitude of bishops, priests, and monks. To him, the Author of our life and Finisher of our faith (Heb 12.2), is the holy Russian Church indebted for her growth, strengthening, and, with the passage of time, her independence. To him be the glory, honor and worship unto ages of ages.

Russian Autocephaly since 1448

5. As far as the beginning of the independent existence of the Russian Church is concerned, this matter is completely clear and was witnessed

to by His Eminence the memorable Archbishop Germanos of Thyateira, the representative of the patriarchal throne of Constantinople, and the representatives of other autocephalous sister churches, when in 1948 in Moscow our holy Russian Church solemnly celebrated the 500th anniversary of its autocephaly. It was with true joy that our holy church welcomed the representative of the most holy patriarch of Constantinople, His Eminence, the most memorable Archbishop Germanos of Thyateira and heard the greeting, full of love, which he addressed to our Holy Council and to the other revered participants of the jubilee celebration in the name of the most holy patriarch and the Holy Synod of the holy Church of Constantinople.

Elevation to Patriarchate in 1589

6. Now, concerning the limits of the Russian Church and the area of her jurisdiction which are spoken of in Your Holiness' letter: As is well known, on January 26, 1589, the primate of the Russian Church, the Metropolitan of Moscow, Job, of blessed memory, was elevated in Moscow to the dignity of "Most Holy Patriarch of Moscow," in which elevation His Holiness Jeremias II Patriarch of Constantinople took part.

On May 8, 1590, the Most Holy and Blessed Patriarchs, Jeremias II of Constantinople, Joachim VI of Antioch and Sophronius of Jerusalem (the throne of the patriarch of Alexandria being at that time vacant), as well as seventy-nine other hierarchs of the Holy Orthodox Church abiding in the East signed the tome, which was delivered to Moscow in 1591 by Metropolitan Dionysius Rhalles. In 1593, Patriarch Meletius Pegas of Alexandria added his signature. In this Tome it is stated that "the archbishop of Moscow, Lord Job, will be the fifth patriarch and will have the dignity and honor of a patriarch and will be joined to and equal to the other patriarchs for all ages ... and in the first place we assert and regularly confirm that the above-mentioned Lord Job is established and named patriarch of Moscow ... so that the newly-elevated patriarch of Moscow, Lord Job, has the title of patriarch and is joined to the other patriarchs and is ranked and commemorated after the patriarch of Jerusalem. He must commemorate our name and the names of the other patriarchs, also he must recognize the first place and primacy of the apostolic throne of Constantinople, as do the other patriarchs. We order and proclaim that this boon and patriarchal honor and title will be known and constant, given at the present time not only to the patriarch of Moscow, Lord Job, but also that every primate who will be appointed after him by the synod of Moscow should be called patriarch according to the order and example extant and set by the patriarch of Moscow, Lord Job, beloved brother in the Holy Spirit and concelebrant of our humility."

"Patriarch of Northern Countries"

7. Thus, it is obvious that the jurisdiction of the patriarch of Moscow, if, as we said, we take it in the context of the above-cited tome, has the same attributes and limits as those of the first four Eastern patriarchs. It is self-evident that our holy Russian Church had to give due respect and honor to the other patriarchal sees, among which, after the Great Schism of churches, in conformity with the canons and tradition, the throne of Constantinople ranks first; the latter, of course, possesses no elements of power over the Russian Church. As far as the boundaries of the Moscow Patriarchate are concerned. the very title given to His Holiness, Patriarch Job, speaks of them—"Patriarch of Moscow and all Russia, and all northern countries."

Practice of Autocephaly Fully Defined

8. A large part of Your Holiness' letter deals with the exposition of the problem of autocephaly from the point of view of church canons and practice. Your Holiness touches upon a truly relevant matter, which concerns the life of the Orthodox Church in its entirety; and we consider it extremely important to have a completely impartial discussion of the issue, so that Orthodox harmony would not be shattered by differences in its understanding.

Your Holiness notes in your letter that, in ecclesiastical law, there is no exact definition of autocephaly. Your Holiness is correct, in the sense that there is no definition in which the holy canons and the practice of holy Orthodoxy on this issue would be presented systematically. We have the hope that our Orthodox Church will in time, as the Lord pleases, produce such a definition together with others. For as Your Holiness knows, the representatives of the local churches, gathered together in the fall of 1961 on the Island of Rhodes, entered the matter of the codification of the holy canons and canonical procedures (III.A) and the question of autocephaly and autonomy in the Orthodox Church (IV.E) into the agenda of the future Orthodox Pro-Synod or Council. However, the absence at the present time of a systematic and precise legislation on autocephaly, as well as on many other canonical questions, does not prevent the holy Orthodox Church as a whole and her local parts from performing their saving mission, already in progress for almost 2000 years, enlightening the whole world with the light of Christ's truth and regenerating innumerable generations of various nations and tongues inhabiting the earth in prior times and filling it at present to life with Christ.

We assert that the divine canons and the practice of the holy Orthodox Church give sufficient evidence to consider the Orthodox teaching concerning autocephaly as fully defined.

Peripheral Concern by Ecumenical Councils

9. Let us turn to the main underlying question: which is the legal authority, granting autocephaly? In Your Holiness' letter, there is the assertion that the granting of autocephaly belongs exclusively to the competence of the entire Catholic Orthodox Church and cannot be considered as the right of an individual autocephalous church. In following passages of Your Holiness' letter it appears clearly that in speaking of the competence in this matter of the Catholic Orthodox Church, you have in mind the ecumenical eouncils, which, as is sufficiently well known, never considered the problems of autocephaly as a whole. The point was taken for granted: no one ever challenged, for instance, the dignity of the churches of Rome, Alexandria, or Antioch (I Ecumenical Council, Canon 6). The decisions concerned disputed matters arising between autocephalous churches, as

well as new issues, which arose from the life of the Orthodox Church. As is known, the fathers of the First Ecumenical Council in their holy canons never mention the bishop of Constantinople, whose territory was under the jurisdiction of the metropolitan of Heraclea. However, the fathers of the Second Ecumenical Council decided on raising the rank of the bishop of Constantinople in the diptychs[2] in view of the fact that his see was located in the new capital of the empire. It is this factor (that Constantinople was the capital) which determined their decision, a factor which was later suppressed and which does not exist today, by will of divine providence, as all things change upon earth. This matter was until then an unknown occurrence, and for this reason the fathers of the council occupied themselves with it. However, in Your Holiness' letter there appeared a new assertion, hitherto unknown in the life of the Orthodox Church, to wit: that those local churches whose autocephaly was confirmed by the ecumenical councils, though undergoing many trials, were preserved, while those local churches whose autocephaly did not have such a confirmation were with the passing of time abolished. And further, there follows a no less astonishing conclusion that the newest autocephalous churches are in need of such confirmation by an ecumenical council for a final and inviolable confirmation of their existence: your letter implies that autocephalies granted by the most holy Patriarchate of Constantinople, are in this situation (i.e., need confirmation by an ecumenical council—*Ed.*).

Ecumenical Councils Respected Tradition

10. There cannot be any doubt that an ecumenical council extends its competence upon matters of autocephaly, as well as any and all matters and questions which exist in the Catholic Orthodox Church at the moment when an ecumenical council is called. However, according to the holy canons, including many of those mentioned in Your Holiness' letter, the fathers of the ecumenical councils carefully maintained the ancient traditions and privileges of the already existing autocephalous churches, and thus were

---

[2]Diptychs: listing of primates by rank and seniority for commemoration at the liturgy. —*Ed.*

concerned in their judgments only with those questions which, as controversial or arising out of the very life of the Church, were set before their divinely inspired scrutiny. For this reason, for instance, the fathers of the First Ecumenical Council in Nicaea, Canon 6, speaking of the privileges of the bishop of Alexandria over Egypt, Libya, and Pentapolis, refer to the identical privileges of the Roman bishop in his territory as similar to the way which "in Antioch and in other regions, the privileges of the churches are preserved." From this canon it follows that for the fathers of the council there was no necessity to list by name the "autocephalous churches" (as we call them today), which existed at that time in various provinces; this should have been done, however, if there was a need for their confirmation on the part of the ecumenical council which was the first in the history of Christ's Church. Also, the fathers of the Second Ecumenical Council in Constantinople, in Canon 2, do not list all the then existing independent churches. And even the fathers of the Sixth Ecumenical Council, in Canon 36, in which is found the diptych of the Eastern patriarchs, fail to mention, for instance, the Church of Cyprus and the Church of Iberia (Georgia), whose independence, incidentally, was established by her mother church of Antioch in 467 (cf. the commentary by Balsamon on Canon 2 of the Second Ecumenical Council), was recognized by the Church of Constantinople, and exists today; though in Your Holiness' letter, for some unknown reason, this ancient Orthodox Church is spoken of as if it were abolished. In view of this, one can obviously recognize that the ecumenical councils did not occupy themselves specifically with confirming the existence of autocephalous churches.

Autocephalies Established and Suppressed

11. It is obvious that there is no greater disappointment for us than that the ecumenical councils have not met for almost 1200 years. However, it would be impossible to suppose that this fact, which is due to historical reasons, could prevent the normal continuity of holy Orthodoxy, inasmuch as the head of the Church is our Lord himself, Jesus Christ. In fact, from the time of the eighth century (the time of the last, Seventh Ecumenical Council

in Nicaea) new and vast territories on earth have become territories of new local churches. Many peoples, existing in the darkness of paganism at the time of the Seventh Ecumenical Council, have found faith in Christ and have become fervent Christians. And we well know that this last circumstance influenced the history of these peoples and the development of their culture and civilization. And it was natural and inarguable that at the proper, God-ordained time new independent churches were established by the lawful canonical authority; in no way did this development transgress the unity of holy Orthodoxy. Some of these churches, in view of well-known circumstances, no longer have an independent existence; but it is painful to recall that some autocephalous churches were abolished as a result of unbrotherly interference by neighboring local autocephalous churches which contributed to their abolition. But some of the abolished churches were reborn, such as, for instance, the Church of Trnovo, also mentioned by you, which exists today as the "Bulgarian Church."

Authority of Council Recognized

12. Of course, an ecumenical council, the convocation of which is now planned by the entire Orthodox community, and which will gather together all Orthodox hierarchs of the world, will have to include in its agenda the listing of autocephalous Orthodox churches as they will exist at that time. However, it would be inconsistent with either the sacred canons or the Church's tradition and life to think that the forthcoming ecumenical council will be obligated to confirm the rights and the existence of already existing autocephalous Orthodox churches.

Mother Churches Grant Autocephaly

13. At this point it seems appropriate to return to the problem of defining the lawful authority, empowered to grant autocephaly. We assert that, besides an ecumenical council, which is a rare and extraordinary occurrence in the life of the holy Orthodox Church, the usual factor in the granting of autocephaly is the will of the episcopate of the already existing autocephalous Orthodox churches. Naturally, the competence of a council

of bishops of an autocephalous Orthodox church is limited to the territory of this local church. To dispute this right of autocephalous churches is to deny their autocephaly, i.e., calling them in name autocephalous, while considering them in fact autonomous, which would appear to be, in view of certain claims to be the world center of the Church in the East, a non-Orthodox tendency, subverting the order according to which a bishop of any, even the highest, rank is forbidden to interfere in ecclesiastical provinces which are not his own. The council of a local church can, when need arises, proclaim the new autocephaly of a part of its own local church. This assertion is based on, and explained in, the sacred canons, which set no limitations to rights of local councils of autocephalous provinces (concerning local councils, see the decrees of the First Ecumenical Council in Nicaea; Canon 2 of the Second Ecumenical Council, and others). It is also confirmed by the age-long practice of autocephalous Orthodox churches, which grant autocephaly to their parts, whenever ecclesiastical necessity arises. Examples of the latter are known to all from the lives of the local churches of Constantinople, Antioch, and Russia.

Constantinople: Primacy of Honor Only

14. The assertion in Your Holiness' letter, that the council of an autocephalous mother church has only the right to receive the first petitions from those parts of the local church which desire to become independent, and to express solely its conclusion in this matter, appears extremely strange to us and inconsistent with the laws and practice laid down by the Church. We understand the reason why Your Holiness' letter makes this affirmation. Later in the letter, there exists an assertion of primacy and supremacy of the Patriarchate of Constantinople over all the rest of the local Orthodox churches. It is wholly unpleasant for us to return to this matter, because both the late Most Holy Patriarch Alexis of blessed memory and his predecessors wrote repeated letters on this subject to the primates of the holy Church of Constantinople. But we cannot avoid in connection with the aforementioned assertion of Your Holiness' letter, to declare again, clearly and categorically, that the primacy of honor, which traditionally

belongs to the throne of the Church of Constantinople, does not give her any basis for asserting a position of power. We remember the precept of the holy fathers of the Third Ecumenical Council in Ephesus, who wrote in their Canon 8: "Let the vanities of worldly power not be brought in under pretext of sacred office; and let us not lose, without knowing it, little by little, the freedom which Our Lord Jesus Christ, the Deliverer of all men, hath given us by his own blood." In addition, we consider that the center of the internal unity of autocephalous Orthodox churches, which in Your Holiness' letter is identified with the most holy Church of Constantinople, is also to be found in our Lord, Jesus Christ. We do not consider that the revered throne of the Patriarchate of Constantinople is an indispensable mediator between autocephalous Orthodox churches in their needs, as again is asserted in your letter; but in accordance with the universal experience of the Church, we witness that each holy local church must exercise mediation for the alleviation of church needs, if it has the possibility of doing so.

Jerusalem, the Only Universal Mother Church

15. Having accepted the light of faith in Christ from the shores of the Bosporus, we revere the Church of Constantinople as our mother church, but to other churches, which did not originate from Constantinople, she is not the mother church. To call her "mother" is to contradict the ancient church tradition, which is expounded in the holy hymn of St John Damascene: "Rejoice holy Zion, mother of churches, the dwelling of God."

Credentials for Autocephaly

16. Now, concerning factors in the autocephaly: we are totally in agreement with Your Holiness that the granting of autocephaly must have as its goal the satisfaction of purely ecclesiastical needs. And during the centuries, certain conditions have been worked out, which an autocephalous Orthodox church must fulfill. Such a church, in the first place, must have a sufficient number of bishops so that she can independently consecrate her own bishops (though as we know, there are exceptions to this condition). Such a

church must have a sufficient number of priests so that the witness and the services of the Church can be adequately performed. She must also have a sufficient flock, so that her material needs can be supplied. Usual factors in autocephaly are also partially found in the distinctiveness of peoples and in coordination with civil government. However, the last principle is not fundamental, for in a single centralized state such as Byzantium there were several patriarchates, autocephalous churches. At the same time, an indispensable factor, as is also asserted in Your Holiness' letter, is the expressed opinion of the Christian fullness, e.g., the bishops, clergy, and laity, who must feel that independence is necessary for the further successful developments of their Church. There are sufficient examples of this in the history of Orthodoxy, and they are known to all.

Unity of Orthodoxy in America before 1921

17. And we assert that the Russian Orthodox Greek Catholic Church in North America has fulfilled all these requirements and conditions in full, in connection with which, her mother church, the Patriarchate of Moscow, granted this holy church autocephaly, which act was expressed in the Patriarchal and Synodal Tomos of 10 April, 1970. The right of the Holy Council of the Patriarchate of Moscow to perform the above-mentioned act, rests on the undisputed fact that the Russian Orthodox Greek Catholic Church of North America is the child and branch of the Moscow Patriarchate. And, though the missionary and enlightening work of the holy Russian Church in North America is strangely evaluated in Your Holiness' letter (in particular, to our amazement, it is considered as propaganda and proselytism, in reference to the pastoral care for the Slavs, former Uniates, who returned to Orthodoxy), the unalterable fact remains that, until the arbitrary establishment by the throne of Constantinople of its own archdiocese in North America in 1921, an act which we have already mentioned in our last letter to Your Holiness, and which was in absolute violation of the sacred canons (Apostolic Canon 34, Carthage 131, Fourth Ecumenical Council 17, Sixth Ecumenical Council 25), strict canonical order was followed on this continent under the hierarchical leadership of the Church of

Russia. This order was challenged by no one, and was recognized by all the local Orthodox churches, including the Church of Constantinople.

Rights of Moscow in America

18. The reasons for granting autocephaly to the Russian Orthodox Greek Catholic Church of North America have already been stated by us in the circular letter of 22 June, 1970.

In our opinion, the assertions in Your Holiness' letter that the Russian Orthodox Greek Catholic Church of North America is an ecclesiastical province separated from the mother church of Russia, that it does not form an integral part of the Moscow Patriarchate, and that it has had no canonical relationships or subordination to it whatsoever, does not support your negative position with respect to this autocephaly. Any unprejudiced person is able to see that this assertion, astounding to us, is baseless.

So much for that which concerns the Autocephaly of the Russian Orthodox Greek Catholic Church of North America.

Constantinople Transgressed Canons in Poland

19. In all frankness, we must further tell Your Holiness that we reject the accusation, found in Your Holiness' letter, that our holy church has reduced to nothing the sacred and holy canons, and that, overstepping her jurisdiction, granted autocephaly to the Orthodox Church of Poland (1948) and the Orthodox Church of Czechoslovakia (1951). We do not consider it necessary to return again to the matter of the anticanonical interference by the throne of Constantinople in the affairs of the autonomous Orthodox Church in Poland, which was under the jurisdiction of the holy Church of Russia—a transgression of the sacred and holy canons committed during the time of one of Your Holiness' predecessors, the Most Holy Patriarch Gregory VII. The Most Holy Patriarch Tikhon and his successors to the throne of the Patriarchate of Moscow, have witnessed substantially and authoritatively on this matter, and their letters are undoubtedly preserved in the archives of the Patriarchate of Constantinople. However, what plunged us into sorrow is that the natural concern and duty of the Russian

mother church about the normalization and development of the life of her daughter Orthodox Church of Poland after the Second World War, has received in Your Holiness' letter an evaluation which is far from objectivity and truth. And further, the development of Orthodox church life in the lands of the Polish state, realized for the glory of God and the salvation of people by the Orthodox Polish Church, was, without any canonical or historical basis, declared in Your Holiness' letter as the reason for the extension over the Polish Church of partial jurisdiction by the holy throne of the Patriarchate of Constantinople. It is well known that the lands covered by the jurisdiction of the autocephalous Orthodox Church of Poland do not belong to the spiritual heritage of the Patriarchal throne of Constantinople. For centuries they were under the hierarchical leadership of our holy Church of Russia, and in the past this fact was never challenged by Your Holiness' throne. Only in the past decades, the sacred canons were trespassed, due to a desire to spread power beyond the boundaries given by God.

The Case of Czechoslovakia

20. We are amazed in the extreme at the accusation, contained in Your Holiness' letter, against the holy Russian Church concerning the arrangement by her of Orthodox church matters in the territory of the state of Czechoslovakia, in which our church became involved during the post-war period. We decidedly reject the assertion that our holy Russian Orthodox Church interfered in the affairs of the Orthodox Church of Czechoslovakia, which purportedly was in the jurisdiction of the patriarchal throne of Constantinople. We also reject the totally astonishing assertion, according to which some kind of pressure was placed by us upon the late Archbishop Sabbatius. We cannot accept the blame for what is called subversion by our church of the canonical order in an autonomous territory, originated by the Patriarchate of Constantinople in Czechoslovakia in 1923, for the following reasons:

Serbia, Moscow, and Constantinople

21. As must be known to Your Holiness, our Patriarchate of Moscow received jurisdiction, in full agreement with the holy canons and traditions of Church life, over the diocese of Mukachevo-Priashev, which was previously under the jurisdiction of the holy Orthodox Church of Serbia, and also over the legitimate diocese of Czechia-Moravia of that same holy church. The transfer was made in strict accord with church statutes and practice, namely, by way of a decision by the holy Bishop's Council of the Serbian Orthodox Church, taken on 15 May, 1948, concerning which official announcement was forwarded to His Holiness, Patriarch Alexis of Moscow, from His Holiness, Patriarch Gabriel of Serbia. All of this was in full conformity with the wishes of the Christian fullness, the Orthodox clergy and laity of Czechia and Slovakia.

The labors of the holy Church of Russia for the development of Orthodox life within the boundaries of Czechoslovakia, and equally the valid reasons for the granting of the right to independent existence, are known to all. Thus, the assertions contained in Your Holiness' letter, that the autocephaly of the Orthodox Church of Czechoslovakia was uncanonical and unwise, are the cause of our bewilderment, sorrow, and objection. It is the holy throne of Constantinople, which by forming the autonomous territory of Czechia in 1923, and by placing Archbishop Sabbatius at its head, violated and scorned the rights of the holy autocephalous Church of Serbia, which for a long time prior to this had her own diocese in Czechoslovakia; and it is known to all concerned with this matter that the Constantinopolitan autonomous territory of Czechoslovakia under Archbishop Sabbatius was an institution both uncanonical and artificial, which neither the clergy nor laity of Czechoslovakia desired.

Hope for Reconsideration

22. Your Holiness, we again assert that the action by the holy Church of Russia with respect to the autocephaly of the Russian Orthodox Greek Catholic Church of North America, was accomplished in full awareness of its legitimacy, its usefulness, and its necessity. We are grieved and

astonished by the position adopted in this important matter by the most holy throne of Constantinople. From our point of view this position harms the cause of Orthodoxy in the modern world and contradicts the holy canons and tradition of the Catholic Orthodox Church. To avoid furthering and deepening of the harm done by this position of Your beloved Holiness to the unity of the holy Catholic Orthodox Church, we call on Your Holiness to reconsider your and the Holy Synod's understanding concerning the question of the autocephalous Orthodox Church in America and thus contribute to the further glory of the holy Orthodox Church, which for all of us, ministers of God's Word, is the receptacle of the fullness of the gifts of the Holy Spirit, giving life to the children of God.

I request the holy prayers of Your Holiness,
The Locum-Tenens of the Patriarchal throne of Moscow
Pimen, Metropolitan of Krutitsa and Kolomna

August 11, 1970
Moscow

www.ingramcontent.com/pod-product-compliance
Lightning Source LLC
Chambersburg PA
CBHW071433300426
44114CB00013B/1418